PERSONAL INFORMATION

Personal Information

Privacy and the Law

RAYMOND WACKS

CLARENDON PRESS · OXFORD

1989

Oxford University Press, Walton Street, Oxford OX2 6DP
Oxford New York Toronto
Delhi Bombay Calcutta Madras Karachi
Petaling Jaya Singapore Hong Kong Tokyo
Nairobi Dar es Salaam Cape Town
Melbourne Auckland
and associated companies
Berlin Ibadan

Oxford is a trade mark of Oxford University Press

British Library Cataloguing in Publication Data
Wacks, Raymond, 1946–
Personal information: privacy and the law
1. England. Privacy. Encroachment. Control.
Law
I. Title
344.202'858
ISBN 0–19–825611–6

Library of Congress Cataloging in Publication Data
Wacks, Raymond.
Personal information: privacy and the law/Raymond Wacks.
Bibliography
Includes index.
1. Privacy, Right of. 2. Data protection. I. Title.
K3263.W33 1989 342'.0858–dc19 [342.2858] 88–32109
ISBN 0–19–825611–6

Set by Cambrian Typesetters, Frimley, Surrey
Printed in Great Britain by
Biddles Ltd.,
Guildford and King's Lynn

For my parents

Preface

Nearly ten years ago in my book, *The Protection of Privacy*, I expressed a general disenchantment with the use of 'privacy' as a legal term of art. A good deal has happened since then. But my uneasiness remains. This book represents a more sustained and systematic attempt to develop an alternative analysis the outlines of which I only sketched there.

Based on a thesis for which the University of London awarded me the degree of Ph.D. in 1986, this book is inevitably informed by the perspective adopted in *The Protection of Privacy* and other writings. However, both the scope and the objectives pursued here are materially different. And they differ even more fundamentally from my much earlier (and considerably narrower) research conducted at the University of Oxford into the protection of 'privacy' by the English and Roman–Dutch law for which I was awarded the degree of M.Litt. in 1974.

I have clearly been preoccupied with the subject of 'privacy' for far longer than should be permitted. In mitigation I plead that this has afforded me the opportunity (or the burden) of reconsidering and, I hope, refining some of the ideas which I originally held. It does not follow, of course, that I am any closer to resolving the problems I have sought to unravel in the pages that follow.

In an attempt to test the extent to which those problems touch the lives of people in Britain, I conducted the survey of solicitors described in Chapter 4. This exercise would not, of course, have been possible without the assistance of the numerous solicitors who took the time and trouble to complete my questionnaires, several of them appending lengthy addenda expressing their views and proposals. I am most grateful to them.

Dr Michael Bryan of the Faculty of Laws, Queen Mary College, University of London, was (as my adviser) a constant and ready source not only of advice, but of friendly support and encouragement. With kindness and patience he greatly assisted, in particular, my journey through the often impenetrable thicket of the law of confidence, sparing me from many a mishap along the way. Responsibility for those that remain must, of course, be laid at my door.

Being away from England since 1982 proved more of an obstacle to my research than I anticipated. Difficulties in obtaining certain materials required periodic visits to Britain. I am indebted to both the Universities of Natal and Hong Kong for their assistance in financing my raids on the Bodleian Law Library and the Institute of Advanced Legal Studies.

No thanks to Mr Peter Wright. The litigation spawned by his revelations inflicted certain wounds on Chapter 3, though, since my chief concern is with 'personal information' the damage was minor. Still, the minds of almost a score of our leading judges have been exercised in a field of law notorious for its ambiguity. And the impact of their decisions extends beyond the narrow confines of the case to the action for breach of confidence in general. Moreover, as I process these words, I understand that the security service is, for the first time, to be placed on a statutory footing. Should the Security Service Bill become law, the Government's pursuit of *Spycatcher* may prove not to have been entirely in vain. And, as far as Chapter 7 is concerned, some of my comments concerning 'intrusion' by MI5 may have to be revised. I hope so.

For my part the *Spycatcher* drama could have been better timed. The First Act coincided with the despatch of my manuscript. Amendments were made just in time for incorporation in the proofs. Act II, however, was performed only after the book was in press. Nevertheless, thanks to the kind indulgence of my publishers, I have been able to squeeze into the footnotes references to the judgments of the Court of Appeal and the House of Lords.

A final word of gratitude. During the long and often difficult years during which I spent on this research, my wife, Penelope, endured what must have seemed like endless evenings and weekends without me. Throughout this period, she selflessly yielded to my wholly unreasonable demands for solitude and even for 'privacy'.

December 1988   R. W.

Acknowledgements

I have drawn on a number of my publications. In particular, 'Breach of Confidence and the Protection of Privacy' (1977) 127 NLJ 328; 'No Castles in the Air' (1977) 93 LQR 492; 'Pop Goes Privacy' (1978) 31 MLR 68; 'The Poverty of "Privacy" ' (1980) 96 LQR 73; *The Protection of Privacy*, Modern Legal Studies, London: Sweet & Maxwell, 1980; ' "Privacy" and the Practitioner' (1983) Public Law 260; 'Controlling AIDS: Some Legal Issues' (1988) 138 NLJ 254, 283; 'The Right to Privacy' in R. Wacks (ed.), *Civil Liberties in Hong Kong*, Hong Kong: Oxford University Press, 1988. I am grateful for permission to use them here.

Contents

Tables

Figures

Table of Cases

Table of Statutes

Statutory Instruments

Foreign Legislation

International Documents

Introduction

The temptation, rarely resisted, to conceive of social life in terms of large, abstract ideas often facilitates an attractive richness of meaning in explaining or interpreting the way we live. But such concepts (like 'freedom', 'democracy', and, of course, 'privacy') while they frequently illuminate, also occasionally obscure. Quite apart from the problem of subjectivism and the various epistemological difficulties (which are touched upon in Chapter 1) the attempts to translate the idea of 'privacy' into intelligible legal language may be described as, at best, unsatisfactory. Nor is it merely a question of terminological or linguistic precision; the generous application of the concept to so wide and varied a field of issues: abortion, contraception, homosexuality, the wearing of crash-helmets or long hair, obscene publications, stretches it close to breaking-point, thereby undermining the very protection it seeks to provide.

Whatever views one may hold of Judge Robert Bork, Mr Reagan's recently unsuccessful nominee to the United States Supreme Court, it is difficult not to sympathize with his uneasiness about the Supreme Court's 'privacy' decisions: 'Nobody knows what that thing [a generalized right to privacy] means. But you have to define it; you have to define it. And the court has not given it definition. That is my only point.'[1]

In an attempt to obviate the confusion that afflicts the question of 'privacy' and obstructs the satisfactory legal protection of the interests with which it is concerned, this book examines the plausibility of an alternative analysis that might facilitate a less obscure account of the problems involved and, in consequence, offer a more effective means of resolving them. The essence of my argument is that at the heart of the concern about 'privacy' is the use, and especially

[1] *Nomination of Robert H. Bork to be an Associate Justice of the United States Supreme Court*, Report of the Committee on the Judiciary, US Senate, Washington: 13 Oct. 1987, 32.

the misuse, of 'personal information' about an individual.

In the English law the principal ambiguity assumes a slightly different but no less problematic form: the organic growth of the equitable jurisdiction of breach of confidence by which the courts have managed to absorb complaints which are often explicitly proclaimed to relate to the plaintiff's 'privacy'. But there are other contexts in which the term 'privacy' has been applied, including the question of protecting individuals against the misuse of computerized data and the problems generated by telephone-tapping and other forms of electronic surveillance.

My purpose is to suggest a more practicable alternative. In each of the areas identified (breach of confidence, the public disclosure of private facts, the collection of personal data, and intrusions upon the individual by simple or electronic surveillance) I argue that, by locating as the core of the problem the protection of 'personal information' (as defined), many of the apparently intractable difficulties that continue to beset this area of the law might be more readily resolved. At the very least, it is hoped that this perspective might point the way to a more coherent analysis of these issues.

The project undertaken in these pages is not, of course, innocent of its own problems, some of which are examined in the chapters that follow. Nor should it be thought that, were the solution proposed here to be adopted, it would provide more than a starting-point for a fresh evaluation of the problems of 'privacy'. Still less does my approach purport to address the wider question of what has come to be called 'information law' of which the subject of this book is merely a small part.[2] A further difficulty of an analysis grounded in the identification and protection of 'personal information'

---

[2] For a useful assessment of the need for a new body of law to deal, in particular, with rapidly growing information technology, see J. Bing, 'A Background Analysis for Information Law' (1987) 1 International Computer Law Adviser 12. Ideally this body of law would incorporate the (presently haphazard) rules about the creation, communication, storing, processing, content, form, structure, and medium of information. This is clearly an ambitious objective and, even if it were practicable, each element would still require its own analysis. The main focus of my discussion is the content of the information, though, as will become evident in the course of this book, it is impossible to treat this or any other aspect independently.

could be said to arise: it might appear to be vulnerable to the charge that it is not only narrower in scope than one based on 'privacy', but that it cannot adequately account for the social, moral, or political value of 'privacy'. To this charge there is a relatively simple defence: it is no part of the argument developed here that 'privacy' (in its most general—and least satisfactory—sense) is not a 'value' worthy of protection. But the mainspring of my thesis is that, precisely because of its importance, the interests that seem to underpin it warrant a far more careful treatment if they are to receive effective legal recognition and protection. The argument advanced here is not, in other words, 'reductionist'; it acknowledges the existence of these interests and the need for their legal control. But it proposes a framework that appears to offer a more perspicuous account than the conventional 'privacy' approach which is steeped in broad generalization and incoherent theory. It therefore offers what seems to be a preferable method of protecting the interests of individuals against the disclosure or misuse of private details about their lives.

After a critical examination, in Chapter 1, of the origin and nature of modern claims to 'privacy', a definition of 'personal information' is proposed which appears to avoid most of the philosophical and legal problems (identified in Chapter 2) of the concept of 'privacy'.

In Chapter 3 it is argued that, though the action for breach of confidence affords certain adventitious protection to 'personal information', there are numerous—neglected—practical limitations and doctrinal difficulties inherent in this application. Thanks, in part, to Mr Peter Wright, the law in this area has been invoked on an unexpectedly large number of recent occasions. And, even prior to the spate of *Spycatcher* cases, the law has developed swiftly, if not systematically, in the last few years. Indeed, the courts have been faced with several actions for breach of confidence which may well render the Law Commission's legislative proposals redundant. This jurisdiction represents the principal means of protecting the 'personal information' which is the focus of the book. It therefore seemed singularly important to consider at some length the extent to which the action might be further fashioned to deal with the issues identified in the pages that follow. In order to offer a reasonably coherent account of the structural and doctrinal limitations of the action identified in Chapter 3, it proved necessary to describe the main features of the action and its operation. This outline may at first appear to be secondary to the analysis of 'personal information', but it was impossible to develop the argument of that chapter except by first sketching the essential elements of the action itself. Readers who are familiar with the terrain are invited to proceed directly to my critical examination of the action's success in the field of non-technical information.

In order to measure the extent to which individuals in Britain seek legal advice concerning 'privacy'-related issues, a survey of 185 solicitors was conducted in 1981 and 1982. The results are reported in Chapter 4. Had I been able to send the questionnaire to this (or a new, randomly selected) group in 1988, the result might have been different, though I am inclined to think that this would not have been the case. It would certainly be intriguing to attempt another survey when the Data Protection Act and the Interception of Communications Act have been in effect for five years.

Chapter 5 briefly describes the conventional 'privacy' analysis of unauthorized publicity given to private facts, and the corresponding legal (and non-legal) developments in Britain. The 'personal information' alternative is suggested as a more rational approach to the problems associated with freedom of speech. The general difficulties raised by, and major forms of, regulating information systems are described in Chapter 6. The question is posed whether 'personal information' is adequately protected by these measures or whether there might be more effective alternatives.

Chapter 7 investigates the problems generated, in particular, by the use of electronic surveillance devices, and the manner and scope of existing and proposed methods of control.

I do not, of course, expect that my efforts to identify as the essence of 'privacy' the notion of 'personal information' will meet with general approbation. And even if my pursuit of the will-o'-the-wisp of conceptual clarity is regarded as fruitful, readers may consider that several other obstacles, no less thorny, beset the path of the zealous law reformer. At the very least, I hope that I have been able to show that, in this 'information age' when there is a steady erosion of the separation between the public and the private, it is only when we can define with much greater lucidity the nature of these concerns that any legal measures designed to safeguard the individual against the ubiquitous depredations of government, commercial agencies, and the media might be expected to hold a reasonable prospect of success.

I.

'Privacy' and 'Personal Information'

1. The Private and the Public

At the heart of the concern to protect 'privacy' lies a conception of the individual and his or her relationship with society. The idea of private and public spheres of activity assumes a community in which not only does such a division make sense, but the institutional and structural arrangements that facilitate an organic representation of this kind are present.

For the Greeks a life spent in the privacy of 'one's own' (*idion*), outside the world of the common, was by definition 'idiotic'. Similarly, the Romans regarded privacy as merely a temporary refuge from the activities of the *res publica*. It is only in the late Roman period that it is possible to detect the beginnings of a recognition of privacy as a zone or sphere of intimacy.[1] As Hannah Arendt puts it,

In ancient feeling the privative trait of privacy, indicated in the word itself, was all-important; it meant literally a state of being deprived of something, and even of the highest and most human of man's capacities. A man who lived only a private life, who like the slave was not permitted to enter the public realm, or like the barbarian had chosen not to establish such a realm, was not fully human.[2]

The modern distinction between public and private realms arose out of a twin movement in modern political and legal thought. On the one hand, the emergence of the nation-state and theories of sovereignty in the sixteenth and seventeenth centuries produced the idea of distinctly public realm.[3] On

[1] H. Arendt, *The Human Condition* (1958), 38.
[2] Ibid. Cf. A. H. Saxonhouse, 'Classical Greek Conceptions of Public and Private', in S. I. Benn and G. F. Gaus (eds.), *Public and Private in Social Life* (1983), 380.
[3] D. Hanson, *From Kingdom to Commonwealth* (1970), 1–19, quoted by M. J. Horwitz, 'The History of the Public/Private Distinction' (1982) 130 Univ. of Pa. Law Rev. 1423.

the other, a delineation of a private sphere free from the
encroachment of the state emerged as a response to the claims
of monarchs and, subsequently, parliaments, to an untrammelled power to make law.[4] Thus the development of
the modern state, the regulation of social and economic
behaviour, the perception of a 'private' zone, and so on are
natural prerequisites to this form of demarcation.[5] But, while
historical or empirical evidence for this phenomenon is
legion,[6] it is best captured by sociological typologies in which
it is shown to be expressive of the values of certain forms of
society. In other words, there is an apparent relationship
between the existence of a public/private dichotomy and
other fundamental features of a society. One such model is
the distinctive representation of societies as exhibiting the
characteristics of *Gemeinschaft* (in which, broadly speaking,
there is a community of internalized norms and traditions
regulated according to status but mediated by love, duty, and
a shared understanding and purpose) or *Gesellschaft* (where
self-interested individuals compete for personal material
advantage in a so-called free market).[7]

In the former there is virtually no distinction between
private and public, while in the latter the division is sharply
demarcated: the law formally regulates that which is conceived
to be public. And this contrast may also illuminate the
economic and political order in which each formation is to be
found; thus *Gesellschaft* has been identified as 'the bourgeois
commercial society in which the cash nexus tends to drive out
all other social ties and relationship, in which men become

---

[4] J. Appleby, *Economic Thought and Ideology in Seventeenth-Century
England* (1978), 62–3, quoted by Horwitz, 'The History of the Public/
Private Distinction'.

[5] See R. H. Mnookin, 'The Public/Private Dichotomy: Political Disagreement and Academic Reputation' (1982) 130 Univ. of Pa. Law Rev.
1429. This raises complex questions of legitimacy which cannot be
examined here; see J. Habermas, *Legitimation Crisis* (1973); T. McCarthy,
The Critical Theory of Jurgen Habermas (1984 edn.), 358–86; R. Austin,
'The Problem of Legitimacy in the Welfare State' (1982) 130 Univ. of Pa.
Law Rev. 1510.

[6] The literature is immense. Some of the more useful anthropological/
cultural accounts are referred to below.

[7] F. Tonnies, *Gemeinschaft und Gesellschaft* (1887) trans. C. P.
Loomis, *Community and Association* (1955).

bound only by contract and commercial exchange, in which the city dominates the country and the trading class converts the whole land into a market, in which the "common social sphere" is based on the fleeting moment when men meet in barter . . .'.[8] And the division between a public and private sphere is a central tenet of liberalism. Indeed, 'liberalism may be said largely to have been an argument about where the boundaries of [the] private sphere lie, according to what principles they are to be drawn, whence interference derives and how it is to be checked'.[9]

1.1. 'PUBLIC', 'PRIVATE', AND THE LAW

The extent to which the law (the 'public') might legitimately intrude upon the 'private' is a recurring theme especially in nineteenth-century liberal doctrine: 'One of the central goals of nineteenth-century legal thought was to create a clear separation between constitutional, criminal, and regulatory law—public law—and the law of private transactions—torts, contracts, property, and commercial law.'[10] And the question of the limits of the criminal law in enforcing 'private morality' continues to vex legal and moral philosophers.[11]

While the drawing of the public–private boundary is logically anterior to any conception of the role of law, it is also constituted by law. And this circularity is compounded by the fact that non-legal regulation of what is apparently

[8] E. Kamenka, 'Public/Private in Marxist Theory and Marxist Practice', in Benn and Gaus, *Public and Private in Social Life*, 267, 273–4.

[9] S. Lukes, *Individualism* (1973), 62. For the argument that the decline of 'privacy' in the common law 'contains a rejection of the traditional liberal view that privacy is essential for human flourishing' see H. Collins, 'The Decline of Privacy in Private Law' (1987) 14 J. of Law & Soc. 91, 102.

[10] Horwitz 'The History of the Public/Private Distinction', 1423, 1424.

[11] This is amply illustrated by the Hart/Devlin debate concerning, in particular, the issue of homosexuality between consenting adults. The liberal position is, of course, exemplified by the Wolfenden Report (*Report of the Committee on Homosexual Offences and Prostitution*, Cmnd. 247, 1957), which based itself on J. S. Mill's 'harm principle' expressed in *On Liberty* (1859). See too the *Report of the Committee on Obscenity and Film Censorship* (chairman: Bernard Williams) Cmnd. 7772, 1979.

'private' may exercise significant controls over such behaviour. Moreover, it would be misleading to assume that—even in liberal thought—there is a consistent or definitive boundary between what is 'private' and what is 'public'.

A prodigious literature devoted to the resolution of these difficulties inevitably raises complex methodological and epistemological questions which frequently obscure rather than illuminate. This chapter makes no attempt to address these issues in detail. Without suggesting that lawyers should neglect sociological and philosophical enquiries of this kind, it is submitted that a more constructive means of resolving some of the *legal* problems encountered in regulating the collection, storage, and use of private facts about the individual might be found by avoiding—as a legal term of art—the concept of 'privacy' altogether. Instead of pursuing the false god of 'privacy', attention should be paid to identifying what *specific interests* of the individual we think the law ought to protect. And it is submitted that at the core of the preoccupation with the 'right to privacy' is the protection against the misuse of personal, sensitive information. This is not to deny the importance of rights or even their formulation in broad terms which facilitate their recognition by the common law,[12] but, as one American commentator has recently acknowledged, 'a natural "right" to privacy is simply inconceivable as a legal right—sanctioned perhaps by society but clearly not enforceable by government . . . Privacy itself is beyond the scope of law.'[13] He proposes instead legislation to regulate clearly identified threats to sensitive information.

By addressing the problems of 'privacy' as problems of the protection of 'personal information' it is submitted that the pervasive difficulties that are generally (and, it is argued, mistakenly) forced into the strait-jacket of 'privacy' might find a less artificial and more effective legal resolution. In particular, it is suggested that the concept of 'privacy' has

[12] The strongest contemporary 'right-based' argument is to be found in the writing of Ronald Dworkin, now most coherently and sysematically stated in *Law's Empire* (1986).

[13] R. F. Hixson, *Privacy in a Public Society: Human Rights in Conflict* (1987), 98.

become too vague and unwieldy a concept to perform useful analytical (and, hence, legal) work. It has grown into as nebulous a notion as 'freedom' (with which it is not infrequently equated) or 'autonomy' (with which it is often confused). This ambiguity has, it is submitted, actually undermined the importance of the value of 'privacy' and impeded its effective legal protection.

1.2. WHY PROTECT 'PRIVACY'?

Accounts of the value of 'privacy' in social life are not immune to similar problems. Thus, quite apart from the importance of 'privacy' in democratic theory[14] it is claimed to be important, for example, to the individual's psychological health,[15] creativity,[16] ability to love,[17] and social relationships.[18] And Westin[19] identifies four functions of 'privacy' which combine its individual and social dimensions. First, it provides personal autonomy; the democratic principle

[14] A. Westin, *Privacy and Freedom* (1967), 23–51; H. J. McCloskey, 'The Political Ideal of Privacy' (1971) 21 Philosoph. Q. 303; Lukes, *Individualism*, ch. 9; W. L. Weinstein, 'The Private and the Free: A Conceptual Inquiry', in J. R. Pennock and J. W. Chapman (eds.) *Privacy, Nomos XIII* (Yearbook of the American Society for Political and Legal Philosophy, 1971), 27; E. Shils, 'Privacy: Its Constitution and Vicissitudes' (1966) 31 Law & Contemp. Probs. 281. Cf. Arendt, *The Human Condition*.

[15] S. M. Jourard, 'Some Psychological Aspects of Privacy' (1966) 31 Law & Contemp. Probs. 307; R. Ingham, 'Privacy and Psychology', in J. B. Young (ed.), *Privacy* (1978); Schwartz, 'The Social Psychology of Privacy' (1968) 73 Am. J. of Sociology 747; O. M. Ruebhausen and O. G. Brim, 'Privacy and Behavioral Research' (1965) 65 Colum. Law Rev. 1184; Westin, *Privacy and Freedom*, 39–42.

[16] M. A. Weinstein, 'The Uses of Privacy in the Good Life' (1971) 13 *Nomos XIII* 88.

[17] C. Fried, *An Anatomy of Values: Problems of Personal and Social Choice* (1971), 25; id., 'Privacy' (1968) 77 Yale LJ 475.

[18] R. Gerstein, 'Intimacy and Privacy', in F. Schoeman (ed.), *Philosophical Dimensions of Privacy: An Anthology* (1984), 265; Fried, *Anatomy of Values*; J. Rachels, 'Why Privacy is Important' (1975) 4 Phil. & Pub. Aff. 323; J. H. Reiman, 'Privacy, Intimacy, and Personhood' (1976) 6 Phil. & Pub. Aff. 26.

[19] A. Westin, *Privacy and Freedom*, 33 ff.

of individuality is linked to the need for autonomy: the desire to avoid being manipulated or dominated by others. Secondly, 'privacy' provides the opportunity for emotional release. Thirdly, it permits self-evaluation: the creative and moral activities, and the formation and testing of ideas. Finally, it provides opportunities for sharing confidences and intimacies: limited and protected communication.

But all of these functional accounts (including those anthropological and cultural analyses of 'privacy' in primitive societies)[20] presume a meaning of 'privacy' which is by no means shared. And even the economic view advanced by Richard Posner[21] that the assignment of 'privacy' rights is actually socially *injurious* because it is economically inefficient, assumes a meaning of 'privacy'.[22]

On the other hand, it is argued that the 'private'

in its positive senses is a record of the legitimation of a bourgeois view of life: the ultimate generalized privilege, however abstract in practice, of seclusion and protection from others (*the public*); a lack of accountability to 'them' . . .[23]

There is, especially amongst Marxists, a mistrust of the concept of the 'private'. The notion that anything stands outside society or is regarded as prior to it is considered to be a 'dangerous illusion'.[24] Yet even in a wholly communitarian

[20] e.g. J. M. Roberts and T. Gregor 'Privacy: A Cultural View' *Nomos XIII* 199; A. Westin, *Privacy and Freedom*, 11–18; id., *Privacy in Western Society* (1967); Shils, 'Privacy'; R. F. Murphy, 'Social Distance and the Veil' in Schoeman (ed.), *Philosophical Dimensions of Privacy*, 35; P. Halmos, *Solitude and Privacy* (1953).

[21] 'Privacy, Secrecy, and Reputation' (1979) 28 Buff. Law Rev. 1; id., 'The Right to Privacy' (1978) 12 Ga. Law Rev. 393; id., 'An Economic Theory of Privacy', in Schoeman (ed.), *Philosophical Dimensions of Privacy*, 333. This account is returned to below, and in ch. 2.

[22] Although he avoids 'defining' the concept (and his focus is 'informational privacy') he includes in his analysis, for instance, 'telephone solicitations even if the caller makes no effort to extract private information': 'Privacy, Secrecy, and Reputation'. Such conduct is by no means a necessary feature of other definitions of 'privacy'. Some elements of this economic theory are considered below.

[23] R. Williams, *Keywords: A Vocabulary of Culture and Society* (1976) 203, quoted by Hixson, *Privacy in a Public Society*.

[24] Kamenka, 'Public/Private', 274.

society the complete separation of the public and the private is neither possible nor desirable.

The mainspring of the approach adopted here is the recognition that at the core of the problem of 'privacy' is the interest claimed by individuals to withhold certain information by virtue of its privateness or sensitivity.[25] That no comprehensive attempt has apparently been made to analyze the issue in this way is surprising, for it was Professor Westin who himself concluded in his monumental (and highly influential) treatise[26] (published almost twenty years ago) that:

The first way we can try to come to grips with [the problem of loss of 'privacy'] is to *develop a new way of classifying information, to identify what is private and 'non-circulating'; what is confidential, with limited circulation; and what is public or freely circulating.* This can also be seen as a distinction between *the facts about ourselves that are intimate*; those that are *part of our life transactions* (education, employment, family, etc.), and those that are *formal public records.*

A definition of 'personal information' is proposed below, but the burden of the present argument is that by applying an informational analysis to the related questions of 'privacy' (breach of confidence, unwanted publicity being given to private facts, electronic eavesdropping, and the collection, storage, and transfer of (mainly computerized) personal data) the conceptual confusion engendered by the use of this abused term might be avoided or, at least, diminished.

2. Defining 'Privacy'

In spite of the huge literature on the subject, a satisfactory definition of 'privacy' remains as elusive as ever. The ambiguity of the concept stems largely from difficulties in respect of its:

(1) status;

[25] See R. Wacks, 'The Poverty of "Privacy" ' (1980) 96 LQR 73; id., *The Protection of Privacy* (1980) ch. 1.

[26] *Privacy and Freedom*, 322 (emphasis supplied).

(2) features; and

(3) coherence.

A brief analysis of each of these questions may demonstrate their complexity (and perhaps even their intractability).

2.1. THE STATUS OF 'PRIVACY'

A particularly ubiquitous and influential definition (especially in the legal literature) conceives of 'privacy' as a *claim*: the 'claim of individuals, groups, or institutions to determine for themselves when, how, and to what extent information about them is communicated to others'.[27] To regard 'privacy' as a claim (or, *a fortiori*, a right)[28] not only presumes the value of 'privacy', but fails to define its content.[29] It is rightly described as a kind of 'logical synecdoche'[30] for it is defining the part by the whole. It would, moreover, include the use or disclosure of *any* information about an individual. A similar criticism may be levelled at those conceptions of 'privacy' as an 'area of life',[31] or a psychological state.

But Westin's definition has exerted even greater influence in respect of its description of 'privacy' in terms of the extent to which an individual has *control* over information about him.[32] For control over information to be co-extensive with 'privacy' an individual would have to be said to have lost

[27] Westin *Privacy and Freedom*, 7.

[28] Westin does, however, add a second definition: 'Viewed in terms of the relation of the individual to social participation, privacy is the voluntary and temporary withdrawal of a person from the general society through physical or psychological means . . .' (ibid.).

[29] See D. N. McCormick, 'Privacy: A Problem of Definition' (1974) 1 Br. J. of Law & Soc. 75.

[30] By T. Gerety, 'Redefining Privacy' (1977) 12 Harv. CR–CL L. Rev. 233, 262.

[31] *Privacy and the Law*, a Report by JUSTICE (1970), para. 19.

[32] Similar 'control' definitions are adopted by several other writers, e.g.: Fried, 'Privacy', 482; R. Parker, 'A Definition of Privacy' (1974) 27 Rutgers Law Rev. 275, 280–1; A. Miller, *The Assault on Privacy* (1971), 25; E. L. Beardsley, 'Privacy: Autonomy and Selective Disclosure', in J. R. Pennock and J. W. Chapman (eds.), *Privacy, Nomos XIII* (1971), 56, 70; H. Gross, 'Privacy and Autonomy', ibid. 169; Gerety, 'Redefining Privacy'; Shils, 'Privacy', 282.

'privacy' if he is prevented from exercising this control: even if he is *unable* to disclose personal information. This suggests a pre-emptive view of 'privacy'[33] by which the value of 'privacy' is assumed. Similarly, if I knowingly and voluntarily disclose personal information I do not thereby lose 'privacy' because I am exercising rather than relinquishing control. But this sense of control does not adequately describe 'privacy', for although I may have control over whether to disclose the information, it may be obtained by other means. And if control is meant in a stronger sense (namely that to disclose information, even voluntarily, constitutes a loss of control because I am no longer able to curtail the dissemination of the information by others) it describes the *potential* rather than the actual loss of 'privacy'. Hence, I may not attract any interest from others and therefore I will be accorded 'privacy'—whether I want it or not. There is a distinction between my controlling the flow of information about myself and my being known about in fact. In order to establish whether such control actually protects my 'privacy', according to this argument, it is also necessary to know, for instance, whether the recipient of the information is bound by restrictive norms. Furthermore, if 'privacy' is regarded as an aspect of control (or autonomy) it is assumed that what is in issue is my freedom to choose 'privacy'. But, as suggested above, I may choose to *abandon* my 'privacy'; the control-based definition therefore speaks to the question of *which* choices I exercise rather than the *manner* in which I exercise the choice. It is, in other words, a definition which assumes the value of 'privacy'.

2.2. THE FEATURES OF 'PRIVACY'

This is a matter of considerable disagreement and confusion in the literature. The best account[34] conceives of 'privacy' as 'limited accessibility', a cluster of three related but independent components:

(a) *secrecy*: information known about an individual;

[33] R. Gavison, 'Privacy and the Limits of Law' (1980) 89 Yale LJ 421, 427–8.   [34] Ibid. 428–40.

(b) *anonymity*: attention paid to an individual;
(c) *solitude*: physical access to an individual.

A loss of 'privacy' (as distinct from an infringement of a 'right' of 'privacy') occurs, in this account, where others obtain information about an individual, pay attention to him, or gain access to him. The claimed virtues[35] of this approach are first, that it is *neutral*, facilitating an objective identification of a loss of 'privacy'; secondly, it demonstrates the *coherence* of 'privacy' as a value (see below); thirdly, it suggests the *utility* of the concept in legal contexts (for it identifies those occasions calling for legal protection); fourthly, it includes *'typical' invasions of 'privacy'* and excludes issues which, though often thought to be 'privacy' questions, are not (noise, odours, prohibition of abortion, contraception, 'unnatural' sexual intercourse, etc.).

Yet even this analysis presents certain difficulties. In particular, in her effort (which is central to her account) to define 'privacy' in such a way as to avoid pre-empting questions as to its desirability, Professor Gavison is driven to rejecting definitions which limit themselves to the *quality* of the information divulged. She therefore dismisses the view[36] that to constitute a part of 'privacy', the information concerned must be 'private' in the sense of being intimate or related to the individual's identity. This issue is returned to below, but it is important to observe in the present context that if a loss of 'privacy' occurs whenever *any* information about an individual becomes known (the secrecy component) the concept loses its intuitive meaning. Indeed, Gavison, in pursuit of a neutral definition, contends that unless we regard the disclosure of *any* information about the individual as a loss of 'privacy', the following situations will not be considered losses of 'privacy':

(i) an estranged wife publishes her husband's love letters to her, without his consent;
(ii) a single data bank containing all census information

---

[35] Ibid. 423, 436–7.
[36] Expressed by, among others, Parker, 'Definition of Privacy', 282 and Gerety, 'Redefining Privacy', 281–95.

and government files is used by all government officials;

(iii) an employer asks every conceivable question of his employees and yet has no obligation to keep the answers confidential.

But even if the view adopted here (that information which is 'personal' needs to be defined in some way) is misconceived, it is still difficult to accept that there is no loss of 'privacy' in (i): the contents of love letters are clearly 'private' on almost any account. In respect of (ii) and (iii), on the other hand, losses of 'privacy' do *not* seem to have occurred at all. Once the information is actually used (or misused) or disclosed, the situations postulated may give rise to losses of 'privacy'.

But this leaves the important issue mentioned above unresolved. While it would appear to be a distortion to describe *every* instance of the dissemination of information about an individual as a loss of 'privacy', the requirement of a value-free definition of 'privacy' dictates that to confine the ambit of 'privacy'-invading conduct to the transfer or communication of *'private'* information is to invoke a value judgment in respect of the desirability of 'privacy'. To the extent, however, that 'privacy' is a function of information or knowledge about the individual, this seems to be inevitable. In (ii), therefore, the objection to the collection of information is not the loss of 'privacy' that it causes, but that the information may be transferred without the knowledge or consent of the individual to whom it relates, that it may be inaccurate, irrelevant, and so on. (These questions are considered in Chapter 6.) Equally in (iii) the employee's objection is that information imparted in confidence ought not to be divulged to a third party without the employee's consent. When such a disclosure is made by the employer, the employee's complaint is not that his 'privacy' is invaded (though, depending on the nature of the information and the extent of its disclosure, this may arise as an additional objection), but that the data have been passed on without his knowledge or consent. (The relationship between questions of 'privacy' and breach of confidence is considered in Chapter 3.)

In other words, in so far as the question of information about an individual is concerned, a limiting or controlling factor is required, and it is submitted that the most acceptable limiting factor is that the information be 'personal' (see below).

To claim that whenever an individual is the subject of attention or when access to him is gained he necessarily loses 'privacy'[37] is again to divest our concern for 'privacy' of much of its intuitive meaning. Having attention focused upon us or being subjected to uninvited intrusions upon our solitude are objectionable in their own right, but our concern for the individual's 'privacy' in these circumstances is strongest when he or she is engaged in activities which we would normally consider 'private'. The Peeping Tom is more likely to affront our conception of what is 'private' than someone who follows an individual in public. This is a subject that is returned to below in attempting to formulate an alternative analytical approach.

2.3. THE COHERENCE OF 'PRIVACY'

Quite apart from its utility or application as a *legal* concept (considered in Chapter 2), the coherence of the very idea of 'privacy' is suspect. This is evident in two respects. First, it is sometimes argued that by protecting the values underpinning 'privacy', (property rights, human dignity, preventing or compensating the infliction of emotional distress, etc.) moral and legal discourse concerning 'privacy' may be dispensed with. This essentially reductionist argument obviously has its major purchase in relation to the need for the *legal* protection of 'privacy' (and is therefore examined in Chapter 2); but if it can be demonstrated that the concept is largely parasitic, that its protection may be secured by safeguarding other (primary) interests, its conceptual distinctiveness is thrown into considerable doubt. Secondly, even among those who deny the parasitical character of 'privacy', there is little agreement concerning its principal defining features. Again, these concerns are especially important in the context of arguments

[37] Gavison, 'Privacy and the Limits of Law', 432–3.

concerning the *legal* protection of 'privacy'. But it is clear that unless a concept is sufficiently distinctive to facilitate coherent analytical identification and description, the prospects for its satisfactory legal recognition and application are bound to be poor.

These difficulties are not, of course, peculiar to the notion of 'privacy'. 'Freedom', 'security', 'liberty', and other values are, to a greater or lesser extent, susceptible to similar criticism. But, unless it is to be argued that subscription to generalized values exhibits our 'clear commitment'[38] to them, it seems perverse not to attempt to refine the nature and scope of the problem—especially if this might actually engender more effective protection.

3. An Alternative Approach

I want to argue that, without undermining the significance of 'privacy' as a value, a less problematic and more direct method of attempting to resolve the difficulties associated with its protection, is to isolate the essential issues that give rise to such claims. Indeed, in view of the confusion that generally afflicts discussions of the concept, there is an overwhelming case for seeking to liberate the subject from the presumptive force of its value-laden starting-point concerning the desirability of 'privacy'. And if it is replied that it is possible to arrive at a *neutral* definition of 'privacy', it must be said that such attempts inevitably strip the concept of much of its intuitive meaning and explanatory power. Thus to conceive of 'privacy' as 'limited accessibility' avoids loading the concept with a positive value, but it also results in *any* loss of solitude by or information about an individual having to be counted as a loss of 'privacy'.

[38] Ibid. 468. 'Some terms, like "liberty" and "equality", are *pervasively indeterminate*. It is not that such terms have no content whatsoever; it is that *every* application, every concretization, every instantiation requires the addition of supplementary premises to apply the general term of specific cases': F. Schauer, 'Formalism' (1988) 97 Yale LJ 509, 524. A similar observation might be made about 'privacy'. But Professor Schauer shows that charges of 'formalism' are often misconceived; sometimes precise language *should* restrict decision-makers including judges.

There are, moreover, a number of associated problems that might be obviated by adopting the alternative approach proposed here. In particular, three specific analytical difficulties might be briefly mentioned.

First, arguments about the meaning of 'privacy' frequently proceed from fundamentally different premises. Thus, for instance, where 'privacy' is described as a 'right'[39] issue is not seriously joined with those who conceive it to be a 'condition'.[40] The former is usually a normative statement about the need for 'privacy' (however defined); the latter merely make a descriptive statement about 'privacy'.

Secondly, claims about the desirability of 'privacy' confuse its instrumental and inherent value. Some of these arguments were alluded to above: 'privacy' is regarded by some as an end itself,[41] while others view it as instrumental in the securing of other social ends such as creativity,[42] love,[43] or emotional release.[44]

Thirdly, there is, among discussions of 'privacy', a confusion between descriptive accounts especially of the law[45] on the one hand, and normative accounts on the other. A fairly considerable effort has been made in an—ultimately futile—attempt to reconcile these two fundamentally antagonistic perspectives.

The essence of the argument presented in this book, then, is that at the centre of the concern about 'privacy' is the use (and especially the misuse) of personal information about an individual. There is little doubt that originally the 'archetypal' complaints in the 'privacy' field related to what, in legal

[39] The *Report of the Committee on Privacy* (chairman: K. Younger) Cmnd. 5012, 1972 (hereafter referred to as Younger) confused 'rights' and 'liberties': D. N. McCormick, 'Right of Privacy' (1973) 89 LQR 23; id., 'Privacy: A Problem of Definition'. Cf. N. Marsh, 'Hohfeld and Privacy' (1973) 89 LQR 183.

[40] L. Lusky 'Invasion of Privacy: A Clarification of Concepts' (1972) 72 Colum. Law Rev. 693, 709; M. A. Weinstein 'The Uses of Privacy in the Good Life'.

[41] Beardsley 'Privacy: Autonomy and Selective Disclosure', 56; S. I. Benn 'Privacy, Freedom and Respect for Persons', in *Nomos XIII*, 1.

[42] Weinstein, 'Uses of Privacy'.

[43] Fried, *An Anatomy of Values*.

[44] Westin *Privacy and Freedom*, 33.

[45] See the discussion of the Prosser–Bloustein debate in ch. 2.

terms, have come to be described as 'public disclosure of private facts' and 'intrusion upon an individual's seclusion, solitude or private affairs'. (These categories are examined in Chapter 2.) More recently the subject of the collection and use of computerized personal data has come to dominate discussions of 'privacy'. (This matter is examined in Chapter 6.) Without at this stage exploring the precise nature and scope of these issues, it is clear that, at bottom, these three questions share a concern to limit the extent to which 'private facts' about the individual are respectively published, intruded upon, or misused.

It is therefore submitted (and it is hoped that the validity of this claim will become evident in the course of the ensuing chapters) that a more rational, direct, and effective method of seeking to address the central questions of 'privacy' is to avoid the conceptual labyrinth that has so far impaired their satisfactory resolution. This is not to suggest that certain conditions (for instance, being alone) or certain activities (such as telephone-tapping) ought not intuitively to be characterized as 'privacy' or 'invasions of privacy' respectively. But, except to describe the underlying value, the term 'privacy' ought to be resisted—especially as a legal term of art. It adds little to our understanding either of the interest that it is sought to protect or of the conduct that it is designed to regulate. But, more importantly, eschewing the concept facilitates a clearer analysis of the problems and their possible solution.

4. 'Personal Information'

In locating the problems of 'privacy' at the level of 'personal information' two obvious questions arise. First, what is to be understood by 'personal', and, secondly, under what circumstances is a matter to be regarded as 'personal'?

4.1. WHAT IS 'PERSONAL'?

For present purposes, nothing turns on the distinction between 'personal' and 'private'; indeed, in defining 'private' the *Oxford English Dictionary* provides 'personal' as one of its meanings and *vice versa*. The word 'personal', however, has the advantage of avoiding some of the difficulties already identified in respect of 'privacy' from which the word 'private' may be inclined to suffer.

In normal parlance, though the term 'personal' has several possible meanings,[46] it is in three particular respects that its usage is of special importance here:

(a) It may mean that the matter is one which does not affect or concern *the community*. I might, for example, refuse to answer a question on the ground that the subject is 'personal'.

(b) Certain *activities* may plausibly be characterized as private or personal (such as sexual or bodily functions) in order to claim the opportunity to withdraw physically to undertake them.

(c) Certain *communications* or conversations may be described as personal or private; a letter marked 'personal' denotes that its contents are for the addressee's eyes only; a similar message is conveyed by the injunction: 'Please leave the room, what we want to say is personal.'

Describing a matter as 'personal' in this way is to invest it with characteristics of intimacy or sensitivity.

4.2. WHEN IS A MATTER 'PERSONAL'?

Is something 'personal' by virtue simply of the claim by an individual that it *is* so, or are certain matters *intrinsically*

---

[46] Six associated usages may be identified. It may be employed (1) to describe what is legitimately *one's own*: 'It is my personal property'; (2) to describe things as *'personal effects'*; (3) to imply a degree of individualism or even *selfishness*: 'He is doing that to suit his personal convenience'; (4) to describe *remarks* made by an individual that are improper or abusive: 'He is getting personal'; (5) to describe a state of being: 'We may talk freely; we are now in private'; it is used in this sense in the Sexual Offences Act to permit homosexual acts *in private* between consenting adults; (6) to mean simply 'of an individual or person' as opposed to, say, the community; this application is commonly found in the context of 'personal information' which is the subject of computerized data banks (discussed in ch. 6).

personal? The assertion, in other words, that something is 'personal' may be norm-dependent or norm-invoking. To claim that my political views are personal must depend on certain norms which prohibit or curtail inquiries into, or unauthorized reports of such views. It may, however, suffice for me to invoke the norm that I am entitled to keep my views to myself.

These norms are clearly culture-relative as well as fluctuating. Anthropological evidence suggests that primitive societies have differential 'privacy' attitudes. And it can hardly be doubted that in modern societies conceptions of what is 'private' will differ and change. There is certainly less diffidence in contemporary Britain in regard to several aspects of private life than characterized the society of even fifty years ago.

But the present argument goes further: there is a class of information that may plausibly be described as 'personal'. Normally it is objected that 'privateness' is *not* an attribute of the information itself; that the *same* information may be regarded as very private in one context and not so private or not private at all in another.[47] Naturally X may be more inclined to divulge, say, his extra-marital affair or his homosexuality (or both!) to his psychiatrist or to a close friend than to his employer or his wife. And his objection to the disclosure of the information by a newspaper might be expected to be even stronger. But *the information remains 'personal' in all three contexts*. What changes is the extent to which he is prepared to permit the information to become known or to be used.

It is counter-intuitive to describe the information in the first context (the psychiatrist) as 'not private at all' or even 'not so private'. We should surely want to say that the psychiatrist is listening to *personal* facts being discussed. Were the conversation to be surreptitiously recorded or the psychiatrist called upon to testify in court to his patient's homosexuality or infidelity, we should want to say that *personal information* was being recorded or disclosed. The

[47] This view is expressed, for instance, in the *Report of the Committee on Data Protection* (chairman: Sir Norman Lindop) Cmnd. 7341, 1978 (referred to hereafter as Lindop) para. 2.07.

context has manifestly changed, but it affects the degree to which it would be reasonable to expect the individual to object to the information being used or spread abroad, not the *quality* of the information itself.

Any definition of 'personal information' must therefore include *both* elements. It should refer both to the *quality* of the information and to *the reasonable expectations of the individual concerning its use.* The one is, in large part, a function of the other. In other words, the concept of 'personal information' postulated here functions both descriptively as well as normatively. Since 'personal' relates to social norms, to so describe something implies that it satisfies certain of the conditions specified in the norms, without which the normative implications would have no validity. Thus if a letter is marked 'personal' or if its contents clearly indicate that it is personal, the implication is that it satisfies one or more of the conditions necessary for its being conceived as 'personal'—and this is a descriptive account.[48]

This approach is taken (from a slightly different perspective) by Sissela Bok in her recent book on *Secrets*:

How then might we sort out what is unduly invasive from all the gossip about private and secret lives? To begin with, there is reason to stop to consider whether gossip is thus invasive whenever those whose doings are being discussed claim to feel intruded upon. But these claims must obviously not be taken at face value: they are often claims to ownership of information about oneself. While such claims should give gossipers pause, *they are not always legitimate.* People cannot be said, for instance to own aspects of their lives that are clearly evident to others and thus in fact public, such as a nasty temper or a manipulative manner, nor can they *reasonably* argue that others have no right to discuss them. Least of all can they suppress references to what may be an 'open secret,' known to all, and half-suspected even by themselves—a topic treated in innumerable comedies about marital infidelity. Similarly, more concealed aspects of their lives may be of legitimate interest to others—their mistreatment of their children, for example, or their past employment record . . . Merely to *say* that gossip about oneself is unduly invasive, therefore, does not make it so. I would argue that additional factors must be present to render gossip unduly

[48] S. I. Benn and G. F. Gaus 'The Public and the Private: Concepts and Action' in Benn and Gaus (eds.), *Public and Private in Social Life*, 3, 12.

invasive: the information must be about matters *legitimately considered private*; and it must hurt the individuals talked about.[49]

In other words, the bald assertion that information is 'personal', 'private', or 'sensitive' does not automatically render it so. The concern expressed by those who have misgivings about the attempt to characterize certain information as 'personal' etc. seems to spring from the relativity of information. It is argued that information cannot be objectively adjudged to belong to this putative category, for what is 'personal' to X may not be to Y. But this neglects not only the fact that (as suggested above) certain information *remains* 'personal' even though the context in which it is imparted changes, but also the fact that, in the absence of some objective test, claims that information is 'personal' might be made in respect of information that cannot *legitimately* be so described. The objective test therefore operates as a limiting factor based on what is both descriptively and normatively acceptable to the society in which such claims arise.

4.3. WHAT IS 'INFORMATION'?

A good deal of the literature treats 'information' as interchangeable with 'data'. It may, however, be useful to distinguish between the two. 'Data' become 'information' only when they are communicated, received, and understood. 'Data' are therefore potential 'information'. Thus when the data assume the form of the printed word they are immediately transformed into information by the reader. Where, however, data consist in acts or signs which require interpretation before they acquire any meaning, they remain in this state of pre-information until they are actually understood by another. For the purpose of the present work (and, I would venture to suggest, for legal analysis in general) it is with 'information' that we are concerned, though in discussing data protection in Chapter 6, unless specifically stated, the two terms are unavoidably used synonymously.[50]

[49] *Secrets: On the Ethics of Concealment and Revelation* (1982) 97. Emphasis supplied (except for the word 'say').

[50] See J. Bing, 'A Background Analysis for Information Law' (1987) 1 Int. Computer Law Adviser 12, 13.

4.4. A DEFINITION OF 'PERSONAL INFORMATION'

The following definition of 'personal information' is proposed:

> *'Personal information' consists of those facts, communications, or opinions which relate to the individual and which it would be reasonable to expect him to regard as intimate or sensitive and therefore to want to withhold or at least to restrict their collection, use, or circulation.*

It might immediately be objected that, by resting the notion of 'personal information' on an *objective* determination of an individual's expectations, the definition is actually an exclusively normative one—and therefore pre-empts enquiries concerning the desirability or otherwise of protecting 'personal information'. But any attempt to classify information as 'personal', 'sensitive', or 'intimate' proceeds on the assumption that such information warrants special treatment. To the extent that it is necessary to define the information by reference to some objective criterion (since a subjective test would clearly be unacceptable) it is inevitable that the classification depends on what legitimately may be claimed to be 'personal'. Only information which it is reasonable to wish to withhold is likely, under any test, to be the focus of our concern. An individual who regards information concerning say, his car, as personal and therefore seeks to withhold details of the size of its engine, will find it difficult to convince one that his vehicle's log book constitutes a disclosure of 'personal information'. An objective test of what is 'personal' will operate to exclude such species of information.

But this becomes more difficult where the individual's claim relates to information which affects his 'private life'. It would not be unreasonable for an individual to wish to prevent the disclosure of facts concerning his trial and conviction for theft. Applying the proposed definition of 'personal information' as a first-order test of whether such information is 'personal' may suggest that the claim is a legitimate one. But such a claim is likely to be defeated on the ground that in our society, the administration of justice is an open and public process. The passage of time may, however, alter the nature of such events and what was once a *public* matter may, several years later, be considered to be one which may reasonably be regarded as private. An individual's desire to withhold details of past offences (accorded limited recognition by the Rehabilitation of Offenders Act 1974) may be thought to turn on his right to control 'personal information'.[51]

Similarly, the publication of what was once 'public' information garnered from old newspapers may several years later be considered an offensive disclosure of personal information. It does not therefore follow that the objective test pre-empts the 'balancing' of the individual's right or claim to withhold 'personal information', on the one hand, and the competing interests of the community in, say, freedom of expression, on the other.

By voluntarily disclosing or acceding to the use or dissemination of personal information, the individual does not relinquish his claim that he retain certain control over it. He may, for instance, allow the information to be used for one purpose (such as medical diagnosis), but object when it is used for another (such as employment). In regard to opinions about an individual expressed by a third party the existence of which the individual is *aware* (such as references sought by him for a job application), it would be reasonable to expect him to permit access to such material only by those who are directly concerned in the decision whether or not to employ him. Where he does *not* know that assessments have been made about him (where, for example, he is described as a 'bad risk' on the computerized files of a credit reference agency) or that his communications have been intercepted or recorded, he may reasonably be expected to object to the use or disclosure (and in the case of surreptitious surveillance, and the actual acquisition) of the information, particularly if it is (actually or potentially) misleading or inaccurate—*were he aware* of the existence of the information.

[51] Though it is argued (in ch. 5) that this generally concerns the individual's reputation rather than his 'privacy'.

There is naturally a whole range of 'items' of 'personal information' the use or disclosure of which one might expect individuals to wish to resist. A complete catalogue of such information would be impossible (and probably pointless), though the classification considered in Chapter 6 incorporates the kinds of data that are most commonly the subject of concern or dispute. And there are some species of 'personal information' (for instance, the provisions of an individual's will) which generate *specific* problems that may call for special analysis. It is not the purpose of this study to examine every such type of information and the possible means of dealing with it. The sort of 'personal information' that is discussed (sometimes in detail) represents what gives rise to the persistent difficulties that have been encountered and continue to arise in most jurisdictions.

5. The Economics of 'Personal Information'

In seeking to withhold or limit the circulation of 'personal information', is the individual not engaged in a form of deception—especially where the information depicts him in an unfavourable light? This is the burden of Posner's application of his 'economic analysis of law' to the subject of personal information.[52] As he asserts, 'To the extent that

[52] Though he employs (with little clarity) the term 'privacy', Posner (rightly, it is submitted) concentrates his attention on the question of personal information. See R. Posner 'Privacy, Secrecy and Reputation'; id., 'The Right of Privacy' (1978) 12 Ga. Law Rev. 393; id., 'An Economic Theory of Privacy' in Schoeman (ed.) *Philosophical Dimensions of Privacy*, R. A. Epstein, 'Privacy, Property Rights and Misrepresentation' (1978) 12 Ga. Law Rev. 455. Cf. C. E. Baker, 'Posner's Privacy Mystery and the Failure of the Economic Analysis of Law' (1978) 12 Ga. Law Rev. 475; E. J. Bloustein, 'Privacy Is Dear at Any Price: A Response to Professor Posner's Economic Theory' (1978) 12 Ga. Law Rev. 429. A symposium on the economic analysis of 'privacy' appears in (1980) 9 J. of Legal Stud.; particularly useful are G. J. Stigler, 'An Introduction to Privacy in Economics and Politics', 623; J. Hirschleifer, 'Privacy: Its Origin, Function and Future', 649; R. A. Epstein, 'A Taste for Privacy? Evolution and the Emergence of a Naturalistic Ethic', 665; E. W. Kitch, 'The Law and Economics of Rights in Valuable Information', 683; J. P. Gould, 'Privacy and the Economics of Information', 827.

people conceal personal information in order to mislead, the economic case for according legal protection to such information is no better than that for permitting fraud in the sale of goods.'[53]

The individual who hides a history of mental illness or some other relevant health defect from his employer, family, and friends, or a history of bankruptcies, from his creditors, or tastes, eccentricities, opinions, attitudes, and the like that if known would impair his reputation among friends and acquaintances is engaged in the same kind of activity as a producer who conceals defects in his products. Only the modern intellectual's prejudice against market activity makes this a startling equation.[54]

The equation is indeed startling, but not for the reason Posner suggests. Even if one were to accept the 'economic' perspective it does not follow that one would accept the assessment of the economic 'value' of withholding personal information; individuals may be willing to trade off their interest in restricting the circulation of such information against their 'societal' interest in its free flow. In other words Posner has not shown, and may be unable to show, that his calculation of the 'competing' interests is necessarily the correct, or even the most likely, one. This analysis cannot be pursued here, but it is worth noting that Posner's claim that his economic theory 'explains' the operation of law produces a certain dissonance if one were to compare the protection of 'privacy' in the United States with that prevailing in England.

He also argues that transaction-cost considerations may militate against the legal protection of personal information. Where the information is discrediting and accurate there is a social incentive to make it generally available: accurate information facilitates reliance on the individual to whom the information relates. It is therefore socially efficient to allow society a right of access to such information rather than to permit the individual to conceal it. In the case of non-discrediting or false information, the value to the individual of concealment exceeds the value of access to it by the community. Information which is false does not advance

---

[53] 'The Right of Privacy', 401.
[54] 'Privacy, Secrecy, and Reputation', 11–12.

rational decision-making and is therefore of little use. Most of his argument rests on an explicit recognition of personal information as 'property', the legal implications of which are discussed in the following chapter.

2

'Privacy', 'Personal Information', and the Law

In this chapter the principal features of the American and English law are traced. My account is not intended to be a comprehensive description of the law relating to 'privacy' obtaining in these jurisdictions, but rather a backdrop against which the subsequent analysis of the law (in the appropriate chapters) is undertaken. In particular, the failure of the English common law (and more specifically the law of tort) to recognize a 'right of privacy' has resulted in several attempts to create such a right by legislation and, following the Report of the Younger Committee,[1] more modest proposals for (and the statutory enactment of) controls over computerized personal data and the interception of communications. Some of the theoretical foundations of these developments are briefly considered (especially the concept of 'personal information' as 'property') in order to examine the specific issues identified in subsequent chapters *from the perspective of the protection of 'personal information'*.

1. The American Law

The impact of the Warren and Brandeis essay[2] upon the American common law and, to a certain extent, constitutional

---

[1] Discussed below.

[2] 'The Right to Privacy' (1890) 4 Harv. Law Rev. 193. Prosser describes the essay as 'the outstanding example of the influence of legal periodicals upon American law' ('Privacy' (1960) 48 Calif. Law Rev. 383). Ronald Dworkin says that the essay is 'sometimes taken to be a kind of brilliant fraud': *Taking Rights Seriously* (1977), 119, though I have not encountered this suggestion in the literature. In Dworkin's view, the thesis was 'sound in its ambition', for the line of precedents was justified by a 'new principle' (ibid.). Further criticism is to be found in W. F. Pratt, 'The Warren and Brandeis Argument for a Right to Privacy' (1975) Public Law 161, and H. Kalven, 'Privacy in Tort Law: Were Warren and Brandeis Wrong?' (1966) 31 Law & Contemp. Probs. 326.

law[3] is sufficiently well known not to require elaborate restatement here. Their thesis that the common law implicitly recognized the right to privacy 'enjoys the unique distinction of having initiated and theoretically outlined a new field of

[3] Until the Supreme Court's controversial decision in *Griswold* v. *Connecticut* 381 US 479 (1965) (declaring unconstitutional a Connecticut statute which prohibited the use of contraceptives, on the ground that it violated the right of marital privacy, a right 'older than the Bill of Rights' (at 486)), the constitutional protection of 'privacy' did not significantly extend beyond the torts recognized by the common law (see below). Though the Constitution itself is silent in respect of the 'right of privacy', through several of the Amendments (particularly the First, Third, Fourth, Fifth, Ninth) the Court has recognized, *inter alia*, the right of 'associational privacy' (*NAACP* v. *Alabama* 357 US 449 (1958)), 'political privacy' (*Sweezy* v. *New Hampshire* 354 US 234 (1957)) and 'privacy of counsel' (*Massiah* v. *U.S.* 377 US 201 (1964)). In attempting to come to terms with its earlier rulings in *Olmstead* v. *U.S.* 277 US 438 (1928) and *Goldman* v. *U.S.* 316 US 129 (1942) that electronic surveillance was *not* a search and seizure within the meaning of the Fourth Amendment and therefore *not* constitutionally regulated, the Court has sought to set the limits of protection against eavesdropping and unlawful searches (see ch. 7). The incremental development of Supreme Court 'privacy' doctrine has continued (notably in *Roe* v. *Wade* 410 US 113 (1973), invalidating abortion statutes on the ground of invading a constitutional right of privacy) but has provoked certain critical responses that suggest the possibility that it might one day be checked: J. H. Ely, 'The Wages of Crying Wolf: A Comment on *Roe* v. *Wade* (1973) Yale LJ 920; R. G. Morgan, '*Roe* v. *Wade* and the Lesson of the Pre-*Roe* Case Law' (1979) 77 Mich. Law Rev. 1724; T. Huff 'Thinking Clearly about Privacy' (1980) 55 Wash. Law Rev. 777. The opportunity arose in the recent decision of the Supreme Court in *Bowers* v. *Hardwick*, 106 S. Ct. 2841 (1986). By 5 to 4 the court held the privacy protections of the due process clause do not extend to homosexual acts between consenting adults in private. The majority judgment, however, rests, not on the basis of the unsatisfactory enlargement of the constitutional concept of privacy, but on the narrower ground that: 'No connection between family, marriage, or procreation on the one hand and homosexual conduct on the other has been demonstrated' (at 2844). For a vigorous attack on the majority's reasoning in this case and in *Thornburgh* v. *American College of Obstetricians and Gynecologists*, 106 S. Ct. 2169 (1986) (invalidating certain provisions relating to abortion on the ground that they burdened the constitutional right of privacy) see D. A. J. Richards, 'Constitutional Legitimacy and Constitutional Privacy' (1986) 61 NYU Law Rev. 800, A. T. Sheppard, 'Private Passion, Public Outrage: Thoughts on *Bowers* v. *Hardwick*' (1988) 40 Rutgers LJ 521. The application of the First Amendment in 'privacy' litigation is examined in ch. 5.

jurisprudence'.[4] Drawing upon English cases of, in particular, breach of confidence, property, copyright, and defamation, they argued that these cases were merely instances and applications of a general right to privacy. The common law, they claimed, albeit under different forms, protected an individual whose privacy was invaded by the likes of snooping journalists. In so doing the law acknowledged the importance of the spiritual and intellectual needs of man. In their rhetoric:

The intensity and complexity of life, attendant upon advancing civilization, have rendered necessary some retreat from the world, and man, under the refining influence of culture, has become more sensitive to publicity so that solitude and privacy have become more essential to the individual; but modern enterprise and invention have, through invasion upon his privacy, subjected him to mental pain and distress, far greater than could be inflicted by mere bodily injury.[5]

The common law, they argued, has developed from the protection of the physical person and corporeal property to the protection of the individual's '[t]houghts, emotions and sensations'.[6] But as a result of threats to privacy from recent inventions and business methods and from the press, the common law needed to go further. An individual's right to determine the extent to which his thoughts, emotions, and sensations were communicated to others was already legally protected—but only in respect of authors of literary and artistic compositions and letters who could forbid their unauthorized publication. And though English cases recognizing this right were based on protection of property, in reality they were an acknowledgement of 'privacy', of 'inviolate personality'.[7]

In 1902 the New York Court of Appeals was given an opportunity to consider the Warren and Brandeis thesis. The plaintiff complained that her picture had been used without her consent to advertise flour.[8] The majority rejected the

[4] D. Larremore, 'The Law of Privacy' (1912) 12 Colum. Law Rev. 693.
[5] Warren and Brandeis, 'The Right to Privacy', 196.
[6] Ibid. 195.   [7] Ibid. 205.
[8] *Roberson* v. *Rochester Folding Box Co.*, 171 NY 538, 64 NE 442 (1902).

'privacy' argument: it had 'not as yet an abiding place in our jurisprudence, and . . . cannot now be incorporated without doing violence to settled principles of law . . .'.[9] The minority, however, saw the matter differently. Gray J. held that the plaintiff had a right to be protected against the use of her image for the defendant's commercial advantage: 'Any other principle of decision . . . is as repugnant to equity as it is shocking to reason.'[10] The case was greeted with unexpected public disquiet,[11] the consequence of which was legislation which rendered the unauthorized use of an individual's name or image for advertising or trade purposes unlawful.[12]

Three years later in a case involving similar facts the Supreme Court of Georgia explictly adopted the reasoning of Gray J.[13] The Warren and Brandeis thesis, fifteen years after its publication, had triumphed. And its power remains undiminished. It has spawned a huge body of case law and academic comment. Almost every American state has incorporated the 'right to privacy' into its law. Yet, despite the authors' almost exclusive reliance on English decisions,[14] no similar development has occurred in England.

For present purposes, it will be necessary to give only a brief account of the American law (in order to show the manner and extent to which the tort of 'invasion of privacy' and the constitutional protection of the 'right of privacy' have developed) and to sketch the attempts in England to legislate on the subject. Little purpose would be served by a detailed historical or comparative analysis of these developments, for, as pointed out above, the main purpose of this chapter is to identify some of the major conceptual difficulties

---

[9] Ibid. at 447.   [10] Ibid. at 450.

[11] A criticism of the judgment by the *New York Times* seems to have been the cause of one of the majority judges taking the unprecedented step of defending the decision: O'Brien 'The Right of Privacy' (1902) 2 *Colum. Law Rev.* 437.

[12] NY Sess. Laws (1903) ch. 132, paras. 1–2, subsequently amended in 1921, NY Civil Rights Law, paras. 50–1.

[13] *Pavesich* v. *New England Life Insurance Co.*, 122 Ga. 190; 50 SE 68 (1905).

[14] The decision on which they largely relied was *Prince Albert* v. *Strange* (1849) 2 De Gex & Sm. 652, 64 ER 293, (on appeal) (1849) 1 Mac. & G. 25, 41 ER 1171. The case is discussed in ch. 3.

that have been generated by the 'privacy' approach. Attention is, moreover, paid to the specific legal problems (and their attempted solutions) in the appropriate places in the chapters which follow.

The American common law, following Prosser,[15] recognizes not one tort, 'but a complex of four'.[16] The four relatively discrete torts are described by Prosser as:

(a) Intrusion upon the plaintiff's seclusion or solitude, or into his private affairs;
(b) Public disclosure of embarrassing private facts about the plaintiff;
(c) Publicity which places the plaintiff in a false light in the public eye;
(d) Appropriation, for the defendant's advantage, of the plaintiff's name or likeness.

This formulation (though it has been criticized)[17] has exercised a considerable influence on the American courts. Indeed, in their willingness to accept it, not only have they resisted the application of the law of 'privacy' to other fact-situations (a largely positive consequence!) but, more importantly, they have failed to question its theoretical coherence. In particular, the inclusion of the 'false light' and 'appro-

[15] 'Privacy', 383. Adopted by the *Restatement, Torts*, para. 867.

[16] Prosser, 'Privacy', 389. Though he argues that each of the four torts invade four distinct interests of the plaintiff, only *three* such interests are actually identified: reputation, property, and mental feelings.

[17] It has been argued, in particular, that Prosser's division undermines the essential unity of the law's protection of 'privacy' based on the right to, in Warren and Brandeis's phrase, an 'inviolate personality' (Warren and Brandeis, 'The Right to Privacy', 205). Professor Bloustein attacks Prosser's atomization on the ground that at the heart of the law's protection of 'privacy' is the recognition of 'human dignity': an invasion of 'privacy' is 'demeaning to individuality . . . an affront to personal dignity' (E. Bloustein, 'Privacy as an Aspect of Human Dignity: An Answer to Dean Prosser' (1964) 39 NYU Law Rev. 962, 973). A similar argument is made by S. Benn, 'Privacy, Freedom and Respect for Persons' (1971) *Nomos XIII* 1. Cf. H. Gross, 'The Concept of Privacy' (1967) 42 NYU Law Rev. 34. The debate seems misplaced for Prosser's account is (despite the normative interpretation it often receives) largely descriptive of the existing law. Bloustein, on the other hand, is identifying (rightly or wrongly) at a higher level of abstraction, a broader explanation for the law's protection of 'privacy'. Issue is never seriously joined.

priation' categories is, at best, a questionable application of 'privacy' to circumstances that have only the most tenuous relationship to the concept—even as conceived by Warren and Brandeis.[18] There is, moreover, a certain irony in the observation by Prosser in 1971 that 'there is as yet no decided case allowing recovery which does not fall fairly within one of the four categories with which the courts have thus far been concerned'.[19] It is precisely because of the courts' alacrity to adopt Prosser's classification as an authoritative statement of the law that no such development had occurred![20]

An extended analysis of the four torts would serve little purpose here, but it is necessary briefly to outline the main features of each (as defined by Prosser) in order to discover their relationship to 'personal information'.

1. *Intrusion upon the plaintiff's seclusion or solitude or into his private affairs.* The wrongful act consists in the intentional interference with the plaintiff's solitude or seclusion. It includes the physical intrusion into the plaintiff's premises and eavesdropping (including electronic and photographic surveillance, 'bugging', and telephone-tapping). Three requirements must be satisfied.[21] (a) there must be an actual *prying* (disturbing noises or bad manners will not suffice); (b) the intrusion must offend *a reasonable man*; (c) it must be an intrusion into something *private*. This third requirement is, for the purposes of the present study, the most important. It is examined in Chapter 7.

2. *Public disclosure of embarrassing private facts about the plaintiff.* Three elements of the tort are indicated by

---

[18] This is so, it is submitted, in the face of the fact that the first decision of the American courts to recognize the tort was an 'appropriation' case: *Pavesich* v. *New England Life Ins. Co.* 120 Ga. 190, 50 SE 68 (1905).

[19] *The Law of Torts*, 4th edn.

[20] Prosser's 'concept of privacy is alluded to in almost every decided privacy case in the last ten years or so' (Bloustein, 'Privacy as an Aspect of Human Dignity, 964). This practice has, in the more than twenty years since Bloustein made this observation, continued unabated.

[21] Prosser and Keeton, *The Law of Torts*, 5th edn. (1984) 855. This work is referred to hereafter simply as Prosser, though occasionally the 4th edn. (1971) is cited in order to reflect Prosser's own view.

Prosser:[22] (a) there must be *publicity* (to disclose the facts to a small group of people would not suffice); (b) the facts disclosed must be *private facts* (publicity given to matters of public record is not tortious); (c) the facts disclosed must be offensive to *a reasonable man of ordinary sensibilities.* Again, it is this third requirement that is of special importance here. It is examined in Chapter 5.

3. *Publicity which places the plaintiff in a false light in the public eye.* According to Prosser[23] this tort normally arises in circumstances in which some opinion or utterance (such as spurious books or views) is publicly attributed to the plaintiff or where his picture is used to illustrate a book or article with which he has no reasonable connection. The overlap with the tort of defamation is at once apparent, and, though the false light 'need not necessarily be a defamatory one', it is argued (in Chapter 5) that an action for defamation will invariably lie in such cases. The publicity must be 'highly offensive to a reasonable person.'[24]

4. *Appropriation, for the defendant's advantage, of the plaintiff's name or likeness.* Under the common law tort the advantage derived by the defendant need not be a financial one;[25] it has, for instance, been held to arise where the plaintiff was named as father in a birth certificate. The statutory tort (which exists in several states) normally requires the unauthorized use of the plaintiff's identity for commercial (usually advertising) purposes; the New York statute[26]—upon which most of the current legislation is modelled—confines itself to advertising or 'purposes of trade'.[27] The recognition of this tort establishes what has

---

[22] Prosser, 856–7; *Restatement*, para. 652D.

[23] Prosser, 863–4; *Restatement*, para. 652E adds the requirement that 'the actor had knowledge of or acted in reckless disregard as to the falsity of the publicized matter and the false light in which the other would be placed'.

[24] *Restatement*, para. 652E, comment b.

[25] Prosser, 853; *Restatement*, para. 652C, comment b.

[26] New York Civil Rights Law 1921, Titles 50–1.

[27] Though this has been given a fairly loose interpretation; see e.g. *Spahn v. Julian Messner, Inc.* 23 App. Div. 2d 216; 260 NYS 2d 451 (1964).

been called a 'right of publicity'[28] under which an individual is able to decide how he wishes to exploit his name or image commercially. It is argued below that the protection of this essentially proprietary interest has little connection even with the protection of a general 'right to privacy'.

2. The American Common Law and 'Personal Information

It is only the torts of 'intrusion' and 'public disclosure' that 'require the invasion of something secret, secluded or private pertaining to the plaintiff'.[29] It might therefore be argued that the torts of 'appropriation' and 'false light' are not properly conceived of as aspects of 'privacy'. To some extent, this is the position adopted in this book. Thus it is suggested (in Chapter 5) that 'false light' bears a relationship to defamation rather than 'privacy', and (below) that 'appropriation' is essentially a proprietary wrong. But this is an argument which does not require to be made for the purposes of the present analysis of the protection of 'personal information'. It is sufficient to show that only the first two torts bear any relation to the question of 'personal information'—and this is conceded by the leading authority.[30]

That neither Prosser nor the American courts have sought specificallly to define what is 'private' seems to be, in part, a consequence of the perspective (which is adopted, as well, by Warren and Brandeis)[31] that regards 'the right of privacy' as equivalent to 'the right to be alone'.[32] If 'privacy' is believed to express a general right of this kind, the need to declare in advance the precise circumstances in which it is invaded is less important than if the starting-point is some conception of 'personal information'. Nevertheless in seeking to draw the boundaries between 'private' and 'public', the courts have, in effect, formulated a relatively clear test of what is protected.

[28] M. B. Nimmer, 'The Right of Publicity' (1954) 19 Law & Contemp. Probs. 203; Kalven, 'Privacy in Tort Law', 331.
[29] Prosser, *Law of Torts*, 4th edn., 814.   [30] Ibid.
[31] 'The Right to Privacy', 195.
[32] Attributed to Thomas M. Cooley in *A Treatise on the Law of Torts*, 2nd edn. (1888), 29.

And, in so doing, they have appealed to what is *reasonable* in the circumstances. Thus in the case of 'intrusion' (discussed in Chapter 7) it has been held that there is no cause of action where, for instance, the plaintiff is photographed in a public place.[33] And, in the case of 'public disclosure' (discussed in Chapter 5) it has been held that the plaintiff cannot complain where publicity is given to matters of public record such as his date of birth or marriage.[34]

A limiting factor in both torts is that the intrusion or disclosure is offensive and objectionable to *a reasonable man of ordinary sensibilities*. In the latter case, it is clear that the law applies 'something in the nature of a "mores" test[35] under which there will be liability only for publicity given to those things which the customs and ordinary views of the community would regard as highly objectionable'.[36] This sort of approach was suggested in Chapter 1 as the proper basis upon which to define the notion of 'personal information'. It was argued there that the objection to the attempt to categorize information as 'personal' (on the ground of what the plaintiff would reasonably wish to withhold) is misconceived. Clearly, even under a general 'privacy' action, a similar test is necessary and, under American tort law, applied. This question is further examined in Chapters 5 and 7.

3. The English Law

In its recognition of the general failure of the common law to mirror American developments[37] the legislature has, on

[33] *Gill v. Hearst Publishing Co.* 40 Cal. 2d 224, 253 P 2d 441 (1953) (see ch. 7).

[34] *Meetze v. Associated Press* 230 SC 330, 95 SE 2d 606 (1956).

[35] First proposed in the lower court in *Sidis v. F.-R. Publishing Corporation* SDNY 1938, 34 F Supp. 19 (see ch. 5).

[36] Prosser, 857; *Restatement*, para. 652D, comment h.

[37] The courts, it has been argued, 'are as free as the American ones to develop a law of privacy. But there is no spirit of adventure or progress, either in judges or counsel in England today. English judges are not the innovators that some of their distinguished predecessors were; in the hands of modern judges the common law has lost its capacity to expand' (H. Street, *Freedom, the Individual and the Law*, 5th edn. (1984), 264.

several occasions, sought (without success) to create a statutory 'right of privacy'.[38] The most comprehensive bill, introduced in 1969,[39] was the result of an investigation by a Committee of JUSTICE into the inadequacies of the common law. Eschewing mere tinkering with the law of, for instance, trespass and nuisance, to provide remedies for invasions of 'privacy', and the enactment of piecemeal legislation, it recommended instead a bill to create 'a general right of privacy applicable in all situations'.[40] The proposed 'right of privacy' was defined to mean:

the right of any person to be protected from intrusion upon himself, his home, his family, his relationships and communications with others, his property and business affairs, including intrusion by:

(a) spying, prying, watching or besetting;
(b) the unauthorised overhearing or recording of spoken words;
(c) the unauthorised making of visual images;
(d) the unauthorised reading or copying of documents;
(e) the unauthorised use or disclosure of confidential information, or facts (including his name, identity or likeness) calculated to cause him distress, annoyance or embarrassment, or to place him in a false light;
(f) the unauthorised appropriation of his name, identity or likeness for another's gain.

The influence of the American law is at once evident in the

---

[38] A Right of Privacy Bill was introduced in the House of Lords by Lord Mancroft on 14 Feb. 1961. It was restricted to the 'public disclosure' element of 'privacy'. Though it attracted the support of Lord Denning in the House of Lords (229 *Hansard* col. 639 (13 Mar. 1961) HL) and, passed its second reading by 74 votes to 21, the bill was withdrawn during the committee stage for lack of government support (232 *Hansard* cols. 289–99 (15 June 1961) HL). A second Right of Privacy Bill was introduced by Mr Alexander Lyon MP under the ten-minute rule on 8 Feb. 1967. It applied to 'intrusion' as well as 'public disclosure', but proceeded no further than its first reading (740 *Hansard* cols. 1663–85 (8 Feb. 1967) HC). A third attempt to introduce a Right of Privacy Bill was made by Mr Brian Walden MP on 26 Nov. 1969 (792 *Hansard* col. 340 (26 Nov. 1969) HC). The bill was similar, in all material respects, to that proposed by JUSTICE (the British Section of the International Commission of Jurists) in its report *Privacy and the Law* (see the discussion in the text above).

[39] The Walden–JUSTICE Bill. It received its second reading one week after the JUSTICE Report was published. See previous note.

[40] *Privacy and the Law* Para. 128.

wholesale (and ill-considered) adoption of the four common-law torts outlined above. During the second reading debate, the Home Secretary, Mr James Callaghan MP, argued (with some justification) that the kinds of activity that were genuinely objectionable required clearer definition. He also expressed concern that the bill vested too much discretion in the courts and that it might generate 'unwarranted litigation'.[41] The matter, he persuaded the House, warranted a full investigation. The proposer, Mr Brian Walden withdrew his bill. (With few modifications it emerged again almost twenty years later as a private member's bill proposed by Mr William Cash MP. Though it attracted considerable support, by the end of 1988 it had not been debated.)[42]

Following the withdrawal of the Walden Bill, a Committee on Privacy was appointed on 13 May 1970 under the chairmanship of Kenneth Younger with the following terms of reference:

To consider whether legislation is needed to give further protection to the individual citizen and to commercial and industrial interests against intrusions into privacy by private persons and organisations, or by companies and to make recommendations.

By excluding 'public sector' invasions of 'privacy' from the committee's consideration—a matter to which its members objected—the Government placed a significant restriction upon its brief. The committee rejected by a majority[43] the creation of a general right of privacy, preferring instead a 'piecemeal approach'.[44] It took the view that 'privacy' was 'a basic need, essential to the development and maintenance both of a free society and of a mature and stable individual personality.'[45] But the 'best way to ensure regard for privacy is to provide specific and effective sanctions against clearly defined activities which unreasonably frustrate the individual in his search for privacy.'[46]

---

[41] 794 *Hansard* col. 943 (23 Jan. 1970) HC.

[42] The Bill (which attracted the support of 307 MPs and the chairman of the Press Council) was not debated in Parliament, but its proposer intends to pursue it in the future.

[43] Mr Alexander Lyon and Mr D. M. Ross QC dissented.

[44] Younger, para. 659.   [45] Ibid. para. 113.   [46] Ibid. para. 633.

The committee concluded that a general right would create uncertainty, although there is less substance in their claim that it would burden the court with 'controversial questions of a social and political character',[47] for this is to accept the dubious proposition that the courts do not concern themselves with such questions anyway.

It recommended:

(a) the creation of a new crime and a new tort of unlawful surveillance;[48]

(b) the creation of a new tort of disclosure or other use of information unlawfully acquired;[49]

(c) the reference to the Law Commissions of the law relating to breach of confidence with a view to its clarification and statement in legislative form.[50]

Subsequent developments (and the relevant common law) are considered in the appropriate chapters below. The proposals of the Law Commission and the Scottish Law Commission are examined in Chapter 3. The *Report of the Committee on Data Protection* is considered in Chapter 6. The Interception of Communication Act 1985 is discussed in Chapter 7. The purpose is not to provide a comprehensive account of the law is so far as it 'protects' aspects of 'privacy', but to analyse the extent to which 'personal information' (as defined in Chapter 1) is accorded explicit or adventitious recognition.

4. 'Personal Information' as 'Property'

One consequence of the extraordinary growth and scale of 'information technology'[51] is the extent to which existing

---

[47] Ibid. para. 653.   [48] Ibid. paras. 560–5.
[49] Ibid. para. 632.   [50] Ibid. para. 630.
[51] In the last twenty years the service sector has been the fastest growing component in international trade. It accounts for about *one-third* of total world trade, and this proportion continues to increase. It has been estimated that the US (the most service-intensive nation) depends on services for *two-thirds* of its GNP and 70% of its jobs. By 1980 more than half of those employed in the service sector were employed in the field of *information technology* (Winham, 'GATT and the New Trade World' (1983) 4 Int. Perspectives 3, quoted in C. J. Millard, *Legal Protection of Computer Programs and Data* (1985), 225).

formal legal concepts are appropriate or adequate to control the numerous ways in which computer data are susceptible of misuse. In particular, the question has arisen whether, by ascribing property rights to information, the law might provide an effective means of regulating this and other instances of its wrongful use.[52]

Breach of confidence litigation has spawned the occasional dictum[53] which employs the concepts (or, at any rate, the term) 'property'. Thus, in *Butler* v. *Board of Trade*[54] Goff J. referred to the plaintiff's 'limited proprietary right in equity to restrain a breach of confidence'. But this is merely a metaphorical use of the term; 'property is not being used in its normal sense as conferring an exclusionary right which operates against the whole world'.[55] As Holmes J. put it in *E. I. Du Pont de Nemours Powder Co.* v. *Masland*:[56]

The word 'property' as applied to trademarks and trade secrets is an unanalyzed expression of certain secondary consequences of the primary fact that the law makes some rudimentary requirements of good faith. Whether the plaintiffs have any valuable secret or not the defendant knows the facts, whatever they are, through a special

---

[52] The subject has generated a doctrinal debate the terms of which extend beyond the question under consideration here: R. Grant Hammond, 'Quantum Physics, Econometric Models and Property Rights to Information' (1981) 27 McGill LJ 47; id. 'Theft of Information' (1984) 100 LQR 252; 'The Misappropriation of Commercial Information in the Computer Age' (1986) 64 Can. Bar Rev. 342. D. F. Libling, 'The Concept of Property: Property in Intangibles' (1978) 94 LQR 103; S. Ricketson, 'Confidential Information: A New Proprietary Interest?' (1977–8) 11 Melb. Univ. Law Rev. 223; J. E. Stuckey, 'The Equitable Action for Breach of Confidence: Is Information Ever Property?' (1981) 9 Sydney Law Rev. 402; E. Kitch 'The Law and Economics of Rights in Valuable Information' (1980) 9 J. Legal Stud. 683. A. S. Weinrib 'Information as Property' (1988) 38 Univ. of Tor. LJ 117. The narrower question of confidential information is considered in R. P. Meagher, W. M. C. Gummow, and J. R. F. Lehane, *Equity: Doctrines and Remedies* (1984) 832–4; F. Gurry, *Breach of Confidence* (1984) 46–56.

[53] For example *Argyll (Duchess)* v. *Argyll (Duke)* [1967] 1 Ch. 302, 320 per Ungoed-Thomas J. Cf. *Nicrotherm Electrical Co. Ltd.* v. *Percy* [1957] RPC 207, 209; *Malone v. Commissioner of Police of the Metropolis (No. 2* [1979] 2 All ER 620, 630 per Megarry VC; *Fraser v. Thames Television Ltd.* [1983] 2 WLR 917, 932–3 per Hirst J.

[54] [1971] Ch. 680, 691.   [55] F. Gurry, *Breach of Confidence*, 47.

[56] 244 US 100, 102; 61 L Ed 1016, 1019 (1916). Emphasis supplied.

confidence that he accepted. The property may be denied, but the confidence cannot be. Therefore *the starting point for the present matter is not property or due process of law, but that the defendant stood in confidential relations with the plaintiffs . . .*

And a similar point was made by Lord Upjohn in respect of confidential information in *Phipps* v. *Boardman*:[57]

In general, *information is not property at all.* It is normally open to all who have eyes to read and ears to hear. The true test is to determine in what circumstances the information has been acquired. If it has been acquired in such circumstances that it would be a breach of confidence to disclose it to another then courts of equity will restrain the recipient from communicating it to another. In such cases such confidential information is often described as the property of the donor, the books are full of such references . . . But in the end the real truth is that it is not property in any normal sense . . .

Thus, though there are certain similarities between trade secrets (which have an obvious economic value) and the traditional notion of property (e.g., trade secrets may be sold[58] or transmitted by will[59]), to employ the concept of property is likely only to create conceptual confusion.[60] The courts have sensibly resisted the temptation to resort to property rights in the context of breach of confidence and have thus far been unimpressed by the argument that information may be stolen.[61]

Sometimes, however, they have appeared to rely on rights

---

[57] [1967] 2 AC 46, 127–8. Emphasis supplied. Lord Hodson, on the other hand, said, 'I dissent from the view that information is of its nature something which is not properly to be described as property.' (At 107.)

[58] *Bryston v. Whitehead* (1822) 1 Sim. & St. 74; 57 ER 29.

[59] *Canham v. Jones* (1813) 2 V. & B. 218; 35 ER 302.

[60] 'Broad brush concepts, it seems, even in the chip economy do not make good legal handmaidens. At best they are crude starting points' (R. G. Hammond, 'Theft of Information' (1984) 100 LQR 252, 263).

[61] *Oxford v. Moss* (1978) 68 Cr. App. R. 183. Cf. *R. v. Stewart* (1983) 5 CCC (3d) 481; 35 CR (3d) 105; 149 DLR (3d) 583. This decision of the Ontario Court of Appeal that confidential information *is* property for the purpose of the general theft provisions of the Canadian Criminal Code is roundly criticized by Hammond, 'Theft of Information'. But see Weinrib, 'Information as Property'. *Stewart* was not followed by the Alberta Court of Appeal in *R. v. Offley* (1986) 45 Alta. LR (2d) 23; 11 CPR (3rd) 231.

of property to found relief for breach of confidence. Indeed, the leading decision of *Prince Albert* v. *Strange*[62] by which Warren and Brandeis set so much store in support of their argument that the common law recognized the right to an 'inviolate personality',[63] seems to rest on the plaintiff's right of property in the etchings which the defendants sought to use without consent (see the discussion of the decision in Chapter 3). The Vice-Chancellor declared:[64]

Upon the principle, therefore, of protecting property, it is that the common law, in cases not aided or prejudiced by statute, shelters the privacy and seclusion of thoughts and sentiments committed to writing, and desired by the author to remain not generally known.

And Lord Cottenham said:

The property of an author or composer of any work, whether of literature, art or science, in such work unpublished and kept for his private use or pleasure, cannot be disputed, after the many decisions in which the proposition has been affirmed or assumed . . . If, then, such right and property exist in the author of such works, it must so exist exclusively of all other persons.[65]

But the operation of this apparent proprietary right is problematic. It is certainly no easy task (without a large measure of artificiality) to distinguish the few decisions in which confidential information has been regarded as property. In any event, it would seem that the recognition of such a right would extend the jurisdiction of breach of confidence only to circumstances in which a third party has acquired confidential information without committing an actual breach of confidence[66] (a matter considered in both Chapter 3 and

[62] (1849) 2 De Gex & Sm. 652; 64 ER 293. On appeal: (1849) 1 Mac. & G. 25, 41 ER 1171.
[63] See ch. 1.   [64] 64 ER 293, 312.
[65] (1849) 1 Mac. & G. 25, 42–3. There are similar statements in *Exchange Telegraph Co. (Ltd.)* v. *Howard* (1906) 22 TLR 375 and *Deta Nominees Pty. Ltd.* v. *Viscount Plastic Products Pty. Ltd.* [1979] VR 167, 190–2.
[66] Gurry, *Breach of Confidence*, 47–8, 53–4 who suggests that, since there is authority to support the right of a person to use confidential information which he has discovered by independent means (*James* v. *James* (1872) 13 LR Eq. 421, 424) or who acquires it by analysing a marketed product in which the secret is embodied (*Estcourt* v. *Estcourt*

Chapter 7). Whether the application of a property right of this kind is useful—or desirable—in such cases (which generally involve the conduct described in Chapter 1 as 'intrusion') is considered in the appropriate places in Chapters 3, 5, and 7. It is submitted that from the point of view of the general protection of trade secrets[67] and, *a fortiori*, 'personal information',[68] the application of the concept of property is 'unsuited to the purpose of resolving the problems relating to the rights and obligations of third parties in the field of information.'[69]

Whatever general theory of property[70] one chooses to adopt, it is not difficult to see why the concept has insinuated itself into decisions on and analysis of information, in particular where the matter is thought to involve 'privacy'. The Warren and Brandeis thesis itself turns, of course, on cases in which relief was founded on an interest in property

Hop Essence Co. (1875) 10 Ch. App. 276), property is not being used in its full (and normal) sense as conferring an exclusionary right which operates against the whole world. Authority for its use would therefore seem to be confined to cases in which the information is acquired improperly (see ch. 7).

[67] Professor Miller describes the designation of personal information as property as 'one of the most facile and legalistic approaches to safeguarding privacy that has been offered to date' (*The Assault on Privacy* (1971), 226). On the other hand, Weinrib, 'Information as Property', 117–18, regards the view that confidential information is property as a natural and desirable application of the concept of property, and of the protection that follows from that catgorization'.

[68] '[I]t is my view that the problem when a defendant should disgorge profits made through the breach of another's confidence cannot be solved by categorising information as property' (G. Jones 'Restitution of Benefits Obtained in Breach of Another's Confidence' (1970) 86 LQR 463, 473).

[69] Law Commission Report, *Breach of Confidence*, para. 2.10.

[70] Though there are several theories (utilitarian, Hegelian, Marxist) the most influential (particularly in the US) is, of course, Locke's. See C. B. McPherson, *The Political Theory of Possessive Individualism* (1962); L. C. Becker, *Property Rights: Philosophical Foundations* (1977). In very broad terms, he argued that since all have a property in their own person and in that which has been mixed with their own labour, they could therefore appropriate to themselves anything which they had converted to their use through their own labour (J. Locke, *Second Treatise of Government* (1690), ch. 5. A modern (and more radical) version of Locke's philosophy is espoused by R. Nozick, *Anarchy, State and Utopia* (1974).

(especially *Prince Albert* v. *Strange*),[71] and, as has already been pointed out, the very first judgment to recognize the common law protection of 'privacy' was one which involved what has now come to be known as the tort of 'appropriation'.[72] This consists in the use, for the defendant's benefit, of the plaintiff's name or likeness, and usually takes the form of the unauthorized use of the plaintiff's identity for commercial (normally advertising) purposes.[73] It is not therefore surprising that, initially at least on the strength of the Warren and Brandeis argument,[74] the American courts have accepted 'appropriation' as one of the four 'privacy' torts. It is, however, difficult to see how the wrong of appropriation relates to 'privacy'[75] (even if the widest

---

[71] See below, 82 ff.

[72] *Pavesich* v. *New England Life Ins. Co.* 120 Ga. 190; 50 SE 68 (1905). The New York Court of Appeals had, three years earlier, rejected by a majority the Warren and Brandeis thesis and denied recovery in a case involving the unauthorized use of the plaintiff's picture for advertising purposes: *Roberson* v. *Rochester Folding Box Co.* 171 NY 64; 64 NE 442 (1902); the resulting public dissatisfaction led to the passing of the New York statute on appropriation of personality for 'purposes of trade' (upon which many of the enactments of other states are based). See *Zacchini* v. *Scripps-Howard Broadcasting Co.* 433 US 562 (1977).

[73] But it is not so confined. There are American decisions allowing recovery where, for example, the plaintiff's name has been put forward as a candidate for political office without his consent (*State ex rel. La Follette* v. *Hinkle* 131 Wash. 86; 229 P. 317 (1924)) or where his name has been used to enable the defendant to pose as the plaintiff's common-law wife (*Burns* v. *Stevens* 236 443; 210 482 (1926)).

[74] They had to look beyond 'property' for a theoretical foundation for their argument, for when they wrote (in 1890) the concept of property was considerably narrower than it is today: Libling, 'The Concept of Property: Property in Intangibles'.

[75] The inappropriateness of the 'privacy' argument is recognized by M. B. Nimmer, 'The Right of Publicity' (1954) 19 Law & Contemp. Probs. 203 and R. Gavison, 'Privacy and the Limits of Law' (1980) 89 Yale LJ 421, 440: 'The essence of privacy is not freedom from commercial exploitation . . . The use of privacy as a label for protection against some forms of commercial exploitation is another unfortunate illustration of the confusions that will inevitably arise if care is not taken to follow an orderly conceptual scheme.' H. Kalven suggests that the rationale for protection 'is the straightforward one of preventing unjust enrichment by the theft of good will' ('Privacy in Tort Law', 331). Cf. T. Frazer, 'Appropriation of Personality: A New Tort?' (1983) 99 LQR 281.

definition of the term is employed: see Chapter 1). It cannot, *a fortiori*, be said to concern the question 'personal information' (as defined here) either.

It has, however, been argued[76] that unless property rights are recognized scarce resources will not be efficiently used because investment will only occur when property is protected and users of scarce resources will ignore the external costs of such use. Property rights are therefore required if resources are to be efficiently allocated and employed. Moreoever, a person will increase his utility when the expected benefits of acquiring property rights in a non-owned resource exceed the cost of enforcing claims over it. When applied to the 'appropriation' aspect of 'privacy' it has been suggested[77] that '[p]urely in terms of economic efficiency . . . there may be a justification for converting personality from no-owner-ship to private property'.[78] Even if this were a valid argument in respect of 'appropriation' (with its peculiarly proprietary characteristics) and trade secrets[79] it would create un-necessary conceptual confusion to apply this sort of approach to 'personal information'.

While certain advantages may accrue from the application of property theories to information in general,[80] and com-

---

[76] The leading advocate of this approach is R. Posner, *The Economic Analysis of Law*, 2nd edn. (1977).

[77] Frazer, 'Appropriation of Personality'.

[78] Posner, *Economic Analysis of Law*. He applies two well-known models used in welfare economics: the Pareto optimality and the Kaldor-Hicks tests. His conclusions, described in the text, are drawn on the basis of the latter.

[79] Posner is consistent in refusing property rights to personal informa-tion, but extending them to trade secrets. For him the disclosure of personal information (in a general, undefined sense) is restricted because it is costly to the person to whom the information relates, and valuable to others. But he is unwilling to allow that this should give rise to vesting property rights in persons both because of the deception involved (see above) and the high transaction-costs of enforcing such rights ('The Right of Privacy' (1978) 12 Ga. Law Rev. 393, 397 ff.).

[80] This is a large question that raises several difficult problems (that lie outside the present study) about the future of the social and institutional management of information technology. There can be little doubt that 'if information is . . . conceived as a *resource*, (as opposed to a *commodity*) then its characteristics as a collective good would lead to quite different

mercial information in particular,[81] there is no compelling case for applying the concept of property to 'personal information' as defined in this book. Adequate legal means already exist without the need to manufacture new property rights.

approaches with respect to the production and distribution of information in society' (Hammond, 'Quantum Physics, Econometric Models and Property Rights to Information' 71).

[81] See S. K. Murumba, *Commercial Exploitation of Property* (1986).

3

'Personal Information' and Breach of Confidence

1. Introduction

Confusion attends both the basis and the scope of the jurisdiction to restrain breach of confidence. Although—or perhaps because—the jurisdiction has its origins in equity, there is a notorious imprecision in respect of the nature and extent of the action, and no single principle—or even clearly related set of principles—can easily be identified as explaining or underpinning it. Little has changed in almost two decades since Professor Gareth Jones wrote:

A cursory study of the cases, where the plaintiff's confidence has been breached, reveals great conceptual confusion. Property, contract, bailment, trust, fiduciary relationship, good faith, unjust enrichment, have all been claimed, at one time or another, as the basis of judicial intervention. Indeed some judges have indiscriminately intermingled all these concepts. The result is that the answer to many fundamental questions remains speculative.[1]

The leading cases[2] do not establish with adequate clarity the circumstances in which (either direct or indirect) recipients of confidential information may be restrained from using or disclosing it. This is often a result of their being applications for interlocutory injunctions which require speedy adjudication. More recent decisions recognize a wider equitable principle of 'good faith' on which to base the jurisdiction (expressed in the maxim: he who has received the information

---

[1] G. Jones, 'Restitution of Benefits Obtained in Breach of Another's Confidence' (1970) 86 LQR 463, footnotes omitted. For a perceptive analysis of the underlying purpose of the law in this area see P. D. Finn, *Fiduciary Obligations*, 5th edn. (1977), ch. 19.

[2] *Prince Albert* v. *Strange* (1849) 1 H. & Tw. 1; 1 Mac. & G. 25, discussed below; *Morison* v. *Moat* (1851) 9 Hare 241.

in confidence shall not take unfair advantage of it),[3] but its scope remains problematic.

A detailed account of the action for breach of confidence would be out of place here; it is not the purpose of this chapter to provide a comprehensive analysis of this branch of the law. Nevertheless, in order to investigate the extent to which the action provides protection for 'personal information' the first section of this chapter sketches the principal elements of liability, the remedies available for breach of confidence, certain important (and controversial) aspects of the developing law of confidence, and some of the Law Commission's proposals to reform the law. It would be impossible to provide a coherent critique of the action's protection of personal information without this preliminary introduction. However, readers who are familiar with the terrain may skip Section 2 and proceed directly to Section 3 where I look at four decisions which concern 'personal' (as opposed, in the main, to technical or commercial non-personal) information to see the extent to which the action provides an adequate or appropriate means of protecting this category of information. This is followed in Section 4 by an analysis of the practical limitations and doctrinal difficulties inherent in the application of the action for breach of confidence to such cases. I have tried to limit the repetition of points already made Section 2, but on occasion, to avoid excessive cross-references, this has been necessary and is, I hope, helpful.

2. The Action for Breach of Confidence.

2.1. THE PRINCIPAL ELEMENTS OF THE ACTION

In order to establish a cause of action, three general requirements must be satisfied:

1. The information itself must 'have the necessary quality of confidence about it'.[4] (This requirement is normally

---

[3] *Seager* v. *Copydex* [1967] 2 All ER 415 at 417 per Lord Denning MR; *Fraser* v. *Evans* [1969] 1 All ER 8 at 11 per Lord Denning MR.

[4] *Saltman Engineering Co. Ltd.* v. *Campbell Engineering Co. Ltd.* (1948) 65 RPC 203, [1963] 3 All ER 413 at 415 per Lord Greene MR.

satisfied by demonstrating that the information is 'not . . . public property and public knowledge'.)[5]

2. The information must have been imparted in circumstances imposing an obligation of confidence. Such an obligation will normally arise when information is imparted—either explicitly or implicitly—for a limited purpose, and extends to any third parties to whom the information is disclosed, in breach of confidence, by the original confidant.[6]

3. There must have been an unauthorized use of the information by the party who was under an obligation of confidence.

Each of these requirements will be briefly examined.

2.1.1. *The Information*

The action has been applied, in the main, to cases involving what may broadly be called 'trade secrets'—a term which includes business secrets[7] and technical secrets;[8] but secrets of government,[9] artistic and literary confidences,[10] as well as 'personal information' have all been accommodated within the jurisdiction. The last-mentioned category will, of course, be the central concern of this chapter.

In respect of the general question of the information that is capable of protection, reference to only two issues need be made here. First, while it is trite law that once information is

---

[5] Ibid.

[6] *Lord Ashburton* v. *Pape* [1913] 2 Ch. 469.

[7] e.g., *Thomas Marshall (Exporters) Ltd.* v. *Guinle* [1978] 3 WLR 116 at 136 where Megarry VC considered the sort of information which was 'capable of being confidential'. Sir Nicolas Browne Wilkinson VC recently expressed the view (rightly, it is submitted) that '[n]either in principle nor on authority [is] there any reason why information relating to sexual matters should not be the subject of an enforceable duty of confidentiality': *Stephens* v. *Avery* [1988] 2 WLR 1280.

[8] e.g., *Ackroyds (London) Ltd.* v. *Islington Plastics Ltd.* [1962] RPC 97 (invention of tool to manufacture plastic 'swizzle sticks').

[9] *Attorney-General* v. *Guardian Newspapers Ltd. (No. 2)* (Scott J.) [1988] 2 WLR 805; (Court of Appeal) [1988] 2 WLR 805; *Attorney-General* v. *Guardian Newspapers Ltd* [1987] 1 WLR 1248; *Attorney-General* v. *Jonathan Cape Ltd.* [1976] 1 QB 752; *Commonwealth of Australia* v. *John Fairfax & Sons Ltd.* (1981) 55 ALJR 45.

[10] e.g., *Fraser* v. *Thames Television Ltd.* [1983] 2 WLR 917 (idea for a television series).

generally accessible (in the 'public domain') it loses its claim to protection,[11] an immediate difficulty, highlighted by the recent *Spycatcher* litigation, is the meaning, especially in a non-commercial context, of the concept of 'public domain'. Another problem arises where the defendant has obtained some of the information in confidence and then subsequently all of it is made public. Can he be heard to say that since the information is now public knowledge he ought to be as free as the next man to use it? The law seems to give a negative reply. The information which he acquired in confidence may not be used as a 'springboard' for activities detrimental to the plaintiff. Moreover, it remains a springboard 'even when all the features have been published or can be ascertained by actual inspection by any member of the public'.[12]

This so-called Springboard Doctrine, first expressed in *Terrapin* has been applied on a number of occasions, including by the Court of Appeal in *Seager* v. *Copydex Ltd.*[13] There has been a tendency to temper the rigour of this doctrine in respect of the duration of the obligation[14] and where the plaintiff has voluntarily disclosed the information in, say, a patent specification.[15] The doctrine has given rise to several difficulties[16] none of which is strictly relevant here; but the problem of information which is in the 'public domain' does assume an important position in respect of 'personal information' and freedom of expression, which is discussed in 2.2 below.

Secondly, confidential information may be disclosed where such disclosure is in the 'public interest'. The recognition by courts of this limitation on the protection of confidentiality

---

[11] *Saltman Engineering Co. Ltd.* v. *Campbell Engineering Co. Ltd.* (1948) 65 RPC 203, 215; [1963] 3 All ER 413, 415: The information must have 'the necessary quality of confidence about it, namely, it must not be something which is public property and public knowledge', per Lord Greene MR.

[12] *Terrapin Ltd.* v. *Builders Supply Co. (Hayes) Ltd.* [1967] RPC 375, 391 per Roxburgh J. But see *Attorney-General* v. *Guardian Newspapers Ltd. (No. 2)* [1988] 3 WLR 776, 809–810 (per Lord Goff).

[14] *Potters-Ballotini* v. *Weston-Baker* [1977] RPC 202, 206 per Lord Denning MR.

[15] *O. Mustad & Son* v. *Dosen* (1928) [1963] RPC 41.

[16] See F. Gurry, *Breach of Confidence* (1984) 245–52.

has recently developed beyond the relatively narrow expression by Wood VC in *Gartside* v. *Outram*[17] that 'there is no confidence as to the disclosure of iniquity' to include not merely disclosures relating to the commission of criminal offences and civil wrongs[18] but to acts which are 'destructive of the country or its people',[19] and even to disclosures which reveal 'the truth' about pop stars.[20] The expansion of this defence—which has a direct bearing upon the relationship between confidentiality and freedom of expression—warrants separate consideration below.

2.1.2. *The Obligation of Confidence*

The recipient of information normally incurs an obligation of confidence by virtue of the relationship in the course of which the information is imparted. Such an obligation may arise, with or without a contract, in a variety of circumstances, ranging from marriage[21] to cabinet meetings.[22]

It is generally the case that even in the absence of an explicit undertaking by the recipient of information to maintain its confidentiality, an obligation of confidence will be imposed upon him if the circumstances are such as to indicate that he knew or ought to have known that the information is to be treated as confidential.[23] Even if a third party receives confidential information, and, at the time he receives it, he is unaware that he has acquired it as a result of

[17] (1857) 26 LJ Ch. (NS) 113, 114.

[18] *Initial Services* v. *Putterill* [1968] 1 QB 396.

[19] *Beloff* v. *Pressdram Ltd.* [1973] 1 All ER 241, 260 per Ungoed-Thomas.

[20] *Woodward* v. *Hutchins* [1977] 1 WLR 760, 764 per Lord Denning MR.

[21] *Argyll* v. *Argyll* [1967] Ch. 302.

[22] *Attorney-General* v. *Jonathan Cape Ltd.* [1976] QB 752.

[23] The objectivity of the test was suggested, *obiter*, by Megarry J. in *Coco* v. *A. N. Clark (Engineers) Ltd.* [1969] RPC 41, 48: 'It may be that the hard-worked creature, the reasonable man, may be pressed into service once more; for I do not see why he should not labour in equity as well as at law. It seems to me that if the circumstances are such that any reasonable man standing in the shoes of the recipient of the information would have realised that upon reasonable grounds the information was being given to him in confidence, then this should suffice to impose upon him the equitable obligation of confidence.'

a breach of confidence, he will, on being given notice of the breach, be prima facie subject to a duty of confidence. This is clear from the judgment of Sir Robert Megarry VC in *Malone* v. *Commissioner of Police for the Metropolis (No. 2)*[24]

> If A makes a confidential communication to B, then A may not only restrain B from divulging or using the confidence, but may also restrain C from divulging or using it if C has acquired it from B, even if he acquired it without notice of any impropriety . . . In such cases it seems plain that, however innocent the acquisition of the knowledge, what will be restrained is the use or disclosure of it after notice of the impropriety.

Where information is obtained by improper means (e.g. bugging or telephone-tapping) it appears that, in the absence of a relationship of confidence between, say, the tapper and the party whose telephone is tapped, the acquirer of the information is under no duty not to use or disclose it. This aspect of 'personal information' and the application of the action of breach of confidence is discussed in Chapter 6. On the other hand, where a third party Z obtains information which is already subject to a duty of confidence by Y to X, Z may, on ordinary equitable principles, be restrained from using or disclosing such information which he knows to be subject to an obligation of confidence. Thus in *Duchess of Argyll* v. *Duke of Argyll*,[25] which is discussed below, the plaintiff was able to prevent confidential information which she had communicated to her husband, the first defendant, from being published by a third party, a newspaper to which her husband had passed the information.[26]

2.1.3. *Unauthorized Use*

Broadly speaking, in order for the plaintiff in a breach of confidence action to establish that the defendant has actually used or disclosed the confidential information, he must prove

---

[24] [1979] 2 All ER 620, 634.   [25] [1967] Ch. 302.

[26] A similar result was reached in, for instance, *Prince Albert* v. *Strange* (1849) 2 De Gex & Sm. 652, 64 ER 293, (on appeal) (1849) 1 Mac. & G. 25, 41 ER 1171 (discussed below) and *Morison* v. *Moat* (1851) 9 Hare 241.

that the information was 'directly or indirectly obtained from (the) plaintiff, without the consent, express or implied, of the plaintiff . . .'.[27] He does not have to show that the defendant has acted dishonestly or even consciously in using the information. Thus in *Seager* v. *Copydex Ltd.*[28] the defendant was held liable for 'unconscious plagiarism'[29] in using the plaintiff's idea for a carpet grip; the two parties had discussed—apparently in very general terms—the plaintiff's idea, but their negotiations broke down and the Court of Appeal found that the defendant honestly believed the idea to be his own.[30]

It is unclear whether the plaintiff need establish that he has suffered (or will suffer) detriment as a result of the breach of confidence. Though Megarry J. (as he then was) in *Coco* v. *A. N. Clark (Engineers) Ltd.*[31] suggested that this might be a requirement of the action, the better view would seem to be that this factor ought to be conceived as relevant only to the determination of the appropriate remedy. Particularly in respect of 'personal information' it would not always be easy to see how, other than the injured feelings, embarrassment, or distress suffered by the plaintiff, he could realistically be said to have suffered any detriment in the strict sense of material disadvantage.[32] In principle, it ought not to matter whether the 'personal information' disclosed was true or false or whether it lowered or enhanced the plaintiff's reputation (a view accepted by Knight Bruce VC in *Prince Albert* v.

---

[27] *Saltman Engineering Co. Ltd.* v. *Campbell Engineering Co. Ltd.* (1948) 65 RPC 203, 213 per Lord Greene MR.

[29] Ibid. at 374.   [28] [1967] RPC 349.

[30] See, too, *Terrapin Ltd.* v. *Builders Supply Co. (Hayes) Ltd.* [1967] RPC 375; (on appeal) [1960] RPC 128.

[31] [1969] RPC 41, 48; see, too, *Dunford & Eliot Ltd.* v. *Johnson & Firth Brown Ltd.* [1978] FSR 143, 148 per Lord Denning MR.

[32] In *Attorney-General* v. *Guardian Newspapers Ltd. (No. 2)* [1988] 3 WLR 776, 782 Lord Keith stated, *obiter*, 'I would think it a sufficient detriment to the confider that information given in confidence is to be disclosed to persons whom he would prefer not to know of it, even though the disclosure would not be harmful to him in any positive way.' Lord Goff (at 806) wished to keep the question open. See, too, *X* v. *Y* [1988] 2 All ER 648, 657. *Li Yau-wai* v. *Genesis Films Ltd.* [1987] HKLR 711; M. Pendleton, (1987) 17 HKLJ 362.

Strange[33] and by Megarry J. in *Coco* v. *A. N. Clark (Engineers) Ltd.*).[34]

Nevertheless, there is no denying the fact that 'some people want privacy largely so that they can turn it to their own financial advantage'[35] and the detriment in such cases would not be different from the normal commercial confidence case. There is also much to be said for Professor Cornish's view[36] that:

It is tempting to say that liability ought to follow simply upon the breaking of the confidence without looking also for detriment. But one should remember that a very wide range of subject-matter is involved, and also that there is always some public interest in the freedom to use information. Restriction of that freedom accordingly requires sufficient reason.

Indeed, if, as Cornish suggests,[37] the test in such circumstances should be an objective one (i.e. detriment should be measured by reference to whether a reasonable man would be injured) the definition I have proposed of 'personal information' with its objective standard, would render the test similar to his analogy of defamation. The plaintiff may only sue on statements which lower him in the eyes of right-thinking members of society. Similarly, the plaintiff in an action for breach of confidence where 'personal information' is involved may only sue on information which a reasonable person would regard as intimate or confidential and would therefore wish to withhold or to restrict its circulation.

2.2. INFORMATION IN THE 'PUBLIC DOMAIN'

The jurisdiction to restrain or redress breaches of confidences is, as was pointed out above, restricted to the unauthorized use or disclosure of information which is 'secret'. It might be thought that this is a simple matter: once a secret has become

[33] (1849) 2 De Gex & Sm. 652, 697.
[34] [1969] RPC 41, 48; see, too, Stott J. in *Cork* v. *McVicar* [1984] *The Times*, 1 Nov.
[35] W. Cornish, *Intellectual Property: Patents, Copyright, Trade Marks and Allied Rights* (1981), 285.
[36] Ibid.
[37] Ibid.

public knowledge, once the information is accessible to anyone who wishes to acquire it, it is no longer possible to obtain relief for a breach of the confidence that may have taken place.[38]

In the recent *Spycatcher* litigation, however, the Master of the Rolls introduced a subtle refinement. Denying that Peter Wright's book was in the public domain, he stated:[39]

> For my part I accept that to the extent that these publications have been read the information to which they related has become public knowledge, but not that it has entered the public domain, so losing the seal of confidentiality, because that only occurs when information not only becomes a matter of public knowledge, but also public property.

The question of 'public domain' normally arises in the more congenial environment of disputes about trade secrets.[40]

[38] *O. Mustad & Son* v. *Dosen* (1928) [1963] RPC 41; [1964] 1 WLR 109.

[39] *Attorney-General* v. *Guardian Newspapers Ltd.* [1987] 1 WLR 1271 at 1275. In the House of Lords, Lord Brandon was unconvinced that the information was 'public knowledge': 'it is, I think, putting the case too high to say that the matters contained in *Spycatcher* have become public knowledge in the United Kingdom. A limited section of the public who feel a strong motivation to acquire knowledge of the matters concerned, can no doubt obtain access to a copy of the book published in America and not prohibited from being imported here. But this does not mean that the matters concerned are already within the knowledge of the public as a whole' (at 1289). On the other hand, Lord Oliver (dissenting) was in no doubt that the information was in the 'public domain' (at 1320). His view was expressly approved by Scott J. in the Attorney-General's application for a permanent injunction, [1988] 2 WLR 805. In the Court of Appeal both Bingham and Dillon L JJ, in dismissing the appeal, regarded the fact that the information was in the 'public domain' as of central importance [1988] 2 WLR 805. The House of Lords took a similar view. It held that since the facts were in the 'public domain' no further damage could be done to the public interest, *Attorney-General* v. *Guardian Newspapers Ltd.* (No. 2) [1988] 3 WLR 776.

[40] See, in particular, *Mustad* v. *Dosen*, see above; *Saltman Engineering Co. Ltd.* v. *Campbell Engineering Co. Ltd.* (1948) 65 RPC 203; [1963] 3 All ER 413; *Under Water Welders & Repairers Ltd.* v. *Street and Longthorne* [1968] RPC 498; *Ackroyds (London) Ltd.* v. *Islington Plastics Ltd.* [1962] RPC 97; *Peter Pan Manufacturing Corporation* v. *Corsets Silhouette Ltd.* [1963] RPC 45, [1964] 1 WLR 96; *Cranleigh Precision Engineering Ltd.* v. *Bryant* [1966] RPC 375; *Terrapin Ltd.* v. *Builders' Supply Co. (Hayes) Ltd.* [1960] RPC 128.

In these cases certain specific considerations relating to the availability, accessibility, or even simplicity of the commercial secrets obtain. It sits far less comfortably in non-commercial cases.[41]

Thus in *Woodward* v. *Hutchins*[42] three well-known entertainers, Tom Jones, Engelbert Humperdinck, and Gilbert O'Sullivan, and their manager employed the first defendant, Hutchins, as public relations officer, consultant, press representative, and literary agent. After leaving the management company through which the entertainers' business was conducted, the first defendant entered into a contract with the *Daily Mirror* to disclose details of his former employers' private lives which the newspaper proposed to serialize. The first two instalments had appeared when the plaintiff entertainers sought and were awarded an interlocutory injunction by Slynn J. restraining the first defendant and the newspaper from making further disclosures concerning the private lives of the plaintiffs. The plaintiffs' claim was based on both breach of confidence and libel. On appeal, the Court of Appeal discharged the injunction, holding that the appellants could continue to publish the disclosures and that the respondents should seek a remedy in damages.

The information that the newspaper published related, in part, to the alleged sexual pursuits of one of the plaintiffs aboard an aeroplane. Lord Denning MR regarded these activities as being 'in the public domain', since 'it was known to all the passengers on the flight'.[43] This conclusion is difficult to criticize and, even under the broad protection accorded to 'privacy' by the American law (see Chapter 2) a plaintiff will not, in general, have a remedy where the activities reported take place in a public place. Yet the use of the concept of 'public domain' in this context has a certain artificiality about it, given the fact that its principal objective (along with the associated Springboard Doctrine discussed above) is to deny protection to information imparted in

---

[41] Lord Bridge, in his dissenting judgment in the *Spycatcher* case remarked, 'I deliberately refrain from using expressions such as "the public domain" which may have technical overtones' ([1987] 1 WLR 1271, 1284).

[42] [1977] 1 WLR 760, discussed further below.   [43] At 764.

circumstances which, at least ostensibly, suggest a desire to preserve or even impose confidentiality even if, because this information subsequently turns out to be 'public property' or 'public knowledge', such confidentiality is nullified. Events (or even information disclosed) in a public place would seem, prima facie, to lack 'the necessary quality of confidence'[44] though the application of the notion of 'public domain' in such circumstances is understandable and by no means illogical.

This is simply another instance of the tenuous doctrinal relationship between the protection by equity of commercial or trade secrets, on the one hand, and 'personal information' on the other. That is not to suggest that by treating the information in question (exploits aboard a jumbo jet) as 'personal' (as defined in this work) the difficulties of limiting protection are automatically resolved. Even if the facts are such that it would be reasonable to expect the individual concerned to regard them as intimate or confidential and therefore to want to withhold them or at least to restrict their circulation (see Chapter 1), it would still be necessary for the court to consider the extent to which their being committed (or disclosed) in a public place would defeat the plaintiff's claim to protection, but this would be undertaken in the context of a proper discussion of the wider issues concerned.

An important limitation on the principle of 'public domain' emerges from the majority decision of the Court of Appeal in *Schering Chemicals Ltd.* v. *Falkman Ltd.*[45] In order to counteract adverse publicity which attended the marketing of a pregnancy-testing drug, Schering employed the services of Falkman to train Schering executives in the subtle art of television interviews. Falkman in turn employed Elstein (the second defendant) to conduct the course. Elstein obtained for this purpose information from Schering which the former regarded as confidential. Elstein nevertheless passed on this information to Thames Television (the third defendant) which used it as the basis of a television film which it intended to broadcast. The Court of Appeal, by a majority (Lord Denning MR dissenting), upheld the decision

---

[44] *Saltman*, see above, 215.   [45] [1981] 2 WLR 848.

at first instance granting an interlocutory injunction against all three defendants.

In respect of Falkman there was clearly a breach of contract: his contract with Schering required him to preserve the confidentiality of information he received from them, and this would apply regardless of whether the information was in the 'public domain'.[46] But the majority based Elstein's liability (and hence that of Thames Television) on a 'fiduciary obligation'[47] and an 'implied promise'[48] to maintain the confidence—despite the fact that the information given by Schering had already been revealed by the press and television and hence was, in a very real sense, in the 'public domain'.

In his dissenting judgment, Lord Denning MR conceded that Elstein owed a duty of confidence to Schering, but, in his view, no breach of that duty had occurred because the defendants 'were at liberty to use public information by going and collecting it themselves'.[49] He attached importance to the fact that the researcher employed by Elstein obtained all her material from newspapers, periodicals, research papers, etc. He said, 'It is, to my mind, quite unfair to accuse him [Elstein], on the present evidence, of a flagrant breach of duty, or of being a traitorous advisor seeking to make money out of his misconduct . . .'.[50]

And echoing his sentiments in *Woodward* (in respect of 'personal information')[51] he declared:

I look at it this way: the correspondence shows that if Schering had approved of the film—if it had been good publicity for them—they would gladly have let it be shown. But, because they disapproved of it, thinking it was bad publicity, they claim to be entitled to ban the showing of it indefinitely—the whole of it.[52]

It must be said that the importance Lord Denning attached, both here and in *Woodward*, (see below) to the question of unfavourable publicity, whatever its appeal to common sense and simple virtue, represents an additional (and inadequately justified) hurdle for the plaintiff to cross. He will be less likely

---

[46] *Saltman*, see above, 215 and 415.   [47] At 869 per Shaw LJ.
[48] At 879 per Templeman LJ.   [49] At 859.   [50] Ibid.
[51] This aspect of the decision is discussed below.   [52] At 859.

to attract the sympathy of the law, in Lord Denning's view, if his objection to the publicity may be construed as springing from a desire to stifle bad publicity. Or, to put it slightly differently, a plaintiff who objects to publicity will be refused relief if it may be inferred that, had the publicity been favourable, he would not have complained. This view, it is submitted, is open to two objections.

First, it ought not, in principle, to matter whether the confidential information disclosed depicts the plaintiff in an unfavourable or in a 'creditable and advantageous'[53] light. Naturally, a complaint is more likely to arise in respect of publicity which is damaging to the plaintiff, but, as was suggested above, the requirement of detriment to the plaintiff may not be a necessary element in the action for breach of confidence.

Secondly, particularly in the case of 'personal information', even if detriment to the plaintiff is a requirement, the objection to the disclosure is not necessarily that it is false (where, in any event, the appropriate action might be one for defamation), but that a breach of confidence has occurred. This subject is returned to below.

Shaw and Templeman L JJ considered the conduct of Elstein to be so morally reprehensible that even the fact that the information was in the 'public domain', could not be allowed to justify its disclosure. And, in arriving at this conclusion, the majority was effectively attaching greater weight to the preservation of trust than to the freedom of the press to publish information which is in the public interest. As Templeman LJ put it, foreshadowing his view in the *Spycatcher* case:

if the injunction is withheld, the court will enable a trusted adviser to make money out of his dealing in confidential information. These consequences must be weighed against the argument that, if an injunction is granted, the public will be deprived of information.[54]

[53] *Prince Albert* v. *Strange* (1849) 2 De Gex & Sm. 652, 697 per Knight-Bruce VC.

[54] At 881. In *Snepp* v. *United States*, 62 L. Ed. 2d (1980) the American Supreme Court was faced with facts strikingly similar to the *Spycatcher* case. A former CIA agent published a book based on his experiences during the American withdrawal from Vietnam. Although it was conceded that his revelations contained no confidential information, the court imposed a

In his view, the latter carried less weight. He remarked that, 'It is not the law that where confidentiality exists it is terminated or eroded by adventitious publicity'.[55]

An 'unfortunate and paradoxical result'[56] of the majority's view is that once information has been acquired in confidence, the recipient's obligation not to disclose it would subsist— even beyond the time when the information was generally available. In other words, anyone would be free to use or disclose the information—save the recipient who obtained it in confidence. Nevertheless, though the decision has attracted considerable criticism, the application of the decision to cases involving 'personal information' may call for a different analysis. In particular, as was suggested above, the concept of information 'in the public domain' is less susceptible of simple categorization in such cases than in cases concerning trade or commercial secrets. Indeed, in its Working Paper[57] the Law Commission suggested that where 'personal inform-ation' was concerned, information should not be treated as being in the public domain unless:

(a) the information can be ascertained by recourse to any register kept in pursuance of any Act of Parliament which is open to inspection by the public or to any other document which is required by the law of any part of the United Kingdom to be open to inspection by the public, or

(b) the information was disclosed in the course of any

constructive trust on Snepp in respect of profits accruing from the book. In the *Spycatcher* case, Lord Ackner was 'unimpressed' by the argument for an account of profits; he pointed out that profit may not be the ex-employee's motive: he 'may be embittered or embarrassed or unbalanced, may publish his memoirs out of spite to embarrass his superiors; to mount some eccentric campaign or publish for any number of other reasons' (at 1307). Cf. Sir John Donaldson MR (at 1277) and, in the appeal against the decision of Scott J. to deny a permanent injunction [1988] 2 WLR 805. Scott J. held the *Sunday Times* had been in breach of the duty of confidentiality in publishing an instalment of *Spycatcher* and was liable to account for any profits resulting from that breach. A majority of the Court of Appeal (Bingham LJ dissenting) and the House of Lords agreed.

[55] At 871.
[56] Law Commission Report, *Breach of Confidence* (Law Com. No. 110) 1981, para. 6.67.   [57] No. 58, para. 103.

proceedings, judicial or otherwise, which the public were by the law of any part of the United Kingdom entitled to attend.

In its Report, however,[58] the Law Commission departed from this formulation, suggesting instead that in any statutory framework for the action the 'public domain' requirement should be stated 'in broad terms'[59] leaving the courts to decide in the circumstances of each case whether the information concerned was 'relatively secret'[60] or 'available to the public'.[61]

The reason for this change of heart appears to be the fact that:

it is often difficult to determine when information ceases to be of commercial value and becomes merely personal. If a person suffers hardship by reason of the repetition of true stories about him which are already in the public domain, the questions whether he should be given a remedy cannot depend on the law of confidence, because the information is public. Any remedy would have to be sought under a law of privacy, which lies outside our terms of reference.[62]

Despite this clear statement of the different theories that underpin the two causes of action, the Law Commission, by abandoning the 'more rigid standard'[63] of what counts as the 'public domain' in respect of 'personal information', allows the very distinction it has drawn to be undermined. The argument appears to run as follows:

1. There is a distinction in the application of the principle of 'public domain' in 'personal information' as opposed to purely commercial information cases;

2. This distinction should not—in the context of a statutory framework of the action for breach of confidence—result in a more rigid standard of what constitutes the 'public domain' for the purposes of dealing with cases involving 'personal information' because the line between 'personal' and 'commercial' information is often difficult to draw;

---

[58] Para. 6.69. [59] Ibid.
[60] *Franchi v. Franchi* [1967] RPC 149, 152–3 per Cross J.
[61] *Ackroyds (London) Ltd. v. Islington Plastics Ltd.* [1962] RPC 97, 104 per Havers J.
[62] Para. 6.69. [63] Ibid.

3. An individual who is subjected to the publication of 'true stories' about him which are in the 'public domain' has no action for breach of confidence, because the information is public: his remedy is to be sought under the 'law of privacy'.

This is a perplexing line of reasoning. The distinction identified in the first proposition is then denied in the second—on the ground that the distinction (already acknowledged) is an extremely difficult one to draw. This is undoubtedly true for what sometimes passes for 'personal information' may well be commercial information: though it is also true that any value ultimately has a commercial value), but the essential distinction between the two categories of information is that the chief interest which is under attack where 'personal information' is disclosed is that of the victim's *personality*. That it may incidentally occasion pecuniary loss does not materially affect the argument.

The move to the third proposition is also suspect. To argue that a plaintiff who is subjected to disclosures of *true* facts cannot rely on the law of confidence 'because the information is public' is to beg the question. It is surely precisely that issue which the court is called upon to determine, (and which the Law Commission is itself attempting to decide and clarify in statutory form) namely, whether the information has, in fact, been made public. Moreover, even supposing that the court finds that it *is* in the 'public domain', it cannot follow that the action for breach of confidence is inapplicable, partly because it is by the very application of the law of confidence that this conclusion has been reached, but, more importantly, because this view is incorrect. Where a breach of confidence has occurred and true facts about the plaintiff are disclosed, there is no reason why he should not, in principle, have a remedy under the law of confidence.

In determining whether the information is in the 'public domain' (the whole object of the Law Commission's formulating a test at all), the court is impicitly raising the very question of whether 'personal information' is to be treated on the same footing as commercial information. In respect of the latter, of course, several decisions have applied certain fairly well-established criteria (including the so-called Springboard Doctrine), but in the only reported case in which the principle of 'public domain' has been applied to 'personal information', *Woodward*, the Court of Appeal treated the issue as unproblematic, and simply regarded it as self-evident that any event that took place in public was in the 'public domain'. Lord Denning MR said:

[The injunction] speaks of 'confidential information'. But what is confidential? . . . Mr. Hutchins, as a press agent, might attend a dance which many others attended. Any incident which took place at the dance would be known to all present. The information would be in the public domain. There could be no objection to the incidents being made known generally. It would not be confidential information. So in this case the incident on this Jumbo Jet was in the public domain. It was known to all the passengers on the flight. Likewise with several other incidents in the series.[64]

Apart from the fact that the test here proposed is unacceptably sweeping (can it really be said that an incident that took place at a dance 'would be known to *all* present'?—it does, of course, depend on the incident (!)—but it is not difficult to imagine an 'incident' being known to merely a handful of guests, even though the dance is a public event), it is clear that the law of confidence (however unsatisfactorily in this instance) was able to measure the extent to which the information was 'confidential'. Nor is it an adequate answer—in this context—[65] to urge that a remedy would have to be sought under a 'law of privacy' for, in respects of events such as the one in issue, a similar test would inevitably have to be applied. In any case, in its discussion of the problem, the Law Commission confined itself to documentary information. It should have considered *Woodward* and the difficulties raised by activities which take place 'in public'. To say that such questions are 'outside our terms of reference'[66] because they related to the 'law of privacy'[67] is to neglect the fact that, in certain circumstances (such as wide publicity being given to

---

[64] At 764.
[65] There is merit in distinguishing analytically between the two causes of action—see below—but this is not the point that the Law Commission is making here.
[66] Para. 6.69.
[67] Ibid.

'personal information' which involves also a breach of confidence, as occurred in *Woodward*), the two interests converge—and this would be the case even if there were an English 'law of privacy'. Moreover the question of 'privacy' (as understood here by the Law Commission) would not, strictly speaking, arise unless the information was given wide publicity, which is not necessarily suggested by the phrase 'repetition of true stories about him'.[68]

Despite their reluctance to stray into the field of 'privacy', the Law Commission nevertheless added that they 'wish[ed] to emphasize that information is not "available" to the public if, to extract the information in respect of which the claim of confidence is made, a member of the public would have to make a significant contribution of labour, skill or money'.[69] They give the example of the back files of a newspaper which, if assiduously combed through, might yield considerable information about a person who lived in the area during his early years. Facts about his family, education, business connections, political views, personal and social problems could therefore be garnered from a 'publicly available' source. If this information is subsequently (perhaps many years later) revealed by the person concerned to another 'in the course of a relationship in which absolute frankness is essential, is it right that the person who accepts the confidence should be able, solely on the ground that the facts are technically accessible to the public, to disclose them to others in breach of his duty of confidence?'[70]

Its earlier view, expressed in the Working Paper[71] was that such information should not be regarded as in the 'public domain' because (following the narrow definition referred to above) it was not available in any formal register or report of proceedings. This position was revised in the Report[72] to facilitate greater flexibility on the part of the courts and allow them to decide on the basis of each case whether or not the information—commercial or personal—was in the 'public domain'. It also recognized[73] that even if the newspaper files are available for reference in a public library, it does not mean that the information revealed by a search—if

---

[68] Para. 6.69. See below.   [69] Ibid.   [70] Para. 6.68.
[71] No. 58, Para. 103.   [72] Para. 6.69.   [73] Ibid. n. 679.

it required 'a significant expenditure of labour, skill or money'[74]—would be in the 'public domain'.[75]

Of course, with computerized retrieval of information, the effort, skill, or expenditure required will be minimal and, hence, the argument that such information is not in the 'public domain' will be far more difficult to sustain. This question is examined below.

2.3. DISCLOSURE 'IN THE PUBLIC INTEREST'

The use or disclosure of information may be justified in circumstances where the public interest in maintaining confidentiality is outweighed by the public interest in its use or disclosure. The difficult and fairly controversial question is whether the information, the use or disclosure of which is claimed to be in the public interest, must relate to the commission of a crime or civil wrong (for it is well established that 'there is no confidence as to the disclosure of iniquity')[76] or whether a wider meaning is to be given to the concept of 'iniquity'. For present purposes, an attempt is made to state the essentials of the principle in order to investigate its importance in the protection of 'personal information'.

There is some confusion in respect of the status and operation of the principle. It is generally considered to be a defence[77] which operates to destroy the original obligation of

---

[74] Ibid.

[75] See clause 2 of the Law Commission's draft bill, app. A.

[76] *Gartside* v. *Outram* (1857) 26 LJ Ch. (NS) 113, 114 per Wood VC.

[77] The Law Commission refrained from treating it as a 'defence', (para. 4.54) despite that fact that it is so characterized in several of the judicial dicta which they quoted (e.g. Lord Denning MR in *Initial Services*, above at 405); and though at certain points (e.g. paras. 4.39, 4.41) they so described it themselves, but preferred to regard it as incumbent on the plaintiff to establish that the public interest in maintaining confidence outweighed the public interest in disclosure (see para. (24) (i)). The balance of authority, however, suggests that it is a defence in the true sense of the term. This is, in any event, an inevitable consquence of the equitable basis of the action: the discretionary nature of the equitable jurisdiction allows the court to recognize the existence of an obligation of confidence while declining to enforce it. See Y. Cripps, *The Legal Implications of Disclosures in the Public Interest* (1986) 22.

confidence between the parties, if any. This will certainly be
the case where the confidential information relates to an
alleged crime or tort. So, for example, where the plaintiff's
former employee revealed to a newspaper information which
showed the plaintiff to be engaged in fraudulent conduct, it
was held that it was a defence to claim that disclosure of this
'iniquity' was justified in the public interest.[78]

But the principle may operate in such a way as to allow the
confidence to survive, even though its breach was justified by
a reasonable suspicion that the confidence did indeed concern
an 'iniquity' (this arose in *Malone* v. *Commissioner of Police
of the Metropolis (No. 2)*).[79] As mentioned above the range
of subject-matter which has been held to justify disclosure in
breach of confidence is not restricted to criminal or tortious
acts, but 'extends to any misconduct of such a nature that it
ought in the public interest to be disclosed to others. . . . The
exception should extend to crimes, frauds and misdeeds, both
those actually committed as well as those in contemplation,
provided always—and this is essential—that the disclosure is
justified in the public interest.'[80]

In *British Steel Corporation* v. *Granada Television Ltd.*[81]
the House of Lords distinguished mere incompetence from
fraudulent misconduct. Only the latter could justify a breach
of confidence. The documents in question suggested that BSC
was being mismanaged; this, in the view of three members of
the court[82] was not sufficient to entitle Granada to breach
confidence.

---

[78] *Initial Services Ltd.* v. *Putterill* [1968] 1 QB 396.
[79] [1979] 2 All ER 620. See Ch. 7.
[80] *Initial Services*, above, 405 per Lord Denning, approved in *British
Steel Corporation* v. *Granada Television Ltd* [1981] 1 All ER 417, 455
and 480; Similar dicta abound: e.g. *Beloff* v. *Pressdram Ltd.* [1973] 1 All
ER 241, 260; *Malone*, above, 634–5; *Weld-Blundell* v. *Stephens* [1919] 1
KB 520, 527; *Fraser* v. *Evans* [1969] 1 QB 349, 362: approved in *Church
of Scientology* v. *Kaufman* [1973] RPC 627, 629, 635, 6499; *Hubbard* v.
Vosper [1972] 2 QB 84, 95; *Distillers Co. (Biochemicals) Ltd.* v. *Times
Newspapers Ltd.* [1975] 1 All ER 41, 52; *Lion Laboratories Ltd.* v. *Evans*
[1984] 2 All ER 417, 422–3; 432–3; *Cork* v. *McVicar* [1984] *The Times*,
1 Nov.   [81] See above.
[82] Lord Wilberforce at 455; Viscount Dilhorne at 461, and Lord Fraser
at 470–1.

The defence of public interest has recently been given its widest and most forthright expression by the Court of Appeal in the *Lion Laboratories* case.[83] The court held that a newspaper was permitted to publish confidential internal correspondence purloined by the plaintiff's former employees which indicated doubts as to the reliability and accuracy of an electronic device designed to measure levels of intoxication by alcohol which had been in use by the Home Office. Discharging the injunction granted by Leonard J., the Court of Appeal unequivocally held that publication was in the public interest. Stephenson LJ said:

There is confidential information which the public may have a right to receive and others, in particular the press, now extended to the media, may have a right and even a duty to publish, even if the information has been unlawfully obtained in flagrant breach of confidence and irrespective of the motive of the informer.[84]

This casts the net of 'public interest' considerably wider than the mere disclosure of 'iniquity': it develops the principle along the lines suggested by Lord Denning MR in *Frazer* v. *Evans*,[85] where he perceived 'iniquity' to be 'merely an instance of a just cause and excuse for breaking confidence'; and it is in keeping also with Sir Robert Megarry's dictum in *Malone*[86] (where he expressly approved of the above statement by Lord Denning MR) that '[t]here may be cases where there is no misconduct or misdeed but yet there is a just cause or excuse for breaking confidence'.[87]

Certainly, in the previous decisions in which the defence has been invoked, if the plaintiff had not been guilty of actual misconduct there was an identifiable risk of harm to the community.[88] And Stephenson LJ offered the following example (which he attributed to Griffiths LJ) to refute the

[83] [1984] 2 All ER 417.   [84] At 422.
[85] [1969] 1 All ER 8, 11.   [86] At 716.
[87] This decision was not referred to by the Court of Appeal in *Lion Laboratories*; cf. Shaw LJ in *Schering*, above, 869; Goff J. in *Church of Scientology* v. *Kaufman* [1973] RPC 635, 649.
[88] e.g. *Hubbard* v. *Vosper* [1972] 2 QB 84 and *Church of Scientology* v. *Kaufman* [1973] RPC 627 ('medical quackery') cf. *Distillers Co. (Bio-chemicals Ltd.* v. *Times Newspapers Ltd.* [1975] 1 All ER 41 and *Schering Chemicals Ltd.* v. *Falkman Ltd.* (the danger no longer existed).

argument that it is only where the plaintiff is guilty of misconduct that the defendants may be restrained from publishing.[89] Suppose the plaintiffs had informed the police that their device was inaccurate, but the police replied that they proposed to use it anyway. If a newspaper sought to publish that confidential information, they could still plead the defence of 'public interest' to justify their publication—even though it was not the plaintiff but the police who were guilty of misconduct. This is a plausible argument, though it is much less likely that in those hypothetical circumstances it would be the manufacturers rather than the police who would in fact be the plaintiffs—and they would, *ex hypothesi*, be guilty of misconduct. Nevertheless, the example does serve to demonstrate the possibility that if 'public interest' is to be taken seriously as a destroyer of confidences, then its application as a justification for publication ought not to be made to turn on the existence of wrongdoing by the plaintiff. As Griffith LJ put it:

I can see no sensible reason why this defence should be limited to cases in which there has been wrongdoing on the part of the plaintiffs. I believe that the so-called iniquity rule evolved because in most cases where the facts justified a publication in breach of confidence the plaintiff had behaved so disgracefully or criminally that it was judged in the public interest that his behaviour should be exposed. No doubt it is in such circumstances that the defence will usually arise, but it is not difficult to think of instances where, although there has been no wrongdoing on the part of the plaintiff, it may be vital in the public interest to publish a part of his confidential information.[90]

This is a robust statement in support of freedom of expression, and, whether or not it may be 'a mole's charter',[91] the court seems to have paid only lip-service to the competing public interest in the maintenance of confidence; indeed there is no real analysis of this question in any of the judgments. On the other hand, the circumstances were 'exceptional':[92] the disclosure concerned a matter which 'affects the life, and even the liberty, of an unascertainable number of Her Majesty's subjects'.[93]

---

[89] At 423.   [90] At 432–3.   [91] At 433 and 435 per Griffith LJ.
[92] At 433 per Griffith LJ.   [93] At 429 per Stephenson LJ.

In any event, had the court found for the plaintiff, it would
be difficult to square the case with, say, the decision in
Woodward where the Court of Appeal refused an interlocutory injunction to the plaintiff pop stars and their
manager on the ground that 'the truth' should be told about
their private lives: 'The public should not be misled.'[94] How
is it to be argued that details of the private lives of
entertainers are to be revealed, whereas information potentially damaging to the lives of members of the public must be
keep confidential?[95] It is no answer to say that the court
should balance the likely injury to be suffered by the plaintiff
(or to the person to whom the confidential information
'relates') if the confidence is breached, against the benefit to
the public that is likely to accrue as a result of publication.
The result of such a test might be that the greater the need for
disclosure (e.g., in the case of a major fraud) the greater the
likely injury to the plaintiff—and this would therefore
operate to prevent disclosure. The most sensible solution
would (inevitably) seem to be that the courts should have 'a
broad power to decide in an action for breach of confidence
whether in the particular case the public interest in protecting
the confidentiality outweighs the public interest in its
disclosure or use.'[96]

Several considerations will need to be taken into account
(e.g., to whom the disclosure was made,[97] whether disclosure

[94] At 764.

[95] Unless it is to be accepted that the real basis of the decision in
Woodward (as well as *Lennon* and *Khashoggi*) was that the information
was already in the 'public domain'. See Cripps, *Disclosures in the Public
Interest*, 69.

[96] Law Commission Report, para 6.77. For two recent judicial
pronouncements which attempt to formulate 'balancing' criteria in
decisions involving personal information see *Stephens* v. *Avery* [1988] 2
WLR 1280, 1287 per Sir Nicolas Browne-Wilkinson VC and *X* v. *Y* [1988]
3 All ER 648, 661 per Rose J.

[97] In *Initial Services Ltd.* v. *Putterill* [1968] 1 QB 396, 405–6 Lord
Denning MR said it should be made 'to one who has a proper interest to
receive the information', but added that, in certain cases, the misdeed in
question may justify disclosure to the press (as it did, in his view, in both
Woodward, above, and *Initial Services*, above; similarly in *Francome* v.
Mirror Group Newspapers Ltd. [1984] 1 WLR 892, 898, Sir John
Donaldson MR expressed the view that publication of incriminating

was, at the time it was made, still in the public interest; and the manner and extent of the disclosure). The question of the manner of acquisition is discussed in Chapter 7.

There are differing views in respect of the relevance of the *motives* of the defendant. Lord Denning MR, in *Woodward* retreated from his remarks, *obiter*, deprecating the sale of 'scandalous information' in *Initial Services*[98] and refused to enjoin the newspaper from publishing the confidential information, even though its informant had received a large sum of money for doing so. Similarly, in his dissenting judgment in *Schering*[99] he was unmoved by the fact that Elstein had acted with a financial motive. This approach is evident also in two recent decisions involving the defence of public interest. In the *Lion Laboratories* case[100] Stephenson LJ declared that where the public has a right to receive certain information, such a right will be recognized by the court 'irrespective of the motive of the informer'. And in *Cork* v. *McVicar*[101] Scott J. allowed a newspaper to publish information which had been obtained by the first defendant by surreptitiously recording parts of conversations with the plaintiff which the first defendant explicitly informed the plaintiffs would not be recorded. The information supported allegations of miscarriages of justice and alleged police corruption. The court expressed the view that:

Newspapers had many functions and practices, some more attractive than others, but one function was to provide a means whereby corruption might be exposed. That could rarely be done without informers and often breaches of confidence. In the present case the corruption alleged concerned the administration of justice. Such corruption was properly a matter of public interest as opposed to matters which should be taken up and dealt with by the appropriate authorities.

evidence about the plaintiffs which had been obtained by the Daily Mirror from electronic eavesdroppers who had tapped the plaintiffs' telephone, did not automatically qualify as being in the public interest: 'it is impossible to see what public interest would be served by publishing the contents of the tapes which would not equally be served by giving them to the police or the Jockey Club. Any wider publication could only serve the interests of the "Daily Mirror".'

[98] At 406.   [99] At 859.   [100] At 422.
[101] [1984] *The Times*, 31 Oct.

A rather different approach is to be found in the majority judgments in *Schering* and in the case of *Francome*. In the former, Shaw LJ declared that the defendants should be denied 'a licence for the mercenary betrayal of business confidences'.[102] While the issue of the defendant's financial reward cannot—in itself—be a proper criterion in determining whether or not his disclosure is in the public interest, it may suggest that his perception of the 'public interest' is an unreasonable one. In *Francome* Sir John Donaldson MR emphasized 'the rarity of the moral imperative'[103] which is invoked to justify a breach of the law, saying that:

it is almost unheard of for compliance with the moral imperative to be in the financial or other best interests of the person concerned. Anyone who conceives himself to be morally obliged to break the law, should also ask himself whether such a course furthers his own interests. If it does, he would be well advised to re-examine his conscience.[104]

And with specific reference to the right claimed by the likes of the editor of the *Daily Mirror*, the Master of the Rolls issued the following counterpoint to dicta (such as the one quoted above from *Cork* v. *McVicar* which tend to neglect the question of who determines what is in the public interest):

The 'media' to use a term which comprises not only the newspapers, but also television and radio, are an essential foundation of any democracy. In exposing crime, anti-social behaviour and hypocrisy and in campaigning for reform and propagating the views of minorities, they perform an invaluable function. However, they are peculiarly vulnerable to the error of confusing the public interest with their own interest. Usually these interests march hand in hand in hand, but not always.[105]

A court is perhaps less likely to countenance a breach of confidence in circumstances in which the plaintiff's belief that his disclosure is in the public interest is objectively obviously unfounded. In *British Steel Corporation* v. *Granada Television Ltd.*[106] the 'mole's' motives were not regarded as significant. Lord Fraser said:

---

[102] At 869.   [103] At 897.   [104] Ibid.
[105] At 898. Stephenson LJ quoted this dictum in *Lion Laboratories*, above, at 423.   [106] [1980] 3 WLR 180.

The informer's motives are, in my opinion, irrelevant. It is said, and I am willing to accept, that in this case the informant neither asked for nor received any money, or other reward, but that he acted out of a keen sense of indignation about the dealings between BSC and the government before and during the strike. No doubt there is a public interest in maintaining the free flow of information to the press, and therefore against obstructing informers. But there is also I think a very strong public interest in preserving confidentiality within any organisation, in order that it can operate efficiently.[107]

If 'public interest disclosure' is to be regarded not as a defence but as a denial of liability (i.e. there is no confidential information to protect) it follows that the defendant's motive ought to be irrelevant.

2.4. POSSIBLE PLAINTIFFS

It is only the person to whom the duty of confidence is owed who is able to sue for breach of confidence. In other words, the only possible plaintiff is the person who imparted the information in confidence or on whose behalf the information was received. An example of the latter would be an employer who, though he does not necessarily impart the information directly to his employee, is entitled to expect the employee to regard certain information which he receives in the course of his employment as confidential. This limitation on potential employees was exemplified in *Fraser* v. *Evans*[108] in which the plaintiff, a public relations consultant, sought to prevent the publication by a newspaper of a report (a copy of which had fallen into the hands of the newspaper) he had made to the Greek Government about its 'image' in Europe. The Court of Appeal refused to grant the injunction on the ground that, although he owed the Greek Government a duty of confidence in respect of the report, no such duty was owed to him by them. He thus had no *locus standi* to sue for breach of confidence. Lord Denning MR stated:

the party complaining must be the person who is entitled to the confidence and to have it respected. He must be a person to whom

[107] At 852. Cf. Lord Salmon at 837.   [108] [1969] 1 1B 349.

the duty of good faith is owed. It is at this point that I think Mr Fraser's claim breaks down. There is no doubt that Mr Fraser himself was under an obligation of confidence to the Greek Government. The contract says so in terms. But there is nothing in the contract which expressly puts the Greek Government under any obligation of confidence. Nor, so far as I can see, is there any implied obligation. The Greek Government entered into no contract with Mr Fraser to keep it secret . . . It follows that they alone have any standing to complain if anyone obtains the information surreptitiously or proposes to publish it.[109]

This is an unavoidable consequence of the distinction between the law's limited concern to protect confidential information (based on the relationship of confidence) on the one hand, and the wider purpose of protecting 'privacy' (or, more specifically, 'personal information' by virtue only of its nature) on the other. It is perfectly consistent with the courts' restricted jurisdiction over confidential information. The Law Commission, in its Working Paper[110] illustrated the limited purpose of the law of confidence, as follows:

Suppose that a newspaper commissioned a journalist to write a candid assessment of a man's life on the understanding that it would be kept confidential until after the man's death and that the journalist furnished an article to the newspaper exposing details of the man's life which were true but likely to cause him distress, or even pecuniary loss; if the article was in fact published by the newspaper before the man's death in breach of their duty of confidence to the journalist, should the man also have a right of action against the newspaper based on their breach of confidence? It is arguable that in this situation the wrong to the man is far greater than that to the journalist and that he should be entitled to recover damages accordingly.

The Law Commission answered the question in the negative, for the man 'has a complaint not because his confidence has been abused but because his privacy has been infringed and . . . to admit an action by him for breach of confidence would amount to using the law of confidence merely as a peg on which to hang a right of privacy in his favour'.[111] And, in its Report, the Law Commission saw no reason to change this view.[112]

---

[109] At 361.   [110] No. 58 (1974), para. 75.
[111] Ibid.,   [112] Paras. 5.9 and 6.60.

The question of possible plaintiffs thus reveals an important doctrinal limitation of the action for breach of confidence: a matter which is more fully canvassed below.

2.5. OTHER DEFENCES

In addition to the defence of 'public interest' (described above), there would appear to be clear authority[113] for the existence of four defences to an action for breach of confidence. First, though the defence of qualified privilege has no application to breach of confidence, it is a defence (which may be regarded as a species of absolute privilege) to show that the confidential information was disclosed in the course of judicial proceedings where the 'private promise of confidentiality must yield to the general public interest that in the administration of justice truth will out'.[114] This normally arises where a party seeks discovery or inspection of documents the diclosure of which would be in breach of confidence.[115]

But, though the House of Lords has held that ' "confidentiality" is not a separate head of privilege'[116] the court may regard it as 'a very material consideration to bear in mind when privilege is claimed on the ground of public interest (in the administration of justice)'.[117]

Secondly, the plaintiff might be met with the equitable defence expressed in the maxim 'he who comes to Equity must come with clean hands'.[118] Thus where the plaintiff has himself acted in breach of confidence or has employed

---

[113] The Law Commission, paras. 4.69–4.70 are (rightly, it is submitted) unconvinced that the defence of absolute or qualified privilege—as applied in the law of defamation—has any application to breach of confidence.

[114] *D.* v. *National Society for the Prevention of Cruelty to Children* [1977] 1 All ER 589, 594 per Lord Diplock.

[115] *Chantrey Martin* v. *Martin* [1953] 2 QB 286; *Alfred Crompton Amusement Machines Ltd.* v. *Customs and Excise Commissioners (No. 2)* [1974] AC 405; *D.* v. *NSPCC*, above, *Science Research Council* v. *Nassé* [1980] AC 1028; *British Steel Corporation* v. *Granada Television Ltd.* [1980] 3 WLR 774.

[116] *Alfred Crompton*, above, at 433 per Lord Cross.

[117] Ibid.

[118] See n. 77 above.

'deplorable means'[119] to protect confidential information, such impropriety may, in the discretion of the court, operate as a defence to his action.

In respect of 'personal information' the decisions in *Duchess of Argyll* v. *Duke of Argyll*[120] and *Lennon* v. *News Group Newspapers Ltd.*[121] suggest that in order for this defence to succeed the plaintiff's impropriety must exceed that of the defendant's. Thus in *Argyll*, though the plaintiff had herself disclosed intimate facts concerning the marriage to a newspaper, Ungoed-Thomas J. regarded the defendant's revelations 'of an altogether different order of perfidy'.[122] And even though the plaintiff exhibited little respect for the sanctity of marriage, this attitude could not destroy confidences relating to the earlier period of their marriage. In *Lennon*, however, Lord Denning MR considered both parties' attitude to marriage sufficiently cavalier to nullify altogether the confidential nature of the relationship and, in consequence, to deny the plaintiff his equitable relief. The plaintiff's hands were thus no cleaner than the defendant's. Whether this is reconcilable with *Argyll* is questioned below.

Thirdly, where the defendant is compelled or authorized by statute to disclose confidential information, he may legitimately breach confidence, but only in respect of the information of which the statute requires disclosure.[123]

Fourthly, a plaintiff who allows too much time to elapse before he commences proceedings may be met with the defence that his delay, by leading the defendant to believe that the plaintiff has acquiesced in the defendant's actions

---

[119] *Hubbard* v. *Vosper* [1972] 2 QB 84, 101 per Megaw J.; see too *Church of Scientology* v. *Kaufman* [1973] RPC 627 and 653. Cf. *Stevenson, Jordan & Harrison Ltd.* v. *Macdonald and Evans* (1951) 68 RPC 190.

[120] [1967] 1 Ch. 302.

[121] [1978] FSR 573 (discussed below, 94–5).

[122] At 331.

[123] e.g., *Hunter* v. *Mann* [1974] QB 767 where a doctor was required to reveal information about a patient in terms of s. 168(2) of the Road Traffic Act 1972; *Tournier* v. *National Provincial and Union Bank of England* [1924] 1 KB 461 lays down qualifications to a banker's obligation of confidence.

(and the defendant to rely thereon), should deprive him of his remedy in equity.[124]

2.6. REMEDIES

The principal remedies available to a plaintiff are the interlocutory or permanent injunction, an order for delivery up or destruction, an account of profits, and damages. A detailed account of these remedies would be inappropriate here; in respect of 'personal information' two questions arise. First, under what circumstances will an injunction be granted to prevent the disclosure of such confidences? Secondly, to what extent are damages available in breach of confidence for injury to feelings?

To an individual whose private life is accorded publicity in breach of confidence, the attraction of an interlocutory injunction is plain: he wishes to prevent any (or any continued) publication.[125] The 'balance of convenience' principle formulated in the *American Cyanamid* case[126] in respect of interlocutory injunctions is noted below. Where a permanent (or final) injunction is sought—either at law or in equity—a court, in exercising its discretion, will generally grant it only where damages would be an inadequate remedy.[127] And, in the case of 'personal information', damages will rarely be an adequate remedy where the plaintiff is faced with the prospect (or continuation) of the disclosure of private facts imparted in confidence. This was

---

[124] *International Scientific Communications Inc.* v. *Pattison* [1979] FSR 429. Cf. *Schering Chemicals Ltd.* v. *Falkman Ltd.* [1981] 2 All ER 321, 346 per Templeman LJ.

[125] May it be used as a deterrent? This application of the interlocutory injunction clearly informed the majority judgment of the House of Lords in *Attorney-General* v. *Guardian* [1987] 1 WLR 1248. Lord Oliver in his dissenting judgment described it as 'a misuse of the injunctive remedy' (at 1317). In the appeal against the granting of a permanent injunction the Master of the Rolls (dissenting) explicitly recognized that an injunction was appropriate 'to discourage other Mr Wrights'. [1988] 2 WLR 805, 887.   [126] [1975] 1 All. ER 504.

[127] *Saltman Engineering Co. Ltd.* v. *Campbell Engineering Co. Ltd.* (1948) 65 RPC 203, 219.

explicitly acknowledged by Megarry J. in *Coco v. A. N. Clark (Engineers) Ltd.*[128] where he distinguished between the use of disclosure of trade secrets on the one hand, and of 'personal information' on the other.

In respect of the former, he expressed the view that 'the essence of the duty seems more likely to be of not using without paying', while in the case of personal confidences, 'the duty may exist in the more stringent form' i.e. 'of not using at all'.[129] The plaintiff normally seeks to prevent *any* disclosure of private facts. There may, however, arise circumstances in which this might be otherwise. The Law Commission gives the example of a defendant who has been put to great expense before discovering (actually or constructively) that the information was subject to an obligation of confidence. The plaintiff now seeks an injunction to prevent the defendant using the information—for the plaintiff proposes to use it *himself* in his autobiography. Here damages would seem to be the appropriate remedy. 'It should . . . be emphasized,' says the Law Commission,[130] 'that the fact that information is personal does not *in itself* rule out the possibility of damages being awarded in lieu of an injunction against a future breach of confidence.' This is, of course, a somewhat unusual situation, and in the quintessential 'personal information' case, the real question is whether damages are available for injured feelings. This question is considered below.

Among other considerations taken into account by a court in determining whether a permanent injunction is to be granted may be the question of whether the plaintiff has suffered (or will suffer) detriment in consequence of the breach of confidence. In awarding damages in lieu of an injunction under Lord Cairns's Act[131] the second, and more

---

[128] [1969] RPC 41, 50. (See too *Argyll v. Argyll* [1967] 1 Ch. 302.) Cf. *Woodward v. Hutchins* [1977] 1 WLR 760, 764 per Lord Denning MR.
[129] At 50.   [130] Para. 4.100.
[131] Chancery Amendment Act 1858, s. 2. Certain difficulties, which cannot be canvassed here, arise in connection with the power to award damages in cases where the action is based on equity rather than law. It is arguable that in such circumstances an account of profits is the appropriate remedy since the Court of Chancery may award damages only where it could be done were the court exercising a common-law jurisdiction. The

difficult, question arises, namely, the extent to which damages for mental distress or injured feelings are exigible. No such damages have been awarded, though in *Woodward* v. *Hutchins*[132] Lord Denning MR, in refusing an application for an interlocutory injunction to prevent the publication of 'personal information' in breach of confidence, suggested that an award of damages might be a suitable remedy when the matter went for trial. The Law Commission concluded that '[s]o far as non-contractual breach of confidence is concerned, there is no authority to support an award of damages for mental distress.'[133]

This is, of course, hardly surprising in view of the commercial considerations that underpin the action. Analogous situations in which damages are recoverable do not, it is submitted, afford a satisfactory doctrinal basis upon which to extend the court's jurisdiction to award damages, even if 'it would seem quixotic to bar this form of monetary compensation . . . for the sake of yet another historical point'.[134]

Statutory analogies in copyright[135] and even the Race Relations Act 1976[136] do not seem particularly convincing.

better view, however, (see Gurry, *Breach of Confidence*, 429) would seem to be that Lord Cairns's Act conferred jurisdiction on the Court of Chancery to award damages in addition to, or in lieu of, an injunction for breach of a purely equitable obligation. On the question of whether the Court of Chancery has an inherent jurisdiction to award damages in equity, see R. P. Meagher, W. M. C. Gummow, and J. R. F. Lehane, *Equity: Doctrines and Remedies*, 2nd edn. (1984), 604–5.

[132] [1977] 1 WLR 760, 764.　　　　　[133] Para. 4.82.
[134] Cornish, *Intellectual Property*, 289.
[135] In *Williams* v. *Settle* [1960] 1 WLR 1072, the defendant, a photographer, sold a photograph he had taken at a wedding two years before to a newspaper after the murder of the bride's father. In awarding £1,000 damages under s. 17(3) of the Copyright Act, 1956 for 'such additional damages . . . as the court may consider appropriate in the circumstances' where there had been flagrant infringement or benefit to the defendant, Sellers LJ, though acknowledging that there had been little benefit to the defendant, regarded his 'scandalous conduct' as being 'in total disregard not only of the legal rights of the plaintiff regarding copyright, but of his feelings and his sense of family dignity and pride' (at 1082).
[136] Section 57(4) provides that damages in respect of an unlawful act of discrimination 'may include compensation for injury to feeling whether or not they include compensation under any other head'.

And, similarly, though they have a certain appeal to common sense and practical reasoning, examples drawn from the law of contract[137] and tort, especially defamation, compound the analytical confusion that has been identified above. In the case of defamation, though damages may be awarded for mental distress[138] the principal object of the law is to protect the plaintiff's reputation rather than his feelings.

3. Cases involving 'Personal Information'

In order to examine the extent to which the action for breach of confidence affords a means of protecting 'personal information' or even 'privacy', five cases are analysed. They represent what might be called the current jurisprudence of 'personal information' cases—even though it will be argued that though the first clearly concerns non-technical information, it does not, strictly speaking, involve personal information.

3.1. *PRINCE ALBERT* v. *STRANGE*[139]

It is ironic that the case upon which reliance is placed, not only by Warren and Brandeis, but by several other commentators and courts, as authority for the recognition by the English law of a 'right of privacy' cannot, save by somewhat tendentious reasoning, be so conceived. I shall attempt to show that only by the use of the most extended—and

---

[137] Damages may be awarded for 'disappointment' of contractual expectations, and this includes 'the distress, the upset and frustration caused by the breach': *Jarvis* v. *Swan Tours Ltd.* [1973] QB 233, 238 per Lord Denning MR. See too *Perry* v. *Sidney Phillips & Son* [1982] 1 All ER 1005. Cf. *Bliss* v. *S. E. Thames Health Authority* (1985) IRLR 308.

[138] See e.g. *Fielding* v. *Variety Inc.* [1967] 2 QB 841, 851 per Lord Denning MR, 853 per Harman LJ, 855 per Salmon LJ. But this is clearly a rare and subsidiary consideration. If it were otherwise publication to the plaintiff alone would suffice—as it does under the Scots and Roman-Dutch *actio iniuriarum*: the plaintiff's loss of *dignitas* as a result of an insulting statement constitutes an actionable *iniuria*. See D. J. McQuoid-Mason, *The Law of Privacy in South Africa* (1978).

[139] (1849) 2 De Gex & Sm. 652, 64 ER 293); (on appeal) (1849) 1 Mac. & G. 25, 41 ER 1171.

artificial—meaning of the notion of 'personal information' could it be argued that the case is authority for this general proposition. Nor can a narrower argument be made to support the view that the decision was principally concerned with personal information. The litigation concerned a series of etchings made by Queen Victoria and Prince Albert. The plates of the etchings had been sent to the Palace printer in order that he might produce impressions for the private use of the Royal couple. A number of these impressions had fallen into the hands of one, Judge, who seems to have acquired them through a 'mole' who was employed by the printer. Strange, in turn, obtained the impressions from Judge in the bona fide belief that they were to be publicly exhibited with the consent of the Queen and Prince Albert. Strange and Judge determined to arrange the exhibition and produce the accompanying catalogue. On discovering that no such consent had been given, Strange decided not to participate in any exhibition of the etchings, but merely to publish the catalogue. His proposal was to offer the catalogue for sale and to provide each purchaser with an autograph of the Queen or Prince Albert. The Prince sought an injunction to prohibit the planned exhibition and the circulation of the catalogue.

It is plain that in his judgment the Vice-Chancellor considered the essence of the plaintiff's claim to be the property[140] he had in his creations. And while he alluded to the 'privacy and seclusion of thoughts and sentiments committed to writing, and desired by the author to remain not generally known'[141] and the right of the plaintiff and the Queen 'to retain in a state of privacy, to withhold from publication',[142] the basis for his granting the injunction was

[140] Cf. Meagher *et al.*, *Equity*, 824 who argue that reference in these early cases to 'property' must be understood to mean the common law of copyright. But there is much in Gurry's view, *Breach of Confidence*, 49–50, that since the court awarded an injunction to restrain not merely the misuse of the impressions, but also the publication of the *catalogue*, and since copyright confers protection only against the misuse of information *in the form* in which it was originally created, the catalogue could hardly be described as piracy of the information published *in the form* of the etchings.

[141] At 312.   [142] Ibid.

the infringement of the plaintiff's property. He expressed this forthrightly when he said:

Upon the principle, therefore, of protecting property, it is that the common law . . . shelters the privacy and seclusion of thoughts and sentiments committed to writing, and desired by the author to remain not generally known.[143]

He added that 'the invasion is of such a kind and affects such property as to entitle the plaintiff to the preventive remedy of an injunction . . .'[144] and '[t]he Defendant appears to me to have been seeking to make use, for his own purpose, of what does not belong to him.'[145]

In particular, the Vice-Chancellor attached considerable importance to the manner in which the etchings came to fall into the hands of Judge and Strange:

The author of manuscripts, whether he is famous or obscure, low or high, has a right to say of them, if innocent, that whether interesting or dull, light or heavy, saleable or unsaleable, they shall not, without his consent be published; and I think, as I have said, that to use a dishonest knowledge of them for the purpose of composing and publishing, and so to compose and publish a catalogue of them, amounts to a publication of them . . .[146]

Equally, in his judgment the Chancellor, Lord Cottenham, though he acknowledged the importance of the 'breach of trust, confidence, or contract'[147] committed by the defendant, based the major part of his decision on the 'exclusive right and interest of the Plaintiff in the composition or work in question'.[148]

Indeed, it would not be unreasonable to describe Lord Cottenham's disposal of the merits of the case (in upholding the granting of an injunction) as fairly cavalier. Not only did he declare that '[i]t would be a waste of time to refer in detail to the cases upon this subject',[149] but he unashamedly acknowledged that '[t]he importance which has been attached to this case arises entirely from the exalted station of the

---

[143] Ibid.   [144] Ibid.   [145] At 313.
[146] At 311.   [147] At 1178.   [148] Ibid.
[149] Ibid.

Plaintiff, and cannot be referred to any difficulty in the case itself.'[150]

Secondly, it is clear that 'the breach of trust, confidence, or contract'[151] upon which the Lord Chancellor based his finding in favour of the plaintiff was committed, not by the defendant, but by the printer's employee. In other words, despite the court's apparent reliance upon the wider concept of breach of confidence, the decision was actually conceived by Lord Cottenham to consist in no more than a breach by an employee of his duty of good faith to his employer by the disclosure of a trade secret. This is evident from the cases cited by the Lord Chancellor in support of his view that there had been a breach of confidence. He referred to the decisions in *Duke of Queensbury* v. *Shebbeare*[152] and *Abernethy* v. *Hutchinson*[153] regarding them as being on all fours with *Tipping* v. *Clarke*.[154]

In *Duke of Queensbury* it was held that the owner of the unpublished manuscript of the Earl of Clarendon's *History of the Reign of Charles II* had an exclusive right to publish it for profit. In *Abernethy* the plaintiff doctor was able to obtain an injunction restraining publication by the *Lancet* of lectures on surgery that he had delivered to students at St Bartholomew's Hospital. *Tipping* v. *Clarke* concerned a bank clerk who, after falling out with his employer, threatened to publish details of the former's accounts. The Vice-Chancellor, Sir James Wigram, was in no doubt that 'every clerk employed in a merchant's counting-house is under an implied contract that he will not make public that which he learns in the execution of his duty as a clerk.'[155] Lord Cottenham, therefore, treated the matter as turning on the relationship of trust between parties arising through an express or implied contract.

Thirdly, the court accorded great importance to the potential profit that the owner of the property stood to make from its use, and the extent to which this economic right was threatened by the defendant. Thus, referring to *Tipping* v. *Clarke* Lord Cottenham stated that, as in that case, 'the

[150] At 1177. [151] At 1178. [152] (1758) 2 Eden 329.
[153] (1825) 1 H. & Tw. 2, 47 ER 1313. [155] At 161.
[154] 2 Hare 383, 67 ER 157.

matter or thing of which the party has obtained knowledge, being the exclusive property of the owner, he has a right to the interposition of this Court to prevent any use being made of it, that is to say, he is entitled to be protected in the exclusive use and enjoyment of that which is exclusively his.'[156]

In short, therefore, it is difficult to characterize *Prince Albert* v. *Strange* as a case relating principally to 'personal information'. And this much was conceded even by the Solicitor-General who stated:

The interference of the Court is not asked for in this case on the ground of decorum or good taste, but on the general principle that this court would protect every person in the free and innocent use of his own property, and will prevent anyone from interfering with that use, to the injury of the owner. A man has a right of property in the production of his mind, and incident to that right is the right of making the same public.[157]

And similarly, in replying to the contention that no property in the catalogue vested in the Prince, he said, 'No such right of property . . . in the catalogue is claimed, but the Plaintiff asserts that he has a right to make public the etchings, and that the publication of the catalogue interferes with that right.'[158]

3.2. *DUCHESS OF ARGYLL* v. *DUKE OF ARGYLL*[159]

The Duchess successfully sought an injunction to prohibit the Duke and a newspaper from publishing confidences she had reposed in her husband in the course of their marriage. Ungoed-Thomas J., relying largely on *Prince Albert* v. *Strange*, held that such communications between spouses were protected against breach of confidence—notwithstanding the Duchess's subsequent adultery and divorce from the Duke. On the face of it this decision would appear to constitute a paradigmatic instance of the protection against

---

[156] At 1179.
[157] At 1175. See the discussion of the 'right of publicity' in ch. 2.
[158] At 1178.   [159] [1967] Ch. 302.

public disclosure of 'personal information'. Yet, again, for four main reasons, this conclusion is not entirely convincing.

First, though it is reasonable to suppose that the communications between the spouses were indeed of an intimate nature, their precise content is not revealed, Ungoed-Thomas J. (remarking that '[i]f this were a well-developed jurisdiction, doubtless there would be guides and tests to aid in exercising it')[160] being satisfied that publication would breach marital confidence. This suggests that it was the relationship between the parties rather than the nature of the information that provided the court's justification for awarding the injunction. Ungoed-Thomas J. declared, 'there could hardly be anything more intimate or confidential than is involved in [the relationship of marriage], or than in the mutual trust and confidence which are shared between husband and wife.'[161]

Secondly, this concern by the court to protect marital confidences was explicitly founded on public policy: the court referred to the statutory rule that a spouse may not generally be compelled to disclose in court proceedings any communication made by the other spouse to him or her during the marriage—a rule which obtains even after the termination of the marriage.[162] Yet in the leading case concerning the admissibility of marital communications[163] the House of Lords, though it articulated the importance of preserving confidentiality of marital communications (expressed as well in the provisions in various statutes relating to the competence of spouses as witnesses), nevertheless held that the evidence in question was admissible. A witness other than the wife was allowed to give evidence of a letter which the husband—subsequently charged with murder—gave to the witness for posting abroad to his wife. The letter came into police possession: it contained, in terms, a confession by her husband to the murder. In other words, the policy which purports to protect the sanctity of marriage will, under certain circumstances, give way to competing policy considerations. It is, moreover, difficult to avoid the conclusion

---

[160] At 330. [161] At 619.

[162] *Rumping* v. *DPP*; Wigmore, *A Treatise on the Anglo-American System of Evidence*, 4th edn., viii, para. 2332.

[163] *Rumping* v. *DPP* [1964] AC 814.

(however cynical it may appear) that the plaintiff's success in *Argyll* v. *Argyll* was not entirely unconnected with the social standing of the parties, for in a similar case (*Lennon* v. *News Group Newspapers Ltd.* discussed below) an injunction was refused. (The plaintiff's success in *Prince Albert* v. *Strange* has also, of course, frequently been ascribed less to the merits of his case than to his position.)

Thirdly, in respect of the breach of confidence argument (the other two grounds upon which the injunction was granted were related to the publication of information in respect of the court proceedings themselves) it is significant that the court rejected the defendants' argument that, since the plaintiff had herself on previous occasions published intimate details concerning the marriage, the plaintiff did not come to Equity with clean hands. But this argument was rejected not by reference to an analysis of the 'personal information' that the defendants now wished to publicize, but rather by balancing the 'perfidy'[164] of the two species of information. Ungoed-Thomas J. was satisfied that the disclosures that the defendants now wished to make were more damning of the plaintiff than the plaintiff's previous disclosures were of the defendant. This suggests that had the reverse been the case (and the present disclosures were less unsympathetic to the plaintiff than her own had been of the defendant) the court might have been disposed to deny the plaintiff her injunction. It is difficult to see how this factor could be relevant if, as is widely believed, the case demonstrates the capacity of the action for breach of confidence to protect 'personal information' *tout court*. If that assessment were correct, it is submitted that the plaintiff's own misdemeanours would not be taken into account either independently or to be balanced against the defendant's present misconduct.

Fourthly, (in similar vein), the court rejected the defendant's argument that since the plaintiff's adulterous past exhibited scant respect for the sanctity of marriage which she now sought to uphold, she could not herself seek equitable relief. Adultery, the court held, undermined only the future confid-

[164] At 331.

ences of a marriage; it did not operate retrospectively to nullify marital confidences of 'earlier and happier days'.[165] But by acknowledging that present adultery might affect the extent to which the court might be willing to protect marital confidences, the decision again exhibits its narrow concerns with the consequences of the confidential relationship of marriage rather than the protection of 'personal information' itself.

The case, therefore, though it marks an important development of the law of confidence in respect of personal (or at least non-technical) confidences, is, not surprisingly, contained by the limitations—doctrinal and practical—set by the equitable jurisdiction of breach of confidence. This is evident not only in the relevance of the relative perfidy of the parties, but also in respect of the avowed policy of the court to uphold the relationship of marriage. Had the parties been friends, or even common-law spouses, it is doubtful whether the court would have exhibited a similar willingness to include the personal information within the restricted compass of the law's protection.

3.3. *WOODWARD* v. *HUTCHINS*[166]

The facts were recounted above. The Court of Appeal refused an application by three entertainers and their manager for an interlocutory injunction against a newspaper that wished to publish 'personal information' about them acquired by the newspaper through a breach of confidence by a former employee of the plaintiffs. In his judgment in the successful appeal to discharge the injunction, Lord Denning MR said:

No doubt in some employments there is an obligation of confidence. In a proper case the court will be prepared to restrain a servant from disclosing confidential information which he has received in the ordinary course of his employment. But this case is quite out of the ordinary. There is no doubt whatever that this pop group [*sic*] sought publicity. They wanted to have themselves presented to the public in a favourable light so that audiences would come to hear them and support them. Mr Hutchins was

---

[165] At 332–3.   [166] [1977] 1 WLR 760.

engaged so as to produce, or help to produce, this favourable image, not only of their public lives but of their private lives also.[167]

He then dealt the following telling blow to the respondents' case (and to the argument that the action for breach of confidence provides 'much greater protection of privacy than is generally realised'):[168]

If a group of this kind seek publicity which is to their advantage, it seems to me that they cannot complain if a servant or employee of theirs afterwards discloses the truth about them. If the image which they fostered was not a true image, it is in the public interest that it should be corrected.[169]

The Master of the Rolls went on to state that in cases involving confidential information the public interest in maintaining the confidence must be balanced against the public interest in knowing the truth. In this case, he held, the balance came down in favour of the truth being told despite the breach of confidence that had been committed: 'As there should be "truth in advertising", so there should be truth in publicity. The public should not be misled.'[170]

It is submitted that this decision in unsatisfactory in several respects. First, in his judgment Lord Denning treated the complaint as one concerning a breach of confidence by an employee. He then distinguished it from an ordinary employment case because of the special circumstances, namely that the respondents had sought publicity and thus forfeited their right to object when that publicity turned out to be unfavourable. Yet it is difficult to see how this is a relevant consideration. If, as Lord Denning himself acknowledged, the court will in a 'proper case'[171] be willing to 'restrain a servant from disclosing confidential information which he has received in the course of his employment'[172] it cannot be the case that a public figure—even (or perhaps particularly) one who inhabits the 'entertainment world'—has no means of preventing his employee from publishing intimate facts about him. It is no answer to say that he might rely on the employee's implied contractual obligation not to make such

---

[167] At 763.   [168] Younger, para. 630.   [169] At 762–3.
[170] At 763–4.
[171] At 762. See R. Wacks, 'Pop Goes Privacy' (1978) 31 MLR 68.
[172] At 762.

disclosures either during[173] or after[174] his term of employment, for the defence of 'just cause or excuse' extends to
breaches of contractual obligations[175] and the same reasoning
would presumably apply. The employer does, of course, have
the opportunity to include an express term in the employee's
contract of employment forbidding disclosure of confidential
information. Such terms are not uncommon in respect of
commercial secrets. But they will afford very limited assistance
to the likes of the respondents in this case for, not only is
much of the harm already likely to have been done by the
time the victim is able to obtain an injunction, but, unlike the
position in the case of commercial confidences, it will be
difficult to determine the extent to which the information is
honestly acquired in the course of employment and, hence,
not strictly in breach of the express term. In any event, it is, in
principle, unacceptable that merely because an individual
seeks favourable publicity (and this description might equally
be applied to politicians or even the royal family) his entire
private life might be laid bare with impunity and, what is
more, by a former employee who will, in most cases, be
moved by motives that are less than altruistic. Indeed,
whereas in previous employment cases in which the defence
of 'public interest' was successfully invoked, the court was
dealing with a public-spirited employee who sought to
expose his employer's (or ex-employer's) dishonesty, Hutchins
acted out of pure self-interest. He approached the newspaper
'no doubt for a very considerable reward' admitted Lord
Denning.[176] In *Initial Services*, however, he strongly disapproved of such conduct, saying, 'it is a great evil when
people purvey scandalous information for reward'.[177]

[173] See e.g. *Tipping* v. *Clark* (1843) 2 Hare 383, 393; 67 ER 157, 161;
Amber Size and Chemical Co. Ltd. v. *Menzel* [1913] 2 Ch. 239, 244–5:
Merryweather v. *Moore* [1892] 2 Ch. 518, 524: *Robb* v. *Green* [1895] 2
QB 315, 317.
[174] See e.g. *Alperton Rubber Co.* v. *Manning* (1917) 86 LJ Ch. 377,
379; *Amber Size and Chemical Co. Ltd.* v. *Menzel* [1913] 2 Ch. 239, 244–
5; *Under Water Welders & Repairers Ltd.* v. *Street and Longthorne* [1968]
RPC 498, 507; *Faccenda Chicken Ltd.* v. *Fowler* [1985] 1 All ER 724.
[175] *Tournier* v. *National Provincial and Union Bank of England* [1924]
1 KB 461, 473.   [176] At 761.
[177] [1968] 1 QB 396, 406. See above.

Secondly, the Court of Appeal's conception of the 'public interest' is curious. Lord Denning expressed the view that the public had interest in knowing 'the truth' about the pop stars. It was argued above that while there may well be a public interest in the truth being told about a fraudulent or dishonest businessmen,[178] the same can hardly be said for the private proclivities of pop singers. Moreover, the extravagant or hyperbolic claims made in public relations literature (by no means restricted to entertainers) ought not to operate to destroy the claims of such public figures to maintain the confidentiality of those aspects of their lives upon which such publicity has little or no bearing.

Thirdly, in denying the respondents an interlocutory injunction, the court applied the rule, long accepted in actions for libel[179] that the remedy will not be granted against a party who intends to justify the libel or plead the defence of fair comment. Lord Denning said 'the courts should not restrain [the disclosure] by an interlocutory injunction, but should leave the complainant to his remedy in damages'.[180]

Yet if the complainant in a breach of confidence action fails to prevent by an interlocutory injunction the threatened disclosure of personal facts about him, there would be little purpose in his pursuing an action for damages. Once broken a secret is no more. In the case of libel the facts which the defendant intends to justify are, *ex hypothesi*, true or the comments he has made, *ex hypothesi*, fair. It is therefore reasonable for the court in a libel case to err on the side of free speech and to deny the plaintiff an interlocutory injunction in such circumstances. Should the defendant subsequently fail to justify the publication the plaintiff may seek damages. In the case of breach of confidence, on the other hand, whatever general test is to be applied in respect to the grounds upon which an interlocutory injunction may be granted,[181] the truth or falsity of the disclosure is less

---

[178] As in *Initial Services Ltd.* v. *Putterill* [1968] 1 QB 396.
[179] See *Bonnard* v. *Perryman* [1891] 2 Ch. 269.   [180] At 763.
[181] The matter is complex and controversial. The principles formulated by Lord Diplock in *American Cyanamid Co.* v. *Ethicon Ltd.* [1975] AC 396 propose essentially that the court should exercise its discretion 'on a

material: indeed, it is often precisely because of its truth that the plaintiff seeks to prevent disclosure of the confidential information. The fact that the defendant intends merely to raise the plea of 'public interest' is not equivalent to the defendant in a libel case who intends to justify.

In *Woodward*, Lawton LJ regarded the action for breach of confidence as 'interwoven with the claim for damages for libel'.[182] He said that the case raised 'the question of balancing freedom of speech and publication against the right of an individual to have his servants treat as confidential that which they have learned in the course of their employment'.[183] And he (and Bridge LJ) considered that the balance of convenience lay against granting the injunction. But it is suggested that the two are, and should be conceived to be, separate. Support for this view was expressed by Sir David Cairns in *Khashoggi* (as quoted—and endorsed—by O'Connor LJ in *Lion Laboratories* v. *Evans*):[184]

It seems to me that there is a fundamental distinction between the two types of action, in that in the one case the plaintiff is saying 'Untrue and defamatory statements have been made about me', and in the other case the plaintiff is saying 'Statements which are about to be published are statements about events which have happened and have been disclosed as a result of a breach of confidence'.

And though he regarded the facts in *Lion Laboratories* as justifying disclosure by the press of the confidential information, O'Connor LJ accepted that different considerations obtained in each action. And Stephenson LJ also agreed with

balance of convenience'. But the application of this test has not been without difficulties. In respect of cases concerning breaches of confidence, the courts appear to have encountered fewer problems than has been the case in certain other contexts (notably trade disputes cases) and in several decisions in addition to *Woodward* (eg. *Dunford & Elliot Ltd.* v. *Johnson & Firth Brown Ltd.* [1977] 1 Lloyd's Rep. 505; *Potters-Ballotini Ltd.* v. *Weston-Baker* [1977] RPC 202; *Schering Chemicals Ltd.* v. *Falkman Ltd.* [1981] 2 WLR 848; *Hadmore Productions Ltd.* v. *Hamilton* [1982] 2 WLR 322; *Lion Laboratories Ltd.* v. *Evans* [1984] 2 All ER 417; *Francome* v. *Mirror Group Newspapers Ltd.* [1984] 1 WLR 892. Sir John Donaldson MR, in *Francome* (at 898) preferred the phrase 'balance of justice' to 'balance of convenience', describing the latter as an unfortunate expression. 'Our business is justice not convenience'.

[182] At 765.   [183] At 764.   [184] [1984] 2 All ER 417, 431.

Sir David Cairns's dictum, preferring his view to those expressed by Lord Denning in *Fraser* v. *Evans*[185] and by Roskill LJ in *Khashoggi* to the effect that a plaintiff should not be better off if he claims for breach of confidence than if he claims for defamation: 'I respectfully agree with Sir David Cairns in *Khashoggi*'s case . . . To be allowed to publish confidential information, the defendants must do more than raise a plea of public interest: they must show "a legitimate ground for supposing it is in the public interest for it to be disclosed".'[186]

3.4. *LENNON* v. *NEWS GROUP NEWSPAPERS LTD.*[187]

The former wife of John Lennon sold the 'story' of her marriage to the ex-Beatle to the *News of the World* which commenced a serialization of it. The articles disclosed intimate details of the relationship between the paintiff and his ex-wife. The Court of Appeal denied an injunction on the ground that 'the relationship of these parties has ceased to be their own private affair . . .'.[188] Lord Denning MR said that since neither of them had had much regard for the sanctity of marriage, the confidential nature of that relationship had ceased to exist. Yet the marriage between the Duke and Duchess of Argyll is no less befitting of such a description. Nor might one distinguish the cases on the possible ground that here 'each of (the parties) is making money by publishing the most intimate details about one another . . .'[189] for in publishing his disclosures in the newspaper the Duke had hardly acted gratuitously.

As in *Woodward* (above) Lord Denning was unwilling to

---

[185] [1969] 1 QB 349.

[186] [1980] 130 NLJ 168. The Court of Appeal in *Francome* v. *Mirror Group Newspapers Ltd.* [1984] 1 WLR 892, discussed below, was disposed to grant an interlocutory injunction since the parties would not be prejudiced if they had to wait until after the trial to publish the information—even though the defendants argued that 'an interlocutory injunction would be contrary to the accepted principles of defamation proceedings' (at 901).   [187] [1978] *FSR* 573.

[188] At 574.   [189] At 575 per Lord Denning.

restrain the publication of confidential information where the plaintiff has courted publicity in respect of his private life. This is an inevitable consequence both of the 'public domain' element in the action for breach of confidence and of the self-evident observation (made above) that if the object of the law was to protect 'personal information' independently of the relationship of confidence in which it is communicated, this factor would, at most, constitute a partial limitation on the plaintiff's right; the fact that the plaintiff has sought publicity will not—in the American 'privacy' cases—nullify his claim to legal protection over every aspect of his life.[190]

3.5. *KHASHOGGI* v. *SMITH*[191]

The former housekeeper of the plaintiff, a wealthy socialite who had attracted considerable publicity, disclosed intimate facts to the *Daily Mirror* concerning the plaintiff. Here, however, there was an investigation proceeding into the alleged commission of an offence by the plaintiff. The Court of Appeal, on an interlocutory motion, refused to enjoin publication on the principal ground that there could be no confidence where it was sought to exploit information for investigation into the commission of alleged offences.[192]

It is significant, first, that the court recognized that if it were concerned 'only with the question of whether or not the intended disclosures regarding Mrs Khashoggi's private life were permissible, different questions would or at least might arise'. This presumably suggests that in the absence of the criminal investigation, the court would have examined the question, which arose in *Woodward*, of the extent to which a former employee may disclose intimate facts concerning his or her former employer. But it is difficult to see how the Court of Appeal could have distinguished its decision in *Woodward*, for the principal motive in both cases was the financial one of selling to a newspaper secrets gained in the course of a relationship of trust. In other words, the action for breach of confidence that failed to assist the plaintiff in

---

[190] See ch. 5. [191] (1980) 130 NLJ 168.
[192] See the discussion of the public interest defence below, 110 *et seq.*

Woodward would be unlikely to have assisted Mrs Khashoggi—even if she had *not* been the subject of a criminal investigation.

Secondly, the fact that Mrs Khashoggi was herself negotiating with the *Daily Mirror* for the sale of her memoirs did not, in the view of the court, deprive her of any right to confidentiality to which she would otherwise be entitled. This appears to be a relaxation of Lord Denning's strict view in *Woodward* that the plaintiffs had forgone their right to the protection of private facts about them because they had themselves courted publicity. Yet it would be somewhat artificial to compare Mrs Khashoggi to three famous entertainers—whatever the extent of her fame or notoriety—and, in any event, since her memoirs were at the time of the hearing little more than a *spes*, the court could hardly be expected to attach any greater importance to them as evidence of her attitude to obtaining a 'favourable image'.[193] It may, therefore, be unwise to read too much into this aspect of the judgment.

3.5. *STEPHENS* v. *AVERY*[194]

The plaintiff disclosed to 'a close friend'[195] details of her lesbian relationship with a third party. The information found its way into the pages of the *Mail on Sunday* and the plaintiff alleged that her 'friend' and the newspaper had acted in breach of confidence.

The Vice-Chancellor, Sir Nicolas Browne-Wilkinson, dismissed an appeal from the master who had refused to strike out the proceedings as disclosing no reasonable cause of action, or as being scandalous, frivolous, or vexatious.

The defendants raised two main arguments. First they claimed that the information ought not to attract legal protection both because it was 'trivial tittle-tattle'[196] and

---

[193] *Woodward*, above, at 763.
[194] [1988] 2 WLR 1280 (Ch. D.).   [195] At 1282.
[196] *Coco* v. *A. N. Cark (Engineers) Ltd.* [1969] RPC 41 at 48 per Megarry J.

because it related to grossly immoral conduct. Secondly they argued that the circumstances in which the plaintiff was alleged to have communicated the information did not give rise to a duty of confidence.

The court rejected both submissions. Sir Nicolas declared: 'I have the greatest doubt whether wholesale revelation of the sexual conduct of an individual can properly be described as "trivial" tittle-tattle.'[197] He added: 'I can see no reason why information relating to that most private sector of everybody's life, namely sexual conduct, cannot be the subject matter of a legally enforceable duty of confidentiality.'[198]

In respect of the second argument, he held, quoting the dicta of Lord Denning MR in *Seager* v. *Copydex*[199] and *Fraser* v. *Evans*,[200] that there was nothing about the relationship between the plaintiff and her 'friend' that suggested the information communicated could not be the subject of a duty of confidence.

This is, with respect, a perfectly sensible judgment. Nevertheless, the court was inevitably required to attach importance to the fact that the 'friend' had accepted the information on the basis that it would be kept secret. Despite his statement that 'the relationship between the parties is not the determining factor',[201] the Vice-Chancellor was obliged to emphasize the fact that 'the express statement that the information is confidential is the clearest possible example of the imposition of a duty of confidence.'[202] Indeed, he refers to the case of *M. and N.* v. *Kelvin Mackenzie and News Group Newspapers Ltd.*[203] in which Garland J. apparently refused an injunction on the ground that 'the mere existence of a homosexual relationship between the two parties did not raise a duty of confidence between them or as against third parties.'[204] In that case there was no express statement that the information was confidential.

In other words, if the newspaper had, through its own devices and without a little help from a 'friend' obtained the information about the lesbian liaison and published it, the plaintiff would have been deprived of an action for breach of

---

[197] At 1285. [198] At 1286. [199] [1967] 1 WLR 923 at 931.
[200] [1969] 1 QB 349 at 361. [101] At 1286. [102] At 1287.
[203] 18 Jan. 1988, unreported. [204] At 1287.

confidence. Yet the court acknowledged that the case raised 'fundamental difficulties as to the relationship between on the one hand the privacy which every individual is entitled to expect, and on the other hand freedom of information.'[205] With respect, the conflict is less between 'privacy' and 'freedom of information' than between 'protecting confidential relationships' and 'freedom of speech'. If the plaintiff had not made it clear that she was communicating the information in confidence, her so-called 'privacy' would have been a fragile thing.

The decision holds merely that the plaintiff's action should not be struck out. Of course the trial, if it takes place, may not necessarily result in judgment for the plaintiff.

3.7. X. v. Y.[206]

An employee of a health authority leaked the names of two practising doctors who had contracted AIDS. The information was given to a newspaper reporter in return for the payment of a sum of money. The plaintiffs, the health authority, obtained an order restraining the newspaper from publishing or using the information. The newspaper nevertheless published an article implying that there were doctors in the health service who were continuing to practise despite having contracted AIDS and suggesting that the DHSS wished to suppress this information. The newspaper intended to publish a further article identifying the doctors. The plaintiffs sought, *inter alia*, an injunction restraining the newspaper from disclosing the identity of the doctors.

The court granted a permanent injunction; it held that the

---

[205] Ibid.

[206] [1988] 2 All ER 648. In addition to the action for breach of confidence, the case also involved a breach of an injunction which prohibited publication of the confidential information. The defendants were convicted of contempt of court and fined £10,000 for the 'deliberate and florid use of information which the injunction prohibited'. (At 666.) The defendants were not, however, compelled to disclose the source of the information because the plaintiffs had failed to prove that disclosure was necessary for the prevention of crime within s. 10 of the Contempt of Court Act 1981.

public interest in preserving the confidentiality of hospital records identifying actual or potential AIDS sufferers outweighed the public interest in the freedom of the press to publish such information, because victims should not be deterred by fear of discovery from coming forward for treatment. Protecting the confidentiality of the names of sufferers would not stifle the free and informed public debate about the disease. Moreover, as Rose J. put it.[207]

The risk of identification is only one factor in assessing whether to permit the use of confidential information. In my judgment to allow publication . . . would be to enable both defendants to procure breaches of confidence and then to make their own selection for publication. This would make a mockery of the law's protection of confidentiality when no justifying public interest has been shown.

The plaintiffs were not, of course, the doctors themselves and there is no evidence of a relationship of confidence between them and the 'mole'. Nevertheless it is likely that they would have had a cause of action against the newspaper on the basis that an obligation of confidence is imposed where a third party knew or ought to have known that the information is to be treated as confidential.[208]

Though the case is yet a further demonstration of the flexibility of the action for breach of confidence, at least two limitations should be recognized. First, it was not the doctors but their employers who brought the action; their primary interest (accepted by the court) was that they may 'be free from suspicion that they are harbouring disloyal employees'. The suffering of the doctors, though acknowledged by the court,[209] was inevitably a secondary consideration.

Secondly, the requirements of the action inevitably obtrude. Though the court was willing to dispose of the requirement that detriment to the plaintiff is a necessary prerequisite for the award of an injunction it nevertheless identified such evidence: it was present 'because patients' records were

---

[207] At 661.

[208] *Coco v. A. N. Clark (Engineers) Ltd.* [1959] RPC 41, 48. See above.

[209] At 657 there is a somewhat cryptic reference to 'the pursuit of one of the doctors as appears from the first defendant's notes of conversation and unpublished draft article and in the information that the other doctor was "very suicidal" '.

leaked to the press in breach of contract and breach of confidence, with the consequences, even without publication, to the plaintiffs and the patients . . . If use were made of that information in such a way as to demonstrate to the public (by identifying the hospital) the source of the leak, the plaintiffs would suffer further detriment.[210] Of course, if detriment were indeed a requirement and if it were the doctors who were plaintiffs, the detriment would be of a different order altogether. Nor, as already mentioned, might it suffice for an award of damages.[211]

4. Breach of Confidence and 'Personal Information'

The least remarkable result of the failure of the English law to develop a law of 'privacy' along American lines is perhaps the paucity of cases in which actions for breach of confidence involving personal information have come before the courts. It may therefore seem rash to attempt to draw definitive conclusions on such limited evidence. On the other hand, there is no shortage of dicta which unequivocally assert the jurisdiction over non-commercial personal confidences.

Indeed, it is mildly unsettling that it was in just such a case[212] that the germ of this development was first identified. It may safely be claimed therefore that, in so far as the doctrinal or conceptual difficulties are concerned, the small body of law on breach of personal confidences (described above) represents a relatively clear statement of the nature of the protection accorded to, and the foundation of liability in respect of, 'personal information', its use and disclosure.

What was less predictable, though equally discomforting, is the extent to which the action would be fashioned by the judges so as to outgrow its less ambitious progenitor. It now provides a forum for the constitutional determination of free speech and the balancing of interests which have long been the hallmark of Supreme Court decisions in the United States,

---

[210] At 657–8. [211] See above, 56.
[212] *Prince Albert* v. *Strange* (1849) 1 Max & G. 25.

but which English judges have traditionally resisted, at any rate, in theory. These cases have not, of course, necessarily involved 'personal information', but, in applying the defence of public interest they have, in the short space of less than twenty years, promoted the narrow principle of 'no confidence in iniquity' into a fully fledged defence of just cause or excuse.

Explanations for this development may be sought in a variety of social and political factors, but, as far as 'personal information' is concerned, the result has been to weaken the protection granted to confidential relationships. The reverse is the case in respect of information concerning national security, dramatically illustrated by the various, and at the time of writing, continuing, attempts by the British Government to restrain the disclosures of erstwhile security agents.

One interpretation of the position is to regard it simply as a demonstration of the capacity of the common law to adapt to new challenges under cover of existing categories. Thus it could be argued that the vacuum created by the absence of a legal 'right to privacy' has been filled by the judicial application of the developing principles of the action for breach of confidence to problems that would, in the American law, probably be subsumed under the protection of 'privacy'. This is most evident in breach of confidence litigation in which the defence of public interest has been raised. But this approach by the courts has generated three kinds of conceptual and practical difficulties which I shall describe as functional, structural, and, somewhat inelegantly, functional–structural. Each may be briefly defined in the following way.

1. *Functional problems.* These are related to the manner in which courts have sought to determine appropriate criteria by which to judge the legitimate use or disclosure of confidential information, both personal and non-personal.

2. *Structural problems.* These arise as a direct result of the application of principles, which are designed largely to protect trade confidences, to disputes involving the disclosure of 'personal information'.

3. *Functional–structural problems.* These occur where, in

evaluating the circumstances under which confidence may justifiably be breached, the court applies principles which, while appropriate to non-personal information, are unsuited to the resolution of cases concerning 'personal information'. The reverse may also occur: the court may apply a 'privacy' argument in order to stifle an action for breach of confidence.

Instances of each of these difficulties will be discussed, and this will be followed by a general consideration of what I call the doctrinal problems: the wider analytical questions pertaining to the action for breach of confidence, the interests that it seeks to protect, and the inadequacy and inappropriateness of the action in cases involving 'personal information'.

4.1. FUNCTIONAL PROBLEMS

They are, broadly speaking, twofold.

1. The courts resort to '*ad hoc* balancing' of the competing interests, and this affords little guidance as to the proper scope of permissible disclosure or use of confidential information;

2. As a result of this process of '*ad hoc* balancing' there is inadequate notice given to confiders and recipients of 'personal information' in respect of the obligation of confidence required; in the case of non-personal secrets, on the other hand, the very nature of the information provides sufficient notice.

Such problems surface most conspicuously in cases in which the 'public interest' is invoked to justify breach of confidence (see discussion in (3.3) above). Support for this approach is to be found in the Report of the Law Commission which expressly proposed that the courts, in such circumstances, should engage in 'balancing the respective public interests in confidentiality on the one hand and in disclosure and use of the information on the other'.[213] But it may be questioned whether 'judges should be encouraged to ride the unruly horse of public policy, to balance a public interest in

[213] Law Commission Report, para. 6.84 (i).

confidentiality against a public interest in disclosure'.[214] This is a problem that extends beyond the present enquiry into the specific application of the law to 'personal information', the 'public interest' aspects of which are considered under the structural difficulties described below. To the extent, however, that the balancing of competing interests affords inadequate guidance to parties who impart and receive 'personal information', there is the serious prospect that such uncertainty and, more particularly, the courts' recent tendency to circumscribe *ad hoc* the legal protection to be given to personal confidences, may inhibit the candour that is an important element in certain relationships (e.g. husband–wife, doctor–patient, employer–employee) which the law is itself committed to sustaining and even encouraging.

It could, of course, be argued that the law is in the process of developing tests which are appropriate to 'personal information', but there remains a significant distinction between such confidences and non-personal information: commercial secrets are invariably imparted in circumstances in which it is clear to both the confider and the recipient that the information is to be treated in confidence; unlike personal confidences, trade secrets, for example, are rarely communicated in a casual manner in which one or both of the parties are left in possible doubt as to the rights or obligations agreed upon. In the case of trade secrets, moreover, relatively unequivocal notice is given to the recipient—by virtue of the nature of the information itself—that he is under a duty not to breach confidence.

4.2. STRUCTURAL PROBLEMS

In the following discussion an attempt is made to show that in each of six areas the application of the law of confidence to 'personal information' yields unsatisfactory or, at best, problematic results. The conclusion is therefore reached that rather than legislating along the lines proposed by the Law Commission, the matter is better dealt with by legislation

[214] G. Jones 'The Law Commission's Report on Breach of Confidence' (1982) Camb. LJ 40, 47. See X v. Y [1988] 2 All ER 648, 661 per Rose J.

that is explicitly designed to protect 'personal information', *whether or not it is imparted in the course of a confidential relationship*. Indeed, the law of confidence in respect of non-personal information appears to be developing satisfactorily in the hands of the judges. It is arguable that no statutory reform is required in that area.[215]

4.2.1. *Requirements of the Action for Breach of Confidence*

There are, as has already been mentioned (see 1 above), several difficulties in connection with each of the three elements of the action:

4.2.1.1. *The information*
Though the categories of confidential information are, like those of negligence, apparently never closed,[216] the application of principles developed to protect trade secrets to other species of information has not been an entirely satisfactory exercise. In particular, in the absence of a definition of 'personal information', the extent to which the law is able to afford clear guidance to those who impart or receive such information of their respective rights and duties, is likely to be fairly limited. It might be argued that such a definition is unnecessary (because the law accommodates all types of confidential information), undesirable (because it might hamper or unduly restrict the proper development of the law), or impossible (because the matter is almost intractably complex). But, though there is

---

[215] Professor Jones goes further. He is unpersuaded that legislation is required at all: 'At the end of the day the large question remains: is it desirable *at this time* to enact legislation on the lines suggested by the Law Commission, legislation which will, in some ways, petrify the development of this branch of the law? Certainly there are few signs in the last few years that the common law has failed to deal adequately with the problems which it has been required to solve. This area of the law is not crying out for reform. It is still in an embryonic state; and there may well be questions lurking unseen in the shadows' ('The Law Commission's Report' (1982) Camb. LJ 40, 47). See too Goff and Jones, *The Law of Restitution*, 3rd edn. (1987), 683. Cf. Cripps, *The Legal Implication of Disclosure*, 251 ff.

[216] Protection will not, however, be given to 'trivial tittle-tattle': *Coco* v. *A. N. Clark (Engineers) Ltd.* [1969] RPC 41 at 48 per Megarry J. Applied in *Church of Scientology* v. *Kaufman* [1973] RPC 635 at 658; *Attorney-General* v. *Guardian Newspapers Ltd. (No. 2)* [1988] 2 WLR 805 (CA); [1988] 3 WLR 776 (HL).

some validity in each of these claims, they do not constitute an overwhelming case against the formulation of such a definition which would, of course, be essential to any separate treatment by the law of 'personal information'.

In its Working Paper[217] the Law Commission acknowledged that '[i]t is clear to us that there is a distinction between a plaintiff who is seeking to protect a trade secret and one who is seeking a remedy for non-pecuniary injury and that the same principles of law will not necessarily be appropriate to both',[218] and it proposed a classification (which was abandoned by the Law Commission in its Report because 'it was criticised on consultation as being unnecessarily complex')[219] divided into three categories:

Category I. The disclosure or use of information which would, in whole or in part, deprive the person to whom a duty of confidence is owed of the opportunity himself to obtain pecuniary advantage by the publication or use of such information.

Category II. The disclosure of information relating to the person to whom a duty of confidence is owed (the plaintiff) which the person subject to the duty (the defendant) knew, or ought to have known, would cause the plaintiff pecuniary loss and which in fact causes the plaintiff pecuniary loss.

Category III. The disclosure of information relating to the person to whom a duty of confidence is owed which would be likely to cause distress to a reasonable person in his position and which in fact causes him distress.

Category I covers the quintessential breach of confidence case involving trade secrets, but could involve 'personal information' where such information (e.g. contained in memoirs to be published by the plaintiff) has an obvious commercial value and where its use or disclosure would occasion straightforward pecuniary loss. Category II incorporates information which relates to the plaintiff, the disclosure of which would cause him financial loss—for instance where the defendant discloses information (which could be 'personal', e.g. that the plaintiff was divorced) to, say the plaintiff's

---

[217] No. 58, paras. 61–8.   [218] Ibid, para. 62.
[219] Ibid, para. 6.3.

employer (whom, the defendant knows, has strong views on the matter) causing him to lose his job. Category III contemplates 'personal information' which was originally imparted in confidence, disclosure of which would cause the plaintiff distress. The example is given of A informing B in confidence that he, A, is a homosexual, and B disclosing this information. A would have a cause of action if he could establish that to be called a homosexual would be likely to cause distress to any reasonable man in his position and that it does in fact cause him distress.[220]

Categories I and III go some way toward identifying a separate branch of obligation to respect confidences which *relate to the plaintiff*, they cover a fairly narrow compass for such disclosures are likely to arise in only a few circumstances, since there obviously needs to be a relationship of confidence between A and B in the first place. In the case of Category III, moreover, any distress that the plaintiff suffers in these circumstances will tend to be a result of *publicity* being given to the information—and this is, of course, not a requirement of the action for breach of confidence, though it is fundamental to the complaint in the context of the American 'privacy' action.

Any attempt to distinguish information on the basis of whether it is of a 'commercial' or 'personal' character is beset with difficulty: 'personal information' has its price, and may be susceptible of commercial exploitation. The Law Commission therefore proposed[221] a twofold test to determine to which category the information properly belonged:

(a) The nature of the harm which a plaintiff is liable to sustain by the misuse of information subject to a duty of confidence, and

(b) Whether the information in question in itself relates to the plaintiff or has no particular relationship to him.

Within the context of the action for breach of confidence the creation of a cognate body of information *relating to the plaintiff* (Categories II and III) requiring the application of different principles of law (the chief issues identified by the

[220] These facts have now materialized in a strikingly similar form, see *Stephens* v. *Avery* [1988] 2 WLR 1280 discussed above.
[221] Ibid, para. 6.3.

Law Commission which might require special treatment are: the question of 'public domain', damages, and jury trials; they might have added the question of 'public interest'—see below) would undoubtedly amount to an improvement in the mode of adjudicating such claims. This could form the basis for the development of a relatively discrete body of law relating to confidential information which pertains to an individual rather than purely commercial secrets (and could also avoid the functional problems identified above). But in view of the central structural requirement of an existing relationship of confidence, such a statutory reform would be of limited utility in the general protection of 'personal information'. Nevertheless, by acknowledging the distinctive character of such information (in respect both of the harm to the plaintiff and the relationship between him and the confidential information) and by suggesting the need for certain structural modifications (in respect of the test of 'public domain' and the appropriate remedy and form of trial) the Law Commission has demonstrated the plausibility of such an approach. It is unfortunate that the proposal did not survive beyond the Working Paper, though, from the point of view of the more comprehensive approach to the protection of 'personal information' proffered in this book, its acceptance (or even, less likely, its legislative enactment) would have solved only some of the problems identified here.

4.2.1.2. *The obligation of confidence* The circumstances under which an obligation of confidence arises have been briefly referred to (see 1 above). It seems reasonably clear that certain relationships import such an obligation (e.g. pre-contractual business negotiations, the doctor–patient relationship) and, in exercising its equitable discretion, a court is willing to recognize that the recipient of information in the context of certain relationships accepts the confidentiality implicit therein. An objective test is employed: would a reasonable man in the position of the recipient have realised that the information was being given to him in confidence?[222] As far as trade secrets are concerned, there will be little doubt

---

[222] *Coco v. A. N. Clarke (Engineers) Ltd.* [1969] RPC 41 at 48 per Megarry J., *obiter*.

in the recipient's mind as to the circumstances under which the information is being communicated to him; it is not unusual for a fair degree of formality to attend such events. With 'personal information', however, this is less likely to be the case, though in respect of certain relationships (e.g. marriage)[223] an obligation of confidence may be implied. Where *no* relationship exists at all, there will probably be no means of preventing the disclosure of private facts. Thus, where my complaint is that you have disclosed intimate facts about me (obtained outside any relationship of confidence) the action for breach of confidence will obviously not apply, but, by virtue of the nature of the information (e.g. it relates to my sex life), it is arguable that you knew, or ought to have known, both that the information is private and that its disclosure is likely to cause me injury. However, the action for breach of confidence is unlikely to assist. Yet, where the defendant is a *third party* I may be able to restrain him from disclosing the information. It is only once a third party has actual or constructive notice of the fact that the information he has received is confidential (i.e. communicated to him in breach of confidence) that he would appear to incur liability for its use or disclosure.[224]

It is an inevitable consequence of the law's concern to protect the relationship of confidence or the express or implied undertaking to respect the confidence rather than the confidential information itself that an innocent third party cannot be restrained from using or disclosing such information—unless and until he has knowledge of its confidentiality. If the purpose of the law were to protect the plaintiff from disclosure of the information itself, the question of notice would not necessarily arise. The issue of the scope of the obligation of confidence assumes particular importance in relation to the obtaining of information by unlawful or improper means. This is returned to in Chapter 7.

4.2.1.3. *Unauthorized use* The question of whether, in

---

[223] *Argyll* v. *Argyll* [1967] Ch. 302.

[224] The clearest statement of the law is still to be found in the judgement of Sir Robert Megarry VC in *Malone* v. *Commissioner of Police of the Metropolis (No.2)* [1979] 2 All ER 620 at 634. Cf. *Francome* v. *Mirror Group Newspapers Ltd.* [1984] 1 WLR 892; *Franklin* v. *Giddens*, above.

order to succeed, the plaintiff must show detriment was discussed above (see 2.1.3) and it was suggested that if this were indeed a requirement of the action such detriment might, in a case involving 'personal information', consist in the injured feelings, embarrassment, or distress suffered by the plaintiff. There is no authority directly in point[225] but the better view is that the existence of detriment goes to the question of the appropriate remedy and is not an element of the action itself. Yet though injured feelings may suffice to allow the plaintiff to win an injunction,[226] the absence of material detriment may preclude an award of damages. The question of the award of damages for mental distress is examined below under Remedies (4.2.6).

4.2.2. *Public Domain*

It has already been argued above that the application of the test of whether the confidential information sought to be protected is in the 'public domain' (a fundamental issue in cases involving trade secrets) to cases concerning 'personal information' has a certain artificiality about it. Thus in *Woodward* v. *Hutchins*[227] the activities of pop stars aboard an aeroplane were classified by the Court of Appeal as being in the 'public domain' since the other passengers witnessed them.[228]

The purpose of the principle (and the associated Springboard Doctrine) is to define the scope of the obligation of confidence to exclude information which though originally communicated in confidence is now 'common knowledge. The secret, as a secret, [has] ceased to exist.'[229]

---

[225] But see the dicta in *Attorney-General* v. *Guardian Newspapers Ltd.* (*No. 2*) [1988] 3 WLR 776 at 782 and 806. See too in *Commonwealth of Australia* v. *John Fairfax & Sons Ltd.* (1981) 55 ALJR 45 at 49; *X* v. *Y* [1988] 2 All ER 648, 657.

[226] *Prince Albert* v. *Strange* (1849) 2 De Gex & Sm. 652 at 697 per Knight-Bruce VC; *Pollard* v. *Photograph Co.* (1889) 40 Ch.D. 345. Cf. *Li Yau-wai* v. *Genesis Films Ltd.* [1987] HKLR 711.

[227] [1977] 1 WLR 760. See too *Attorney-General* v. *Guardian Newspapers Ltd.* (*No. 2*) [1988] 2 WLR 805.

[228] At 764.

[229] *O. Mustad & Son* v. *Dosen* (1928) [1964] 1 WLR 109 at 111 per Lord Buckmaster. *Attorney-General* v. *Guardian Newspapers Ltd.* (*No. 2*) [1988] 3 WLR 766, 809–813 (Lord Goff).

It was suggested above that the rejection by the Law Commission of the 'more rigid standard'[230] of what constitutes 'public domain' in the case of 'personal information' (as proposed by the Law Commission in its Working Paper)[231] is premissed on questionable logic, and that the narrower formulation is to be preferred. A more general test would, of course, be necessary where the court is faced with the publication of 'personal information' outside a relationship of confidence—as in the American tort of public disclosure of private facts.

4.2.3. *Disclosure 'in the Public Interest'*

The reluctance by the courts to permit a plaintiff to prevent the disclosure of 'iniquity' is, in part, a function of the fact that the action for breach of confidence has its origins in Equity. In the absence of clearly formulated privileges, this principle has occasionally been extended to circumstances in which to enjoin disclosure would be to give unwarranted primacy to the protection of confidential information. It is perhaps too abstract a claim to argue that where 'personal information' is concerned, this kind of evaluation is better made in the explicit context of the protection of those interests of the personality which are associated with the protection against the gratuitous publication of 'personal information'. This is so because it is manifestly the case that where confidential information relates to facts about the plaintiff the disclosure of which would cause him distress, a court in weighing up the competing interests of, on the one hand, the public interest in preserving the plaintiff's right to maintain the confidence against, on the other, the interest of the public to be informed about matters of real public concern,[232] might satisfactorily apply similar considerations to those which it would apply in a case involving *other* species of confidential information. But it may do so, it seems, only in circumstances in which the 'personal information' is communicated *within a relationship of confidence.*

---

[230] Law Commission Report, para. 6.69.

[231] Working Paper, para. 103.

[232] *Lion Laboratories Ltd.* v. *Evans* [1984] 2 All ER 417 at 422–3 per Stephenson LJ.

The plaintiff's right in such a case is against a specific individual who has notice of the obligation to maintain the confidentiality of certain identifiable information. In balancing the interests involved, a court is therefore faced with different issues from those that would arise where no relationship of confidence exists, where the 'personal inform-ation' is disclosed as a result, say, of the efforts of a journalist who publishes intimate facts about the plaintiff that he has himself obtained in the course of his own investigations without the aid of a 'mole'.

Here the question of whether disclosure was in the public interest ought to have less to do with balancing this factor against the public interest in the *preservation of confidence* than with balancing it against the *harm to the plaintiff* that the disclosure would cause. Indeed, in protecting confidential *relationships* the court's principal concern is to encourage the preservation of trust—and the fact that its breach would occasion harm to the plaintiff, though it might be alluded to as an element in determining the public interest in confidenti-ality, is merely one possible factor in the balancing exercise.

In a recent statement of the defence of public interest[233] Stephenson LJ reiterated the four considerations that were to be taken into account in determining the extent to which 'the

---

[233] *Lion Laboratories* 423. This decision of the Court of Appeal represents the high-water mark of the development of the defence of just cause or excuse where disclosure is in the public interest, but it is not inconsistent with previous formulations of the principle, notably by Lord Denning MR: *Initial Services* v. *Putterill* [1968] 1 QB 396; *Fraser* v. *Evans* [1969] 1 QB 349; *Hubbard* v. *Vosper* [1972] 2 QB 84; *Woodward* v. *Hutchins* [1977] 1 WLR 760; *Schering Chemicals Ltd.* v. *Falkman Ltd.* [1982] QB 1 (dissenting). See too the speeches of Lords Wilberforce, Salmon, and Fraser in *British Steel Corporation* v. *Granada Television Ltd.* [1981] AC 1096. The Court of Appeal regarded 'public interest' as a *defence*. The Law Commission, however, preferred not to do so (para. 4.41). They therefore omit it from the defences in clause 12 of their bill as well as from clauses 8(3) and 8(4) which deal with the limitations on the obligation of confidence, and from clause 9 which provides for the termination of the obligation. Their reason was that in the balancing of the competing public interests it is for the *plaintiff* to show that there is a public interest in preserving confidence, not for the *defendant* to establish that the public has an interest in learning of the information. In view of the importance of the principle of 'public interest' it is treated separately in this chapter. In section 5 below the *other* defences are considered together.

privacy of confidential matters'[234] might legitimately be infringed:

1. There is an important distinction between what is interesting to the public and what it is in the public interest to make known.[235] The latter is the proper requirement to be satisfied.

2. The 'media' have their own private interest in publishing what appeals to the public since it may increase their circulation or the numbers of their viewers or listeners.

3. In some cases the public interest is best served by an informer giving confidential information not to the press but to the police or some other responsible body.

4. The public interest did not arise only where there was 'iniquity' to be disclosed, and a defendant ought not to be restrained solely because what he sought to publish did not show misconduct on the part of the plaintiff.

It has already been argued above that, while these considerations are appropriate to a balancing of interests in decisions which involve the plaintiff's personality interests, to apply them in cases in which the plaintiff's chief complaint is that a confidence has been breached may give rise to what I have called functional/structural problems (which are discussed in 4.3 below.) Similarly, where information relating to the government is concerned, it is arguable that the court should 'look at the matter through different spectacles' from those which are appropriate in respect of 'the personal, private and proprietary interests of the citizen'.[236]

---

[234] *Lion Laboratories* 423.

[235] The difficulties raised by the failure of courts to distinguish between the 'descriptive' and 'normative' meanings of the term, and the general preference for the latter (expressed also by Lord Wilberforce in *British Steel Corporation* v. *Granada Television Ltd.* [1981] 1 All ER 417 at 455), occurs in the American 'privacy' cases; see Note, 'The Right of Privacy: Normative–Descriptive Confusion in the Defence of Newsworthiness' (1963) 30 Univ. of Chicago Law Rev. 722.

[236] *Commonwealth of Australia* v. *John Fairfax and Sons Ltd.* (1980) 55 ALJR 45 at 49 per Mason J. This dictum has been quoted with approval in a number of decisions including, most recently, the House of Lords in *Attorney-General* v. *Guardian Newspapers Ltd.* (No. 2) [1988] 2 WLR 776, 783–785, per Lord Keith, and the Court of Appeal in Australia in *Attorney-General* v. *Heinemann* [1987]. According to the (so far un-

In the absence of a relationship of confidence between the plaintiff and the person alleged to owe an obligation of confidence to him, the action for breach of confidence is unlikely to assist the plaintiff where the information has been obtained by reprehensible means such as electronic surveillance. But it is suggested by the Law Commission that 'in assessing the public interest in protecting the confidentiality of information the court should take all the circumstances into account, including the manner in which the information was acquired whether by the original acquirer or by a third party'.[237] It is submitted, however, that, though this proposes only that the means of acquisition be regarded as *one* factor in the balancing exercise, the two questions ought as far as possible to be kept separate. Disclosure ought not to be prohibited merely because the means employed to obtain the information are reprehensible. And the reverse should apply: reprehensible means ought not to be permitted merely because the eventual disclosure is justified as being in the public interest.

Support for this view is expressed by Stephenson LJ in the *Lion Laboratories* case,[238] where he remarked:

There is confidential information which the public may have a right to receive and others, in particular the press, now extended to the media, may have a right and even a duty to publish, *even if the*

reported) transcript of the Australian decision, Street CJ (dissenting) added: 'The question before the Court is not whether the UK Government has lost its proprietary interest, or the value of its exclusivity, in knowledge of these confidential matters; that is a consideration relevant to *private* litigation founded on principles of the protection of equitable proprietary rights. The basis of the UK Government's claim is to be found in the legitimacy of its assertion that, in the national interest, publication of these confidential matters should be restrained. The test is not detriment to proprietary interest; it is damage to the national interest. Viewed in this light, defensive assertions of prior publication will have different significance in a case such as the present from the significance they have in ordinary *private* equity litigation' (at 34–5, stress supplied). This important distinction between 'private' and 'public' litigation (which is adumbrated in the text of this chapter) informs also the analysis of the issue by McHugh JA (especially at 15–16 of his judgment). Lords Keith, Griffiths, and Goff explicitly endorse Mason J's approach.

[237] Law Commission Report, para. 6.79.

[238] See above, at 422, emphasis supplied. See X v. Y [1988] 2 All ER 648, 658.

information has been unlawfully obtained in flagrant breach of confidence and irrespective of the motive of the informer.

Other difficulties raised by the application of the public interest defence have already been mentioned. The central problem generated by the judicial balancing of competing interests in the context of actions for breach of confidence seems to be that, in their enthusiasm to espouse the value of free speech, the courts may have neglected the protection of the relationship of confidence.

In the light of the flurry of criticism that greeted the House of Lords decision to maintain the interlocutory injunction against the newspapers in the *Spycatcher* case, this may seem a singularly captious view. It must be emphasized, however, that the present discussion is confined to what might be called *private* confidences: different considerations must obtain when it is the *government* that seeks to restrain the disclosure of confidential information. It is worth quoting in full Mason J.'s important dictum in *Commonwealth of Australia* v. *John Fairfax & Sons Ltd.*[239]

The equitable interest has been fashioned to protect the personal, private and proprietary rights of the citizen not to protect the very different interests of the executive government. It acts, or is supposed to act, not according to the standards of private interest, but in the public interest. That is not to say that equity will not protect information in the hands of the government, but it is to say that when equity protects government it will look at the matter through different spectacles.

It may be a sufficient detriment to the citizen that disclosure of information relating to his affairs will expose his actions to public discussion and criticism. But it can scarcely be a relevant detriment to the government that publication of material concerning its actions will merely expose it to public discussion and criticism. It is unacceptable in our society that there should be a restraint on the publication of information relating to government when the only vice of that information is that it enables the public to discuss, review and criticise government action. Accordingly, the court will determine the government's claim to confidentiality by reference to the public interest. Unless disclosure is likely to injure the public interest, it will not be protected.

[239] See above, no. 217.

Recent decisions on private confidences do suggest that the courts have been less than enthusiastic to protect the interests of the plaintiff who has imparted confidential information.[240] For example in *Francome* and *Lion Laboratories*[241] the protection of the confidential information and the circumstances under which confidence was breached did not weigh heavily with courts determined to encourage the free flow of information which they regarded as the public's right to know. In neither case, however, was the court faced with a confidential relationship of a kind that it would be unreasonable to expect it not to wish to protect.

Suppose, however, that the facts resembled *Woodward*[242] except that the information disclosed by Hutchins to the newspaper affected not only the interests of the entertainers but also 'the life, and even the liberty,' of an unascertainable number of Her Majesty's subjects'.[243] It is doubtful whether the same alacrity to permit disclosure would have been exhibited by the court. And certainly, as the *Spycatcher* cases demonstrate, considerably more attention would have been paid to the possible social consequences of allowing a newspaper to publish information imparted in the course of a relationship it is the law's policy to protect. And the same would surely be true in the case, say, of the relationship between doctor and patient, lawyer and client, or banker and customer. Though none of these relationships is immune to legitimate breach where this is justified by reference to some countervailing interest or group of interests, greater caution would be exercised by the courts in conducting the balancing exercise.

It may be therefore that one should not read too much into those cases which have interpreted the public interest defence widely, for the relationship has either been one which the

[240] The same could be said of the recent judgment by Scott J. in the application for a permanent injunction in the *Spycatcher* case. *Attorney-General* v. *Guardian Newspapers Ltd. (No. 2)* [1988] 2 WLR 805. Similar sentiments are expressed by the Court of Appeal including the Master of the Rolls in his dissenting judgment, [1988] 2 WLR 805, 866 ff, and the House of Lords [1988] 3 WLR 776.

[241] See above and *Cork* v. *McVicar* [1984] *The Times*, 1 Nov.

[242] [1977] 1 WLR 760.

[243] *Lion Laboratories*, above, at 429 per Stephenson LJ.

judges could not have been expected to accord vigorous protection (e.g. between confider of corruption and interviewer)[244] or in which there was an independent—usually contractual—means of maintaining confidentiality so that a judgment in favour of disclosure would not necessarily be read as a significant inroad into the obligation of confidence in question (e.g. the relationship between employer and employee—normally transformed into ex-employee at the time of the action).[245] Indeed, in the two most recent decisions involving the publication of confidential information about homosexuality[246] and AIDS[247] there is evidence of a greater willingness to award injunctive relief.

Morever, many of the cases based on the 'wider' principle of 'public interest' disclosure (with the conspicuous exception of *Woodward*) could equally have been decided on narrower 'iniquity' grounds. And, on the other hand, where the defence *has* received a narrower construction, the circumstances in which disclosure occurred or was threatened were such that the relationship of confidence was either not a material consideration because there was an independent ground upon which the maintenance of confidence could be made to rest, or the information was obtained unlawfully. Thus in *Schering Chemicals Ltd.* v. *Falkman Ltd.*[248] since the majority[249] accepted the fact that the information concerned was *already* in the public domain, the question of whether its publication was in the public interest did not really arise. And in *Francome*[250] where the Court of Appeal restrained publication of information obtained as a result of a criminal offence under the Wireless Telegraphy Act 1949, the Master of the Rolls did not attempt to conceal his distaste for the newspaper's attempt to justify publication of the contents of the tapes in breach of the statute:

I hope that Mr. Molloy [the editor of the *Daily Mirror*] will acquit me of discourtesy if I say with all the emphasis at my command that I regard his assertion as arrogant and wholly unacceptable.

[244] *Cork* v. *McVicar*, above.
[245] See *Lion Laboratories, Initial Services, Woodward*, above.
[246] *Stephens* v. *Avery* [1988] 2 WLR 1280. See p. 96 above.
[247] *X* v. *Y* [1988] 3 All ER 648.   [248] [1981] 2 WLR 848.
[249] Shaw LJ at 869; Templeman LJ at 881.   [250] [1984] 1 WLR 892.

Parliamentary democracy as we know it is based upon the rule of law. That requires all citizens to obey the law, unless and until it can be changed by due process. There are no privileged classes to whom it does not apply. If Mr. Molloy and the 'Daily Mirror' can assert this right to act on the basis that the public interest, as he sees it, justifies breaches of the criminal law, so can any other citizen. This has only to be stated for it to be obvious that the result would be anarchy.[251]

Nor was there the 'corruption' which was held to justify publication in *Cork* v. *McVicar*[252] for here the information obtained from intercepting the plaintiffs' conversations suggested merely that they might have committed offences or breaches of the rules relating to horse-racing. The public interest might have been adequately served by such information being placed in the hands of the police or the stewards of the Jockey Club. In *Cork*, on the other hand, the information 'revealed alleged miscarriages of justice and alleged police practices of a corrupt and disgraceful nature'.[253] Such corruption was, in the court's view, 'clearly a matter of public interest as opposed to matters which should be taken up and dealt with by the appropriate authorities'.[254]

Moreover, with the exception of *Woodward*, since the disclosures in those cases in which the defence of public interest has been widely interpreted did not involve 'personal information' it would be unreasonable to conclude that more weight might not be given to preserving the confidentiality of such information—even though (as has been suggested above) the policy of the law of confidence is to promote confidentiality (in order, presumably, to encourage candour and trust) and thus to attach importance to the *origin* rather than the *nature* of the information.

A further structural problem (which is returned to under 4.2.6 below) is the fact that in deciding not to award an injunction, a court, in accepting the defence of public interest, may do so on the basis that the plaintiff should be left to his remedy in damages[255] or an account of profits but, in the case of 'personal information', this may be a hollow form of redress.

---

[251] At 897.   [252] See above.   [253] Ibid.
[254] Ibid.   [255] *Schering*, above, at 435 per Grifiths LJ.

4.2.4. *Possible Plaintiffs and Defendants*

A conspicuous manifestation of the limited scope of the action for breach of confidence is the principle that the action is available only to the person to whom the obligation of confidence is owed: 'the party complaining must be the person who is entitled to the confidence and to have it respected. He must be a person to whom the duty of good faith is owed'.[256]

This demonstrates the distinction between the protection of the confidential *relationship* (where the origin of the information is paramount), on the one hand, and the protection of *'personal information'* (where the nature of the information is the principal issue), on the other. Hence, in the prototypical case of unwanted publicity being given to private facts, this structural requirement will probably operate to prevent the victim from obtaining relief against a newspaper which, in consequence of its own investigation, publishes such information: there will normally be no duty of good faith owed by the journalist or the newspaper to the victim.

Equally, it is only a person who knows or ought to have known that he is receiving confidential information in breach of confidence, who is under an obligation not to use or disclose it. It is therefore only he who may be liable for any such unauthorized use or disclosure.[257] A third party who, at the time he acquires the information, is innocent, i.e. unaware of the breach of confidence as a consequence of which he acquired the information, becomes liable for its misuse—once he receives notice of the breach.[258] This apparently far-reaching principle (which may not extend to an innocent third party who is a bona fide purchaser who has changed his position in reliance on the information he

---

[256] *Fraser* v. *Evans* [1969] 1 QB 349 at 261 per Lord Denning MR.

[257] *Prince Albert* v. *Strange* (1849) 2 De Gex & Sm. 652 at 714; *Lord Ashburton* v. *Pape* [1913] 2 Ch. 469 at 473–4.

[258] See *Malone* v. *Commissioner of Police of the Metropolis (No. 2)* [1979] 2 All ER 620 at 634 for Sir Robert Megarry VC's statement of the principle.

received)[259] still, of course, requires the existence of an initial relationship of confidence before it may operate. It will therefore not assist a plaintiff whose complaint is that the confidential information is disclosed by a newspaper without any breach of confidence—actual, imputed or constructive, having taken place. Nor may it avail an individual from whom such information is obtained surreptitiously by the use of electronic surveillance methods.[260]

4.2.5. *Other Defences*

The conceptual difficulties involved in the characterization of a particular rule as either, on the one hand, a 'defence' or, on the other, a constituent of the action itself, are no less present here than in other areas of the law. Thus, for instance, the question whether a specific breach of confidence is in the 'public interest'[261] may be concieved either as a defence against an action to restrain publication of information communicated in confidence, or as relevant to the fundamental consideration of whether the information is of such a nature that it warrants legal protection at all. This question is not, however, central to the present enquiry, and it suffices to observe that, in the case of 'public interest' the courts in recent cases[262] have treated it as a defence, whereas, in their analysis of the law, the Law Commission[263] preferred to

---

[259] *Morison* v. *Moat* (1851) 9 Hare 241, (on appeal) (1852) 21 LJ Ch. (NS) 248; *Printers and Finishers Ltd.* v. *Holloway* [1965] RPC 239. Cf. *Stevenson, Jordan & Harrison Ltd.* v. *Macdonald and Evans* (1951) 68 RPC 190, (on appeal (1952) 69 RPC 10. For a useful analysis see the Vice-Chancellor's judgment in *Attorney-General* v. *Guardian Newspapers Ltd.* [1987] 1 WLR 1248 at 1264–6.

[260] *Malone*, above, at 376. Cf. *Francome*, above. See ch. 6. Cf. the Report of the Scottish Law Reform Commission, *Breach of Confidence*, No. 90, Cmnd. 9385, para. 4.22 and clauses 1(2) and 1(3) of their draft bill.

[261] The question of whether the information is public knowledge or in the 'public domain' (discussed above) is susceptible of a similar analysis: is it a defence or is such information simply not protectable? The matter has not really been properly addressed by the courts. The Law Commission preferred the latter view (para. 6.74) though they too do not directly consider the issue. Cf. the approach of the Scottish Law Commission (paras. 4.77–80, 4.87).

[262] *Francome*, see above; *Lion Laboratories* see above.

[263] Law Commission Report, para. 6.91.

regard the matter as one which goes to the question of whether the information is protectable at all. They proposed that in their statutory remedy for breach of confidence there should be a general requirement that, to prevent disclosure, the public interest in preserving the confidence should outweigh the public interest in its use or disclosure. If the defendant satisfies the court that there is a public interest in such use or disclosure, it should then be for the plaintiff to show that this interest is outweighed by the public interest in preserving the confidentiality of the information concerned.[264]

In *Lion Laboratories*,[265] on the other hand, the Court of Appeal held that, at the interlocutory stage, it was for the defendant to establish that 'there is a serious defence of public interest which may succeed at the trial'.

There would appear to be clear authority for the existence of the four other defences described, namely:

(a) that the disclosure was made in the course of judicial proceedings;
(b) that the plaintiff does not come to Equity with clean hands;
(c) that the disclosure was made under statutory compulsion or authority; and
(d) that the plaintiff delayed too long before bringing his action.

It is only the second of these defences that has been applied to cases concerned with 'personal information' (notably *Argyll*),[266] which has already been discussed, in which Ungoed-Thomas J. refused to deny relief to the plaintiff merely because she had herself published information relating to the marriage. On a 'balance of perfidy', the defendant's disclosure of 'the most intimate of confidences'[267] constituted 'an altogether different order of perfidy'.[268] It was argued above that the application of this test reveals that the court's principal concern was to protect the relationship of marriage rather than to prevent the publication of the 'personal

---

[264] Paras. 6.77.84.   [265] See above, at 548.
[266] [1967] 1 Ch. 302.   [267] At 331.   [268] Ibid.

information' itself. The main structural problem caused by the application of this defence to a case involving 'personal information' is therefore the fact that it is premised on the relative wrongdoing of the parties. This implies that had the situation been reversed, and the plaintiff's own breaches of confidence were of a greater magnitude (or number?) the court would have denied her relief.

4.2.6. *Remedies*

Two main issues were identified above, namely: (a) under what circumstances will an injunction be granted to prevent the disclosure of 'personal information', and (b) to what extent are damages available for breach of confidence to compensate the plaintiff for the distress, annoyance or embarrassment caused by the disclosure of 'personal information'? In respect of an interlocutory injunction, a difficulty that was alluded to above is the fact that in *Woodward*[269] the court applied the rule adopted in libel cases that no interlocutory injunction will be granted where the defendant intends to justify the libel or plead the defence of fair comment. The court will leave the plaintiff to his remedy in damages. This is all very well in the context of defamation for, should the defences fail, the plaintiff may still vindicate his reputation by a subsequent award of damages. Where a breach of confidence has occurred, however, the position is very different: the confidential information has been made public; an award of damages can do nothing akin to the rehabilitation of esteem that is possible in the context of defamation. And where the information is of a personal kind, damages are, in any event (see below), unlikely to be awarded to assuage the plaintiff's mental distress. This fact was recognized by the Court of Appeal in its recent decision in *Francome* v. *Daily Mirror Group Newspapers Ltd.*[270] in which the plaintiffs sought an interlocutory injunction to restrain a newspaper from publishing information obtained through the tapping of the plaintiffs' telephone by persons unknown. The newspaper argued that since the tapes revealed breaches of the rules of racing by the first defendant,

[269] See above, at 763.   [270] [1984] 1 WLR 892.

a well-known jockey, publication of the contents of the tapes was 'justifiable in the public interest'.[271]

In awarding a (modified) interlocutory injunction, the Court of Appeal refused to accept that publication was in the public interest, Fox LJ, referring to the fact that if inter-locutory relief were denied, the plaintiff's subsequent remedy would be a limited one, said,

> If the 'Daily Mirror' is permitted to publish the tapes now, the consequent harm to Mr. Francome might be such that he could not be adequately compensated in damages for any wrong thereby done to him whatever the result of subsequent proceedings. Unless Mr. Francome is given protection until the trial, I think that a trial might be largely worthless from his point of view even though he succeeded.[272]

It is hard to see why similar considerations should not have obtained in *Woodward*, even if in that decision the Court of Appeal accepted that there was a public interest in the publication concerned. Surely in *Woodward*, as in *Francome*, to have granted an order restraining publication by the newspaper until the trial of the action would 'merely postpone for a time the publication of a possible sensational story'?[273]

In deciding on the appropriateness of a final injunction, a court may consider whether the plaintiff has suffered (or is likely to suffer) detriment as a result of the breach of confidence. In the case of 'personal information' such detriment (if it is indeed a requirement)[274] would normally consist in the mental distress suffered by the plaintiff. Thus in *Pollard* v. *Photographic Co.*[275] the plaintiff obtained an injunction to prevent the unauthorized use of a photograph taken by the defendant of the plaintiff. The only apparent detriment was the mental distress she would have suffered had the photograph been used.

Failing the award of an injunction (or even after obtaining one)[276] the plaintiff in a case involving 'personal information'

---

[272] At 900.   [273] At 902 per Stephen Brown LJ.   [271] At 897.
[274] See above p. 56 and 109.   [275] (1889) 40 Ch.D. 345.
[276] There is authority for the award of damages in addition to an injunction being issued by a court exercising its direction under Lord Cairns's Act; see e.g. *Cranleigh Precision Engineering Ltd.* v. *Bryant* [1966] RPC 81 at 98.

is likely to seek damages[277] and such damages will normally be for mental distress or injury to feelings. As pointed out above, damages have not been awarded in such a case, though this structural impediment is not insurmountable; indeed in *Woodward* itself both Lord Denning MR[278] and Bridge LJ[279] intimated that damages would be the appropriate remedy when the matter was tried. And both the Law Commission[280] and the Scottish Law Commission[281] recommend in their proposed legislation that damages should be available to the plaintiff. A reform of this sort, while confronting the specific issue of damages, would not, of course, address the other more fundamental problems that spring from the application of the action for breach of confidence to cases involving 'personal information'.

4.3. FUNCTIONAL–STRUCTURAL PROBLEMS

It is, of course, inevitable that in certain cases the courts should have applied principles which are appropriate to the general policy of the preservation of confidence to situations in which the central issue is the extent to which the plaintiff may be entitled to protection against unauthorized publicity being given to intimate facts. (See, in particular, the discussion of *Woodward* above). There is, on the other hand, a measure of irony in the fact that in certain cases courts have employed what might be described as 'privacy' arguments to justify breaches of confidence. This has occurred where a court, in considering the circumstances under which a breach of confidence is permissible, employs principles which would be entirely appropriate to cases involving 'personal information'—*where there is no necessary relationship of confidence.*

[277] It may occasionally be the case that even where the breach of confidence involves 'personal information' an account of profits may the appropriate remedy: if in *Woodward*, for instance, the information about the plaintiffs reflected them in a favourable light, they may have suffered no damage while their ex-employee would have incurred a profit as a result of his sale of the information to the newspaper.

[278] See above, at 764.

[279] At 765.

[280] Paras 6.106 and 6.114.

[281] Paras. 4.92–3 and 4.98.

In *Woodward* the Court of Appeal did both. Refusing to enjoin publication of 'personal information' concerning the plaintiff, the court held *inter alia* that the exploits of the plaintiffs, since they took place aboard an aeroplane, were in the 'public domain', and could not be the subject of an action for breach of confidence. The application of this principle (which has as its chief object the restriction of legal protection to information which is inaccessible)[282] to the facts of the case produces a somewhat artificial result. (See above.) Secondly, the court effectively licensed the press to publish such information—obtained in breach of confidence—because the plaintiffs had courted publicity and could not therefore complain 'if a servant or employee of theirs afterwards discloses the truth about them'.[283]

In so deciding, the court seems to be using a 'privacy' argument to deny an injunction for breach of confidence. To balance properly the competing interests of confidence and 'truth' (which the court claimed to be attempting to do), the fact that the plaintiffs had *sought* publicity (like all well-managed entertainers?) ought not to have been a consideration—for it would mean, not only that virtually all public figures (the most likely plaintiffs) would be denied injunctive relief but that a relationship of confidence in which 'personal information' is imparted (or even observed) would be considerably undermined.

The irony is that in the context of full-blown 'privacy' litigation (in the American law) a court could consider the extent to which the plaintiff was a public figure—but in so doing its principal objective would not be to protect confidential relationships. And the determination of whether the plaintiff was a 'public figure' would be based on clearer grounds which are likely to be less moralistic than the test used by the Court of Appeal and not made to turn exclusively on the plaintiff's preference for favourable publicity.

[282] The test is whether any special effort is needed for the information to be reproduced. If so the court will regard the information as confidential: see *Saltman Engineering Co. Ltd.* v. *Campbell Engineering Co. Ltd.* (1948) 65 RPC 203 at 205 per Lord Greene MR. But see *Attorney-General* v. *Guardian Newspapers Ltd.* [1987] 1 WLR 1248.   [283] At 763.

Similarly, in the recent decision in *Lion Laboratories*[284] (as pointed out above) the Court of Appeal exemplifies the limited extent to which, in balancing the competing interests of confidence and the public's right to receive information, the harm suffered by the plaintiff is taken into account. This seems to be a consequence of the law's concern to protect the *relationship* of confidence, rather than to protect the plaintiff against (or compensate him for) the damage the disclosure may cause (or has caused) him.

4.4. DOCTRINAL PROBLEMS

The most obvious way to illustrate the different doctrinal bases of the action for breach of confidence, on the one hand, and the general protection of 'personal information' on the other, is to compare the former with the American tort of 'public disclosure of private facts' or what is called in the *Second Restatement of the Law of Torts*[285] 'publicity given to private life'.

This exercise has the merit both of drawing on distinctions based on the actual experience of the courts, and, by confining itself to a jurisdiction in which not only is the action for breach of confidence recognized, but in which this equitable remedy provided the mainspring for the development of this particular privacy tort, of pointing up the distinctive (and hence potentially illuminating) developments that have occurred in both legal systems.

But a word of caution is necessary. Though it plays an important part in the common-law and constitutional recognition and expression of the 'right to privacy', the American tort has generated less litigation than might have been anticipated, and in formulating certain—sometimes fundamental—elements, there is a degree of imprecision and even speculation. Furthermore, some of the deficiencies of the tort may be partly explained by the existence of a remedy for breach of confidence.

Nevertheless it is submitted that the following brief

[284] [1948] 2 All. ER 417.
[285] Para. 652D.

account, which is confined to what is relatively settled law, does help to identify the significant doctrinal features of the American tort and so to substantiate the argument suggested above that the application of the action for breach of confidence to cases involving 'personal information' is fraught with problems.

The *Restatement*[286] defines the tort as follows:

One who gives publicity to a matter concerning the private life of another is subject to liability to the other for invasion of his privacy, if the matter publicized is of a kind that (a) would be highly offensive to a reasonable person, and (b) is not of legitimate concern to the public.

As has been pointed out before, the tort has the following three elements:

1. There must be *publicity*: to inform his employer or a small group that the plaintiff is, say, a homosexual, would not suffice;

2. The information disclosed must be *private* facts: publicity given to matters of public record will not be actionable;

3. The facts disclosed must be offensive to *a reasonable man of ordinary sensibilities*.[287]

The American tort therefore differs in a number of respects from the equitable remedy for breach of confidence. Table 1 identifies the essential differences.

The fundamental distinction lies, of course, in the fact that while the tort of unwanted publicity is based on the protection against the disclosure of certain information which is categorized as 'private', the action for breach of confidence rests on the more limited protection against disclosure of certain information which is categorized as 'confidential' and is subject to an obligation of confidence owed normally to the person who has confided it. That 'private facts' (or 'personal information') may be protected by the action for breach of confidence is plain, but it results in the application of a doctrinal approach—developed largely to justify the protection of commercial information—to essentially different circumstances.

[286] Ibid.
[287] See the discussion of *Sidis* and *Melvin v. Reid* in ch. 5.

TABLE 1. Public disclosure and breach of
confidence compared

Public disclosure	Breach of confidence
Publicity given to 'private facts'	Use or disclosure of confidential information
Wide publicity generally required	Not required
Not required	Information must be imparted in circumstances imposing a duty of confidence
Facts disclosed must be 'highly offensive'	Not required, but 'trivial tittle-tattle' not protected
Disclosures in the public interest not actionable	Similar limitation obtains
Public figures may forfeit some protection	Similar limitation obtains
Anyone who is subject to unauthorized publicity may sue	Only the person to whom the duty of confidence is owed may sue
Anyone who publishes private facts without without authority may be sued	Only the person who is subject to a duty of confidence may be sued

In particular, in the 'privacy' tort, the purpose of the law would seem to be to protect the plaintiff against wide publicity being given to certain classes of information. The purpose of the law of confidence, on the other hand, though it requires the information to be 'confidential', is essentially to maintain the fidelity or trust that the plaintiff has reposed in the person to whom he has confided (or, at any rate, who ought to recognize that he is breaching such trust). The policy of the law is essentially to promote the honesty (or, at any rate, absence of deception) which is an important aspect of commercial transactions. It is not therefore illogical that the action for breach of confidence should concentrate on the *source* rather than, as in the 'privacy' tort, the *content* of the information.

There is, moreover, no requirement in the case of the action for breach of confidence that the disclosure be 'highly offensive' (or indeed offensive at all) since its principal object is not to prevent harm to the plaintiff, but to ensure that information communicated in confidence (actually or constructively) will, in general, be protected. I will not, under the American tort, have a cause of action where the published information about me is, by reference to an objective standard, innocuous—even if its disclosure causes me embarrassment or distress. Where, however, I impart the *same* facts in the course of a confidential relationship, it is arguable that, because I might not have revealed them in the absence of an expectation of confidentiality, I should be able to prevent their disclosure by the action for breach of confidence.

Thus, in the case of 'personal information', the action for breach of confidence is potentially able to protect a wider range of subject-matter relating to the plaintiff—subject, of course, to the existence of a relationship of confidence or, at any rate, circumstances in which the defendant knew or ought to have known that he was acting in breach of confidence. This is consistent with the law's objective in protecting the interest in the maintenance of confidential relationships. And even if the present revelations made in breach of confidence were innocuous it would not be unreasonable for the confider to fear that possible future disclosures may be less trivial.

Similarly, whereas the 'privacy' tort requires wide publicity,[288] in the case of breach of confidence the plaintiff will have a legitimate objection if disclosure is made in breach of confidence to a single individual, for example, his employer. The currently expanding principle that permits breach of confidence where it is considered that there is a public interest in the disclosure of the information has been analysed above. In applying the 'privacy' tort the American courts have engaged in a similar 'balancing' of the competing interests involved, and have generally sought to deny or limit

---

[288] *Peterson* v. *Idaho First National Bank* 367 P 2d 284 (1967). Cf. *Beaumont* v. *Brown* 257 NW 522 (1977).

protection to 'public figures' or to facts the revelation of which is conceived to be 'newsworthy', or of 'legitimate public interest'. (See Chapter 5.)

These (related) factors are ultimately functions of community values. The *Second Restatement of the Law of Torts*[289] attempts to strike a balance between these two perceived interests and the American courts have self-consciously formulated a ' "mores" test'[290] which incorporates both the question of 'public interest' and the standard of what is 'highly offensive'. Thus in the leading case of *Sidis v. F.-R. Publishing Corporation*[291] (discussed in Chapter 5) the plaintiff was denied recovery because he had once been a 'public figure' and hence his present activities were of legitimate public interest, and because the revelations were not 'so intimate and so unwarranted in view of the victim's position as to outrage the community's notion of decency'.[292] This is a direct 'balancing' of the interests in issue.

In attempting to reconcile the maintenance of confidentiality on the one hand, with the public interest in the dissemination of information on the other, the English courts have recently applied a similar balancing act (invariably without any—explicit—reference to the offensiveness of the disclosure and the harm to the plaintiff).[293] But, as has already been argued, the action for breach of confidence involves different interests and calls for the application of different considerations. In particular, the fact that the plaintiff has entrusted the information to a confidant— whether or not its disclosure is regarded as being in the public interest—ought to be given considerably more weight than is manifest in these recent decisions. Suppose, for instance, that Sidis had confided in his doctor or lawyer or spouse. Even as a (recently resurrected) 'public figure', his action for breach of confidence against the party divulging this information would surely have given rise to a different evaluation of the interests concerned. And, *a fortiori*, if he were a 'private' figure.

---

[289] Para. 652, comment h. The section is set out on p. 126 above.
[290] W. L. Prosser, 'Privacy' (1966) 48 Calif. Law Rev. 383, 397.
[291] 113 F 2d 806 (1940).   [292] At 809.
[293] See above.

In the case of public figures, moreover, it is at least arguable that, since they are more likely to attract publicity concerning their private lives, the court ought to confer even greater protection to the information that they impart in the course of a confidential relationship. Certainly it should be no less than that which is accorded to private figures. It would perhaps be unreasonable to expect the English courts to have formulated a systematic—or even a precise—analysis of these different considerations in the context of breach of confidence litigation in respect of 'personal information' for, as Ungoed-Thomas J. conceded in *Argyll*[294] '[i]f this were a well-developed jurisdiction, doubtless there would be guides and tests to aid in exercising it.' But, as was suggested above, the courts have, in extending the scope of the public interest defence, exhibited a somewhat lop-sided approach to the reconciliation of confidentiality and the dissemination of information. In the process the legitimate expectations of those who divulge information in the course of a relationship of confidence have been eroded. This is not to suggest that the recent expressions of judicial support for the principle of the public right to know are to be disparaged, but the reasonable expectations of confiders of information warrant more careful and perhaps more sympathetic evaluation. Such an approach is evident in the majority's judgment in *Schering Chemicals Ltd. v. Falkman Ltd.*[295] where the Court of Appeal attached greater importance to the preservation of confidence than to the circulation of information in the public interest.

It is unfortunate, however, that the court in that case was dealing with information which had already become public knowledge—a factor which, along with the repugnance with which both Shaw and Templeman L JJ clearly viewed the breach of faith involved, renders the majority's approach of rather limited persuasive force. But it does represent a more balanced view (and this is true, to some extent, even of Lord Denning's dissenting judgment) of the competing interests in issue than is exhibited in the decisions concerning informa-

---

[294] A conspicuous exception is the recent case of *X v. Y* [1988] 2 All ER 648.

[295] [1981] 2 WLR 848, discussed above, 60 ff.

tion relating to the plaintiff. In the *absence of a confidential relationship*, of course, the approach adopted in cases such as *Woodward*, *Lennon*, *Khashoggi*, and *Lion Laboratories* (which broadly approximates to the American view in cases involving unwanted publicity) is an entirely proper one, but where the court is faced with a newspaper that wishes to publish information which it has obtained in breach of confidence, different issues arise. Some acknowledgement of this is evident in *Francome* v. *Daily Mirror Group Newspapers Ltd.*[296] in which the Master of the Rolls issued a firm warning to the 'media' which were, in his view, 'peculiarly vulnerable to the error of confusing the public interest with their own interest. Usually these interests march hand in hand, but not always.'[297]

Admittedly this case involved the use of 'reprehensible means' (telephone-tapping) to obtain the information which was offered to the newspaper for sale, and it is therefore probable that the court was less disposed to deny an injunction than it might have been if faced with facts of a *Woodward* variety.[298] Yet the observation that the defendants would not be 'substantially prejudiced, if they have to wait until after the trial of the action'[299] suggests a more general application of this consideration to cases involving information relating to the plaintiff.

5. Conclusion

The jurisdiction in respect of breach of confidence clearly affords certain adventitious protection to information relating to the plaintiff in general and to 'personal information' in particular. Nevertheless, this jurisdiction (whether it is based on equity, contract, property, or even the general preservation

---

[296] [1984] 1 WLR 892.

[297] At 898. See too the Vice-Chancellor's dictum in *Stephens* v. *Avery* [1988] 3 WLR 1280, 1287.

[298] 'The fact that coincidentially publication would be a criminal offence which the defendants say they are prepared to commit strongly reinforces the case for an injunction' (per Stephen Brown LJ at 902).

[299] At 898 per Sir John Donaldson MR.

of confidence) is conceptually grounded in policy considerations which, for the most part, require a strained interpretation in cases involving non-technical information. While it is too extravagant to assert that the action for breach of confidence 'does not deal with cases in which the information relates to matters in one's life outside of his business',[300] there is much to be said for the observation that the protection of 'privacy' and the protection of confidence are based on 'two alternative theories',[301] the former being 'primarily designed to protect feelings and sensibilities'.[302] But even if this were not so, even if it could be demonstrated that the action for breach of confidence—either actually or potentially—afforded a satisfactory means of protecting 'personal information', the numerous difficulties identified in this chapter constitute a fairly formidable limitation on the scope of the remedy. These may be summarized in the following ten points.

1. There must be a relationship of confidence between the person who confides the information and the person to whom it is confided. Such a relationship will not necessarily (or even normally) be present where the plaintiff's complaint is that 'personal information' has been published without his consent (e.g. by a newspaper which has obtained the information without any breach of confidence).

2. In the absence of a definition of 'personal information' little guidance is given as to the respective rights and duties of those who impart or receive such information, as opposed to commercial confidences.

3. The possible requirement that in order to succeed the plaintiff must show detriment may mean, in a case involving 'personal information', that the only detriment suffered would be mental distress. This may suffice for the plaintiff to be awarded an injunction, but may deprive him of an award of damages.

4. The plaintiff must establish that the information was inaccessible to the public, not in the 'public domain'; the

---

[300] American *Restatement of the Law of Torts* (1939) para. 759. The *Restatement, Second, Torts* (1977) omits the chapter on Miscellaneous Trade Practice from which this comment is taken.

[301] *Copley* v. *Northwestern Mutual Life Insurance Co.* 295 F. Supp. 93 at 95 (1968). [302] Ibid.

application of this requirement produces artificial results in cases involving 'personal information'.

5. The defence of 'public interest' in cases where the breach of confidence involves information relating to the plaintiff in general and 'personal information' in particular (as opposed to commercial confidences) has generally eroded the protection accorded to information communicated in confidence. This is largely because the courts in such cases inevitably (and perhaps even unavoidably) pay little attention to the possible harm to the plaintiff caused by the disclosure of 'personal information'.

6. The action is available only to the person to whom the obligation of confidence is owed, and it is only the person who has actual, imputed, or constructive knowledge that he is acting in breach of confidence who may be sued. It may not therefore normally assist a plaintiff who is subjected to the unauthorized disclosure of 'personal information' by the publications media.

7. The application of the defence of 'clean hands' to an action for breach of confidence involving the disclosure of 'personal information' results in the court refusing relief where, on a 'balance of perfidy', the plaintiff has himself disclosed information which is of a greater order of impropriety or where he has himself exhibited little concern for the maintenance of the confidential relationship. This demonstrates the law's limited concern to protect the relationship rather than the 'personal information' imparted within it.

8. The application in certain cases of the rule accepted in libel cases that an interlocutory injunction will not be granted against a defendant who intends to justify or plead fair comment, is inappropriate in the case involving breach of confidence—especially where 'personal information' is concerned, for not only is the disclosure of a secret irrevocable, but, since compensation is unlikely to be awarded for mental distress (the plaintiff's usual injury in such cases), to leave the plaintiff to his remedy in damages is effectively to deprive him of relief altogether.

9. In some breach of confidence litigation, the courts have applied principles which, while appropriate to non-personal information, are unsuited to cases involving 'personal in-

formation' (for example, the principles relating to accessibility of information) and, on the other hand, principles appropriate to the protection of 'personal information' have been applied in circumstances which undermine the confider's expectation of confidentiality (e.g. the use of the defence of 'public interest' to deny protection to the trusting and permit the publication of intimate facts which titillate rather than inform).

10. In general the action for breach of confidence is inadequate to deal with the archetypal complaint concerning the disclosure of 'personal information' for the action is largely concerned with:

(a) disclosure or use rather than publicity;
(b) the source rather than the nature of the information;
(c) the preservation of confidence rather than the possible harm to the plaintiff caused by its breach.

4

Measuring the Extent
of the Problem

In almost all the literature on 'privacy' it is assumed that a
'problem' exists: that modern industrial societies constitute,
in themselves, a threat to 'individual privacy', and that a
legislative or judicial response is required to protect the
citizen against these depredations upon his security and
freedom. Quite apart from the difficulties of definition
described in Chapter 1, these generalizations are rarely
rooted in any empirical measurement of the extent or form of
the 'problem'. It might be replied that in such matters
intuition or impression are more than reliable guides; or that
an intelligent observation of certain phenomena (the increase
in the sale of electronic surveillance devices, the rise in the
number of complaints to the Press Council, letters to *The
Times* and so on) affords ample evidence of the advance of
Big Brother or the irresponsibility of the news media.

Even if this kind of evaluation were adequate to account
for the forces that were actually operating in any given
society, and even if it were valid (in the sense of providing
accurate and objectively ascertainable 'proof' of these facts),
it would not follow that there was a 'problem' which
required a legal solution. Nor would it have necessarily been
demonstrated that the 'problem' was perceived to exist in the
minds of those who are regarded as its victims. Indeed, even
an attitudinal survey, of the kind conducted by the Younger
Committee[1] (see Tables 2 and 3) can, at best, illustrate only
that a certain proportion of those questioned regard their
'privacy' invaded by certain forms of conduct or that they
have experienced particular forms of such invasions to a
greater or lesser extent. And, though such research may
reveal interesting attitudes, they do not directly address the

---

[1] Younger, 236, Table F; 239, Table J.

TABLE 2. Types of invasion of privacy within the last
year[a] (per cent)

	Mentioned spontaneously	Prompted	Total
Invasion of home life			
by neighbours or friends	6	8	14
by people from work	n	n	n
by private detectives	—	1	1
by callers at the door	3	11	14
through the post	1	9	10
over the telephone	1	5	6
in other ways	4	3	7
Invasion of privacy			
by newspapers	n	1	1
radio or television	n	n	n
other forms of publication	n	n	n
Collection and use of private information			
by employer	1	1	2
school or college	n	1	n
computer or data bank	—	—	n
credit rating agency	n	1	1
Unnecessary personal questions	6		
Other forms of invasion of privacy	2	3	11
No incident mentioned	80	68	56

a. Total sample = 1,596.
n = negligible.

question of whether there is a social 'problem' of sufficient gravity to warrant legal control or regulation.

A more valuable exercise is to attempt to measure which forms of activity are regarded by respondents as the most objectionable. The Younger Committee[2] selected thirteen examples of possible invasions of privacy, and asked respondents to say whether they would regard the activity as an invasion of privacy, whether they would be annoyed or upset by the activity concerned, and whether they thought the activity should be prohibited by law. (See Table 4.)

[2] Younger 238, Table H.

TABLE 3. Number objecting to publication of various
personal details[a]

	Object	Not object
Address	33	67
Telephone	34	66
(Wife's) maiden name)	18	82
Nationality	8	92
Race	10	90
Occupation	12	88
Education	17	83
Political views	42	58
Religious views	28	72
Leisure activities	22	78
Income	78	22
Details of sex-life	87	13
Medical history	51	49

a. Total weighted sample = 1,596.

TABLE 4. Reactions to examples of invasion of privacy[a]
(per cent)

Example	Invasion of privacy?		Annoyed/upset?			Should be prohibited?	
	Yes	No	No	A bit	Very	Yes	No
Neighbours watching	83	16	18	28	53	55	44
Closed-circuit TV	62	36	37	21	40	49	49
Private detective	39	60	61	19	19	30	69
Religious canvassers	78	24	22	34	46	59	43
Holiday brochure	14	84	87	7	4	14	84
Sex manual	67	34	34	21	46	72	29
Publication of will	77	23	26	28	46	71	29
TV Programme	56	44	46	26	28	47	53
Application form	57	44	51	27	23	48	53
Newspaper report	78	23	16	21	64	69	32
Credit-rating agency	46	53	55	19	25	37	62
Electoral register	35	65	73	18	9	31	69
Central computer	87	12	13	15	71	85	14

a. Total weighted sample = 1,596.

If one is willing to overlook the formidable problems of definition that arise in questionnaires of this kind[3], they do, at least, provide some information that, even in its raw state, may direct one to possible areas of concern. But the subtle and complex difficulties that are inherent in formulating questions that both accurately describe the facts in issue and do so dispassionately are—especially when a simple and brief question is required—considerable. The facts describing the 'central computer', for instance, make no allowance for any controls on accessibility of information, saying simply that the data is 'available to anyone who asks for it'. It is hardly surprising therefore that this incident produced the strongest reaction: 87 per cent responded that this would constitute an invasion of privacy, 71 per cent that they would be very annoyed or upset, and 85 per cent that it should be prohibited by law.

These surveys do not (nor were they designed to) establish the extent to which individuals are (or conceive themselves to be) subjected to assaults on their 'privacy' of a sufficiently serious nature for them to take action, legal or otherwise, to prevent its recurrence or to seek to remedy their loss of 'privacy'. It is not necessary, of course, in order to establish that there exists a 'problem', to demonstrate that persons

[3] The meanings of the examples are in most cases self explanatory, but the references to 'holiday brochure' and 'sex manual' contemplate the unsolicited delivery of these items by post. 'TV programme' refers to responses to the following question: 'While you are watching a television programme about Christmas shoppers, the camera shows you yourself trying on a hat. The commentary is rather scathing at this point. You had no idea you were being photographed.' The example summarized as 'application form' refers to the following facts: 'When you apply for an attractive new job, the application form asks for details of your father's birthplace, occupation, and career. National Security does not seem to be involved in the job.' 'Newspaper report' describes the following example: 'One evening you attend a reunion of some of your old friends whom you have not seen for many years. Unfortunately you have too much to drink and on your way home are arrested for being drunk and disorderly. When the case comes before the magistrates you are discharged without being punished. The following week your local paper reports the case and gives your name, age, occupation, and address.' 'Central computer' refers to the existence of a data bank which holds details of family circumstances, financial situation, political views, etc., with any of the information being available to anyone who asks for it.

who are its victims are driven to action. But if it could be shown that, at the very least, legal advice were sought in these circumstances, the degree to which this was the case would provide powerful support for the intuitive and impressionistic arguments both for the existence of the 'problem' and, possibly, for its legal solution.

The most obvious manner of obtaining rudimentary empirical data in respect of advice sought would be to question a random sample of solicitors about their experience in the 'privacy' field. But this apparently simple approach conceals four main difficulties. First, unlike most wrongs, many attacks on an individual's 'privacy' are—by definition—unknown to him. Secondly, even if the attack is known to him, he might not regard it as a *legal* problem, either because it is, quite simply, *not* one (e.g. 'bugging') or because he does not *perceive* it to be one (whether or not it is, in fact, one). Thirdly, in the (unlikely) event that he does regard the wrong as sufficiently serious to seek advice, he may look to someone other than a solicitor. Fourthly, he may regard legal action as aggravating the loss of 'privacy' he has already suffered, and may therefore be reluctant even to seek advice with a view to initiating legal proceedings. Nevertheless, while the information thereby obtained would provide only a fairly crude index of the scale and the distribution of complaints about invasions of 'privacy', it would at least assist to confirm or deny what are largely speculative or intuitive assumptions.

During 1981 and 1982 I sent a simple questionnaire to a random sample of 253 firms of solicitors in metropolitan England, Wales, and Northern Ireland (including the existing law centres and the National Council for Civil Liberties). The principal objectives of the survey were threefold. To establish:

(a) the extent to which individuals had sought legal advice in respect of six 'privacy issues' in the previous five years and, in consequence;

(b) which of the six complaints attracted the most complaints, which the least;

(c) whether those solicitors who replied regarded the existing law as adequate to deal with the six activities mentioned.

The replies incidentally furnished other information such as the relationship between the group of solicitors which regarded the law as adequate/inadequate and the number of complaints they received in each of the areas identified. Certain interesting disparities between the cities were also revealed, though the samples for provincial cities are probably too small to base any useful conclusions on this question.

Replies from 85 firms were received (a response of 33.59 per cent). But 185 individual solicitors completed the questionnaire (each form providing space for up to seven replies, and some respondents appended pages where this space was inadequate!). In some cases an entire firm was included in the reply, and even where this is not stated on the reply, the solicitor completing the questionnaire may have been speaking for the experience of the whole firm. It is therefore likely that the number of solicitors responding to the questionnaire is actually a good deal higher than 185. But, unless it was explicitly stated that the reply reflected the experience of more than one solicitor, I treated it as a reply from a single solicitor. It seemed important to obtain the responses of *individual* solicitors rather than the corporate view of their firm since they might have received the complaint(s) while employed by a firm other than their present one.

The largest component of the sample was drawn from Greater London (where, of course, the greatest concentration of solicitors is located), but the major cities are represented, though not in direct proportion to the numbers of firms of solicitors either actually in that city or relative to the number in London. (See Table 5.)

My questionnaire is reproduced as Fig. 1 on p. 142.

Formulating the questions to be asked presented more than the usual difficulties associated with questionnaires. In particular, there is an (inevitable) brevity in the descriptions of the activities mentioned. Thus, for example, in question 1(f) there is no suggestion of what is to be understood by 'confidential'. Obviously, if one is seeking to obtain a high response rate, the simpler the questionnaire, the greater the chance that it will be completed. And, by virtue of the fact that this was achieved (anything above a response rate of 20

TABLE 5. Distribution of questionnaires sent and replies received

	Question-naires sent	Replies received	% response	No. of solicitors
Greater London	140	47	33.6	107
Belfast	8	4	50.0	14
Birmingham and vicinity	30	8	26.6	22
Bristol	6	1	16.6	2
Cardiff	6	2	33.3	4
Leeds	6	3	50.0	3
Liverpool	6	3	50.0	3
Manchester and vicinity	30	8	26.6	14
Newcastle	6	3	50.0	5
Law centres and NCCL	15	6	40.0	11
TOTALS	253	85	33.59	185

per cent in surveys of this sort is, I am given to understand, considered high) and without any apparent or, at least expressed, confusion, it suggests that the questions asked were not entirely unsatisfactory.

From an analytical point of view, my own misgivings about the tendency (particularly in the United States) to allow these issues to coalesce into a unitary concept and so to obscure the peculiar characteristics of each activity and, especially, the appropriate controls and remedies, could not be permitted to affect the information sought from the respondents in each of the specific cases identified. In other words, the grouping of these activities together is not an acknowledgement that they ought to be so conceived, either conceptually or legally. Indeed, by separating the relatively discrete aspects (to the point even of dividing, what in the American law is generally regarded as the single wrong of intrusion, into three independent activities ('tapping', 'bugging', 'spying'; see question 1 (a), (b), and (c)) an attempt was made to secure their independent treatment both in the mind of the respondent and in the subsequent analysis by the researcher. And since the principal purpose of the survey was to gather information, my disenchantment with the inclusion

QUESTIONNAIRE

These questions have one simple object: to determine (in so far as it may be possible by reference to the number of individuals seeking legal advice) the extent to which the present law (civil and criminal) adequately protects aspects of personal 'privacy'. Your co-operation is greatly appreciated.

R. I. Wacks, 45 Southmoor Road, Oxford OX2 6RF.

1. In the last five years, approximately how many persons have sought advice in respect of possible legal action they might pursue arising from:

(Each solicitor completing the Questionnaire should use a separate column.)

(a) The alleged 'tapping' of their telephone?							
(b) The alleged 'bugging' of their home or office?							
(c) The alleged spying upon, photographing or electronic surveillance of their private activities?							
(d) The publication without their consent of private facts by the news media?							
(e) The use without their consent of their name or picture for advertising or other commercial purposes?							
(f) The alleged misuse of confidential information (computerized or otherwise) e.g. by credit rating agencies or the National Health Service?							
2. Do you regard the present law as adequate to deal with the activities mentioned above? (Please write Yes or No).							

3. If not, how would you wish to see the law changed?

4. Any further comments you have may be written overleaf.

FIG. 1

of the American tort of 'appropriation of name or image' (which has no direct counterpart in English law) within the concept of 'privacy' (see Chapter 2) was not an adequate reason for its exclusion from the questionnaire. In the case of the tort of 'placing the plaintiff in a false light in the public eye' its almost inextricable relationship with defamation, if not analytically then certainly in the practice (and, one presumes, the minds) of solicitors, presented a convincing argument for its omission.

It was to be expected that in the six areas identified (and fairly broadly defined) as 'privacy' issues, an overwhelming majority of solicitors would be likely to report that they had no experience whatever of any such complaints in the previous five years. The significant feature was therefore likely to be the number of respondents who reported having received *some* complaint(s) in any of the areas mentioned in the questionnaire. In Tables 6–11, therefore, in respect of each of the six activities, the number of solicitors who had received *some* complaint is expressed as a percentage of the total number of solicitors who responded (185). Thus in Table 6, in the case, for instance, of telephone-tapping, 15

TABLE 6. Complaints received in previous five years (all solicitors)

	Solicitors with some complaint	% of 185	Actual complaints	% of total
Telephone-tapping	15	8.1	33	9.9
Bugging	13	7.0	25	7.5
Spying	15	8.1	45	13.5
Unwanted publicity	25	13.5	67	20.0
Appropriation of name or image	6	3.2	19	5.7
Misuse of confidential data	30	16.2	145	43.4

	Yes No.	%	No No.	%	Other No.	%
Is the existing law adequate?	71	38.4	45	24.3	69	37.3
Ignoring 'Other'		61.2		38.8		

TABLE 7. Complaints received by Greater
London solicitors

	Some complaint	%	Actual complaints	% of total
Telephone-tapping	10	9.3	13	9.6
Bugging	6	5.6	8	5.9
Spying	7	6.5	14	10.4
Unwanted publicity	14	13.0	50	37.0
Appropriation of name or image	4	3.7	13	9.6
Misuse of confidential data	13	12.1	37	27.4

	Yes No.	%	No No.	%	Other No.	%
Is the existing law adequate?	42	39.2	25	23.4	40	37.4
Ignoring 'Other'		62.7		37.3		

TABLE 8. Complaints received by provincial solicitors

	Some complaint	%	Actual complaints	% of total
Telephone-tapping	4	6.0	16	17.8
Bugging	6	9.0	9	10.0
Spying	5	7.5	5	5.5
Unwanted publicity	8	11.9	13	14.4
Appropriation of name or image	2	3.0	6	6.7
Misuse of confidential data	12	18.0	41	45.5

	Yes No.	%	No No.	%	Other No.	%
Is the existing law adequate?	29	43.3	12	17.9	26	38.8
Ignoring 'Other'		70.7		29.3		

solicitors reported having received *some* complaint in the
previous five years, i.e. 8.1 per cent of 185. The *actual
number* of complaints is listed separately (in the case of

TABLE 9. Complaints received by law centres (including NCCL)

	Some complaint	%	Actual complaints	% of total
Telephone-tapping	1	9.0	4	3.7
Bugging	1	9.0	8	7.3
Spying	3	27.3	26	23.9
Unwanted publicity	3	27.3	4	3.7
Appropriation of name or image	–	–	–	–
Misuse of confidential data	5	45.5	67	61.5

	Yes No.	No %	No.	Other %	No.	%
Is the existing law adequate?	–	8	72.7	3	27.3	
Ignoring 'Other'	–	100.0				

telephone-tapping it is 33), and then this number is expressed as a percentage of the total number of *actual complaints* received (334, which is not shown in the tables since, in global terms, it is not a particularly meaningful or useful statistics) i.e. 9.9 per cent.

It was important to separate the reporting of *some* complaint from the *actual number* of complaints not only because it assists in determining the distribution of complaints in respect of each of the six activities, but also because in certain cases a solicitor reported a disproportionately high number of actual complaints of a specific activity: by failing to distinguish this figure from the number of complaints *per se*, a small number of inflated returns could easily distort the overall result.

Conclusions

The results of the survey suggest at least four possible conclusions. First, the preponderance of complaints (145 or 43.4 per cent of the total number of actual complaints received) related to the alleged misuse of confidential information (computerized or otherwise). This unexpectedly large number must, however, be read in the context of the pervasiveness of credit transactions and the consequent potential for errors in respect of applications for credit references to agencies which provide such information from their data banks. It is self-evident (and, in many ways, reassuring) that the proportion of citizens whose lives are touched by the increasing computerization of records is likely to be considerably higher than that which is subjected to, say, the tapping of their telephones. And this fact is, to some extent, confirmed by the replies from the law centres (and NCCL) which indicate that the misuse of confidential data accounts for a very substantial percentage (61.5 per cent) of all of the actual complaints received (see Table 9.)

On the other hand, the large number of actual complaints of the misuse of confidential data (relative to the actual number of complaints relating to the other five categories) might be interpreted as suggesting that this activity is perceived by many individuals as having some *legal* dimension or that it is regarded as sufficiently serious to warrant obtaining legal advice (and this may, in turn, suggest that— whether or not such 'misuse' does have a legal dimension—it *ought* to have) or both. Of course, since the question referred only to 'misuse' in a very general sense, the precise nature of the complaint (and hence the possible methods of its resolution) is (save in those instances where the respondents volunteered particulars) not stated. Moreover, as the information was garnered before the passing of the Data Protection Act 1984, it is hard to say (but intriguing to speculate) whether the rate of complaints taken to solicitors would be higher or lower with the Act in full operation.

Secondly, though (as suggested above) the actual number of individuals who are subjected to intrusions in the form of telephone-tapping (and bugging and spying) is, at least in Britain, likely to be small and, in any event, one hopes, considerably smaller than those whose confidential data have been misused, taking these three categories together, 43 of the 185 solicitors (i.e. 23.2 per cent) reported having received *some* complaints, and the total number of *actual complaints* is 103 (or 30.9 per cent of the total of all actual complaints received). This seems a remarkably high figure, especially when it is borne in mind that these activities are generally likely to occur without the knowledge of the victim. Among the law centres (and NCCL) also, such intrusions feature fairly prominent (34.9 per cent of all actual complaints reported) with spying accounting for 23.9 per cent of all actual complaints (see Table 9.)

Thirdly, a surprisingly high proportion of complaints were received from individuals who had suffered the allegedly unauthorized disclosure of private facts by the news media. 13.5 per cent of the respondents reported *some* complaints (though the *actual number* of reported complaints (67 or 20 per cent of the total) is inflated by the reply of one solicitor who estimated that in the previous five years he had received complaints relating to this category from as many as 20 individuals). Admittedly, in the case of unwanted publicity it is reasonably safe to assume that the client was *aware* of the fact (and consequently more likely to take action) than is the case in respect of most of the other categories. But it is frequently supposed that publicity of this kind (generally described in the American law as the tort of 'public disclosure of private facts', see Chapter 2) is reserved for 'public figures'. It is therefore counter-intuitive to find that this category should attract so significant a proportion of clients; indeed, among London solicitors it constitutes the highest number of *actual complaints* reported (50 or 37 per cent of the total); see Table 7. This phenomenon may be explained, in part, by the fact that, while such disclosures are apparently not restricted to the rich and famous (the number of complaints is simply too large for this to be the case), the number of persons who are the subject of unwanted publicity is likely to consist of a higher proportion of those who are economically better off. And they, in turn, are more inclined to seek legal advice. In other words, those who are relatively affluent are more likely to (a) have ready access to a legal adviser and (b) therefore consider the possibility of seeking legal advice. This generalization may, of course, be applied equally to the other five categories (or, indeed, to most instances of civil wrongs), but since the better off are, on this hypothesis, likely to be more attractive, and therefore more vulnerable, to this form of attack, it is reflected in the remarkably high number of complaints reported by their solicitors.

Fourthly, in response to the question whether they regarded the existing law as adequate, 61.2 per cent of those who answered this question answered in the affirmative (see Table 6). The percentage was even higher among provincial solicitors who responded either affirmatively or negatively to this inquiry: 70.7 per cent were satisfied with the law. In marked contrast, *none* of the law centre (and NCCL) respondents regarded the law as adequate to deal with the six categories of activity (see Table 9).

It is arguable that the general satisfaction with the state of the law at the time of the questionnaire expressed by so large a percentage of solicitors in conventional practice may be related to their very limited experience of dealing with matters of this kind. Yet of those practitioners who reported *some* complaints in one or more of the six areas (41 solicitors) 24 or (58.5 per cent) who answered the question yes or no regarded the law as adequate. In other words, even among that group of solicitors who reported having encountered *some* complaints in one or more of the six categories (and might, therefore, in a very weak sense, be described as experienced in such matters) there was a majority who expressed no dissatisfaction with the law. This is not, however, a particularly valuable or reliable statistic for two reasons. First, though an individual respondent may have reported a single complaint in the previous five years, his 'experience' in such matters is hardly a sound basis upon which to build any really reliable conclusions. Secondly, though a small number of solicitors actually answered Question 3 ('If [you do not regard it as adequate] how would you wish to see the law changed?') and some in fair detail, to have required all to have answered this question would, it seems reasonable to fear, have substantially reduced the number of responses. Thus in view of the (deliberately) wide range of activities on which information was sought in the questionnaire, a simple yes or no response to this question is useful chiefly as an index of a very general attitude to the legal protection (or non-protection) of 'privacy' in its broadest (and least satisfactory) sense.

An attempt to elicit the views of 'solicitors' presupposes a homogeneity and shared experience of certain legal matters that do not exist in what is often a highly specialized profession. Certain firms are by their very nature unlikely to attract clients whose complaint is in the 'privacy' field— either because they are, quite simply, almost exclusively devoted to, say, shipping law, or because their clients are predominantly corporations rather than individuals. Any random sample of 'solicitors' (such as the one used here) would therefore inevitably include firms whose specialist preoccupation would preclude their having any experience in the six categories mentioned. To improve the reliability of the data already received, it therefore seemed necessary to separate the returns on the basis of the likelihood that individuals would turn to a particular firm for advice on any of the six activities. A follow-up questionnaire was sent to all original respondents (excuding the ten law centres and the NCCL, on the ground that individuals could reasonably be expected to look to them for advice in such matters) in the following terms:

Some months ago you very kindly answered a questionnaire which I sent you on the subject of 'privacy'. I am now analysing the information which I received, but, in order to improve its statistical reliability, I should greatly appreciate your answering the following question:

Would a client or an individual with a complaint in the 'privacy' field be likely to turn to your firm for legal assistance or advice (or are you mainly concerned with the law unrelated to such matters, e.g., conveyancing, company law etc)?

The responses (51, expressly representing 119 solicitors) were then matched up with the original replies from these solicitors. In the following tables (Table 10 and Table 11) the first group ('The Privacy Group') is composed of those who answered this question in the affirmative. The second group ('The Other Group') consists of those who replied in the negative.

The most extraordinary result of this grouping is the high

TABLE 10. The Privacy Group

	Some complaint	%	Actual complaints	% of total
Telephone-tapping	7	15.2	12	12.4
Bugging	4	8.7	4	4.1
Spying	5	12.2	10	10.3
Unwanted publicity	10	21.7	36	37.1
Appropriation of name or image	4	8.7	14	14.4
Misuse of confidential data	8	17.4	21	21.6

	Yes No.	%	No No.	%	Other No.	%
Is the existing law adequate?	14	25.4	13	23.7	28	50.9
Ignoring 'Other'		51.8		48.2		

TABLE 11. The Other Group

	Some complaint	%	Actual complaints	% of total
Telephone-tapping	3	4.1	13	16.9
Bugging	5	6.8	8	10.4
Spying	4	5.5	5	6.5
Unwanted publicity	10	13.7	14	18.2
Appropriation of name or image	1	1.4	9	11.6
Misuse of confidential data	13	17.8	28	36.4

	Yes No.	%	No No.	%	Other No.	%
Is the existing law adequate?	26	40.6	10	15.6	28	43.8
Ignoring 'Other'		72.2		27.8		

number of solicitors in the Other Group who, despite the fact they did not consider themselves likely recipients of such complaints, reported receiving them anyway. In fact, in the case of the alleged misuse of confidential data, there are among the Other Group, considerably more solicitors who reported having received *some* complaint than there are among their counterparts in the Privacy Group (13 as opposed to 8)! Even the *actual number* of complaints received is higher in the Other Group (see Tables 10 and 11).

It is now possible to *rank* the three sets of responses in terms of the specific categories of complaints received. This is shown in Fig. 2 and Table 12.

Those reporting some complaint

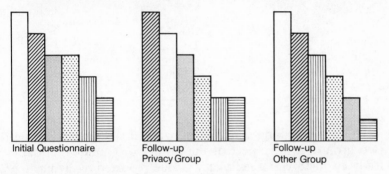

Initial Questionnaire   Follow-up   Follow-up
                               Privacy Group   Other Group

Actual number of complaints

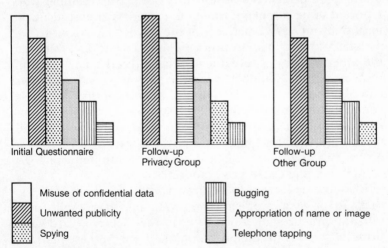

Initial Questionnaire   Follow-up   Follow-up
                               Privacy Group   Other Group

	Misuse of confidential data		Bugging
	Unwanted publicity		Appropriation of name or image
	Spying		Telephone tapping

FIG. 2 All Complaints in Order of Importance

TABLE 12. Ranking of actual number of complaints

Initial questionnaire	*Follow-up questionnaire*
Misuse of confidential data	*Privacy group*
Unwanted publicity	Unwanted publicity
Spying	Misuse of confidential data
Telephone-tapping	Appropriation of name or image
Bugging	Telephone-tapping
Appropriation of name or image	Spying
	Bugging
	Other group
	Misuse of confidential data
	Unwanted publicity
	Telephone-tapping
	Appropriation of name or image
	Bugging
	Spying

The most striking disparity between the responses of the two groups is in respect of the misuse of confidential data (only 8 solicitors in the Privacy Group reported receiving any complaints; in the Other Group the figure is 13). Interestingly, though, the percentage of solicitors of the total number who reported some complaint, is, in this category, almost identical in both groups (17.4 per cent of the Privacy Group and 17.8 per cent of the Other Group: see Tables 10 and 11). But even the other categories reveal a surprising discrepancy. Both in respect of the number of solicitors who report *some* complaint, and in respect of the *actual number* of these complaints, the self-confessed Other Group report an unexpectedly high figure. Indeed, the total numbers of actual complaints is, in the Other Group, 77. In the Privacy Group it is 97, but with one solicitor in this group reporting 20 complaints, the difference evaporates.

A simple deduction to be drawn from this comparison is that the 'privacy' problem is so prodigious that it spills over into the practices of solicitors who themselves regard their firms as unsuited to the provision of advice on these matters. On the basis of the data collected, it is difficult to find a compelling argument to reject this attractively facile conclusion. How else is one to explain, in particular, the fact that the Other Group actually received more complaints relating to the alleged misuse of confidential information than did the Privacy Group?

Perhaps even more curious is the fact that of those who answered yes or no to the question, 'Do you regard the present law as adequate to deal with the complaints mentioned above?' little more than a bare majority of the Privacy Group replied in the affirmative (51.8 per cent). In the Other Group, however, the proportion of those who express dissatisfaction with the law is appreciably higher (72.2 per cent). (See Tables 10 and 11.) One is left with the somewhat awkward conclusion that there is a greater degree of unhappiness with the present law (or, at any rate, what is perceived to be the present law) among those who regard themselves (or their firms) as likely recipients of 'privacy' complaints than on the part of those who do not (but who receive almost as many complaints anyway!) Comparing the replies of the Privacy Group with those of the group who actually *reported* 'privacy' complaints, there is only a small difference: among the latter 58.5 per cent regarded the law as adequate, while, among the Privacy Group, the figure is 51.8 per cent. In other words, among both those who actually received such complaints and those who regard themselves as likely recipients, there is a small majority who are satisfied with the law, and a large minority who are not.

On the basis of the data obtained, the following conclusions may be drawn:

1. The highest number of reported complaints relates to the alleged misuse of confidential information (probably, though not excusively, held by computer data banks).

2. There is an unexpectedly high number of complaints in respect of 'intrusion' (which includes telephone-tapping, bugging, and spying upon, photographing, or the electronic surveillance of private activities).

3. Considering the nature of the activity (in particular, the fact that it is normally only 'public figures' who are thought to attract such publicity), there is a surprisingly high number of complaints reported relating to the unauthorized publication by the news media of private facts.

4. Solicitors who do not consider themselves likely recipients report a remarkably large number of clients with complaints in the 'privacy' field.

5. The relatively high numbers of complaints (especially in the categories mentioned) suggest both that complainants consider the activities sufficiently serious to consider pursuing legal action and, of course, that they perceive the problems in legal terms.

6. There is apparent satisfaction (by a very small majority) with the state of the law at the time of the questionnaire— even on the part of those solicitors who are (and/or think they are) appropriate recipients of complaints in the 'privacy' field. But the responses do not admit of easy construction on this point (for the large minority might equally be interpreted as exhibiting a considerable degree of dissatisfaction with the law).

5

The Public Disclosure of 'Personal Information'

The subjection of an individual's private life to unwanted or unauthorized publicity—since it is normally conducted by the publications media—raises important (and difficult) questions concerning the apparently competing claims of 'privacy' and freedom of expression. Attempts to reconcile or 'balance' these rights or interests have been neither consistent nor especially convincing. Whatever formula is actually applied ('*ad hoc* balancing', a general theory of 'political speech', arguments from 'truth', and so on—see below) the law has inevitably to enunciate principles which, in effect, circumscribe freedom of speech (and especially of the press) on the one hand, in order to give effect to the individual's interest in protecting 'personal information' on the other. In the United States the matter is debated in the context of the purport and scope of the First Amendment's injunction that 'Congress shall make no law . . . abridging the freedom of speech, or of the press'. And this debate has brought forth a prodigious literature which need not be pursued here. Nevertheless, since both the common law and constitutional law in the United States continue to grapple with the problems of reconciling 'privacy' and 'free speech', a brief review of these developments forms an important element of this chapter.

The experience of the American courts in both tort and constitutional cases is instructive. It suggests that the conventional legal analysis (initiated, of course, by Warren and Brandeis) is no more successful in this sphere than it has been in other elements of 'privacy' doctrine and that, here too, the alternative approach proposed in this book might assist in avoiding some of the intractable difficulties the 'privacy' theory has generated. It is reassuring in this respect to find support for this alternative view from several American commentators. After a detailed discussion of the 'public disclosure' tort, one writer concludes.[1]

Privacy law might be more just and effective if it were to focus on identifying (preferably by statute) those exchanges of information that warrant protection at their point of origin, rather than continuing its current, capricious course of imposing liability only if the material is ultimately disseminated to the public at large . . . [A] careful identification of particularly sensitive situations in which personal information is exchanged, and an equally careful delineation of the appropriate expectations regarding how that information can be used, could significantly curtail abuses without seriously hampering freedom of speech. At the very least, this possibility merits considerably more thought as an alternative to the Warren and Brandeis tort than it has received thus far.

And even Professor Thomas Emersen,[2] the distinguished freedom of expression theorist, has recently suggested[3] that there might be '[a]nother approach, and one that seems to me to be more fruitful' that would:

place more emphasis on developing the privacy side of the balance. It would recognise the first amendment interests but it would give primary attention to a number of factors which derive ultimately from the functions performed by privacy and the expectations of privacy that prevail in contemporary society.[4]

The first such factor is:

the element of intimacy in determining the zone of privacy. Thus so far as the privacy tort [of 'public disclosure'] is concerned, *protection would be extended only to matters related to the intimate details of a person's life: those activities, ideas or emotions which one does not share with others or shares only with those who are closest. This would include sexual relations, the performance of bodily functions, family relations, and the like.*[5]

[1] D. L. Zimmerman, 'Requiem for a Heavyweight: A Farewell to Warren and Brandeis's Privacy Tort' (1983) 68 Cornell Law Rev. 291, 363–4. No such identification or delineation is proffered by Professor Zimmerman in this essay. Similar misgivings are expressed by R. F. Hixson, *Privacy in a Public Society: Human Rights in Conflict* (1987), ch. 8.

[2] T. I. Emerson, *The System of Freedom of Expression* (1970); id. 'Toward a General Theory of the First Amendment' (1963) 72 Yale LJ 877.

[3] 'The Right of Privacy and Freedom of the Press' (1979) 14 Harv. Civ. Rights-Civ. Libs. Rev. 329, 343.

[4] Ibid.   [5] Ibid. Emphasis supplied.

That the pursuit of an elusive equilibrium between 'privacy' and 'free speech' has induced a measure of scepticism in respect of the conventional legal analysis need not be taken to mean that an approach which is postulated on an alternative theory of 'personal information' will necessarily obviate the problems identified in this book and by Emerson and others.[6] But, as has been pointed out before, such difficulties spring, in large part, from a failure adequately to define the kind of information that it is sought to protect. As one commentator has recently put it,[7] 'To complain of unwanted publicity of one's private affairs there must be matters *sufficiently private, the publication of which would cause an average person distress, or humiliation, or deep embarrassment.*'

This chapter attempts to demonstrate the manner in which the conventional analysis adopted by the American law has approached the problem of gratuitous publicity, and the corresponding developments in Britain. The 'personal information' alternative is then suggested as a preferable perspective from which to seek a resolution of the problems (briefly discussed) associated with freedom of speech.

1. The Conventional Analysis

1.1. DEFINING THE ISSUE

The three elements of the tort of 'public disclosure of private facts' (recognized by most American states) were described in Chapter 3 where it was compared with the action for breach of confidence. Since their principal concern was the extent to which individuals have a legitimate objection to 'idle gossip' which though 'apparently harmless, when widely and persistently circulated, is a potent for evil',[8] Warren and Brandeis

---

[6] Similar misgivings have been expressed by L. Lusky, 'Invasion of Privacy: A Clarification of Concepts' (1972) 72 Colum. Law Rev. 693, 709, and T. Gerety, 'Redefining Privacy' (1977) 12 Harv. Civ. Rights-Civ. Libs. Rev. 234, 268–71.

[7] S. Stoljar, 'A Re-examination of Privacy' (1984) 4 Leg. Stud. 67, 81. Emphasis supplied.

[8] S. D. Warren and L. D. Brandeis, 'The Right to Privacy' (1890) 4 Harv. Law Rev. 193, 196.

did not require that the information published be particularly intimate or even offensive by objective standards. Rather, they argued that private information 'belonged' to the individual to whom it related, and could be used by others only with that person's consent. With the development of the tort and its reformulation by Prosser, the law has, to a limited extent, sought to define the species of information that might qualify as sufficiently 'private' to warrant protection against publicity. Thus Prosser, in addition to the requirements of (1) wide publicity and (2) objective offensiveness (see below) states (3) that the facts disclosed 'must be private facts, and not public ones'.[9]

The American *Restatement*[10] attempts to formulate what is to be understood by 'private facts':

The extent of the authority to make public private facts is not . . . unlimited. There may be some intimate details of her life, such as sexual relations, which even the actress is entitled to keep to herself. In determining what is a matter of legitimate public interest, account must be taken of the customs and conventions of the community; and in the last analysis what is proper becomes a matter of community mores. The line is to be drawn when the publicity ceases to be the giving of information to which the public is entitled, and becomes a morbid and sensational prying into private lives for its own sake, with which a reasonable member of the public, with decent standards, would say that he had no concern. The limitations, in other words, are those of common decency, having due regard to the freedom of the press and its reasonable leeway to choose what it will tell the public, but also due regard to the feelings of the individual and the harm that will be done to him by the exposure.

But, while this attempt at definition contains certain criteria (such as the objective test of what accords with the 'customs and conventions of the community') which are elements of the concept of 'personal information' proposed in this book, it confuses the question of what is 'private' with the question of what it is legitimate to publish. It is submitted that, if 'personal information' and 'press freedom' are to be given proper recognition and protection, the determination of

---

[9] Prosser, *The Law of Torts*, 856.
[10] *Torts, Second* (1977), para. 652D, comment h.

actionability for unauthorized publicity ought to depend on the separation of the two enquiries. In other words, the test of whether information is 'personal' must first be satisfied (by reference to the objective criterion suggested); it is then necessary to consider whether—despite the information being 'personal'—its disclosure is justified by virtue of its being in the 'public interest'.

Apart from the problem of what is 'private' (which is returned to below), the requirement of wide publicity and the notion of 'newsworthiness' have also given rise to several difficulties. In particular, since in general only publication on a wide scale is actionable, the press has, despite Supreme Court assertions to the contrary,[11] been accorded less constitutional protection under the First Amendment than individuals who broadcast 'private facts' on a limited scale.[12]

In seeking to measure what is 'highly offensive' the courts have developed what Prosser[13] calls a ' "mores" test'. In the leading case of *Melvin* v. *Reid*[14] the plaintiff's past, as a prostitute and defendant in a sensational murder trial, was revealed in a film called *The Red Kimono* which was based on these events. She had, in the eight years since her acquittal, been accepted into 'respectable society', married, and moved in a circle of friends who were ignorant of her past. Her action for the invasion of her privacy caused by the defendant's truthful[15] disclosures was sustained by the California court (which had not hitherto recognized an action for invasion of privacy).

---

[11] See *Houchins* v. *KQED* 438 US 1, 11 (1978); *Branzburg* v. *Hayes* 408 US 665, 684–5; *Pell* v. *Procunier* 417 US 817, 833–5 (1974).

[12] A. Hill, 'Defamation and Privacy under the First Amendment' (1976) 76 Colum. Law Rev. 1205, 1285–90. Cf. H. Kalven, 'Privacy in Tort Law: Were Warren and Brandeis Wrong?' (1966) 31 Law & Contemp. Probs. 326.

[13] Prosser, 857.

[14] 112 Cal App 285; 297 P. 91 (1931).

[15] Where the account is fictionalized, the plaintiff may bring the action under the 'false light' tort. It has already been suggested that this tort is virtually indistinguishable from defamation or, as one writer puts it, 'belongs with defamation as its unacknowledged but not illegitimate offspring': Gerety, 'Redefining Privacy', 258. See the discussion of the Supreme Court's decision in *Time, Inc.* v. *Hill* below.

On the other hand, in *Sidis* v. *F.-R. Publishing Corporation*[16] the plaintiff, a former child prodigy who, at 11, lectured in mathematics at Harvard, had become a recluse and devoted his time to studying the Okamakammessett Indians and collecting streetcar transfers. The *New Yorker* published an article, 'Where Are They Now? April Fool' written by James Thurber under a pseudonym. Details of Sidis's physical characteristics and mannerisms, the single room in which he lived, and his present activities were revealed by the article, which acknowledged that he had informed the reporter who had tracked him down for the interview that he lived in fear of publicity and changed jobs whenever his employer or fellow workers learned of his past. The New York District Court denied his action for invasion of privacy on the ground that it could find no decision 'which held the "right of privacy" to be violated by a newspaper or magazine publishing a correct account of one's life or doings . . . except under abnormal circumstances which did not exist in the case at bar'.[17] On appeal[18] the Second Circuit affirmed the dismissal of the privacy action, but appeared to base its decision on a balancing of the offensiveness of the article with the public or private character of the plaintiff.

Indeed, in both *Melvin* and *Sidis* there is little attempt made to consider the extent to which the information divulged was 'private'. The invocation of the conceptually vague notions of 'community customs', 'newsworthiness', and the 'offensiveness' of the publication render these and many other decisions concerning 'public disclosure'[19] singularly unhelpful in an area of considerable constitutional importance. And this is equally true of the attempts by the Supreme Court to fix the boundaries of the First Amendment in respect of publications which affect the plaintiff's 'privacy'. Thus in *Time, Inc.* v. *Hill*[20] the Court held that the plaintiff's action for invasion of privacy failed where he (and his family)

---

[16] 113 F. 2d 806 (1940). [17] 34 F. Supp 19, 21.

[18] 113 F. 2d 806 (1940).

[19] For example, *Cason* v. *Baskin* 159 Fla. 31, 30 So. 2d 243 (1944) and *Virgil* v. *Time, Inc*, 527 F. 2d 1122 (1975).

[20] 385 US 374 (1967). See too *Cantrell* v. *Forest City Publishing Co.* 419 US 245 (1974).

had been the subject of a substantially false report. The defendant had published a description of a new play adapted from a novel which fictionalized the ordeal suffered by the plaintiff when he and his family were held hostage in their home by a group of escaped prisoners. Adopting the test that it had applied in respect of defamation[21] the Supreme Court held, by a majority,[22] that unless there was proof of actual malice (i.e. that the defendant knowingly published an untrue report) the action would fail. Falsity alone did not deprive the defendant of his protection under the First Amendment—if the publication was newsworthy. And since the 'opening of a new play linked to an actual incident is a matter of public interest'[23] the plaintiff, because he was unable to show malice, failed. Yet, as is suggested below, the decision was not really concerned with the public disclosure of 'private information',[24] whether or not it was even a defamation action![25]

It is often argued that an action in defamation provides a means of protecting the plaintiff's 'privacy'. Professor Nimmer[26] claims that the libel standard adopted in *Sullivan* was wrongly applied in the *Time* case because the Hill family was not defamed by the account of their experience. But it does not follow from this argument that the interests protected by the 'false light' tort are sufficiently distinguishable from those that underpin defamation to justify separate treatment. Indeed, Nimmer himself suggests that the 'false light' category ought to be dealt with in the same way as 'public disclosure' cases. It is submitted, however, that the 'false light' category is both redundant (for almost all such cases might equally have been brought for defamation) and

---

[21] *New York Times* v. *Sullivan* 373 US 254 (1964).

[22] The dissenting judgment of Fortas J. (at 304–5) is referred to below. Cf. *Time, Inc.* v. *Firestone* 424 US 448 (1967). See M. B. Nimmer, 'The Right to Speak from *Times* to *Time*: First Amendment Theory Applied to Libel and Misapplied to Privacy' (1968) 56 Calif. Law Rev. 935.

[23] At 388.

[24] Harlan J. (at 476) proclaims, 'To me this is not 'privacy' litigation in its truest sense.' See Douglas J. (at 401). The information concerned would not, on the account offered in this study, be regarded as 'personal'. The 'intimacy factor was weak or nonexistent,' Emerson, *The System of Freedom of Expression*, 345.

[25] See below. [26] 'The Right to Speak from *Times* to *Time*'.

only tenuously related to the protection of the plaintiff against aspects of his private life being exposed. The Younger Committee recognized that 'placing someone in a false light is an aspect of defamation rather than privacy',[27] and several distinguished commentators have raised the question 'whether this branch of the tort is not capable of swallowing up and engulfing the whole law of defamation'.[28]

'The fundamental difference', it has been suggested,[29] 'between a right to privacy and a right to freedom from defamation is that the former directly concerns one's own peace of mind, while the latter concerns primarily one's reputation.' This, however, is not a distinction that has ever been a sharp one, and not only has the jurisdiction of defamation been enlarged, but (more to the point) recovery has been allowed for invasion of privacy in several American decisions[30] where the plaintiff has been depicted in a 'false light' and it is the plaintiff's reputation, rather than his 'privacy' that would appear to be affected.

[27] Younger, para. 70.

[28] Prosser, *The Law of Torts*, 4th edn., 813; J. W. Wade, 'Defamation and the Right of Privacy' (1962) 15 Vand. Law Rev. 1093; J. Skelly Wright, 'Defamation, Privacy and the Public's Right to Know: A National Problem and a New Approach' (1968) 46 Texas Law Rev. 630; F. Davis, 'What Do We Mean By "Right to Privacy"?' (1959) 4 S. Dak. Law Rev. 1; Kalven, 'Privacy in Tort Law' 341. See too F. S. Haiman, *Speech and Law in a Free Society* (1981) 85–6. In comparing 'defamation' and 'privacy', however, there are several difficulties, not least of which is the fact that these writers share only the most general conceptions of both issues. For example, Davis (at 8) regards the two as 'identical' since they are both concerned largely in protecting the plaintiff's mental feelings. Wade (at 1124) expresses a similar view, but appears to regard disclosure and 'false light' as offending the plaintiff's reputation. Prosser (at 401) and Bloustein, 'Privacy as an Aspect of Human Dignity: An Answer to Dean Prosser' (1964) 39 NYU Law Rev. 962, 993, both identify an overlap, but of different interests. If one conceives (as Prosser does) the interest protected by the tort of public disclosure as reputation, the overlap becomes even more substantial.

[29] *Themo v. New England Newspaper Publishing* Co. 27 NE 2d 753 (1940) 755.

[30] *Marks v. Jaffa* 26 NYS 908 (1893); *Pavesich v. New England Life Ins. Co.* 50 SE 68 (1905); *Foster-Milburn Co. v. Chinn* 120 SW 364 (1909); *Flake v. Greensboro News Co.* 195 SE 753; *Munden v. Harris* 134 SW 1076 (1911); *Hinish v. Meier & Frank Co.* 113 P 2d 438 (1941); *Gill v. Hearst Publishing Co.* 40 Cal 2d 224, 253 P 2d 441, *Cantrell v. Forest City Publishing Co.* 419 US 245 (1974).

It is an obvious enough claim that while defamation is concerned with *false* statements, the falsity or otherwise of the disclosure is irrelevant in an action for public disclosure. A plaintiff who is faced with a *true* statement by which he is embarrassed may obtain relief by bringing his action under the public disclosure tort (provided, it seems, that there is the requisite publicity). In Prosser's view, the tort protects his reputation.[31] But this seems mistaken, for the rationale behind the tort of public disclosure is not merely 'to prevent inaccurate portrayal of private life, but to prevent its being depicted at all.'[32] Moreover, even though the disclosure of sensitive information actually portrays the plaintiff in a *favourable* light, there is no reason why he should in principle be barred from recovery.[33]

On the other hand, if the statement is false, the tort of 'false light' might have been committed, and here too Prosser, more plausibly, suggests that it is the plaintiff's reputation that is affected. But, since the 'false light' cases appear to be equally actionable in defamation (or perhaps 'appropriation': see Chapter 2) it is arguable that 'the overlap (between defamation and privacy) might be thought substantial enough to make the approach via privacy superfluous'.[34]

The suggestion is occasionally made that by modifying the defence of justification many of the actions brought to vindicate the plaintiff's loss of 'privacy' might be accommodated within the tort of defamation. The proposal is that in order for the defence to succeed, the defendant ought to be required to show not only that the statement is true, but that its publication is in the public interest—the position which obtains in several Australian and American jurisdictions and in the Roman–Dutch law in Sri Lanka and South Africa.

[31] Prosser, 'Privacy', 398. Cf. Prosser, 864–5.

[32] Warren and Brandeis, 'The Right to Privacy', 197.

[33] See above.

[34] Kalven, 'Privacy in Tort Law', 332. 'Practically all the cases (i.e. 'false light' cases) . . . are covered by the existing remedies of defamation and injurious falsehood and it seems as if the American concept of privacy has been grafted on to these traditional causes of action *ex abundanti cautela*' (G. Dworkin, 'The Common Law Protection of Privacy' (1967) 2 Univ. Tas. Law Rev. 418, 426). Younger, para. 70; Prosser, 401; Bloustein, 'Privacy as an Aspect of Human Dignity', 993.

This conclusion was, of course, open to Warren and Brandeis to have adopted, though Brandeis might then 'have been marked as a Lorentz, certainly not an Einstein of legal thought'.[35] But since they regarded the principles of the law of defamation as 'radically different'[36] from those underlying the protection of 'privacy', this modification would hardly be consistent with their general thesis. In any event, even if the law of defamation were to be so modified,[37] many actions would still not succeed where the plaintiff's reputation has not, in fact, been affected by the private facts disclosed.

In so far as these issues have arisen in England the conventional analysis has received a certain acceptance. It has already been seen in Chapter 3 how the courts in cases of breach of confidence involving personal information have adopted a 'balancing' of the interests in confidentiality against the public interest in receiving certain information. It was there submitted that there has been a failure to identify and analyse the specific questions that relate to information *relating to the plaintiff* as opposed to commercial confidences. This, it was suggested, has resulted in a tendency to neglect (or even to ignore) the harm caused to the plaintiff by the publication of personal information. By attempting to formulate a more precise identification of the information which merits legal protection the plaintiff's interests might be more effectively protected.

Equally, in dealing with complaints concerning alleged invasions of 'privacy' by the press, the Press Council has attempted, with little success,[38] to strike a balance between

[35] P. Freund, 'Privacy: One Concept or Many?' *Nomos XIII* 182.

[36] Warren and Brandeis, 'The Right to Privacy'.

[37] The sugestion has been made on several occasions and rejected, most recently by the Committee on the Law of Defamation (chairman: Mr Justice Faulks) 1975, Cmnd. 5909, para. 137 *et seq.*

[38] The council's decisions, though compared by a former chairman, Lord Devlin, to the methods used by 'generations of judges who produced the common law of England,' (H. P. Levy, *The Press Council: History, Procedure and Cases* (1967), xi) are frequently terse, unreasoned, and even difficult to understand. Nor does it seem that any attempt is made to offer any real guidance as to the manner in which its 'policy' is applied to the facts of particular cases. In particular, there have been a number of adjudications which are in direct conflict with each other. Successive Royal Commissions on the Press have shown little sympathy for the council's claim that it is 'respected, feared and obeyed' (Younger, paras. 147 and

these interests. It has declared[39] that,

The publication of information about the private lives or concerns of individuals without their consent is only acceptable if there is a legitimate public interest overriding the right of privacy ... The public interest ... must be a legitimate and proper public interest and not only a prurient or morbid curiosity.

But, quite apart from the deficiencies in the council's methods of implementing this 'policy',[40] the *ad hoc* resolution of particular complaints and the lack of a systematic code of conduct[41] make it impossible adequately to deal with the difficult and complex problems of protecting 'personal information'. In particular, in the absence of a proper account of what information is 'personal', the adjudications fail to provide very useful guidance in respect of what might prima facie be expected to warrant protection. In any event, since the council has no power to award compensation, and since it is often not even the victim who is the complainant,[42]

151); see Royal Commission on the Press 1977, para. 20.75, and R. Wacks, *The Protection of Privacy* (1980) 106–9. For a recent comprehensive indictment of Press Council practice and procedure, see G. Robertson, *People Against the Press: An Enquiry into the Press Council* (1983).

[39] In its 'Declaration of Principle on Privacy', *23rd Annual Report* 1976, 151. Similar views are expressed in the council's evidence to the Younger Committee, published as *Privacy, Press and Public* (1971).

[40] Several difficulties arise in any attempt to interpret the adjudications. For instance, in one decision the council found that the newspaper was 'seriously at fault' in publishing private facts, yet declared that the complaint was 'not substantiated': *7th Annual Report* (1960), 25. In another, the council 'deprecated' the publication and yet found that 'no harm' was done by it: *10th Annual Report* (1963), 48. The 1977 Royal Commission recognized some of these deficiencies: para. 20.54.

[41] The 1977 Royal Commission recommended that the council should issue a code of conduct (para. 20.59). But this proposal and various others which hold a limited prospect of improving the council's practices were opposed by the council (paras 20.61 and 20.71; *Privacy, Press and Public*, para. 82; Younger, paras. 190–3.

[42] Moreover, the complainant is required to waive his right to sue the newspaper after the adjudication, a practice which the Royal Commission urged the council to reconsider (paras. 20.43–9), and the Annan Committee on the Future of Broadcasting described as 'an unjustifiable interference with individual rights', Cmnd. 6733, 1977, para. 6.18. See G. Robertson, *People Against the Press*, 28–31; G. Dworkin, 'The Younger Committee Report on Privacy' (1973) 36 MLR 404.

the procedure cannot be seriously advanced as an alternative to legal regulation.[43]

1.2. WHAT ARE 'PRIVATE FACTS'?

While it is relatively clear that if the information is to be protected it must not be a matter of public record[44] or observable in a public place,[45] little attempt is made to specify precisely what it is that is 'private'. It appears to have escaped many courts that, in the most trite sense, '[i]f we wish to compensate people when they are hurt by the truth because the information is "personal", we must be able to

[43] See below.

[44] It is largely on this basis that information disclosed in the course of judicial proceedings is generally excluded from protection: *Cox Broadcasting Corporation* v. *Cohn* 420 US 469 (1970) in which the Supreme Court held that the publication of a rape victim's name was privileged: it was part of an accurate report of a matter contained in a public record. Under s. 6 of the Sexual Offences (Amendment) Act 1976 both the victim and the defendant in a rape trial are entitled to anonymity. There are several other statutory restrictions upon the reporting of various judicial proceedings, e.g., s. 3 of the Criminal Justice Act 1976, s. 39 of the Children and Young Persons Act 1933 and s. 57 of the 1963 Act, s. 21 of the Childrens Act 1975, s. 12(1)(a) of the Administration of Justice Act 1960, Contempt of Court Act 1981. But they are not concerned primarily with 'personal information' or, if they are, they simply buttress the argument that such facts 'are without question events of legitimate concern to the public and consequently fall within the responsibility of the press to report the operations of government' (*Cox*, at 492 (per White J.)). Another statute which has a different objective, but is sometimes conceived to be concerned with 'privacy' is the Rehabilitation of Offenders Act 1974 which permits an individual who is 'rehabilitated' to conceal certain 'spent' convictions.

[45] *Gill* v. *Hearst Publishing Co.* 40 Cal. 2d 224, 253 P. 2d 441 (1953) in which a photograph of the plaintiffs embracing in public was published by the defendant to illustrate an article on the subject of love. The court denied recovery. On the other hand, where the same photograph was used to illustrate a feature on 'the wrong kind of love' the plaintiffs succeeded because they had been 'robbed of their public esteem' (*Gill* v. *Curtis Publishing Co.* 38 Cal. 2d 273, 239 P 2d 630 (1952). It is therefore possible to frame the action in libel (or, indeed, 'appropriation of name or likeness') where the publication does not merely expose the plaintiff to unwanted publicity.

distinguish what is personal from what is not.'[46] The conventional legal analysis, by allowing the determination of what is 'private' to coalesce with considerations of newsworthiness etc., impedes a clear expression of the extent and form of the law's protection. The Australian Law Reform Commission has attempted to define the scope of the legal protection against unauthorized publicity by adopting a category of 'sensitive private facts'.[47] Its draft Unfair Publication Bill provides that,

A person publishes sensitive private facts concerning an individual where the person publishes matter relating to or purporting to relate to the health, private behaviour, home life or personal or family relationships of the individual in circumstances in which the publication is likely to cause distress, annoyance or embarrassment to an individual in the position of the first-mentioned individual.

The intention of the clause is reasonably clear (even if it begs certain questions, e.g., what is 'private behaviour'?) and it offers a better basis than the conventional analysis for a sensible determination of what publications are 'in the public interest.'

1.3. WHAT IS IN THE PUBLIC INTEREST?

Once it has been established that the plaintiff's complaint is that 'personal information' relating to him has been published, the question arises of the extent to which the press may legitimately publish such information. This is a function of the proper bounds of 'press freedom' which, in turn, depends ultimately on larger political considerations concerning the role of the press in a democratic society (touched on below). In simple terms, the courts of both America and (in respect of breach of confidence) England, as well as the Press Council, adopt the broad view that persons who enter the public arena forsake a measure of their claim to prevent information about them being published. This does not, of course, necessarily resolve the difficulties of the *extent* of this waiver

[46] Zimmerman, 'Requiem for a Heavyweight' 344.
[47] *Unfair Publication: Defamation and Privacy* (Report No. 11), 1979, Clause 19 (1) and (2).

or the definition of what it is to be a 'public figure'. Nor does it always explain the function of the harm to the plaintiff occasioned by the disclosures or the application of 'offensiveness' or 'unconscionability', all of which have been employed in the case law in an ostensible effort to strike a 'balance' between the apparently competing interests. (See below.)

The following four, related, issues appear to be the major (but not the only)[48] considerations that feature more prominently in the determination of whether 'personal information might legitimately be published.

1.3.1. *The Status of the Plaintiff*

'Peculiarities of manner and person, which in the ordinary individual should be free from comment,' declared Warren and Brandeis,[49] 'may acquire a public importance, if found in a candidate for public office.' But the American law,[50] the Younger Committee,[51] and the Press Council[52] recognize that this does not constitute a wholesale waiver of the plaintiff's right to complain about those matters and transactions of private life which are wholly unconnected to his public office or his ability to exercise it.

The Supreme Court's landmark decision in *New York Times* v. *Sullivan*[53] (that in order to recover for libel, public figures must prove that the defendant either knew that the

---

[48] Other questions invariably enter into the exercise, for example: Was it necessary for the plaintiff's name to be mentioned? What was the defendant's motive in publishing? Was the disclosure sufficiently serious to warrant liability? Was the disclosure true or false? How much time has elapsed between the occurrence of the events described and the publication in question? See R. Wacks, *The Protection of Privacy*, 99–106.

[49] Warren and Brandeis, 'The Right to Privacy', 215–16.

[50] *Restatement, Torts, Second*, para. 652D, comment h. The courts have not spoken with one voice, and the issue has given rise to certain problems. In addition, the decision is sometimes reached on the basis of '*ad hoc* balancing': *Youssoupoff* v. *Columbia Broadcasting System, Inc.* 41 Misc. 2d 42, 19 App. Div. 2d 865 (1963); and on other occasions on more general principles: *Briscoe* v. *Reader's Digest Association* 483 P. 2d 34 (1971).

[51] Younger, paras 156–7; 181.

[52] *23rd Annual Report* (1976), para. (iii).

[53] 376 US 254 (1964). Applied to private plaintiffs (by a majority) in *Rosenbloom* v. *Metromedia, Inc.* 303 US 29 (1971) which decision was abandoned in *Gertz* v. *Robert Welch, Inc.* 418 US 323 (1974).

publication was false or published it in reckless disregard of its truth or falsity) is, of course, informed by a particular perception of political speech and its functions. Applying this doctrine to the facts of *Time, Inc.* v. *Hill*,[54] required a rather tortuous logic, for it is hard to see how (false) information about the opening of a new play should have been protected under the principle whereby the First Amendment defends disclosures concerning 'all issues about which information is needed or appropriate to enable the members of society to cope with the exigencies of their period'.[55] This effectively permits the press to define as matters of public importance those which they decide to report, and virtually 'swallows' the tort of public disclosure.[56]

1.3.2. *Unconscionability of the Publication*

Recovery is, in some American decisions, made to turn on the offensiveness of the publication. This is especially evident in *Sidis*[57] in which the court suggested that certain revelations 'may be so intimate and so unwarranted . . . as to outrage the community's notion of decency'.[58] This is a standard that is difficult to apply; the notions of 'offensiveness' or 'unconscionability' are inherently vague and subjective. Nor does it follow that the disclosure of information that the plaintiff may—on reasonable grounds—wish to conceal would necessarily be regarded as offensive.

1.3.3. *The Manner of Acquisition*

It was submitted in Chapter 3[59] that in determining the

[54] 385 US 374 (1967).

[55] At 388 quoting the portentous words from *Thornhill* v. *Alabama* 310 US 88 (1940) 102.

[56] Kalven, 'Privacy in Tort Law' 336. The Court has, it was pointed out above, retreated from its *Time* decision (at least in libel actions): *Gertz*, see above; *Time, Inc.* v. *Firestone* 424 US 448 (1976).

[57] See above. A similar view is expressed in *Virgil*, see above.

[58] It is arguable that on this basis Sidis ought to have succeeded: E. Karafiol, 'The Right to Privacy and the Sidis Case' (1978) 12 Ga. Law Rev. 513, 523–9.

[59] Discussing, in particular, the trilogy of recent decisions in *Lion Laboratories Ltd.* v. *Evans* [1984] 2 All ER 417; *Cork* v. *McVicar* [1984] *The Times*, 1 Nov.; *Francome* v. *Daily Mirror Group Newspapers Ltd.* [1984] 1 WLR 892.

extent to which the disclosure of personal information in breach of confidence is in the public interest, the fact that the information has been acquired by improper means ought to be irrelevant. The Law Commission,[60] however, propose that the manner of acquisition ought to be a relevant factor:

We think that in assessing the public interest in protecting the confidentiality of information the court should take all the circumstances into account, including the manner in which the information was acquired whether by the original acquirer or by a third party.

But this could lead to a possible confusion between the issues that arise in respect of 'intrusion' (discussed in Chapter 7) and the different considerations that occur when material is actually published. It may be that fine distinctions need to be drawn in respect of whether it is the defendant who acquires the information or whether the methods employed are unlawful or merely improper. Generally, however, it is preferable to keep the two issues distinct, an approach adopted in some American cases.[61] In *Pearson* v. *Dodd*,[62] for instance, sensitive documents were removed from the files of a Senator and passed on to two journalists who published their contents. In denying the plaintiff Senator's action for invasion of privacy, the court held that the publication did not give rise to liability, because it was of 'general public

---

[60] Law Commission Report, para. 6.79. By recommending the creation of a new tort consisting in the use or disclosure of information *unlawfully obtained*, the Younger Committee is implicitly adopting the position that the two issues are necessarily connected; the proposed cause of action would arise only in respect of information which has been acquired as a result of an unlawful intrusion (Younger, para. 632).

[61] For example, *Metter* v. *Los Angeles Examiner* 35 Cal. App. 304 (1939); *New York Times* v. *United States* 403 US 713 (1971). Cf. *Corliss* v. *Walker* 27 F. 434 (1893); *Barber* v. *Time, Inc.* 159 SW 291 (1942) at 295–6. Where the intrusion and publication are almost inseparable (as in *Barber* in which the plaintiff, who was suffering from a rare disease, was surreptitiously photographed in her hospital bed, the photographs then being published) the argument for liability is naturally stronger. The reverse proposition (namely that a publication which is in the public interest does not exclude liability for the intrusion by which the information was obtained) is—logically—applied in *Dietemann* v. *Time, Inc.* 449 F. 2d 244 (1971) referred to in ch. 7.

[62] 410 F. 2d 701 (1969).

interest'.[63] That the defendants *knew* of the unlawful mode of acquisition did not affect their protection under the First Amendment.[64] As one commentator[65] puts it,

it is unthinkable that a newspaper should incur liability solely because it has knowledge that the information is 'tainted' because [it is] derived [by] trespass, conversion, or invasion of privacy—or through breach of confidence made actionable by law ... The values of the first amendment would be seriously subverted if such protection were withdrawn on the ground of knowledge on the part of the media that the truth had come to light through legally reprehensible means employed by others.

1.3.4. *Newsworthiness*

In their quest for a definitive interpretation of the First Amendment, American courts and commentators have developed several theories of free speech. While these approaches, sometimes consequentialist, often deontological in nature,[66] attempt to account for the exercise of the freedom in every imaginable context, it would be an extraordinarily rich and versatile theory that was able to offer a comprehensive rationalization of speech in all its protean forms. Nevertheless, though it would be artificial to conceive of the problems encountered by the efforts to reconcile 'privacy' and 'free speech' as a discrete question, the American law does appear to have developed the contours of a particular 'privacy/free speech' theory which have been sketched above.

[63] At 703.

[64] A similar view, in respect of the public's right to receive certain information even if it is published in breach of confidence is expressed by Stephenson LJ in *Lion Laboratories*, see above, at 422, see ch. 3.

[65] Hill, 'Defamation and Privacy under the First Amendment' 1279–80.

[66] For an analysis of theories of free speech based on these competing perspectives see F. Schauer, 'The Role of the People in First Amendment Theory' (1986) 74 Calif. L. Rev. 761, 769–78. Professor Schauer finds deontological theories (i.e. that free speech is good *in itself* because, for example, it encourages self-fulfilment) to be unsound. But he is also critical of consequential theories (such as Meiklejohn's) which are premissed on popular participation. He concludes that 'it is time to face up to the paternalism of the first amendment', and 'the fact that a system of government has essentially been forced on us, and there is little we can do about it' (788).

In particular, there is a discernable tendency to view the matter from the standpoint of a purposive construction of the First Amendment. To ask, in other words, what forms of speech or publication warrant protection by virtue of their contribution to the operation of political democracy. This is evident in the decisions (mentioned above) which distinguish, with variable consequences, between 'public figures' and ordinary individuals. Indeed, the Supreme Court's satisfaction with this doctrine appears to account for its (widely criticized) application of the principle adopted in the libel case of *Sullivan* to the 'privacy' case of *Hill* (see above). In the former decision, the Court expressed its philosophy in unequivocal terms,[67]

we consider this case against the background of a profound national commitment to the principle that debate on public issues should be uninhibited, robust and wide open, and that it may well include vehement, caustic, and sometimes unpleasantly sharp attacks on government and public officials.

The principal purpose of the First Amendment is, in this theorem, the protection of the right of all citizens to understand political issues in order that they might participate effectively in the operation of democratic government. This theory—which was advanced most effectively by Alexander Meiklejohn[68]—has an obvious appeal in the context of the protection of 'personal information'. It permits considerable scope for actions by private individuals who have been subjected to gratuitous publicity. In practice, however, it is frequently those who are in the public eye that (for this very reason) attract the attention of the gossip columnist. The difficult question which the theory is then required to answer is the extent to which such public figures are entitled to protection of aspects of their personal lives. And this, in turn, involves a delicate investigation of what features of a public figure's life may legitimately be exposed—in the furtherance of political debate.

Though the law seeks to distinguish between 'voluntary'

[67] *New York Times* v. *Sullivan* 376 US 254 (1964) 270 (per Brennan J.). See too *Whitney* v. *California* 274 US 357 (1927) 375–8 (per Brandeis J.).
[68] *Political Freedom: The Constitutional Powers of the People* (1965).

and 'involuntary' public figures,[69] the application of this theory, except as a useful general rationale for the existence of the freedom of speech itself,[70] provides uncertain guidance as to the respective rights and obligations in cases involving the public disclosure of 'personal information'. Unless some attempt is made to define the kinds of information in respect of which all individuals might prima facie expect to receive protection (even if such protection is subsequently to be outweighed by considerations of 'public interest') one of the central purposes of recognizing the interest in restricting information (the trust, candour and confidence it fosters) is attenuated.

Another theory in support of free speech is John Stuart Mill's argument from truth.[71] Its essence is that any suppression of speech is an 'assumption of infallibility' and that only by the unrestricted circulation of ideas can the 'truth' be discovered. But this theory, taken to its logical conclusion, would prevent any inroads being made into the exercise of the right to speak (at least truthfully). Apart from Mill's questionable assumption that there *is* some objective 'truth', and his confidence in the prevalence of reason, his theory makes the leal regulation of disclosures of 'personal information' (as well as several other forms of speech which cause harm) extremely difficult to justify.

A further theory (which seems to offer more support for the restriction of speech in order to protect 'personal information') views freedom of speech as an aspect of individual fulfilment. To limit an individual's right to express himself is to restrict his intellectual and spiritual development.[72] The apparent attraction of this argument in the

[69] *American Restatement, Torts, Second*, para. 652D, comments e and f.

[70] E. Barendt, *Freedom of Speech* (1985) 23; F. Schauer, *Free Speech: A Philosophical Enquiry* (1982) 85–6.

[71] J. S. Mill, *On Liberty* (1859) ch. 2. Milton advanced a similar argument in *Areopagitica* (1644). It received a certain acceptance by American judges, notably Holmes J. in *Abrams* v. *United States* 250 US 616 (1919) in which (at 630–1) he referred to the relativity of the truth and the need for it to be tested 'in the competition of the market'.

[72] Similar arguments for 'privacy' are, of course, made. See the discussion in ch. 1.

context of 'privacy' lies in the fact that, at first blush, it seems to provide a coherent basis for claiming that publications which harm other individuals cannot seriously be thought to advance the publisher's self-fulfilment. But this cannot logically be deduced from the theory: who is to say whether or not certain forms of speech are instrumental in achieving this object? Moreover, the argument 'suffers from a failure to distinguish intellectual self-fulfilment from other wants and needs, and thus fails to support a distinct principle of free speech'.[73] It is also founded on the principle of the free dissemination of *ideas* rather than *information*, which renders it of limited utility in the present context.[74]

Numerous difficulties attend the attempt to formulate a coherent theory of free speech which is both sufficiently broad to capture the complexities of the exercise of the freedom, and sufficiently specific to account for its variable applications. The argument from democracy appears to attract considerably more support than the Millian or autonomy-based theories, but all provide at best only the most general guidance in respect of the legitimate controls on the public disclosure of 'personal information'. It may be that the matter is best pursued from the perspective of an interest-based theory which seeks to specify the particular interests of the parties involved in the disclosure. However, this approach raises numerous problems of its own (not dissimilar from the interest-based accounts of 'privacy' identified in Chapter 1). In addition, while it is useful to distinguish, say, the 'personality' interests affected by the disclosure of private facts from the 'reputational' interests that are affected by defamatory publications or the 'commercial' interests affected

[73] F. Schauer, *Free Speech*, 56.

[74] A more sophisticated (and arguably more successful) version of this theory is advanced by Thomas Scanlon who proposes that 'the powers of a state are limited to those that citizens could recognise while still regarding themselves as equal, autonomous, rational agents' (T. Scanlon, 'A Theory of Freedom of Expression' in R. Dworkin (ed.), *The Philosophy of Law* (1977) 153, 162). It may not suppress speech on the ground that its audience will form harmful beliefs or act in consequence of them. 'The value of the argument from autonomy is that it is an argument that is directed at *speech*, rather than at the entire range of interests that might with some minimal plausibility be designated "individual" ' (F. Schauer, *Free Speech*, 71).

by breach of confidence, it fails to explain which species of information warrant protection in the face of the competing claims of free speech.

In mediating between the two interests the American Supreme Court has, despite the invitation to adopt an 'absolutist' interpretation of the First Amendment,[75] resorted to the process of 'balancing', by which the interest in free speech is weighed against other interests such as national security, public order, and so on. If such interests are found to be 'compelling' or 'substantial' or where there is a 'clear and present danger' that the speech will cause a significant harm to the public interest, the Court has upheld the restriction of free speech.[76]

2. The Alternative Analysis

The most conspicuous feature of the conventional analysis is its failure to specify with clarity or consistency the circum-

---

[75] By Black and Douglas JJ.

[76] The English courts have occasionally—and perhaps less portentously—applied the 'balancing' process: see the cases discussed in ch. 3, in particular *Francome, Lion Laboratories,* and *Cork*. See too *Secretary of State for Defence* v. *Guardian Newspapers Ltd.* [1984] 3 WLR 986; *Attorney-General* v. *Guardian Newspapers Ltd.* [1987] 1 WLR 1248; *Stephens* v. *Avery* [1988] 2 WLR 1280 at 1287 per Sir Nicolas Browne-Wilkinson VC. In respect of the newsworthiness of a particular publication, the Younger Committee took the view that 'because it is impossible to devise any satisfactory yardstick by which to judge, in cases of doubt, whether the importance of a public story should override the privacy of the people and personal information involved, the decision on this point can be made only in the light of the circumstances of each case. The question we have to answer, therefore, is who should make that decision . . . We are in no doubt that the initial decision can only be made by those responsible for the publication: that is by the press themselves . . . we do not think that this is the sort of duty that should be given to the courts' (Younger, paras. 187–8). The Committee's general conclusion has already been considered (see ch. 2), but, while obviously recognizing the justiciability of the claim, the Supreme Court has itself occasionally accepted the judgment of the press concerning what is and what is not newsworthy (e.g. *Daily Times Democrat* v. *Graham* 276 Ala. 380, 162 So. 2d 474 (1964); *Briscoe* v. *Reader's Digest Association,* see above). This view is supported by a leading American theorist: Z. Chafee, *Government and Mass Communication: A Report from the Commission on Freedom of the Press* (1965) 138.

stances under which the public disclosure of private facts is actionable. The leading decisions of the American courts (and, as was suggested in Chapter 3, of the English courts in respect of breach of confidence) afford limited guidance as to the legitimate expectations of individuals concerning the restriction of intimate or sensitive information. Can it really be said that, say, *Sidis, Melvin, Hill* or *Woodward, Argyll,* or *Francome* (let alone the deliberations and declarations of the Press Council) provide an adequate statement of the rights of the individual and the obligations of publishers of 'personal information'?

Nor is it possible to obtain any real guidance on the wider question of free speech from the recent *Spycatcher* litigation, outlined in Chapter 3. Quite apart from the *public* nature of the case which, as was suggested in Chapter 3, gives rise to special problems, on one level it concerns merely the duty of confidence of an ex-employee. Moreover, the whole matter is so heavily tinged by several moral factors,[77] complicated by the national security question, that the judgments should be treated with caution. Thus while several of the judges allude to the importance of the public interest in free speech[78] and even refer to Article 10 of the European Convention on Human Rights, this was within the narrow context of the Attorney-General's application for an interlocutory injunction to prevent republication by the British press of Wright's memoirs. On the question of whether an interlocutory injunction should be granted, therefore, though the majority of the House of Lords decided that there was a more potent public interest in preserving confidentiality in order to maintain the morale and effectiveness of the security services,

---

[77] Consider the tendentious manner in which Lord Templeman formulated the possible defences open to the newspapers: 'Three defences were put forward by the appellant newspapers, first, that Mr Wright intended his treachery to be helpful to the British public, secondly, that damage to the Security Service arising from Mr Wright's treachery had already been fully inflicted, and thirdly, that the public interest in receiving information entitled the press to publish treachery at home provided it had been published abroad' ([1987] 1 WLR 1248 at 1293).

[78] See Sir Nicolas Browne-Wilkinson VC at 1269, Ralph Gibson LJ at 1279, Lord Bridge at 1286, Lord Templeman at 1296–8, Lord Ackner at 1307, Lord Oliver at 1320–1.

they did so without knowing whether the disclosures would indeed be in the public interest.[79] And even the considerably more libertarian view espoused in the dissenting judgments of Lord Bridge and Lord Oliver, by Scott J. in the application for a permanent injunction,[80] and by Dillon and Bingham L JJ in the Court of Appeal,[81] needs to be read in the context of the importance attached by these judges to the fact that the information was already in the 'public domain'.[82]

The conceptual uncertainty that obtains in this branch of the law (widely acknowledged as almost a truism) is, in large part, a consequence of its signal failure to identify, except in the most general terms, the type of information that deserves protection. This is not to suggest that by adopting the approach proposed here an instant solution would be found to the persistent problem of reconciling the plaintiff's interest in protecting 'personal information' on the one hand, with the interest in freedom of speech, on the other. But it is submitted that by locating as the core of the issue the regulation of 'personal information' (as defined in Chapter 1) the subject is liberated from the vague generality that continues to impede its systematic protection in this and the other areas identified in this book.

[79] The Vice-Chancellor asserted that Wright's allegations were, 'in a number of respects "old hat" ' (at 1267). The Master of the Rolls, however, was more cautious: 'mere allegations of iniquity can never override confidentiality. They must be proved . . .' (at 1275). Cf. Lord Oliver at 1320 with whose formulation Scott J. expressly agreed: [1988] 2 WLR 805, 863.

[80] 'The Press has a legitimate role in disclosing scandals in Government. An open democratic society required that it be so' [1988] 2 WLR 805, 858.

[81] [1988] Dillon LJ declared that he 'preferred, without hesitation, the views of Lord Bridge and Lord Oliver', 2 WLR 805 (at 894).

[82] This factor is the basis of the House of Lords' decision in discharging the injunctions. In the words of Lord Keith, 'all possible damage to the interest of the Crown has already been done by the publication of *Spycatcher* abroad and the ready availability of copies in this country.' [1988] 3 WLR 776, 786. See too the decision by the Scottish Outer House of the Court of Session in favour of publication of the book *Inside Intelligence*. The Lord Advocate failed in his application for an interim interdict (interlocutory injunction) against the *Scotsman* who wished to publish extracts from the book by Anthony Cavendish, an ex-member of the security services: *Lord Advocate* v. *Scotsman Publications Ltd* [1988] *The Times*, 9 Mar.

6
The Collection of 'Personal Information'

It has become commonplace to identify, as a principal feature of modern industrialized societies, their dependence on the large-scale storage of information. It is undeniable that the everyday functions of the organs of the state as well as private institutions require a continual supply of data about individuals in order to administer efficiently the numerous services that are an integral part of contemporary life and of the expectations of modern man. Thus the provision of medical services, social security, credit, insurance, and the prevention and detection of crime, to mention only the most obvious examples, assume the availability of a considerable amount of such data and, hence, a willingness on the part of individuals to furnish it.

The widespread use of computers facilitates, of course, incomparably speedier and more efficient methods of storing, retrieving, and transferring information than is possible with conventional manual filing systems. To what extent, one is impelled to ask, will the dictator or even the bureaucrat prove capable of resisting the temptation to abuse this power? Already there are alarming signs that the drift toward centralized data banks is inexorably posing disturbing threats to individual freedom. And there can be little doubt that, in the absence of clearly formulated legal controls, we are in serious danger of creating an automated, authoritarian society from which there is no escape.

We should, however, be careful not to overstate the case. Dystopian versions of Big Brother frequently endow the computer with a life and identity of its own—as if it were beyond the ingenuity of man to control the monster he has spawned. It is all too easy to express a vague, unspecified bundle of fears that coalesce around the computer's threat to 'privacy'. But, as Colin Tapper puts it,[1]

---

[1] *Computer Law*, 3rd edn. (1983), 130.

[T]he exaggerated and hysterical approach of some commentators has done immense harm. By whipping up fear and suspicion they have themselves created the evil they have blamed on the machine . . . The clue to a successful approach lies, as it usually does, in drawing distinctions, and in adopting a flexible approach which treats each different problem in the light of its own special difficulties and complexities.

This is not to deny, of course, that the greatest vigilance is required in respect of the uses to which computers are put. Nor should we neglect the fact that in Britain and elsewhere there are increasing signs of serious abuses committed in the name of efficiency. But it is imperative that the precise nature of the problem is carefully identified. Only then will it be possible to formulate rational and effective means of control.

To this end I want to attempt in this chapter to specify the problems engendered by information systems (computerized as well as manual). The major approaches to these difficulties, especially in the form of data protection legislation, are examined. The question is then raised whether 'personal information' is adequately protected by these measures or whether there is perhaps a more attractive alternative. Except to provide a concrete example, it is not my purpose to catalogue the data banks currently in use in Britain or elsewhere. Other books provide such information with considerable flair.[2] Nor do I propose to offer a detailed account of the various domestic and international data protection measures currently in force. Reference to the Data Protection Act 1984, the enactments in other jurisdictions, and the international regulation of data banks will inevitably be made. But this is done in order to pursue the central question of the protection of the use of 'personal information'.

The concept of 'personal information' in the present context, however, immediately raises a difficulty. When applied to data held in computers 'personal information' normally means information relating to an *identifiable individual*. Thus section 1 (3) of the Data Protection Act 1984 defines 'personal information' as consisting of 'informa-

---

[2] For a useful and deeply disturbing account of the position in Britain, see D. Campbell and S. Connor, *On the Record: Surveillance, Computers and Privacy: The Inside Story* (1986).

tion which relates to a living individual who can be identified from the information'. While this broad notion of 'personal information' obviously incorporates the category of sensitive or intimate information that is the concern of this book, its very breadth neglects the peculiar problems of sensitive data and the special treatment they may call for. But though the Act neglects this species of data; it does not ignore it altogether. Section 2 (3) declares[3] that the Secretary of State may by order provide additional safeguards in relation to personal data consisting of information as to:

(a) the racial origin of the data subject;
(b) his political opinions or religious or other beliefs;
(c) his physical or mental health or his sexual life; or
(d) his criminal convictions.

Recognition is therefore given to sensitive information (or what I have called 'personal information') as constituting a special category of data warranting special protection. But this is inadequate. If the individual is to be effectively protected from the misuse of such information, if (to use the unhappy language widely in vogue) his 'privacy' is to be safeguarded, the *main* purpose of the legislation ought to be controlling and regulating this species of information.

So, for example, the Danish legislation of 1978 identifies three classes of information: 'trivial data', 'private data', and 'sensitive information'. The legislation applies only to 'financial data' or 'private data . . . or any other data on any personal matter that may reasonably be demanded to be withheld from members of the general public'. The phrase 'private data' is a reference to section 264d of the Penal code; examples of this category of data include family relations, sexual relations, and medical information. The phrase 'other data' includes certain personal information which is not, strictly speaking, 'private data'; examples are personal identification numbers (UPIs) and criminal convictions. The Act which deals with the public sector contains (in sections

[3] This is a restatement of Article 6 of the Council of Europe *Convention for the Protection of Individuals with regard to Automatic Processing of Personal Data*, Strasburg, 1981. Despite its title it may be applied by a Convention State to *manual* records (article 3).

2 (3) and 9 (2)) a category of 'extra sensitive information'. This attracts special legal protection; it includes data on race, religious belief, political and sexual matters.[4]

Of course, it is frequently claimed that attempts to formulate an objective category of sensitive or personal information are futile or even impossible. This argument rests on two related assumptions: first, that sensitivity is a function of the context in which the information is used rather than the type of information itself; secondly, that sensitivity is relative to the individual: what I regard as trivial information you may consider highly personal. I have tried, in Chapter 1, to show that this argument is misconceived. I am likely to consider the intimate details of my sex life personal *whatever* the context in which they are being discussed. The fact that you become aware of this information does not transform its *quality*. You are in possession of 'personal information' about me. Should the context change, it is not the nature of the information that changes, but my *attitude* towards its use. I am likely to have considerably different views about your conduct if, instead of my volunteering this information to you, you obtain it by spying on my bedroom.

Nor, it seems to me, is the second assumption a particularly helpful one. Of course, we will disagree about what is 'personal'. It has become a truism that Scandinavians have little objection to disclosing details of their earnings, whereas this is, in Britain, a delicate subject. And within a society similar differences obtain. What does this prove? The same could presumably be said about varying standards of what is defamatory. Yet the law necessarily adopts an objective test: whether the publication complained of lowers the plaintiff in the eyes of right-thinking members of the community. It is no good to claim that my calling you a poltroon is 'defamatory'

---

[4] A similar classification is adopted in the Swedish Data Act 1973 (s. 4) and the Norwegian Personal Data Registers Act 1978 (ss. 6, 9). The French Act (78–17) also employs the concept of 'extra sensitive information' defined to include data 'which directly or indirectly reveals racial origin, political and religious convictions or membership of trade unions'. I am very grateful to Dr John Bing of the Norwegian Research Centre for Computers and Law for drawing my attention to this aspect of the Scandinavian legislation.

unless the reasonable man shares your view. As in the case of defamation, the law cannot protect persons against their subjective idea of wrongdoing. It is both possible and necessary to identify a class of data which warrants control.

The identification of this species of information is not, however, a simple solution to the problems generated by data banks. But, as I hope to demonstrate, it may enable us to address these problems more effectively.

1. The Problems

Information data banks, computerized or otherwise, pose a variety of problems—and hence challenges—to both private and public law. The obtaining, collection, storage, use, disclosure, and transfer of information each generate their own special difficulties. And while these issues are naturally interrelated and even overlapping, to regard them as a unified, undifferentiated 'threat to privacy' or 'Orwellian nightmare' as is frequently done in the popular (and even occasionally the academic) literature, is to invite analytical confusion and hamper their careful and rational resolution.

There would seem to be four associated, but nevertheless relatively discrete kinds of problems that may arise when information is collected and stored. The solution to one kind of problem may not resolve another; nor may certain possible solutions reside at the same institutional or social level: one particular kind of problem may call for a legal response, while an associated problem may not necessarily require a similar response. Even *within* the categories identified below, each of a set of objections may summon up different sorts of approaches, and it is occasionally the case that the possible solution to a particular problem may depend on the *context* in which it arises: the potential misuse of medical information, for example, may give rise to questions that would not necessarily occur in the case of, say, financial data. These observations have only to be expressed in order for them to appear self-evident; yet it is surprising how little attempt has been made to disentangle, distinguish, and define these complex and difficult issues. One ironical consequence of this conceptual confusion, it will be argued, has been the failure to address the central concern in whose name the assault on data banks has ostensibly been waged, namely the protection of 'privacy' or 'personal information'.

The following four major sets of problems (and their often related, sub-sets) may be identified:

1.1. Data-collection problems
    1.1.1. Confidentiality of data
    1.1.2. Consent by the data subject to the use of data
    1.1.3. Knowledge by the data subject of the existence of the data bank
    1.1.4. Knowledge by the data subject of the use to which the data are being put
1.2. Data bank system problems
    1.2.1. Security of the system
    1.2.2. Unauthorized access to the data bank
1.3. Data-usage problems
    1.3.1. Incorrect or erroneous data
    1.3.2. Relevance of data
    1.3.3. Subjective data
    1.3.4. Retention of old data
    1.3.5. Consent of data subject to the use of data
    1.3.6. Knowledge of the data subject of the use to which the data are being put
1.4. Problems relating to the movement of data
    1.4.1. Linkage of data from different data banks
    1.4.2. Centralization or synthesis of data banks
    1.4.3. Transborder data flows

These problems may arise in the case of virtually any data collected and stored in any data bank, though they are most relevant to information about identifiable individuals, and (in respect of the fourth, almost exclusively) to data held in computerized data banks. The present emphasis, is, of course, on 'personal information' defined to include object-ively sensitive or intimate information. The following dis-cussion, while it obviously relates to data about identifiable individuals, focuses upon 'personal information'. And, since most major data banks are computerized (though, to escape legislative control, manual storage of sensitive information may be resorted to!) the principal concern is with such data banks. References to specific computer applications are intended to serve only as examples of the kinds of data banks in existence in most industrialized societies—and their effects on 'personal information'.

1.1. DATA-COLLECTION PROBLEMS

A number of objections may be made to the collection of data itself: Is it necessary? Need the data be in identifiable form? How are the data obtained? Is the information given willingly? Such objections may apply equally to manual systems, but it is widely believed (and feared) that computerization poses more insidious and less controllable threats to individual liberty, and, hence, a further objection is often raised: Need the data be held in a computer? Certain specific questions arise in respect of the collection of data, and, in particular, of 'personal information'.

1.1.1. *Confidentiality of Data*

Individuals may be willing to impart the most sensitive information on the basis that it will not be given to anyone save the recipient or, perhaps, those who have an obvious and explicit interest in receiving it. There is a variety of circumstances in which this is likely to occur. The following discussion is not intended to provide a comprehensive account of these circumstances—this would serve little purpose. But in order to illustrate the extent to which the problems of confidentiality intrude into the workaday activities of most citizens,[5] some of the more significant examples are briefly described. In many cases, the individual himself is unaware that the ostensible confidentiality of 'personal information' about him has been breached, and this poses special difficulties in respect of its protection. Thus, for

---

[5] My survey (described in ch. 4) revealed an unexpectedly high percentage of complaints relating to the misuse of confidential data (computerized or manual) in a general sense: 43.3% of all complaints received by solicitors.

example, job-applicants may have legitimate fears concerning the confidentiality of 'personal information' about them. A consequence of the apparent growth in the 'democratization' in the procedures of employment and promotion is the extent to which information concerning the applicant—revealed either by himself (in documents, in response to questionnaires, or in interview) or, in testimonials, by others—is circulated to persons other than his prospective employer. An applicant for appointment (or promotion) may be taken to have consented to such data (some of which may be sensitive) being known to those who have a direct interest in them. A similar expectation is shared by authors of testimonials or references who will normally assume that the applicant himself will be denied access to such materials. While those who are privy to this information will generally be under an express or implied obligation of confidence, there can be little doubt that there is an increased risk in the authorized disclosure of 'personal information' of which the applicant is unlikely himself to learn. Section 18 (1)(c) of the Employment Protection Act 1975 affords limited protection by providing an exception to the employer's statutory obligation to disclose certain information to employees or to trade union representatives; he need not disclose information which he has received in consequence of the confidence reposed in him by another person.[6]

The clearest instance of the application of the principle of confidentiality described above, arises in the case of the relationship of solicitor and client, a privilege which is recognized by the law[7] in order to 'facilitate the obtaining

[6] See the discussion of access to staff records below. For an admirable discussion of the numerous issues generated by AIDS in the context of employment, see Christopher Southam and Gillian Howard, *AIDS and Employment Law* (1987).

[7] R. Cross, *Evidence*, 6th edn. (1985), 388 ff; Wigmore, *A Treatise on the Anglo-American System of Evidence*, 4th edn., viii, para. 2290; *Lord Asbhurton* v. *Pape* [1913] 2 Ch. 469; *Parry-Jones* v. *Law Society* [1969] 1 Ch. 1; *Alfred Crompton Amusement Machines Ltd.* v. *Commissioners of Customs and Excise (No. 2)* [1974] AC 405; *Waugh* v. *British Railways Board* [1979] 2 All ER 1169; Law Reform Committee 16th Report, 'Privilege in Civil Proceedings', Cmnd. 3472, 1967; *United States* v. *Miller*, 425 US 435 (1976); *Fisher* v. *United States*, 425 US 391 (1976).

and preparation of evidence by a party to an action [or, one might add, defendant in a criminal trial] in support of his case'.[8] This privilege is narrower in scope than the solicitor's general duty of confidence to his client. The former prevents a solicitor from disclosing in any legal proceedings communications between his client and himself without the consent of the client.[9] The latter extends to any confidential information which he has obtained in his capacity as legal adviser: he may not use such information except in the interests of his client.[10] Depending on the circumstances this principle may operate to preclude a solicitor from acting for a former client's opponent.[11]

The special privilege attaching to the solicitor-client relationship is, of course, a function of the position of legal advisers in the administration of justice[12] and its extension to other relationships which rely equally on trust and candour has been resisted: the courts have refused to recognize its application to the relationship with priest,[13] doctor,[14] accountant,[15] banker,[16] or to the claimed right of journalists

---

[8] Law Reform Committee, 'Privilege in Civil Proceedings', para. 20; Wigmore, *Evidence*, para. 2301.

[9] In this respect the position of the solicitor—and barrister (*Carter v. Palmer* (1839) 1 Dr. & W. 722; (affirmed) (1842) 8 Cl. & F. 657, 8 ER 256)—is no different from that of other professional advisers such as accountants, surveyors, or financial advisers who are in a fiduciary relationship with their client: *Brown v. Inland Revenue Commissioners* [1965] AC 244, 265 (per Lord Upjohn).

[10] *Rakusen v. Ellis, Munday & Clarke* [1912] 1 Ch. 831.

[11] As it did in *Davies v. Clough* (1837) 8 Sim. 262; 59 ER 105. Cf. *Re Flint Coppock v. Vaughan* [1885] WN 163; *In re John Holmes (a solicitor)*; *In re The Electric Power Co. Ltd.* (1977) 25 WR 603; *In re Sarah C. Getty Trust* [1985] *The Times*, 28 May.

[12] *D. v. NSPCC* [1977] 1 All ER 589, 606 per Lord Simon.

[13] *Wheeler v. Marchant* (1881) 17 Ch. D. 675, 681; *Pais v. Pais* [1971] P 119, 121.

[14] *R v. Duchess of Kingston* (1776) 20 How. St. Tr. 355, 373, *R v. Gibbons* (1832) 1 Car. & P. 97.

[15] *Chantrey Martin v. Martin* [1953] 2 QB 286; *Clough v. United States*, 425 US 322 (1973).

[16] *Lloyd v. Freshfield* (1826) 2 Car. & P. 325; *Foster v. The Bank of London* (1862) 3 F. & F. 214; *Attorney-General v. Mulholland* [1963] 2 QB 477, 489; *California Bankers Association v. Schultz*, 416 US 21 (1974).

not to disclose their sources.[17]

One of the most pervasive collectors of 'personal informa-tion' in Britain is the National Health Service. Patients routinely divulge the most intimate information to their doctors who, according to the Hippocratic oath,[18] the ethics of the profession,[19] and the law[20] are under a general duty to maintain the confidentiality of such information. This duty is occasionally overridden by the competing public interest in, for example, the protection of others against contagious disease[21] or the administration of justice.[22]

In the particular context of AIDS a number of arguments have been raised to justify the violation of medical confidenti-

[17] *Attorney-General* v. *Mulholland*, see above, at 489; *Attorney-General* v. *Clough* [1963] 1 QB 773.

[18] The modern form is: 'Whatever in connection with my professional practice, or not in connection with it, I see or hear, in the life of men, which ought not to be spoken of abroad, I will not divulge, as reckoning that all such should be kept secret.'

[19] The Handbook of Medical Ethics of the British Medical Association, (1984 edn.), paras. 2.16, 17, and 18, and the General Medical Council's 'Blue Book', *Professional Conduct and Discipline: Fitness to Practice* (1983 edn.), 20, both impose a duty on medical practitioners to maintain the confidentiality of various information which they encounter or of which they are informed in the course of their practice.

[20] *Hunter* v. *Mann* [1974] 1 QB 676, 722. *Furniss* v. *Fitchett* [1958] NZLR 396, 400.

[21] For instance under the National Health Service (Venereal Diseases) Regulations 1974, SI 1974/29; the Public Health (Infectious Diseases) Regulations 1968, SI 1968/1399, as amended. A similar provision requiring disclosure is the Misuse of Drugs (Notification of and Supply to Addicts) Regulations 1973, SI 1973/799.

[22] Under the Administration of Justice Act 1970, ss. 31 and 32, parties (or potential parties) to an action for damages for personal injury or fatal accidents may obtain an order in the High Court compelling a person who is not a party to the proceedings to disclose relevant documents. In *McIvor* v. *Southern Health and Social Services Board* [1978] 2 All ER 625 the House of Lords extended such discovery beyond the applicant's medical advisers, Lord Diplock rejecting the view that this might result in misinterpretation and possible distress by the patient and his relatives. He said that these consequences might be avoided by the assistance of the medical advisers in interpreting the documents, or by covering up 'irrelevant parts of a document' (at 628) so as to prevent possible distress or perhaps to prevent violence. Sections 33 and 34 of the Supreme Court Act 1981 empower the court to order disclosure as it sees fit either to the applicant, his legal or medical advisers.

ality.[23] In particular it is urged that in order to contain the spread of the disease it may be necessary for doctors to report cases of AIDS to public health authorities.[24] The need for accurate information is obviously vital if research into the aetiology and spread of AIDS is to be properly conducted. Yet there is no compelling reason why such data cannot be anonymous. In view of the traumatic consequences that their disclosure will cause, the onus should be on the authorities to demonstrate that the benefits outweigh carriers' rights to have their medical histories kept confidential.[25] Similarly, there is a considerable risk that a person who is rejected for individually screened small group coverage—because he has been tested positive—may find that the insurance company has passed on this information to his employer, resulting in discrimination.

Failure to enforce a strong duty of medical confidentiality is likely to prove counter-productive. Many individuals will simply be deterred from being tested for the virus. This will have the obvious consequence of drying up sources of information and, at the same time, contributing indirectly to the further spread of the disease. Hence the argument in

[23] Though some have argued for an unqualified duty of confidentiality; see Michael H. Kottow, 'Medical Confidentiality: An Intransigent and Absolute Obligation' (1986) 12 J. Med. Ethics 117. Some of the central issues are usefully analysed by the court in X v. Y [1988] 3 All ER 648.

[24] In some jurisdictions AIDS is a notifiable disease and there is therefore a legal duty imposed on doctors to report cases to the authorities. This is not the case in the UK, but the Public Health (Infectious Diseases) Regulations 1985 (SI 85/434) and the Public Health (Control of Diseases) Act 1984 recognize that 'in exceptional circumstances' orders may be made to compel individuals believed to be infected with the AIDS virus to be examined and to enforce the compulsory detention in hospital of AIDS patients.

[25] In the US, California, Wisconsin, and, most recently, the District of Columbia have enacted legislation protecting the confidentiality of those who are tested. The District of Columbia Act restricts the use of the results of all AIDS-related tests for a five-year period. The Act specifically prohibits the use of personal information such as age, marital status, area of residence, occupation, sex, or sexual orientation for the purpose of predicting whether an individual may develop AIDS. California has also passed legislation prohibiting the disclosure of personally identifying research records without the prior written consent of the research subject. Similar legislation, though not as far-reaching, exists in New York.

favour of confidentiality has strong appeal on both deontological grounds—the doctor's duty of confidentiality is
respected—as well as utilitarian grounds—the public is likely
to suffer if confidentiality is breached.

What, it is often asked, should a doctor do when his
patient is tested positive for AIDS and the doctor knows or
suspects that the patient is likely to continue engaging in sex
with his (uninfected) partner? He has failed to persuade the
patient to inform his partner or to desist or even to take
precautions. Should the doctor breach his patient's confidence
and inform the partner? It is difficult to see how an absolute
duty of confidence could be maintained in such circumstances,[26] but it does not follow from this somewhat
extreme—and rather unlikely—example that we should
readily allow exceptions to the general duty. It merely
suggests that, while maintaining a strict duty of confidence,
doctors may, on rare occasions, have to consider breaching it.

The common law is an inadequate tool to protect patients
from the various forms of breach of medical confidence that may befall him, and the most effective means of
striking a fair balance between the rights of AIDS sufferers,
on the one hand, and the community, on the other, is the
enactment of carefully drafted legislation.[27] Such legislation
should, at the very least, protect the confidentiality of AIDS
testing and research. This would be subject, of course, to
certain limited exceptions such as the disclosure of the results
of tests to doctors and medical personnel directly responsible
for treating the patient, or under a court order. It should be
clearly provided that the details of positive test results should
exclude information relating to the identity of the subject,

---

[26] Though it has been argued that even in this sort of case the duty
should not be breached for it is 'self-defeating': 'if physicians become
known as confidence-violators, problem-ridden patients will try to lie,
accommodate facts to their advantage or, if this does not work, avoid
physicians altogether . . . It is better to treat and advise the syphilitic
husband without informing the wife than not to have him come at all for
fear of undesired revelations.' Kottow, 'Medical Confidentiality', 119–20.
See Margaret Brazier, *Medicine, Patients and the Law* (1987) 36 ff.

[27] See Peter J. Nanula 'Protecting Confidentiality in the Effort to
Control AIDS' (1986) 24 Harv. J. on Legis. 315–49; Southam and
Howard, *AIDS and Employment Law, passim.*

and that employers and insurance companies should not be permitted to require anyone to reveal the results of an AIDS test. Further legislation is necessary to prohibit discrimination on the grounds merely that an individual is an AIDS sufferer.

In *Gillick* v. *West Norfolk and Wisbech Area Health Authority and the DHSS*[28] the House of Lords held, by a majority, that parental rights were not necessarily infringed where a doctor, in exceptional circumstances, gave contraceptive advice and treatment to a girl under 16 without her parents' knowledge or consent. The judgment which has become something of a *cause célèbre*, turned in part on the confidential relationship between doctor and patient, Lord Fraser declaring that 'to abandon the principle of confidentiality for contraceptive advice to girls under 16 might cause some not to seek professional advice at all, thus exposing them to "the immediate risks of pregnancy and sexually transmitted diseases" '.[29]

The collection, storage, and transfer of sensitive medical information are good examples of the difficulties encountered in ordinary manually recorded systems. For, even though there is an increasing number of computerized medical data banks in the United Kingdom the risk of misuse of information arises quite independently of computerization. Thus, for example, the (possibly inevitable) bureaucratization of the National Health Service has resulted in a growing number of non-medical personnel having access to sensitive information. And, unless a duty of confidence is imposed on them contractually, such individuals may disclose this information with impunity.[30]

Medical data transferred within the NHS assume three main forms.[31] The first type consists in medical records used

[28] [1986] AC 112.
[29] Phrase from DHSS circular. Following *Gillick* the Medical Council advised general practitioners that the decision does not guarantee confidentiality for children whom the doctor believes to be inadequately mature to give consent. Cf. (1987) 17 Family Law 101.
[30] This fact was acknowledged by the British Medical Association in its evidence to the Younger Committee (Younger, para. 366) and by the Royal College of Psychiatrists in its evidence to the Lindop Committee (Lindop, para. 7.10).
[31] See Campbell and Connor, *On the Record*, 126–7.

in hospitals and primary health care by general practitioners. With the apparent exception of Exeter,[32] these data are manually recorded and transferred. The second type consists of registers maintained to monitor community health developments such as the Cancer Registration Scheme, the control of infectious diseases, and the recording and surveillance of child health. Thirdly there is administrative information on hospital bed occupancy and so on.

All Regional Health Authorities' records are computerized; the largest is the. hospital activity analysis system which contains more than five million records of patients. Much of these data are anonymous and hence the system is not required to be notified to the Data Protection Registrar under the 1984 Act. There is, however, a risk that information relating to identified patients may be linked to the statistical data for epidemiological purposes.[33] Following recommendations of the Korner Committee,[34] all hospitals and Area Health Authorities will in 1988 be required to collect standard items of information on all patients. It proposed computerizing data on women attending family planning clinics (including details of contraception) and sexual-contact tracing services operated by sexually transmitted disease (STD) clinics. While these data are to be anonymous, in the case of STD clinics the identity of patients and their contacts is obviously an important instrument in attempting to control the spread, in particular, of AIDS.

The confidentiality of medical records may be protected by the action for breach of confidence (see below) for should a doctor, hospital or other holder of medical information disclose it without the patient's consent to a party who has no legitimate interest in receiving it,[35] an action would lie. But

---

[32] Its system 'suppresses' data of special sensitivity. This means that they appear on the screen only when a password is used. The principal object appears to be to control access to subjective data recorded by doctors about their patients.

[33] Campbell and Connor, *On the Record*, 127.

[34] *Steering Group on Health Services Information*, First Report, HMSO, 1982.

[35] Another difficulty is that the range of persons who might be said to fall into this category continues to expand: 'Medical confidentiality has become increasingly diluted by the development of the principle of

this is a hollow remedy, not only because the plaintiff will not generally know that the information has been disclosed, but also because even if he does know, the damage will have been done. His objection would be to any unauthorized disclosure, and an injunction is likely to be the most effective remedy— but this, of course, presupposes that he is aware that a disclosure is about to take place, an unlikely eventuality. (An injunction may, of course, enable him to prevent the information—if he is aware of its disclosure—being given wider circulation.) Even if he is awarded damages for distress and embarrassment, it is improbable that this will satisfy a plaintiff whose objection is to the disclosure itself.

Under the Data Protection Act 1984 (considered below) where the information is held in a computer, sections 22 and 23 provide that a court may award compension for any 'distress' suffered by the data subject as a result of the 'inaccuracy of the data' (s. 22) or the loss, unauthorized destruction or disclosure of or access to the data (s. 23). Again, such compensation is unlikely to be of much use once the sensitive information has been disclosed. Similarly, the disclosure of sensitive medical facts (say, that the patient is suffering from AIDS) may give rise to a cause of action for defamation, though since the information is likely to be true, the plaintiff may be met by the defence of justification, or if it has been transferred to an agency with an interest in receiving it, with the defence of privilege.

It is sometimes argued that some of these difficulties might be met by granting the patient a legal right of access to his medical file. It is hard to see how this would assist—except perhaps to avoid errors being recorded in the file, a fairly unlikely possibility in the context of medical information. The general question of access to data is considered below.

The use of sensitive financial information[36] held by

"extended confidence": medical records may be seen not only by the patient's doctors but also by the health care team, secretaries, administrators and in some cases by social workers', G. Dworkin, 'Access to Medical Records—Discovery, Confidentiality and Privacy' (1979) 42 MLR 88, 90.

[36] The Younger Committee found that 78% of those questioned objected to information concerning their income being available to anyone who sought it: Younger, para. 254 and app. E. See the discussion of 'personal information' in ch. 1 above.

bankers[37] is exemplified by the leading decision of the Court of Appeal in *Tournier* v. *National Provincial and Union Bank of England*.[38] T's account with the N Bank was overdrawn. He agreed with N to seek to reduce his overdraft, but failed to do so. X, another of N's customers, drew a cheque in T's favour, which T endorsed to Y. On receiving the cheque for payment, N learned from Y's bank that Y was a bookmaker. N subsequently informed T's employers that T had endorsed X's cheque to a bookmaker, whereupon T's contract of employment was terminated. The majority of the Court of Appeal (Bankes and Atkin L JJ)[39] held that disclosure of this information, since it was acquired by N in their 'character as the plaintiff's banker',[40] was in breach of the bank's obligation of confidence. All three members of the Court accepted that no information *received from the customer himself, from the state of his account, and from the transactions that go through his account or securities, if any, given in respect of the account* could be disclosed by the bank, save under compulsion of law.[41] The Court's power to order disclosure was described by Lord Widgery CJ[42] as 'a

[37] Another important repository of financial information is the credit reference bureau. The Lindop Committee stated that 'the growing number of agencies which sell information and the free circulation of information firms in the consumer credit industry bring greater risk that information will become available to persons other than credit grantors' (Lindop, para. 13.33). It has occurred that on the liquidation of a credit agency its files were offered for sale.

[38] [1924] 1 KB 461.

[39] Scrutton LJ preferred the view that since the identity of the bookmaker was obtained from X's account, rather than from T's, any complaint against N could be brought by X not T.

[40] At 474 per Bankes LJ.

[41] There are several legislative provisions which allow the banker to disclose information concerning bank records. Section 7 of the Bankers' Book Evidence Act 1879, for instance, provides that on the application of a party to legal proceedings a court may order that the applicant be at liberty to inspect and take copies of any entries in a banker's book for the purpose of such proceedings. Similar provisions are to be found in, e.g., Schedule 6 to the Finance Act 1976. Disclosure may also be permitted in the public interest, for the protection of the banker's own interests (a good example is *Sunderland* v. *Barclays Bank Ltd.* (1938) *The Times*, 25 Nov.), or with the customer's express or implied consent (see below).

[42] In *Williams* v. *Summerfield* [1972] 2 QB 513, 518.

very serious interferences with the liberty of the subject' and 'a gross invasion of privacy'.[43]

Ethical evaluations of the collection by social scientists of what are often extremely intimate facts about their 'subjects' seek to strike a balance between the individual's interest in the anonymity and confidentiality of information, on the one hand, and 'the needs of the search for knowledge',[44] on the other. But this is not a judgment in which the social scientist can reasonably be expected to be entirely dispassionate; where his research calls for this kind of information to be published, he is likely to be peculiarly ill-suited to resolving the problem.[45] The Lindop Committee, though it regarded as satisfactory the codes of practice adopted by bodies such as the British Sociological Association and the Medical Research Council, nevertheless recommended that all research workers be subject to the Codes of Practice (having the force of law) which it envisaged would be drafted by the Data Protection Authority. This approach was, of course, rejected by the Government and though the Registrar is to 'encourage' the dissemination of voluntary codes of practice prepared by data users under the Data Protection Act 1984, (section 36 (4)) they will not be legally binding on data users, let alone social researchers whose information is, in any event, often likely to be manually collected and stored.

[43] The Inspectors of Taxes are vested with far-reaching powers under ss. 13, 17, 24, and 26 of the Taxes Management Act 1970 to obtain information from banks in respect of customers' accounts.

[44] J. A. Barnes, *Who Should Know What? Social Science, Privacy and Ethics* (1979) 13. Professor Barnes, himself an eminent social scientist, concedes that the acquisition of personal data by researchers 'constitutes a much greater invasion of privacy' than the Census (91).

[45] In an Australian decision (*Foster v. Mountford and Rigby Ltd* (1976), 14 Austr. LR 71) an anthropologist who had collected data concerning the customs and rites of an aboriginal tribe was, 35 years later, enjoined from publishing a book which contained this information. The court held that an obligation of confidence was owed to the members of the tribe who argued that the publication of the book would severely harm their tribal lives, for uninitiated or female members of the tribe would discover details that were regarded by the tribe as secret. Though this case does not, strictly speaking, concern 'personal information' in the sense proposed here, it suggests (apart from the flexibility of the action for breach of confidence, already considered in ch. 3) that this kind of (fairly sensitive) evaluation is best made by a disinterested party.

Disquiet is periodically voiced concerning the confidentiality of sensitive information obtained by the Census. In particular, the adequacy of the measures used by the Office for Population Census and Surveys to protect the anonymity of individuals has been questioned. In its White Papers *Computers and Privacy*[46] the Government acknowledged the need for 'special precautions against risks for the privacy of the individual, especially as the data may be very sensitive indeed'.[47] One means of protecting anonymity is the use of 'randomised response techniques' which was recommended by the Lindop Committee[48] in view particularly of the availability on magnetic tape of individual records—as is the case with the General Household Survey.[49] Concern is also expressed that information obtained in the Census might be made available to other bodies (for example, 'in the interest of national security') though there is little evidence that disclosures of this kind have actually taken place, not that such evidence would be easily obtained.[50] Nor does the Data Protection Act provide any special protection for Census data.

1.1.2. *Consent by the Data Subejct to the Use of the Data*

An associated problem concerns data which, though obtained or collected for one purpose, are used for another. This is normally a data-usage problem (and is therefore considered in 3 (e) below), but may arise at the collection stage as well since information may willingly be given on the understanding

[46] See above, para. 21.

[47] In response to criticism that information obtained from a proposed question concerning the race of respondents was susceptible to misuse, the question was dropped from the 1981 Census.

[48] Lindop, para. 26.09.

[49] The fear that complete anonymity might not be maintained is aggravated by the suggestion in the 1975 White Paper on the Census that information is to be compiled for areas smaller than local authorities, thus facilitating easier identification of respondents.

[50] From time to time assurances have been given by ministers concerning the absolute confidentiality of the data obtained in the Census, and, in particular, that 'information about individual people or families will under no circumstances be released to any authority outside the Census organisation itself' (Mr William Whitelaw MP, Leader of the House, 815 *Hansard*, cols. 814–21 (19 Apr. 1971) HC).

that it is to be used for a specific purpose only. Consent may therefore extend only to such use; had the data subject been informed that the data were to be disclosed or transferred to some other agency, his original consent to their collection might have been withheld.

1.1.3. *Knowledge by the Data Subject of the Existence of the Data Bank*

With a rapid rise in the number of computer applications, it is hardly surprising that individuals may actually be ignorant of the very existence of certain data banks. The Data Protection Act, broadly in line with the proposals of the Lindop Committee,[51] provides for a register of computer bureaux dealing with personal data to be available for public inspection (see below).

1.1.4. *Knowledge by the Data Subject of the Use to which the Data is Being Put*

An individual cannot be expected to be consenting to uses of data he supplies if he is unaware of what these uses are. The Government's White Paper, *Computers and Privacy*[52] recognized that 'people asked to provide information should have a right to know for what purposes it will be used, and who is likely to have access to it'.[53] Some recognition is given to this general requirement in two of the Principles adopted by the Data Protection Act (see below) in terms similar to those used in the 1981 Council of Europe Convention and the 1980 Guidelines of the Organization for Economic Co-operation and Development (OECD) which are considered below.

[51] The principle, which was supported in the White Paper, *Computers and Privacy*, para. 34, met certain resistance from data users in their evidence to the Lindop Committee who were concerned about the practicalities and cost of the idea (Lindop, paras. 5.19 and 5.22; see too, paras. 5.56–8). It was also argued that the register might itself be 'a potential threat to data privacy' for it would provide the snooper with a 'major new work of reference' (ibid. para. 5.21) or a threat to their commercial secrets (ibid. para. 5.20).   [52] Para. 5.21.

[53] The British Computer Society proposed that data subjects be told whether the questions asked were compulsory, and the consequences to them if they declined to answer them (*Computers and Privacy*, para. 5.23).

1.2. DATA BANK SYSTEM PROBLEMS

The literature is replete with descriptions of unauthorized access to computer data banks being obtained by so-called 'hackers' who, through the application of ingenious devices, are able to 'crack the code' and 'gain entry' to systems containing highly sensitive data. Such methods may have an additional attraction, for 'the volume of data and the opportunities for selecting and correlating them may be much greater, and in some cases the intruder may be able to break into the system without risk to himself via a remote terminal or even by telephone'.[54] On the other hand, it may be argued that since both ingenuity and expertise are required in order to achieve these feats, computerized systems are actually more secure than their manual counterparts, access to which normally involves only the conventional skills of burglary or snooping. The problems connected with maintaining the integrity of computer data banks have arisen in the following two closely related forms.

1.2.1. *Security of the System*

Though a number of computer-based measures have been developed to protect the security of data banks (see below), public concern is likely to be allayed only by the rigid and demonstrable enforcement of such measures to data users as well as the provision of the right to compensation for the consequences of breaches of security. Principle 8 of the Data Protection Act 1984, based on article 7 of the Council of Europe Convention and Paragraph 11 of the OECD Guidelines, (discussed below) provides for the taking of 'appropriate security measures'.

1.2.1. *Unauthorized Access to the Data Bank*

The point at which the cost of obtaining data exceeds its value to the intruder will in some cases be reached sooner in

---

[54] Lindop, para. 5.10.

respect of computerized systems than manual ones.[55] A simple deterrent may therefore exist in the form of the cost of obtaining unauthorized access. But the potential for obtaining a large quantity of personal data from a centralized computer bank, once access has been obtained, is likely to produce a more attractive cost–benefit calculation, indeed, 'the computer-age snooper's cost per unit of dirt actually may be lower for poaching electronically stored records than it is for pilfering paper files.'[56]

1.3. DATA-USAGE PROBLEMS

Once information is stored, a number of related problems arise in respect of the use to which the information is put or sought to be put. At least six principal problems may be identified as follows.

1.3.1. *Incorrect or Erroneous Data*

While the extent to which the use of computers produces errors is often exaggerated,[57] and there is some evidence to suggest that manually held data may actually be more susceptible to mistakes than their computerized counter-

---

[55] Based on a survey of 55 private and public data banks, Westin and Baker found, *inter alia*, that most of them 'have not been convinced that unauthorised persons want their information about people badly enough to try and get it without permission. As a result, the information security measures . . . have, thus far, been distinctly minimal' (*Data Banks in a Free Society* (1972), 315). Cf. Peterson and Turn, 'Systems Implications of Information Policy' (1967) 30 *AFIPS Conference Proceedings*; Turn, *Privacy and Security in Personal Information Databank Systems* (1974). See below.

[56] A. Miller, *The Assault on Privacy* (1971), 46–7. R. C. Goldstein, *The Cost of Privacy* (1975).

[57] In their survey of 55 data banks, Westin and Baker concluded: 'Our two principal findings about the accuracy of records can be summarised as follows: computerisation has in many cases reduced omissions from standardised records and increased logical consistency and/or timeliness of the records that are converted to machine-readable form; many computerised operations keep their records more accurate in these respects by software and personnel supervision. But human and machine errors are still possible and present in computerised systems, with some kinds of mistakes capable of affecting very large numbers of individual records. Even when these mistakes are noticed, very important damage may have been

parts,[58] there is nevertheless a real prospect of erroneous computerized data being circulated on a scale far larger than is likely in the case of manual records.

1.3.2. *Relevance of Data*

A particularly insidious difficulty arises where data collected for one purpose are used for another. Not only may such data have been initially collected in circumstances in which their relevance to the stated purpose of their collection is questionable (see above): for instance, a prospective employee or applicant for credit may be asked questions (about his political, sexual, or religious attitudes or activities) the answers to which have no bearing whatever on his suitability for the appointment or his creditworthiness. But (unlike these sorts of cases) the individual may in other contexts have no knowledge that the data even exist. Thus students have, on 'occupying' university administration offices, found files describing the political and sexual behaviour of students[59]— done in the elapsed time to the rights and interests of those persons affected. And computerisation has not affected the substantive correctness of the facts about people collected at the source' (*Data Banks in a Free Society*, 302).

[58] For instance, according to a Canadian report, the disclosure of the contents of *manual* files prior to their automatic processing revealed that out of 406 respondents 301 had discovered mistakes in their manual files, while only 25 out of 480 respondents reported similar errors in their computerized systems. Report of the Task Force established by the Canadian Department of Commerce and Department of Justice (1972) app. 213, quoted by C. Tapper, *Computers and the Law*, 121. There is clearly a potential for error on a wider scale where computer data banks are concerned. A program error may, for instance, be repeated in a large number of files, and many of these may pass undetected. This may result in an individual suffering, say, refusal of credit, in consequence of a confusion between himself and someone who has a similar name or who previously occupied his present address. The prospect of such a problem arising may, of course, be considerably reduced by permitting the data subject access to his file in order that such errors might be corrected (see below).

[59] Such files were obtained during 'sit-ins' at the University of East Anglia in 1971 (when 'cohabitation memos' were found), and the University of Exeter in 1977. In 1970 at Warwick University students came upon correspondence between the university and the schools attended by prospective students, which suggested that the university was interested in several factors other than those that could legitimately be regarded as pertaining to aptitude for higher education.

matters which, in the admission of the Committee of Vice-Chancellors, were 'not the business of a university'.[60]

1.3.3. *Subjective Data*

The almost inevitable subjectivity that attends assessments of individual ability renders much information relating, in particular, to employees,[61] peculiarly vulnerable to abuse. The career of an individual could be permanently blighted as a result of an opinion committed to his file by a superior who may be moved by malice. But the use of opinion (rather than 'fact': though this is not always a simple distinction) has recently assumed an even more disturbing dimension in its institutional application by the police and security service. The Police National Computer (PNC)[62] is routinely fed subjective data in respect of suspected criminals.[63] In the absence of the most rigorous supervision and regulation, this practice represents a potentially sinister feature of police control. In the view of the Lindop Committee, 'The linking of factual personal information about an identifiable individual with speculative data about criminal activity could pose a grave threat to that individual's interest.'[64]

What is of particular concern to civil libertarians is the fact that the Data Protection Act exempts the PNC from the controls over sensitive data that apply to other systems. Thus it may with impunity collect information about racial origin, political views, health, sex life, and criminal convictions. Personal information about witnesses and victims will now

---

[60] Following the Warwick incident the Committee issued a declaration stating that 'the political opinions and affiliations of students and staff are not the business of a university' (Younger, para. 343).

[61] In their evidence to the Lindop Committee, the NCB, ICI, and Esso all admitted that they stored subjective data on their employees: Lindop, para. 12.20.

[62] The PNC holds 5 major files consisting of some 5 million records: the index to national records in the Criminal Records Office (CRO), a file of vehicle-owners, a file of stolen and suspect vehicles, an index to the national fingerprint collection, and a file of missing or wanted persons. The data banks are used more than 70 million times a year.

[63] *TechnoCop: New Police Technologies*, British Society for Social Responsibility in Science (1985) 25–39; Campbell and Conner, *On the Record*, ch. 8   [64] Lindop, para. 8.16.

be stored as well. According to Campbell and Connor[65] eleven million people are checked against the PNC annually, most of them by police officers on the street. Nineteen million vehicles are checked against the PNC every year; almost all of these checks are on vehicles which are neither stolen nor wanted.

The potential for abuse of the system—which is growing at an alarming rate—is enormous.

1.3.4. *Retention of Old Data*

While it may be sensible, in the case of certain statistical data, to retain such information for a fairly considerable length of time,[66] the passage of years renders much information misleading or incorrect. Failure to update or destroy old data can impose upon an individual the burden of facts which have long ceased to be true or, at any rate, relevant to his present circumstances.[67]

1.3.5. *Consent of the Data Subject to Use of Data*

The individual, it was pointed out above, while he may at the collection stage readily consent to the giving of information

[65] *On the Record*, 227–8

[66] Schools are called upon to provide academic records for former pupils many years after they have left the school. And institutions of further or higher education may be expected to provide transcripts of academic results for former students several years after they have completed their studies. Concern has, however, been expressed in respect of the maintenance for long periods of information about students that extends beyond the exclusively academic; the Further Education Statistical Record contains detailed records relating to all students who enrol at maintained institutions of further and higher education which is sent to the Department of Education and Science. The Lindop Committee commented: 'The fact that this is a nationally centralised system held on a computer and that it appears to be likely to continue into the future raises the possibility, which has worried some of our witnesses, that this scheme could be the beginning of a cradle-to-grave educational record on computer for a large part of the whole population' (Lindop, para. 11.20).

[67] An individual may be refused credit as a result of his name appearing on a County Court register of judgment debtors—even though he has paid the debt. The Lord Chancellor's Office proposed some years ago that names be automatically removed on payment of the debt instead of awaiting the subject's application and payment of a fee under s. 101 of the County Courts Act 1959 (now s. 73) of the County Courts Act 1984). This does not appear to have been adopted.

of the most sensitive kind, may be less willing to impart such data if he is aware that there exists some other purpose to which they could be put. Where the data are already on file it becomes a relatively simple matter to transfer them to another data bank. Thus a consumer applying for credit may disclose personal data which are subsequently passed on to a credit reference bureau without his consent.[68] Or medical information relating to an identifiable individual may be transferred for research or other purposes without the individual's consent.[69]

In certain cases active steps may be taken to acquire information that an individual would not himself normally disclose. Thus a creditor who is unable to obtain information concerning his debtor's financial position directly from the latter, may request his banker to seek a reference from his debtor's banker—without the debtor's consent, a practice disparaged by the Younger Committee,[70] and which appears to rest on dubious authority.[71]

1.3.6. *Knowledge of the Data Subject of the Use to which the Data are Being Put*

Closely connected to the problem of consent is the problem of knowledge: a data subject who is unaware of the use to

[68] The Lindop Committee recommended that the regulations governing credit grantors should require that the consumer's consent is obtained prior to the transfer of this information: Lindop, para. 13.37. This does not seem to have happened. The cost of securing the data subject's consent, referred to by witnesses to the Committee (para. 5.30), is clearly a significant factor.

[69] For example, when registering a birth a number of questions of an intimate nature are asked (including the parents' race, country of origin, and 'home conditions'). How many parents know or consent to the fact that these data are stored in the computers of the National Standard Register and Recall System?

[70] 'It recommended that banks should make clear to all customers, existing or prospective, the existence and manner of operation of their reference system, and give them the opportunity either to grant a standing authority for the provision of references or to require the bank to seek their consent on every occasion' (Younger, para. 307).

[71] According to Chorley, *Law of Banking*, 6th edn. (1974), 248 the practice 'would appear to be a breach of the duty which the banker owes to his customer of treating the account as confidential'. See the discussion of *Tournier* and *Sunderland* above.

which data concerning him are being put can hardly consent to such use. In its White Paper, *Computers and Privacy*, the Government expressed the view that the public be informed not only of the existence and purpose of information systems, but the categories of data which they handle, what they do with data, and which interests have access to them: 'People asked to provide information should have a right to know for what purpose it will be used, and who is likely to have access to it.'[72] This proposal has found its way (in a less assertive form) into the principles incorporated into the Data Protection Act 1984, discussed below.

1.4. PROBLEMS RELATING TO THE MOVEMENT OF DATA

1.4.1. *Linkage of Data from Different Data Bases*

Reciprocal or one-way linkage between data banks combines many of the problems associated with both the collection and the use of information. The simplicity, speed, and economy of linking data banks are powerful arguments in support of its transfer—whether or not the subject consents to or even knows about such movement.[73]

1.4.2. *Centralization or Synthesis of Data Banks*

Foremost amongst the fears of those who prognosticate the future of life with (or under) computers is that of a large centralized data bank which, facilitated by a universal personal identifier (or UPI), is able to synthesize data from a variety of sources. These fears are not easily allayed by assurances from the Government that no such plan is under

---

[72] Para. 34.

[73] Details of licensed motor-vehicles are, for example, transferred automatically by the Driver and Vehicle Licensing Centre to the Police National Computer and, on request, to the Board of Inland Revenue. As mentioned above, credit grantors transfer data obtained from consumers to credit reference bureaux, without the consent or knowledge of the consumer.

consideration.[74] The process may be taking place in a gradual, almost imperceptible manner. The inevitable drift toward government centralization is evident particularly in the case of the merging of the data banks of the DHSS and the Departments of Inland Revenue and Employment. It has been suggested[75] that by the year 2000 there will, in effect, be a complete integration of these computer operations. Moreover, there is a disturbing trend toward the granting the Inland Revenue and perhaps other government departments the power to gain access to the centralized DHSS network. It is already the case that the police and MI5 use two major national data banks—the NHS Central Register at Southport and Edinburgh and the DHSS National Insurance General Index near Newcastle-upon-Tyne—as central population registers through which individuals are traced.[76]

1.4.3. *Transborder Data Flow*

A growing international trade in information and data-processing services ensures that data are no longer confined within national borders. They are typically transferred (by satellite, microwave, or landline) from the originating computer in country A to the 'host' computer in country B where

[74] In its White Paper Supplement, *Computers: Safeguards for Privacy*, the Government alluded to the dangers of centralized data banks and declared that it had no plans to introduce one (Cmnd. 6354, 1975). The Lindop Committee was nevertheless concerned that, despite the difficulty and cost of this development, growing computerization of records and the use of National Health Service numbers might encourage a 'drift' in this direction, as has occurred in some countries. It concluded: 'As regards the implications for privacy, there can be no doubt that the UPI would greatly reduce the British citizen's traditional anonymity, because his identity number would remain with him for life and be used in most transactions, making it easier in principle for the state to trace his change of name and address' (Lindop, para. 29.19).

[75] Campbell and Connor, *On the Record*, 86. 'Whatever may be omitted from a national register, however, there will by the year 2000 be a government central computer network recording the name and number, current address, date of birth, sex, identity number, family relationships and many other particulars of virtually the entire population. Linked to the network will be at least 60,000 VDU terminals, to which 200,000 civil servants may have access. Most of these terminals will be installed by 1990' (88).   [76] Ibid. 87.

they are stored or processed and then either returned to the originating computer or redistributed to a computer in country C (and/or D, E, etc.).[77] While most data transferred tends to be of a technical nature, personal data may also be moved to a so-called 'data haven'—a country which has little or no control over data banks, thereby evading regulation in the originating country.[78] It is plain that the only effective means of controlling transborder data flow is through international convention (see below).

2. The Remedies

Both the domestic and the international responses to the general problems identified above have, in large part, been confined to the formulation of rules and principles which, while they address the broad question of data collection, usage, and movement, do not adequately regulate the specific applications in which 'personal information' is concerned.

Sensitive information raises specific issues which need to be specifically addressed. The conventional solution in most countries (including, most recently, Britain) has been to enact legislation which attempts to establish a framework for the use of data—widely defined to include what is here called 'personal information'—in both the public and private sectors. Though the ostensible objective of these statutes is normally to protect the individual's 'privacy', the very information which might be thought to warrant 'protection' in the name of 'privacy' receives little special or explicit attention. Moreover, in seeking to resolve the frequently competing interests of national security, industry, record-

---

[77] The movement may assume complex proportions which may be described as a 'multinational data network' in which data flows 'are characterised by multiple-user, multiple-host interactions, where information and processing can be centralized, distributed or both' (Novotny, 'Transborder Data Flow Regulation: Technical Issues of Legal Concern' (1981) 3 Computer Law J. 1095, 1112, quoted in C. J. Millard, *Legal Protection of Computer Programs and Data* (1985), 210.

[78] Gassman, 'Privacy Implications of Transborder Data Flows: Outlook for the 1980's' in L. J. Hoffman (ed.) *Computers and Privacy in the Next Decade* (1980), 114.

keeping, police investigation, and the individual, these statutes tend to envelop the special problems of sensitive or intimate information in their broad sweep of 'data protection'.

It will be argued that if it is genuinely intended to control or regulate the use of 'personal information', the present approach exhibited in the legislation of several countries and the associated international conventions is likely to prove inadequate. There are, it is submitted, two methods of achieving this objective. The first is to prohibit the storage of 'personal information' altogether. This radical proposal has, for a number of reasons, little prospect of adoption in legislative form. The second suggestion, which is less far-reaching, is explored below: to accord special treatment to 'personal information'.

While the principal purpose of this discussion is to examine the extent to which sensitive data are (and might be) effectively protected against misuse, some of the problems already identified obviously occur to a greater or lesser extent, in respect of data which are non-personal. In order to investigate the methods by which it is sought to resolve these problems—especially in Britain—it will be necessary briefly to consider the relevant provisions of the Data Protection Act 1984. But, as pointed out above, a comprehensive analysis of the Act would be out of place here. Nor would it be particularly useful in this context to discuss in detail the bills preceding the enactment of the Data Protection Act 1984 or, except where they are directly relevant, the recommendations of the Younger and Lindop Committees in 1972 and 1978 respectively. (See Chapter 2.)

2.1. INTERNATIONAL INSTRUMENTS

A useful starting-point is the approach adopted in the two principal (and most directly relevant) international instruments already referred to: the *Guidelines on the Protection of Privacy and Transborder Flows of Personal Information* (hereafter called the *Guidelines*) adopted by the Council of the OECD on 23 September 1980, and the *Convention for* the *Protection of Individuals with regard to Automatic Processing of Personal Data* (hereafter called the *Convention*) drafted by the Committee of Ministers of the Council of Europe, which was opened for signature on 28 January 1981.

The *Guidelines*[79] seek to attain four main objectives: to protect the 'privacy' of personal data, to foster the free flow of information, to avoid unjustified restrictions on this free flow caused by domestic 'privacy' legislation, and to harmonize the provisions of various domestic laws. They are intended to form the 'minimum standards' of legislation in OECD countries and have been followed by a Declaration on Transborder Data Flows which was adopted by OECD Member States on 11 April 1985 and which commits them to the introduction of general regulation of the transborder movement of data.

The *Convention*[80] seeks to 'secure in the territory of each Party for every individual . . . respect for his rights and fundamental freedoms, and in particular his right to privacy, with regard to automatic processing of personal data relating to him ("data protection")' (article 1).[81] The relevant principles contained in these documents are referred to below.

[79] The *Guidelines* are part of the Recommendations made by an expert committee of the OECD. They are reproduced in the Government's White Paper of April 1982 (Cmnd. 8539).

[80] The Committee of Ministers of the Council of Europe, following a Recommendation of the Parliamentary Assembly of the Council, adopted two Resolutions in 1973 and 1974 in respect of electronic data processing systems in the private and public sectors and their effect on the 'privacy' of individuals: *Protection of the Privacy of Individuals vis-à-vis Electronic Data Banks in the Private Sector*, Resolution (73) 22 of 26 Sept. 1973; *Protection of the Privacy of Individuals vis-à-vis Electronic Data in the Public Sector*, Resolution (74) 29 of 20 Sept. 1974. The legislation of several Member States (Sweden: Data Act 1973; West Germany: Federal Data Protection Act 1977; Australia: Data Protection Act 1978; Denmark: Private Registers, etc. Act 1978, Public Authorities' Registers Act 1978; France: Act 78–17; Norway: Personal Data Registers Act 1978; Luxemburg: Nominal Data Processing Act 1979) incorporates the principles contained in these resolutions. On 23 Jan. 1981 the Committee adopted Recommendation (R81)1) concerning Regulations for automated medical data banks.

[81] The Convention has been signed by the United Kingdom, West Germany, Italy, Spain, Portugal, Austria, Luxemburg, Belgium, Norway, Denmark, Greece, Iceland, Turkey.

2.2. DATA PROTECTION PRINCIPLES

The general principles to be found in the domestic legislation of most industrialized states (including Britain) mirrors, to a large extent, those expressed in the Council of Europe *Convention*[82] and the OECD *Guidelines*:

1. *Collection limitation principle.* There should be limits to the collection of personal data and any such data should be obtained by lawful and fair means and, where appropriate, with the knowledge or consent of the data subject.

2. *Data quality principle.* Personal data should be relevant to the purposes for which they are to be used, and, to the extent necessary for those purposes, should be accurate, complete, and kept up-to-date.

3. *Purpose specification principle.* The purpose for which personal data are collected should be specified not later than at the time of data collection and the subsequent use limited to the fulfilment of those purposes or such others as are not incompatible with those purposes and as are specified on each occasion of change of purpose.

4. *Use limitation principle.* Personal data should not be disclosed, made available or otherwise used for purposes other than those specified in accordance with the *Guidelines*[83] except: (a) with the consent of the data subject; or (b) by the authority of law.

5. *Security safeguards principle.* Personal data should be protected by reasonable security safeguards against such risks as loss or unauthorized access, destruction, use, modification, or disclosure of data.

6. *Openness principle.* There should be a general policy of openness about development, practices, and policies with respect to personal data. Means should be readily available of

---

[82] Article 5 provides that personal data undergoing automatic processing shall be: (a) obtained and processed fairly and lawfully; (b) stored for specified and legitimate purposes; (c) adequate, relevant, and not excessive in relation to the purposes for which they are stored; (d) accurate and, where necessary, kept up-to-date; (e) preserved in a form which permits identification of the data subjects for no longer than is required for the purpose for which those data are stored.   [83] Para. 9.

establishing the existence and nature of personal data, and the main purpose of their use, as well as the identity and usual residence of the data controller.

7. *Individual participation principle.* An individual should have the right: (a) to obtain from a data controller, or otherwise, confirmation of whether or not the data controller has data relating to him; (b) to have communicated to him, data relating to him (i) within a reasonable time; (ii) at a charge, if any, that is not excessive; (iii) in a reasonable manner; and (iv) in a form that is readily intelligible to him; (c) to be given reasons if a request made under subparagraphs (a) and (b) is denied, and to be able to challenge such denial; and (d) to challenge data relating to him and, if the challenge is successful, to have the data erased, rectified, completed or amended.

8. *Accountability principle.* A data controller should be accountable for complying with measures which give effect to the principles stated above.

The Data Protection Act contains[84] the following 'data protection principles':

---

[84] Schedule 1, Para. 4. Other formulations exist which have influenced the draftsman here and abroad, notably the principles of 'fair information practice' proposed by the Advisory Committee to the United States Department of Health in its 1973 Report *Records, Computers and the Rights of Citizens* (which formed the basis of the 1974 Privacy Act): (1) there must be no personal-data record keeping systems whose very existence is secret: (2) there must be a way for an individual to find out what personal information is in a record and how it is used; (3) there must be a way for an individual to prevent personal information obtained for one purpose from being used or made available for other purposes without his or her consent; (4) there must be a way for an individual to correct or amend a record of his or her own identifiable information; (5) any organization creating, maintaining, using, or disseminating records of identifiable personal data must assure the reliability of the data for their intended use and must take reasonable precautions to prevent misuse of the data. In its report, *Personal Privacy in an Information Society* of 1977, the United States Privacy Protection Study Commission proposed 8 central concerns: oppenness, individual access, individual participation, collection limitation, use limitation, disclosure limitation, information management, and accountability. The Younger Committee identified ten 'principles for handling personal information': (1) information should be regarded as held for a specific purpose and not be used, without appropriate

(a) The information to be contained in personal data shall be obtained, and personal data shall be processed, fairly and lawfully.

(b) Personal data shall be held only for one or more specified and lawful purposes.

(c) Personal data held for any purpose or purposes shall not be used or disclosed in any manner incompatible with that purpose or those purposes.

(d) Personal data held for any purpose or purposes shall be adequate, relevant and not excessive in relation to that purpose or those purposes.

(e) Personal data shall be accurate and, where necessary, kept up to date.

(f) Personal data held for any purpose or purposes shall not be kept for longer than is necessary for that purpose or those purposes.

(g) An individual shall be entitled: (i) at reasonable intervals and without undue delay or expense: (1) to be informed by any data user whether he holds personal data of which that individual is the subject; and (2) to access to any such data held by a data user; and (ii) where appropriate, to have such data corrected or erased.

authorization, for other purposes; (2) access to information should be confined to those authorized to have it for the purpose for which it was supplied; (3) the amount of information collected and held should be the minimum necessary for the achievement of the specified purpose; (4) in computerized systems handling information for statistical purposes, adequate provision should be made in their design and programs for separating identities from the rest of the data; (5) there should be arrangements whereby the subject could be told about the information held concerning him; (6) the level of security to be achieved by a system should be specified in advance by the user and should include precautions against the deliberate abuse or misuse of information; (7) a monitoring system should be provided to facilitate the detection of any violation of the security system; (8) in the design of information systems periods should be specified beyond which the information should not be retained; (9) data held should be accurate. There should be machinery for the correction of inaccuracy and the updating of information; (10) care should be taken in coding value judgments. The influence of these principles is immediately apparent in the 8 data protection principles set out in Schedule 1 to the Data Protection Act 1984.

These principles provide the essential framework of the Act's general objectives.[85]

Part II of Schedule 1 sets out directions in respect of the manner in which each of these principles are to be interpreted, though in the directions are not intended to be exhaustive. Moreover, as is discussed below, the Secretary of State may by order under section 2(3), modify or supplement the principles for the purpose of providing additional protection to 'sensitive' data.

2.3. THE DATA PROTECTION ACT 1984

The limitations of the Act's protection of 'personal information' are considered below, but it is worth first briefly examining the manner in and extent to which the Act attempts to deal with each of the problems identified above.

2.3.1. *Data Collection Problems*

2.3.1.1. *Confidentiality of data* Though no explicit reference is made to 'confidentiality' in any of the principles stated

[85] Though it rejected the Lindop Committee's central proposal that an independent Data Protection Authority be established with powers, *inter alia*, to issue detailed and specific Codes of Practice in the form of statutory instruments, breaches of which would be punishable as criminal offences, the Government accepted several of its recommendation (e.g., that the law should cover both the public and private sectors, but that it should not cover institutions or bodies, but only individual data subjects). The essential feature of the 1984 Act is the requirement that data users (including the police, central and local government, nationalized industries) be required to register details of their data banks with an independent Registrar. The register is open to public inspection. The Act extends to both automated and 'automatable' data, i.e. data (even if manually held) which can be processed by computers. There are several exemptions from the Act (most notably in favour of those data banks where a Minister of the Crown certifies that exemption is required in the interests of national security). A Data Protection Tribunal is established to deal, *inter alia*, with appeals against the Registrar's decision to reject the application for registration (where, for instance, he apprehends that the application is likely to breach one of the data protection principles). The individual is provided with a right of access (subject to various exceptions, see below) and a right to receive compensation where he suffers damage and distress as a result of the presence in a data bank of incorrect or misleading information about him (see below).

above, the Act's first principle ('personal data shall be obtained . . . fairly and lawfully')[86] is sufficiently broad to incorporate many of the problems concerning possible breaches of confidence mentioned above. And, of course, since the plaintiff's cause of action in a breach of confidence case involving personal information normally rests on the unauthorized disclosure of such information imparted in circumstances giving rise to a duty of confidence, the principles relating to 'incompatible use or disclosure'[87] and security of the data[88] provide a certain amount of protection. The Act also provides for compensation in respect of damage suffered as a result, *inter alia*, of unauthorized disclosure of data (Section 23 (1) (c)).

There is some irony in the fact that, whereas in the case of actions for breach of confidence involving non-technical information, the plaintiff is not required to prove the existence of damage (see Chapter 3), damages under the Act are dependent on proof of damage. Since the plaintiff's complaint in a case concerning personal information is usually founded on the embarrassment or emotional effects of the disclosure, this is a rather odd consequence; it suggests that the action for breach of confidence is a more appropriate cause of action in a case involving sensitive data than the statutory remedy designed for that purpose! On the other hand, there are some respects in which an individual may find the statutory remedy more congenial: he need not establish that the information was 'confidential' or that it was obtained in circumstances imposing an obligation of confidence. To obtain the Act's protection, of course, the data need only be 'personal' in the very general sense of its relating to an identifiable individual. Clearly the law of confidence will continue to have a part to play in circumstances in which the confidential information is not automatically processed (which, thus far at least, accounts for almost all of the cases in this area) and in respect of technical and commercial confidences.

[86] The phrase is common to both the *Convention* (art. 5(a)) and the OECD *Guidelines* (para. 7).
[87] Principle 3; *Convention* (art. 5(b)); OECD *Guidelines*, (para. 9).
[88] Principle 8; *Convention* (art. 7); OECD *Guidelines* (para. 11).

The Act's provisions relating to the data subject's right of access to personal data (see below) explicitly exempt from such access certain categories of information (particularly relevant here is information in respect of which a claim to legal professional privilege could be maintained in legal proceedings (s. 31 (2)). But no such exemption is extended to circumstances in which there exists 'any enactment or rule of law prohibiting or restricting the disclosure, or authorising the withholding of information' (s. 26 (4)).[89] In the usual relationship of confidence, therefore, if 'personal information' about Z is imparted by X to Y in circumstances which impose a duty of confidence on Y, Z may nevertheless obtain access to the data about him held by Y. Y's obligation of confidence to X will not avail him against Z's statutory right of access, though X may, of course, have a cause of action against Y for breach of confidence.

2.3.1.2. Consent by the data subject to the use of the data The general statement contained in Principle 1 of the Act (and article 5 (a) of the *Convention*) fails to state expressly the requirement that the data subject consent to the use of data he has given. The Principle is to be interpreted, according to Paragraph 1 (2) of Part II of the First Schedule, to mean that information is to be treated as having been obtained 'fairly' if it is obtained from a person who

(a) is authorised by or under any enactment to supply it; or
(b) is required to supply it by or under any enactment or by any convention or other instrument imposing an international obligation on the United Kingdom . . .

This is less satisfactory than the more forthright formulation in Paragraph 7 of the OECD *Guidelines* which requires that the data should be obtained 'where appropriate, with the knowledge or consent of the data subject'.

2.3.1.3. Knowledge by the data subject of the existence of the data bank In addition to the generalities expressed in

---

[89] The data subject may recover compensation from the data user, unless, *inter alia*, the data user proves that he had taken such care as in all the circumstances was reasonably required to prevent the disclosure in question (s. 23(3)).

Principles 2[90] and 3,[91] section 4 (3) (b) of the Act provides that a register entry in respect of a particular data user shall include a description of the purpose(s) for which the personal data to be held by him are to be held or used. And section 4 (3) (d) requires that the register entry contain a description of the person/s to whom the data user intends or may wish to disclose the data.

2.3.2. *Data Bank System Problems*

2.3.2.1. *Security of the system*   Principle 8 of Schedule 1 provides that appropriate security measures shall be taken against unauthorized access to, or alteration, disclosure, or destruction of personal data and against accidental loss or destruction of personal data. The Principle may be enforced through the exercise of the Registrar's powers, and this is buttressed by the provision in section 23 of a right to compensation for damage and distress suffered by reason of loss of, or unauthorized destruction or disclosure of, or access to personal data (see below).

2.3.2.2. *Unauthorized access to the data bank*   Principle 8 (and the similar provisions of the *Convention* and OECD *Guidelines*—including the Use Limitation Principle expressed in the latter, see above) extends to unauthorized access to the data bank.[92] In the event of either unauthorized disclosures of or unauthorized access to personal data (as well as their

[90] 'Personal data shall be held only for one or more specified and lawful purposes' (interpreted in para. 2 to mean those purposes described in particulars registered under the Act in relation to data). Art. 5 (b) of the *Convention* provides that data shall be stored for 'specified and legitimate purposes and not used in a way incompatible with those purposes'. The Purpose Specification Principle and the Openness Principle contained in the OECD *Guidelines* (set out above) are less imprecise.

[91] 'Personal data held for any purpose or purposes shall not be used or disclosed in any manner incompatible with that purpose or those purposes.' Art. 5 (b) of the *Convention* is to similar effect.

[92] Para. 6 of Schedule 1 provides that in interpreting the Principle, regard shall be had: (a) to the nature of the personal data and the harm that would result from such access, alteration, disclosure, loss or destruction; and (b) to the place where the personal data are stored, to security measures programmed into the relevant equipment, and to measures taken for ensuring the reliability of staff having access to the data.

loss or unauthorized destruction) the individual's right to compensation under section 23 is (subject to certain general exceptions) available against a registered data user who discloses personal data or permits access to any person described in the relevant register entry as a person to whom the data user intends or may wish to disclose the data (s. 23 (3)).

2.3.3. *Data-usage Problems*

2.3.3.1. *Incorrect or erroneous data*   The requirement of accuracy is expressed in Principle 5.[93] In interpreting this Principle, however, no contravention will, generally speaking, arise in the case of data which accurately record information received or obtained by the data user from the data subject or a third party where the data (or the extracted information) indicate the source, and any objections by the data subject are included in the data.

Apart from the enforcement of this Principle by the Registrar, the data subject is, under section 22, afforded the right to compensation (subject to certain exceptions)[94] for damage suffered in consequence of the inaccuracy of data, and to correction and erasure of inaccurate data (in terms of section 24 (1) and (2)). The prospect of inaccurate or erroneous data arising, is, of course, substantially reduced by permitting the data subject access to the information held concerning him. This is now expressed in Principle 8 of Schedule 1 (see above) along the lines of Article 8 of the *Convention* and Paragraph 9 of the OECD *Guidelines* (the Individual Participation Principle). And section 21 of the Act sets out the details of the operation of the right of access.[95]

[93] It is based on art. 5 (d) of the *Convention* and para. 8 (the Data Quality Principle) of the OECD *Convention*.

[94] Part IV of the Act includes, for example, the national security exemption (s. 27 (1)); the domestic or recreational exemption (s. 33 (1)) the public information exemption (s. 34 (1)), and the 'ex-UK' exemption (s. 39).

[95] It raises several issues which lie outside the question of sensitive data being considered here. Many of these issues are no longer especially controversial since a right of access is adopted by the legislation in Austria, Canada, Denmark, France, Iceland, Israel, Luxembourg, Norway, Sweden, the US and now, the UK. Most recently the UK has passed the Access to

Though it represents an important recognition of the need for individuals to control the data concerning them, the right is subject to certain important exemptions and exceptions, which limit its scope. In particular, section 21 (4) permits a data user to deny access in circumstances where it would necessitate his revealing the source of data held by him. The object is to avoid the prospect of unrestricted access causing the sources of information to disappear. But the provision could well result in the denial of access even where the data source does not actually object to the disclosure to the data subject of information he has supplied. A second (un-warranted) limitation is expressed in section 29 and allows access to be denied where data are held by the police[96] or taxation authorities, and disclosure would be prejudicial to the prevention or detection of crime, the apprehension or prosecution of offenders, or the collection or assessment of any taxes.

A third limitation relates to data which the Secretary of State may (in terms of section 34 (2)) by order exempt from the subject-access provisions 'personal data consisting of information the disclosure of which is prohibited or restricted by or under any enactment if he considers that the prohibition or restriction ought to prevail over those provisions *in the interests of the data subject or of any other individual*'. The breadth of this provision is, at least in theory, restricted by the stressed phrase, which was absent from the original bill.

As mentioned above, there are several reasons why the patient's right of access to his medical record has been Medical Reports Act 1988 which gives individuals access to medical reports about themselves made by their general practitioners for insurance companies or employers. The Australian Law Reform Commission has proposed a similar right of access: *Privacy* (Report No. 22), paras. 1230–77. The Access to Personal Files Act 1987 provides individuals with a right of access to and the correction of a class of information relating to themselves held by the Housing Act local authority and local social services authority. It extends to manual files.

[96] In their evidence to the Lindop Committee, the representatives of the police argued that police data should be totally exempt from access: Lindop, paras. 8.27–30. The Act, however, permits an individual who is refused access to appeal to the Registrar who may seek an explanation for the refusal and if not satisfied with the explanation may serve an enforcement notice to compel access to be given.

resisted.[97] In particular, there is the suggestion (articulated, for instance, by Lord Diplock)[98] that this might occasion harm or distress to the patient and his relatives or inhibit the candour with which doctors write such reports.

Though the court has no power under section 24 to order rectification or erasure of, or supplementation with regard to, personal data within the classes of general exemption or where the Act does not apply (see above), section 22 (1) provides that an individual who is the subject of personal data held by a data user (whether registered or not), and who suffers damage in consequence of the inaccuracy of the data is entitled to compensation from the data user for that damage as well as for any distress the individual has suffered by reason of the inaccuracy.

2.3.3.2. *Relevance of data*   Principle 4[99] requires that data be 'adequate, relevant and not excessive'. Quite apart from the effects on the data subject, the use of irrelevant data is inherently unreliable and dangerous to the data user.

2.3.3.3. *Subjective data*   The use of opinion data or information which is based on subject judgment is—surprisingly—not explicitly mentioned in any of the domestic or international legislation. Some recognition was given to the dangers of subjective data by the Younger Committee which, in its tenth 'principle for handling personal information', recommended that '[c]are should be taken in coding value

[97] Section 29 provides for the modification or exclusion of the subject-access provisions where the data relate to the mental or physical health of the individual. The Data Protection (Subject Access Modification) (Health) Order 1987 (SI 1987 No. 1903) restricts access which 'would be likely to cause serious harm to the physical or mental health of the data subject' or 'to disclose to the data subject the identity of another individual (who has not consented to the disclosure of the information)'. Section 29 (1) allows for exclusions in respect of social work information.

[98] In *McIvor* v. *Southern Health and Social Services Board* [1978] 2 All ER 625, 627-8. Who owns the files? The British Medical Association takes the view that the patient's files are the property of the doctors. The DHSS, on the other hand, asserted in its evidence to the Lindop Committee, that ownership vests in the Secretary of State.

[99] Similar terms are to be found in art. 5 (c) of the *Convention* and para. 8 (the Data Quality Principle) of the OECD *Guidelines*.

judgments', pointing out that the practice 'often entails the loss of shades of meaning and emphasis. For example, a numeral indicating "fair" in evaluating an employee's performance is capable of wide interpretation.'[100] The potential for misuse is even graver in respect of subjective data used by the police (mentioned above).

To the extent that the Act's definition of 'personal data' (in s. 1 (3)) includes any expression of opinion about the individual, subjective information falls within the general purview of the Act. Thus a statement in an employee's file that he is ill-suited to his present position would qualify as 'personal data'. But the section expressly excludes an indication of the intentions of the data user in respect of that individual. It does not require a great deal of skill or imagination for an opinion to be cast in the form of an intention and so fall outside the Act. Instead, therefore, of recording the above opinion about an employee, the data user need merely record his intention not to promote him. The principle attraction of this subterfuge might be to avoid the subject access provisions and so deny the employer access to this information. It is to be hoped that the Registrar will not permit data users to employ such cynical devices to frustrate the individual's right of access.

2.3.3.4. *Retention of old data*   Principle 5[101] ('personal data shall be accurate and, where necessary, kept up to date') and Principle 6[102] ('Personal data . . . shall not be kept for longer than is necessary [for the purpose of their storage]') seek to deal with the difficulties mentioned above in respect of old data. The special problems posed by statistical data (mentioned above) are addressed in paragraph 7 (b) of Schedule 1 which provides that in interpreting Principle 6, personal data held for historical, statistical or research purposes and not used in such a way that damage or distress

---

[100] Younger, para. 600. It adds that in such cases it would be preferable to refer the interrogator of the computer to a more detailed report.

[101] Based on art. 5 (d) of the *Convention* and para. 8 of the OECD *Guidelines*.

[102] Based on art. 5 (e) of the *Convention* and para. 9 of the OECD *Guidelines*.

is, or is likely to be caused to any data subject, may—notwithstanding this Principle—be kept indefinitely.[103]

2.3.3.5. *Consent of the data subject to use of the data*   The requirement that the individual consent to the use of data concerning him is stated only elliptically in Principle 3: 'Personal data held for any purpose or purposes shall not be used or disclosed in any manner incompatible with that purpose or those purposes.'[104] The principle is expressed with greater force and precision in the OECD *Guidelines* Use Limitation Principle (above) which stipulates that personal data should not generally be disclosed without the consent of the data subject.[105]

2.3.3.6. *Knowledge by the data subject of the use to which the data are being put*   That data should be processed 'fairly and lawfully', as provided in Principle 1[106] might be interpreted to mean that the data subject ought to know the purpose to which the data are being put. Paragraph 1 (2) of the Schedule 1 provides that in interpreting the Principle, regard shall be had to the method by which data were obtained (see above), but no mention is made of the criteria by which fair and lawful *processing* is to be determined.

---

[103] Such data are, in addition, exempt from the subject-access provisions, provided they are held only for preparing statistics or carrying out research, they are not used or disclosed for any other purpose, and that the resulting statistics or research are not made available in a form which identifies the data subjects: s. 33 (6). Para. 7 (a) of the Schedule 1 provides that in interpreting Principle 1 ('fair and lawful' obtaining and processing) personal data held for historical or statistical purposes, the use of which causes no damage or distress, are not to be regarded as unfairly obtained by reason only that their use for any such purpose was not disclosed when it was obtained.

[104] Similar terms are contained in art. 5 (b) of the *Convention* and para. 9 of the OECD *Guidelines*.

[105] The Act confers an entitlement to compensation from a data user upon an individual who suffers damage and distress as a result of the disclosure of personal data *without the authority of the data user* (s. 23 (1) (c))—unless the latter can prove that he had taken reasonable care to prevent the disclosure (s. 23 (3)).

[106] The phrase is common to art. 5 (b) of the *Convention* and para. 7 of the OECD *Guidelines*.

However, since consent implies knowledge, the express provisions of the OECD *Guidelines* (the Use Limitation and Purpose Specification Principles) imply that the data subject knows of the use to which data about him are being put.

2.3.4. *Problems Relating to the Movement of Data*

2.3.4.1. *Linkage of data from different data bases*   The Act seeks to contain the linkage of data largely by imposing certain controls on the 'disclosure'[107] of data by persons registered (or treated as registered) as data users. Subject to the 'non-disclosure exemptions',[108] such persons are prohibited from disclosing personal data held by them to 'undescribed'[109] persons. A person who carries on a computer bureau, whether or not it is registered, must not disclose the 'serviced' personal data without the consent of the person for whom the services are provided.[110]

2.3.4.2. *Centralization or synthesis of data banks*   Neither the Principles contained in the Act nor the declarations on which they are based make explicit reference to the related issues of a IPU, a Central Data Bank, and the general question of the synthesis of data banks which hold information relating to different aspects of an individual's life.

---

[107] Section 1 (9) provides that 'disclosing' in relation to data includes disclosing information extracted from the data; and where the identification of the individual who is the subject of personal data depends partly on the information constituting the data and partly on other information in the possession of the data, the data shall not be regarded as disclosed or transferred unless the other information is also disclosed or transferred. It will generally include the electronic transmission of the data, their physical transmission (e.g. by posting the floppy disk or print-out containing the data), oral or written communication of information extracted from the data, and the permitting of access to the data or information extracted therefrom.

[108] See above. These include disclosure for the purpose of protecting national security (s. 27 (3)); for the prevention of crime etc. (s. 28 (3)); to the data subject (s. 34 (6) (a)); urgently required to prevent injury to health etc. (s. 34 (8)).

[109] This refers to persons who are not described in the entry in the register of data users who carry on computer bureaux: s. 5 (2) (d).

[110] See above: s. 15 (1).

Whether the rigid implementation of the Data Protection Act (or even its more stringent foreign counterparts and international conventions) and the statements by certain governments that this development is not contemplated, are adequate reassurance in the face of the inexorable drift toward state control of information is a matter which raises questions that extend beyond the present enquiry.

It is, however, important that consideration be given to the fact (suggested below) that the regulation and control of 'personal information' may call for a more comprehensive approach than is generally recognized.

2.3.4.3. *Transborder data flow* The rapidly developing traffic in data manifestly calls for an international solution. Both the OECD *Guidelines*[111] and the Council of Europe *Convention*[112] express the need to restrict the untrammelled transfer of data while at the same time encouraging the free flow of information. Again, this raises questions[113] which lie beyond the scope of the present study.

---

[111] Part 3, para. 16 provides, *inter alia*, that member countries should 'take all reasonable and appropriate steps to ensure that transborder flows of personal data . . . are uninterrupted and secure'. Para. 17 adds that member countries should refrain from restricting transborder flows of personal data between themselves and other member countries except where the latter do not yet substantially observe the *Guidelines* or where the re-export of the data would circumvent their domestic privacy legislation. A member country 'may also impose restrictions in respect of certain categories of personal data for which its domestic privacy legislation includes specific regulations in view of the nature of those data and for which the other member country provides no equivalent protection'.

[112] Art. 12 provides, *inter alia*, that a party 'shall not for the sole purpose of the protection of privacy, prohibit or subject to special authorisation transborder flows of personal data going to the territory of another Party'. It allows, however, for parties to 'derogate' from this provision in so far as their legislation includes specific regulations for certain categories of personal data because of their nature, except where the regulations of the other party provide an equivalent protection. See now the Declaration on Transborder Flows adopted by OECD member states on 11 Apr. 1985.

[113] See I. Pool and R. B. Solomon, 'Intellectual Property and Transborder Data Flows' (1980) 16 Stanford J. Int. Law 113.

3. Data Banks and 'Personal Information'

The domestic legislation of most states[114] and the principal international documents acknowledge and identify the special character of personal or sensitive information. They do, moreover, recognize the need to accord such data special protection. Thus article 6 of the Council of Europe *Convention*,[115] declares:

Special categories of data

Personal data revealing racial origin, political opinions or religious or other beliefs, as well as personal data concerning health or sexual life, may not be processed automatically unless domestic law provides appropriate safeguards. The same shall apply to personal data relating to criminal convictions.

In order to comply with this provision, section 2 (3) of the Data Protection Act 1984, mentioned above, provides:

The Secretary of State by order modify or supplement [the data protection principles] for the purpose providing additional safeguards in relation to personal data consisting of information as to
  (a) the racial origin of the data subject;
  (b) his political opinions or religious or other beliefs;
  (c) his physical or mental health or his sexual life;
  (d) his criminal convictions . . .[116]

---

[114] This is the case in respect of the European data protection statutes (see below), but neither the Canadian Privacy Act 1982 nor the Acts of most of the Australian states (with the minor exception of certain statutes, such as Victoria's Credit Reporting Act 1978, s. 11, and South Australia's Fair Credit Reports Act 1974, s. 6, which proscribes the collection or use of certain data by credit bureaux) stipulate special treatment for sensitive data. The US federal legislation also fails to impose special requirements in respect of sensitive data, though the Privacy Act 1974 entitles agencies to establish 'special procedures', if deemed necessary, for the disclosure to an individual of medical records, including psychological records (s. 552A (f) (3)).

[115] The OECD *Guidelines*, on the other hand, expressly refrain from identifying certain information as *'per se* sensitive', OECD Explanatory Memorandum, paras. 50–1. See below.

[116] This might occur, for example, where sensitive medical data are disclosed by a health authority to the police in order to assist the prevention or detection of crime. Since such a disclosure will normally fall

The difficulties attending any formulation of criteria by which to characterize certain information as 'sensitive' or 'personal' have already been mentioned in Chapter 1. The definition of 'personal information' suggested in this book obviates the need to catalogue the precise species of data which warrant special safeguards. By making the sensitivity turn on an objective evaluation of the legitimate expectations of the individual, the problems of context and culture-relativity are rendered less intractable. Even if the classes of data identified in Article 6 of the OECD *Guidelines* (and adopted by the Data Protection Act 1984) convey the essence of what is widely conceived to be 'sensitive', any rigid identification or definition of such categories is likely not only to invite controversy,[117] but to impose unnecessary rigidity on the determination of what forms of information may call for more stringent protection. This is not to suggest that in regulating the collection, use, and disclosure of personal data, special categories of information should not be explicitly identified,[118] but this should be accompanied by a general formulation of the kind proposed here. This approach is, as pointed out above, to be found in the Danish

within the 'non-disclosure exemptions' described in s. 28 (3) (see above), and since it is unlikely to constitute an offence under s. 5 (d) (which permits registered data users to disclose information ('sensitive' or otherwise) to a party named in the relevant register entry as one to whom the data user intends or may wish to disclose the data (ss. 4 (2) (d) and 5 (2) (d)) or where the disclosure is permitted by the 'non-disclosure exemptions', the Secretary of State may consider that the protection afforded by the data protection principles is inadequate, and therefore make an order under s. 2 (3) to the effect that sensitive medical data may be disclosed to a third party only with the patient's consent.

[117] There is, almost inevitably, no unanimity amongst the draftsmen of the various European statutes. For example, in the data protection legislation of Denmark, France, Luxemburg, Norway, and Sweden, sexual activities are regarded as sensitive in the legislation of Norway and Denmark: race in Norway, Denmark, and France; religion in Norway, Denmark, Sweden, France, and Luxemburg; trade union affiliation in France and Luxemburg; criminal records in Norway, Denmark, Sweden, and Luxemburg; credit-worthiness in Denmark; alcohol or drug abuse in Norway, Sweden, and Denmark; 'family intimacies' in Norway. Significantly, it is only political affiliations and beliefs that are regarded as sensitive in all 5 countries.

[118] See below.

legislation[119] which, in addition to detailing various forms of data as sensitive (see above) provides that personal information comprises 'private or financial data on any individual, institution, association or business enterprise or other data on any personal matter *that may reasonably be demanded to be withheld from members of the general public'.*[120]

But, while the definition of 'personal information' suggested here does admit of an important open-texture in the determination of what kinds of data ought to be subject to regulation, there is an additional need for specific definition of data which though 'personal' in the sense described, may be particularly sensitive and therefore require special protection. It is submitted that inadequate attention has been paid to developing a classification of 'personal information' which recognizes the *levels of sensitivity* of such information. The formulation of a hierarchy of sensitivity may suggest that certain *types* of personal data should not be collected at all. It has already been seen how, in response to public concern, the Home Office decided to omit a question relating to race from

---

[119] The Private Registers, Etc. Act 1978. One of the more comprehensive attempts to define the information in issue is to be found in the Canadian Privacy Act 1982, s. 3, which refers to: (a) information relating to race, national or ethnic origin, colour, religion, age, or marital status of the individual; (b) information relating to the education of the medical, criminal, or employment history of the individual or information relating to financial transactions in which he has been involved; (c) any identifying number, symbol, or other particular assigned to the individual; (d) the address, fingerprints, or blood type of the individual; (e) records of the personal opinions or views of the individual; (f) correspondence sent by the individual that is implicitly or explicitly of a private or confidential nature, and replies to such correspondence that would reveal the contents of the original correspondence; (g) the views or opinions of another individual where it appears with other personal information relating to the individual or where the disclosure of the name itself would reveal information about the individual.

The US Federal Privacy Act 1974 (5 USC 552a (a) (4)) defines personal information to include 'any item, collection, or grouping of information about an individual . . . including, but not limited to his education, financial transactions, medical history, and criminal or employment history . . . [which contains] his name, or the identifying number, symbol, or other identifying particular assigned to the individual, such as a finger or voice print or a photograph'.

[120] S. 1 (1), emphasis supplied.

the last Census. Similar arguments might be made in respect of the collection of other classes of personal data the sensitivity of which ought to place on the collector the onus of demonstrating that the social justification for their collection outweighs the likely harm it may cause to the data subjects involved. The Data Protection Act 1984, it has been pointed out above, acknowledges the special character of certain types of data and, under section 2 (3), provides for the Secretary of State by order to supplement the data protection principles for the purpose of according additional protection to sensitive data (relating to the data subject's race, political opinions or religious or other beliefs, physical or mental health, sexual life, or criminal convictions). This constitutes an important recognition of the fact that 'personal' information (as defined in the Act) is not necessarily 'sensitive' data, and that, while the former may be adequately protected by the Act's general principles and mechanisms (outlined above), the latter warrants special treatment.

Thus, to take a simple example, the definition of 'personal information' contained in the Act would include an individual's name. It would be difficult to describe this as 'sensitive' information. An individual's objection to his name being collected, used, or disclosed will not normally be strong, though where his name is *linked* to 'sensitive' data, different considerations will obviously apply. On the other hand, information concerning an individual's sexual life is clearly more 'sensitive' and hence stands in need of greater protection.

But though the Act (and the European declarations upon which it is based) accept that 'sensitive' data require additional safeguards, it is inadequate merely to render the determination of the nature and scope of these safeguards subject to the discretion of the Secretary of State. The objective demarcation of information as 'personal' (proposed in this book) facilitates a flexibility in the protection to be granted to personal data, but, within this category, it will be necessary to provide specific guidelines in respect of the data themselves. In other words, if legislation is to be effective in solving many of the problems associated with 'personal information' which have been identified above, it will need not only to construct a proper framework for the regulation of data collection and use as well as satisfactory institutional means of control, but it will also have to institute *as a central feature of its operation* the detailed management of personal data. And this calls for an explicit formulation of what might be called an 'Information Sensitivity Grading'. Such a process is not entirely value-free, and there is an inevitable measure of relativity involved in arranging the classification. But, as with the wider category of 'personal information', the sensitivity of information is determined by reference to the reasonable expectations of the individual. Any sensitivity grading consists in the application of this general criterion to particular classes of information *for the purpose of regulating their collection and use*. The concept of 'personal information' (which is proposed here partly to attempt to identify the central concerns of the 'privacy' question and which is essential in order to distinguish, for example, 'personal' information from information which merely relates to identifiable individuals) is a limiting first-order category which provides an important basis for a second-order analysis of 'personal information' to refine the characteristics of 'intimacy', 'sensitivity', and 'confidentiality' contained within it. In this sense, the grading is normative rather than descriptive.[121]

In seeking to formulate a sensitivity index it is therefore assumed (since this is an essential feature of the definition of 'personal information' suggested here) that all personal data are potentially sensitive. Any index is likely to be incomplete and susceptible to change; to attempt a comprehensive catalogue valid for all time is naturally futile. Indeed, one of the virtues of such an index is that it might be modified in the light of social and political developments as well as the experience of those who administer the system. But it should be emphasized that in formulating the degree of sensitivity of data, the competing requirements of efficiency, economic management, accessibility of data, and so on ought to be *suspended*. These factors will, of course, have already

---

[121] See J. Bing, 'Classification of Personal Information with Respect to the Sensitivity Aspect', *Proceedings of the First International Oslo Symposium on Data Banks and Society* (1972). This classification forms the basis of the one proposed in the text.

insinuated themselves into the more fundamental social and political determination of what is 'public' and what is 'private' (see Chapter 1), but for the purpose of grading the data themselves, they should be treated independently of the broader question of the social needs for personal data.

It ought, in addition, to be assumed that the data (which are, of course, by definition related to identifiable individuals: one is here not concerned with purely statistical, anonymous data)[122] may fall into the *wrong* hands. That is to say that in evaluating their sensitivity, one ought to err on the side of the probability that the data will be misused. But in attempting to predict the relative probability of this occurring, certain judgments will need to be made which will reflect the functional, institutional, and ethical context in which the information is handled.

The suggested indexes are based on a threefold classification of data which may be described as being of:

(1) High sensitivity (HS);
(2) Moderate sensitivity (MS); and
(3) Low sensitivity (LS).

While no index can be expected to anticipate the circumstances under which all data are obtained or used, (and, this will itself be a consideration in formulating the index) the following six factors would be among those which could materially affect the sensitivity of personal data:

1. *The reasonable expectations of the data subject.* Judged objectively the collection, use, or disclosure of certain classes of information will not give rise to expectations of control on the individual's part. Thus information revealed by a patient to his doctor concerning his sexual activities could reasonably considered to be highly sensitive (HS), whereas whether one is a car owner would normally be regarded as only of low sensitivity (LS).

---

[122] Similarly, certain data, such as one's NHS number (or equivalent means of identification) which are not sensitive *per se*, may have a secondary or derived sensitivity by virtue of the fact that access to substantive sensitive data may be gained through their use. Such data may therefore require protection in the form of additional security: Bing, ibid. 107–8.

2. *The recipient of the data.* A patient will clearly have little objection to medical information about him being held by his doctor and, perhaps, health service personnel directly involved. He could reasonably be expected to adopt a different view if the data were to be disclosed to his employer. Determining whether medical information (or some of it) is highly sensitive (HS), moderately sensitive (MS), or of only low sensitivity (LS) will require, in part, a judgment as to the potential misuse of such data by virtue of the likelihood of its being disclosed to parties other than the intended recipients, and the extent to which the likely (or possible) recipients do (or are likely to) protect against misuse the personal data they receive.

3. *The scale of the disclosure.* The individual's objection against disclosure of even the most trivial data which may be categorized as LS (such as his address) will—legitimately— grow in proportion to the number of persons to whom the information is given. Equally, such information when it relates to the inhabitants of an entire district may give rise to objections based on the use of the data for the purpose of sending unsolicited post.

4. *The age of the data.* While, as has been seen above, raking up the ashes of an individual's past may occasion distress and embarrassment, generally speaking, the older the data the less sensitive they are likely to be. In determining sensitivity it must be assumed that the data are up-to-date or, at any rate, that they still accurately describe or relate to the data subject.

5. *The context of the collection, use or disclosure.* The extent to which the sensitivity of information is dependent upon the context in which it is given or disclosed was considered in Chapter 1 (where it was suggested that though this is clearly a factor to be taken into account, the concept of 'personal information' incorporates the related questions of *both* the quality of the information *and* the reasonable expectations of the individual concerning its use). It is when evaluating the degree of sensitivity to be ascribed to specific data that contextuality will become important. Thus any sensitivity index must contain certain predictive variables in respect of the likely usage of the data and, in particular, the

probable data users who are likely to have access to the data (factor 2 above).

6. *The purpose of collection, use or disclosure.* An individual is unlikely to resist the giving of information (and, in most cases, its use or disclosure) the purpose of which is to advance his own interests. Thus personal data concerning an individual's medical condition will be given with less reluctance to health authorities investigating the need for improved health facilities than to those pursuing less benign purposes. This presupposes, of course, that he is aware of and consents to the initial collection and subsequent use of the data, in accordance with the principles examined above. But even if he is or does not, one of the objects of a sensitivity grading is to provide protection where it is most needed—where data are especially sensitive. The *quality* of the data is therefore of greater significance than the *purpose* to which they are to be put.

Broadly speaking, the classification is based on the following evaluation of personal data:

1. *High sensitivity (HS)*. These are, in general, *intimate data* about an individual, relating in particular to some facts of his medical history, sexual behaviour, or other aspects of his life which may accurately be described as 'private' or 'personal'. It is in respect of this class of information that the 'privacy' argument is strongest, and there is a persuasive case for maintaining that at least some of these data should not be collected at all.

2. *Moderate sensitivity (MS)*. This is information of considerable sensitivity in the sense that the potential for harm when such data are misused is of a very high order. It includes what may be called *judgmental data* about an individual which extend to almost every aspect of his life. Yet it is difficult to argue that such information, unlike that graded HS, should not be collected at all.

3. *Low sensitivity (LS)*. These are *biographical data* concerning the individual; they are sensitive in that they might facilitate the acquisition of information which may be of a higher order of sensitivity. Thus information about a former employee may provide access to data which are of a greater degree of sensitivity.

It should be stressed that attempting to apply these categories to data normally held by public and private agencies in Britain is not a precise exercise, and it may be that certain types of data ought to be classified differently (or, indeed, that the classification itself stands in need of greater refinement). But the purpose is to demonstrate that personal information is susceptible of this sort of analysis, and that it might offer a more effective means of regulating the collection and use of such data.

TABLE 13 Sensitivity grading of personal information

	01—0000	BIOGRAPHICAL INFORMATION
LS	01—0101	Name
MS	01—0102	NHS number
LS	01—0103	Previous (or maiden) name
MS	01—0104	Aliases or pseudonyms
LS	01—0201	Date of birth
LS	01—0202	Place of birth
LS	01—0301	Domicile
LS	01—0302	Nationality/citizenship
LS	01—0303	Residence status
LS	01—0304	Previous nationality/citizenship
LS	01—0401	Physical characteristics (height, hair and eye colour)
MS	01—0402	Special marks of identification (birthmarks, finger-prints, etc.)
LS	01—0501	Sex
MS	01—0601	Race
	02—0000	HOME
LS	02—0101	Address (including postcode)
LS	02—0201	Type of dwelling
LS	02—0202	Size of dwelling
LS	02—0203	Number of rooms
LS	02—0204	Use of rooms
LS	02—0205	Utilities (gas, electricity)
LS	02—0206	Sewerage
LS	02—0301	Number of persons living in dwelling
LS	02—0302	Tenants or sub-tenants
LS	02—0303	Subsidiary uses of property
LS	02—0401	Details of owner(s) or tenant(s)

TABLE 13. *(continued)*

LS	02–0402	Date of acquisition
LS	02–0403	Freehold or leasehold
MS	02–0404	Monthly mortgage repayments or rent
LS	02–0405	General and water rates
LS	02–0406	Local authority improvement grants
LS	02–0501	Garden
LS	02–0502	Specifications
LS	02–0503	Additional installations or structures
LS	02–0601	Telephone number
LS	02–0602	Television licence
LS	02–0603	Distance from public facilities
MS	02–0701	Previous address
MS	02–0702	Date of moving to and from previous address
MS	02–0703	Reason(s) for moving
LS	02–0801	Historic facts about the dwelling
	03–0000	FAMILY RELATIONSHIPS
LS	03–0101	Marital status
LS	03–0102	Spouse or 'common-law' partner
MS	03–0103	Marriage date and details
MS	03–0104	Former spouse
MS	03–0105	Cause of dissolution of previous marriage
LS	03–0201	Parents
MS	03–0202	Marital status of parents at birth of individual
MS	03–0203	Foster parents
MS	03–0204	Institutions attended
LS	03–0205	Guardian(s)
LS	03–0301	Children born during present marriage (names and sex
LS	03–0302	Children born during previous marriage (names and sex)
MS	03–0303	Children born out of wedlock (name and sex)
LS	03–0304	Place of children's birth
MS	03–0305	Adopted children (names and sex)
MS	03–0306	Real parents of adopted children
MS	03–0401	Registered disputes with present spouse
MS	03–0402	Registered disputes with former spouse
MS	03–0403	Registered disputes with parents
MS	03–0404	Registered disputes with children
MS	03–0405	Registered disputes with other relatives
	04–0000	EMPLOYMENT
LS	04–0101	Name of employer
LS	04–0102	Address of workplace

TABLE 13. *(continued)*

LS	04–0103	Description of employer
LS	04–0202	Occupation
LS	04–0203	Job description
LS	04–0204	Immediate superior
LS	04–0205	Immediate subordinate
MS	04–0301	Wages/salary (cf. Financial Information)
LS	04–0302	Manner of payment
LS	04–0303	Normal working hours
LS	04–0304	Overtime
LS	04–0305	Part-time or additional employment (including agencies etc.)
LS	04–0306	Holidays
LS	04–0307	Pension or superannuation
LS	04–0308	Additional benefits
LS	04–0401	Shareholding in registered companies
LS	04–0402	Board membership of registered companies
LS	04–0403	Other business relationships
MS	04–0501	Opinion data (reports on progress etc)
MS	04–0502	Applications for promotion, transfer etc
MS	04–0503	Confidential testimonials
MS	04–0504	Absences from work
MS	04–0601	Trade union membership
MS	04–0602	Trade union office(s) held
MS	04–0603	Business association membership
MS	04–0604	Business association office(s) held
	05–0000	FINANCIAL INFORMATION
MS	05–0101	Annual income
MS	05–0102	Distribution of income from various sources
MS	05–0201	Liquid assets
MS	05–0202	Deposit accounts (bank, building society, etc.)
MS	05–0203	Securities
MS	05–0204	Fixed assets
MS	05–0205	Movable assets
MS	05–0301	Mortgage(s)
MS	05–0302	Hire purchase contracts
MS	05–0303	Bank loan(s)
MS	05–0304	Private loans
MS	05–0305	Local Education Authority grant(s)
MS	05–0306	Debts incurred by administration of estate
MS	05–0307	Regular deductions from wages/salary
MS	05–0308	Other debts of loans
MS	05–0401	Life assurance policies (and beneficiaries)

TABLE 13. *(continued)*

MS	05–0402	Property insurance policies
MS	05–0403	Liability insurance policies
MS	05–0404	Beneficiary under life assurance policies
MS	05–0405	Third party insurance
MS	05–0406	Other insurance policies
MS	05–0407	Loans from insurance companies
MS	05–0501	Personal bankruptcies
MS	05–0502	Default in payments
MS	05–0503	Credit rating
MS	05–0601	Registered will and other testamentary dispositions
MS	05–0602	Registered will(s) etc. with subject as beneficiary
MS	05–0603	Unsettled estates
MS	05–0604	Maintenance orders
MS	05–0701	Tax code
MS	05–0702	Tax office
MS	05–0703	Tax liability
MS	05–0704	Taxable income
MS	05–0705	Tax allowance
MS	05–0706	Tax paid
MS	05–0707	Disputes with Inland Revenue
MS	05–0801	DHSS Office
MS	05–0802	Social Security contributions
MS	05–0803	Social Security benefits (Family Allowance/Child benefits, Sickness benefits, etc.)
MS	05–0804	Unemployment benefits
MS	05–0805	Other benefits or claims
MS	05–0806	Disputes with DHSS
MS	05–0807	Manner of payment (Post Office account no. etc.)
LS	05–0901	Copyright to literary productions
LS	05–0902	Copyrights to visual productions
LS	05–0903	Patents
LS	05–0904	Licences
LS	05–0905	Pattern rights
LS	05–0906	Trade mark rights
MS	05–0907	Capital invested in know-how
MS	05–1001	Transactions of purchase/sale of fixed assets
MS	05–1002	Transactions of purchase/sale of investment items (antiques, precious metals, etc.)
MS	05–1003	Purchases or sale of securities
MS	05–1101	Cheque account(s) (banks, numbers)
MS	05–1102	Credit card accounts (companies, numbers)
MS	05–1103	Methods of payment (cheque, credit card, standing order, money order, cash)

TABLE 13. *(continued)*

	06–0000	MEDICAL INFORMATION
MS	06–0101	NHS number
LS	06–0102	Area Health Authority (current and previous)
MS	06–0103	Local health centre
MS	06–0104	General practitioner (current and previous)
MS	06–1015	Private health insurance policies
LS	06–0201	Blood group
HS	06–0202	State of health (including history)
HS	06–0203	Results of blood tests for contagious diseases
HS	06–0204	Medical examinations
HS	06–0205	Congenital dispositions to illness
HS	06–0206	Congenital physical handicaps
HS	06–0207	Inflicted physical handicaps
HS	06–0301	Stays in hospital (details)
HS	06–0302	Surgery
HS	06–0401	Mental illness
HS	06–0402	Suicide attempts
HS	06–0403	Psychological tests
HS	06–0404	Psychiatric treatment
HS	06–0405	Special treatment
HS	06–0501	Misuse of alcohol
HS	06–0502	Misuse of drugs
HS	06–0503	Treatment
LS	06–0601	Required to wear spectacles
LS	06–0602	Required to wear hearing aid
LS	06–0603	Required to use crutches, stick, etc.
LS	06–0604	Required to use artificial limb(s)
MS	06–0605	Constant supervision required
MS	06–0606	Permanent supervision required
MS	06–0607	Medicine required (prescription details)
MS	06–0608	Dependent on mechanical apparatus (dialysis, breathing apparatus, etc.)
	07–0000	EDUCATIONAL INFORMATION
LS	07–0101	School/s attended
MS	07–0102	Dates of admission and leaving
MS	07–0103	Reasons for change of school
MS	07–0104	Examination results ('GCSE' and 'A' Level)
MS	07–0105	Details of teachers, head teachers, etc.
MS	07–0106	Progress reports etc.
MS	07–0201	Special schools attended
MS	07–0202	Reasons for attending
MS	07–0203	Progress reports etc.

LS	07–0301	Colleges attended
LS	07–0302	Dates attended
LS	07–0303	Courses taken
LS	07–0304	Examination results
LS	07–0305	Qualification obtained
MS	07–0306	Reasons for non-completion of course
MS	07–0307	Progress reports etc.
LS	07–0308	LEA grant
LS	07–0309	Scholarships, prizes
LS	07–0401	University or polytechnic attended
LS	07–0402	Course taken
LS	07–0403	Dates attended
MS	07–0404	Examination results (class of degree etc.)
MS	07–0405	Reason for non-completion of course
MS	07–0406	Progress reports, references, etc.
LS	07–0407	LEA grant
LS	07–0408	Scholarships, prizes
LS	07–0501	Practical training
LS	07–0502	Employer details
MS	07–0503	Results or performance report
MS	07–0504	Progress reports
MS	07–0505	Reason for non-completion of training
	08–0000	IDEOLOGICAL INFORMATION
MS	08–0101	Membership of political party (current and previous)
MS	08–0102	Offices held in political party (current and previous)
MS	08–0103	Membership of political organization, pressure groups, etc. (current and previous)
MS	08–0104	Offices held in political organizations etc (current and previous)
HS	08–0105	Voting at last general election
HS	08–0106	Voting at last local election
HS	08–0107	Previous voting behaviour
MS	08–0108	Conscientious objection (and consequences)
MS	08–0201	Religious denomination
MS	08–0202	Attendance at church etc.
MS	08–0203	Offices held in congregation
MS	08–0204	Membership of religious organizations
MS	08–0205	Offices held in religious organizations
MS	08–0206	Baptism, confirmation, etc.
MS	08–0207	Change of religion and reason
MS	08–0308	Religious denomination of parents

TABLE 13. *(continued)*

MS	08–0309	Religious denomination of spouse
MS	08–0310	Religious education of children
MS	08–0401	Membership of charitable organization
MS	08–0402	Offices held in charitable organizations
MS	08–0403	Donations to charitable organizations
	09–0000	POLICE AND OTHER HOME OFFICE INFORMATION
LS	09–0101	Driving licence(s)
LS	09–0102	Vehicle log book(s)
LS	09–0103	Passport number and particulars
LS	09–0104	Other licences (firearms, boats, pets)
MS	09–0201	Investigations concerning subject
MS	09–0202	Reports of complaints concerning subject
MS	09–0203	Reports or complaints lodged by subject
MS	09–0304	Convictions
MS	09–0305	Charges dropped
MS	09–0306	Acquittals
MS	09–0307	Traffic offences
MS	09–0308	Admissions of guilt
MS	09–0309	Sentences (custodial, suspended, fines, etc.)
MS	09–0310	Sentences served
MS	09–0311	Probation
MS	09–0312	Parole (applications and results)
MS	09–0401	Fingerprints
MS	09–0402	Other identification marks
MS	09–0403	Aliases
HS	09–0404	Non-factual information concerning subject recorded by police or obtained from informers
MS	09–0501	Missing
MS	09–0502	Wanted
MS	09–0503	Suspected (may fall under 09–0404)
MS	09–0601	Immigration status (including details of spouse, children, work permit (Department of Employment), etc.)
MS	09–0701	Jury service (eligibility, details of service)
	10–0000	LEISURE ACTIVITIES
LS	10–0101	Sporting activities
LS	10–0102	Performance
LS	10–0103	Membership of clubs
LS	10–0104	Offices held in clubs
MS	10–0201	Cultural activities

TABLE 13. *(continued)*

MS	10–0202	Reading habits
MS	10–0203	Television viewing habits
MS	10–0204	Cinema attendance
MS	10–0205	Listening habits (radio, recorded music, etc.)
MS	10–0206	Visits to theatre, ballet, opera
MS	10–0207	Attendance at concerts, recitals
MS	10–0208	Extra-mural courses, lectures, etc.
MS	10–0209	Time spent on each of above
MS	10–0301	Membership of societies or associations
MS	10–0302	Offices held
MS	10–0303	Function of society
MS	10–0304	Time spent on society activities
MS	10–0401	Hobbies
MS	10–0402	DIY
MS	10–0403	Time spent
MS	10–0404	Money earned/spent on these activities
MS	10–0501	Social activities (parties, dinners, etc.)
MS	10–0502	Restaurant visits (expenses, invitors/invitees)
MS	10–0503	Week-end activities
MS	10–0504	Holidays (resorts, trips abroad, home, etc.)
MS	10–0601	Pets
MS	10–0701	Boats
MS	10–0702	Aeroplane
	11–0000	HABITS
MS	11–0101	Time of rising in the morning
MS	11–0102	Typical breakfast, lunch, dinner
MS	11–0103	Where meals are eaten
MS	11–0104	Time of retiring at night
MS	11–0201	Shops normally frequented
MS	11–0202	Merchandise normally purchased
MS	11–0203	Brands normally purchased
MS	11–0204	Normal times of shopping
HS	11–0301	Frequency of sexual intercourse with spouse
HS	11–0302	Intercourse with persons other than spouse
HS	11–0303	Divergent sexual habits
MS	11–0401	Types of associates
MS	11–0402	Frequency
MS	11–0403	Venue
MS	11–0404	Smoking
MS	11–0405	Drinking, drug-taking

TABLE 13. *(continued)*

	12–0000	TRAVEL AND COMMUNICATION INFORMATION
MS	12–0101	Regular use of public transport
MS	12–0102	Destination
MS	12–0103	Expenses incurred
MS	12–0201	Distance covered in private car
MS	12–0202	Frequency of use
MS	12–0203	Use of private boat/aeroplane
MS	12–0204	Travel abroad (countries visited)
MS	12–0204	Frequency
MS	12–0205	Purpose
MS	12–0206	Means of transport used
MS	12–0301	Private telephone usage (expenses)
MS	12–0302	Office telephone usage
MS	12–0303	Telephone numbers contacted
MS	12–0304	Telegrams (addressees)
MS	12–0305	Telexes (addressees)
MS	12–0401	Newspaper subscriptions
MS	12–0402	Periodical subscriptions
MS	12–0403	Books borrowed from libraries
MS	12–0404	Books obtained from book clubs
MS	12–0501	Overnight stays away from home
MS	12–0502	Frequency
MS	12–0503	Purpose
MS	12–0504	Accommodation (hotel, boarding-house, pub)

4. Conclusion

The threefold classification used in the above index of 'personal information' is based on the extent to which the collection and use of the data holds a potential for *serious harm* to the subject. This cannot, of course, be a scientific exercise; the index is neither definitive nor complete. It provides no more than a suggested method of grading information in such a way as to ensure that legal protection and control are supplied where they are most needed. It postulates a means of alerting legislators to the special measures that are required to safeguard individuals against the misuse of information relating to them. In particular, it may help to demonstrate that data protection calls for a more refined range of measures which depend on the type of information in question.

The Data Protection Act, though it recognizes in section 2 (3) the special character of 'sensitive' information, fails to provide adequate protection for this data. This is so not only because of the absence of regulations under this section to protect this information, but on at least five other grounds. First, there is little coherence in the group of 'sensitive' data. It will be recalled that the section singles out information relating to the subject's race, political opinions or religious or other beliefs, physical or mental health, sexual life or criminal convictions. These matters may superficially appear to share a sense of being 'sensitive'; they do so however, only in the most general sense. Moreover, the justification for treating them as a group seems inconsistent with the declared purpose of the Act and the international declarations on which this section is based—the protection of 'privacy'. For example, in the case of the subject's race, though a strong case can be (and has been) made even for prohibiting altogether the collection of data on racial origin, this argument rests less on the dangers associated with the use or disclosure of intimate information (as in the case, say, of data about one's sex life), than on the potential for racial discrimination, though the two are often closely related.

Similarly, the unauthorized disclosure or use of one's religious or political beliefs may harm the individual. Again, however, this is based less on the infringement of the personality interests identified here (though this information is undeniably 'sensitive' in the way that one's race may not be), than on the possibility of prejudice against the subject arising from the knowledge of this information. For this reason I have classified these items as being 'moderately sensitive'. Equally, details of one's criminal convictions are 'sensitive' information (and the Rehabilitation of Offenders Act 1974 reflects a concern that certain past offences should, following the offender's rehabilitation, be wiped out), but the case for storing this information is based surely on the fact that, unlike the other data identified in this section of the Act, the commission of an offence and the trial and conviction, or acquittal, of the defendant are generally matters of *public* record and interest.

Secondly, the Act fails adequately to protect personal information by excluding from its purview data which are manually collected. This is an invitation to data users to transfer their most sensitive (and hence potentially most harmful) data to conventional files. The right of access is therefore rendered a singularly hollow remedy. This exclusion of manual or 'mixed' records contradicts Article 2 of the European Convention on Human Rights which requires ratifying states to control data processed by 'operations . . . carried out in whole or in part by automated means'.

Thirdly, by the simple device of the data user couching information in the form of 'intentions' rather than 'opinions' the right of access is avoided. This undermines one of the most important means of correcting errors available to data subjects under the Act.

Fourthly, personal information may be held by exempted 'national security' data banks; indeed such systems may be completely exempted from the Act's registration provisions. This means that the most sensitive information (as identified by the Act itself in section 2 (3)) may be held 'for the purpose of safeguarding of national security' and is exempt from registration, regulation, supervision, and access. Nor need this information be obtained or processed 'fairly or lawfully' as required generally by the Act's first Data Protection Principle. And section 27 provides that 'a certificate signed by a minister of the Crown certifying that the exemption is or at any time was so required shall be conclusive evidence of that fact'. There can be no judicial review of the minister's decision. Nor do the Registrar or the Tribunal have any jurisdiction over this matter.

Fifthly, data to which access is not permitted (e.g. that which relates to the 'prevention and detection of crime') are neither inspected nor supervised by the Registrar.

These are only some of the weaknesses of the Act in so far as it purports to protect 'privacy'. A number of other criticisms of the general regulation of data banks could be made. But they are not strictly relevant in the present context.

It must be said, in conclusion, that the legislation is, in several respects, a disappointment. In the words of two recent commentators it is

woolly, ambiguous and formless. The Act's supervisory body, the Data Protection Registry, is small, weak, burdened with some excessive regulation, constrained from entering the few real danger areas, and bereft of necessary powers of investigation, inspection and surveillance. Were the Registrar and Registry now to disappear in a sea of paper, never to be seen or heard of again in Whitehall, the mandarins might well exchange thin, reserved smiles over a morning's sherry, and reflect quietly that data protection was less of an impediment to efficient public administration than first they had feared.[123]

It could, of course, be argued that information classified as 'highly sensitive' should not be collected or stored at all.[124] Such a claim is unlikely to appeal to legislators who may readily be expected to regard this data as relevant to the function of various public and private agencies. But this response is rarely based upon an adequate consideration of the competing right of the individual to withhold sensitive data. Nor does it examine the particular *type* of information in issue. Unless this 'balancing' (if this is what it is) is conducted in the context of a proper analysis of the nature of the particular data, their social function, and their potential for misuse and harm to the individual, the result is inevitably lop-sided: primacy is given to the demands of ostensible order and efficiency.

How might this balance be more satisfactorily struck? Suppose the collection of the data classified above as 'highly sensitive' were to be prohibited. What consequences might

[123] Campbell and Connor, *On the Record*, 319.

[124] Thus the model Information Reporting Act drafted by the Uniform Law Conference of Canada in 1977 prohibits the storage of data relating to, *inter alia*, race, creed, political affiliation, 'and any other adverse information more than seven years old which has not been supplied by the agency of the subject' (s. 9 (3)). This has not been adopted by any of the provinces, and the Federal Privacy Act provides merely that the collection of personal information by the government should be restricted to that which is directly necessary to 'an operating program or activity of the institution' (Schedule I).

follow? The following are the items of information that I have characterized as 'highly sensitive' in Table 13;

Medical information

06–0202	State of health (including history)
06–0203	Results of blood tests for contagious diseases
06–0204	Medical examinations
06–0205	Congenital dispositions to illness
06–0206	Congenital physical handicaps
06–0207	Inflicted physical handicaps
06–0301	Stays in hospital (details)
06–0302	Surgery
06–0401	Mental illness
06–0402	Suicide attempts
06–0403	Psychological tests
06–0404	Psychiatric treatment
06–0405	Special treatment
06–0501	Misuse of alcohol
06–0502	Misuse of drugs
06–0503	Treatment

Ideological information

08–0105	Voting at last general election
08–0106	Voting at last local election
08–0107	Previous voting behaviour

Police and other Home Office information

09–0404	Non-factual information concerning subject recorded by police or obtained from informers

Habits

11–0301	Frequency of sexual intercourse with spouse
11–0302	Intercourse with persons other than spouse
11–0303	Divergent sexual habits

Medical information accounts for the preponderance of 'highly sensitive' data. The normal argument deployed in support of the collection, and often the transfer, of such data is that it is in the patient's own interests: it facilitates proper or improved diagnosis and treatment. But, unless a wholly paternalistic view is to be adopted, the logical consequence of this argument is that it ought to be for *the patient* to decide whether the data should be given.

The question of the autonomy of the patient has already assumed an important place in the current debate about the control of AIDS. But the resolution of several medico-moral dilemmas turns ultimately on what position is taken in respect of the rights of the patient. Thus the difficult questions of abortion, euthanasia, reproductive technology, and informed consent—to mention only a few—often turn out to be conflicts between the rights or expectations of the patient, on the one hand, and the 'duty' of the doctor to serve the best interests of the patient or even the community, on the other. A conflict, in other words, between autonomy and paternalism.[125]

I cannot here explore the moral debate between Kantians (who argue for autonomy as a logically necessary feature of being a rational being) and Millians (who justify autonomy on utilitarian grounds).[126] Suffice it to say that, without pretending that this is always an easy balance to strike, it is submitted that, save in exceptional circumstances, (for example where the patient is incapable of rational thought) we should seek to allow the patient rather than the doctor to decide. This is not to say, of course, that the doctor should not try to persuade his patient of the best course of action. Indeed, many patients would happily allow the doctor to take the decisions for them. But, the Hippocratic oath notwithstanding, doctors in a democratic society must acknowledge that their patients have the right to decide what is to be done to their bodies.[127]

[125] See R. Gillon, 'Autonomy and Consent' in M. Lockwood (ed.), *Moral Dilemmas in Modern Medicine* (1985), 111–25; S. Gorovitz *et al.*, (eds.), *Moral Problems in Medicine* (1976); C. M. Culver and D. Gert, *Philosophy and Medicine: Conceptual and Ethical Issues in Medicine and Psychiatry* (1982); A. Buchanan, 'Medical Paternalism', in M. Cohen, T. Nagel, and T. Scanlon (eds.), *Medicine and Moral Philosophy* (1981), 214–34. See too I. Kennedy, *The Unmasking of Medicine* (1983).

[126] For a useful discussion see Gillon, 'Autonomy and Consent'.

[127] The question of 'informed consent' has generated a prodigious literature. See H. Teff, 'Consent to Medical Procedures: Paternalism, Self-determination or Therapeutic Alliance?, (1985) 101 LQR 432; P. D. G. Skegg, *Law, Ethics, and Medicine: Studies in Medical Law* (1984), 47–117.

It must be conceded, however, that the question of the autonomous patient assumes a significantly more difficult (some would say intractable) dimension when the patient is a carrier or victim of AIDS. For in such a case it is reasonable for a doctor to consider not merely the interests of his patient, but also those of the patient's family and sex partners, the community, and even his own interests as potential victim. There are no simple answers to this dilemma, but we should try to resist the clamour for curtailing the legitimate rights of AIDS victims.[128]

Even if it is contended that the doctor, or health authority, is best placed to decide whether the collection of the information is in the patient's interests, it does not follow that the data should not be recorded *at all*, merely that it ought not to be stored in a form that permits access to it *without the patient's consent*. To make the argument that certain data are so sensitive that their collection should be forbidden, requires an evaluation of the competing claims in issue. Thus in order to establish that certain 'highly sensitive' information should not be collected it would need to be shown that the interest of the individual in restricting or even preventing access to such data outweighs the interest of the decision-maker who requires it to reach a proper decision. But this is more complex than may first appear. Not only the individual, but the decision-maker has an interest in ensuring that personal data are complete, accurate, and relevant. In the case of 'highly sensitive' data, however, it is sometimes argued that it is *never* relevant to any legitimate social purpose. This clearly goes too far; the most sensitive medical information (e.g. that an individual is an AIDS victim) may serve an important and legitimate social purpose. But, as already argued above, even in such a case there is no compelling reason why the identity of the victim needs to be disclosed. In certain countries (which so far does not include the United Kingdom) AIDS is a 'notifiable disease' and doctors are therefore under a legal obligation to report cases to public health authorities. But there is no compelling reason why such information cannot be anonymous. Nor need the

[128] R. Wacks, 'Controlling AIDS: Some Legal Issues' (1988) 138 NLJ 254, 283.

identity of carriers or victims be disclosed for the purpose of research into the causes and spread of the disease.

In the less dramatic (though not unrelated) case of information concerning an individual's sexual behaviour the subject maintains an interest in these data being accurate and complete. It would be preferable therefore to say that in respect of such information he may be willing to trade off his interest in restricting or preventing its circulation against his interest in its correctness. Here a blanket prohibition is unlikely to prove the most practical or even the most effective solution. In each case it ought to be for the data subject himself to decide whether or not, and under what conditions, he is willing to allow the data to be collected and used. The importance of the subject's knowledge of and consent to collection and use therefore assumes a position of fundamental importance in the regulation of data banks.

Though the Act and, in particular, the 'Collection Limitation Principle' (article 7 of the Council of Europe *Convention*) and the 'Use Limitation Principle' (article 10) recognize the need to inform the data subject of, and seek his consent to, the collection and use of personal data, this ought to be a central concern of the legislation which should, in its Regulations, stipulate the detailed character and form of both the information-giving and consent-obtaining requirements. And though this ought to apply to all personal information, it is essential in the case of 'highly sensitive' data. There should be a statutory duty imposed on data users to inform data subjects of the fact that 'highly sensitive' data about them are being held. Before the data are used in any way the data subject ought, along with being informed of his rights of access and correction, to be asked whether he consents to the data being held at all, and whether he consents to their being used for certain stated specific purposes. The Act pays far too little attention to this principle.

7

Personal Information
and Intrusion

Watching, following, spying, and the use of monitoring and listening devices do not, of course, have as their sole objective the obtaining of 'personal information' as defined in this book. But since this is often what they do obtain, it is necessary to examine the extent to which the law does or can protect such information from the manifold forms by which 'personal information' is, either deliberately or incidentally, acquired. It is, moreover, often difficult to separate the *acquisition* of information (personal or otherwise) from the *use* to which such information is put. Thus in discussing, for example, the question of the public disclosure of 'personal information' by the news media (see Chapter 5), the issue of the manner in which the information was collected is sometimes thought to be a relevant consideration. And, as was pointed out in Chapter 3, the use of 'reprehensible means' to obtain confidential information is a live issue in the action for breach of confidence.

It is not, however, the purpose of this chapter to provide a comprehensive or detailed account of the various electronic devices presently in use or of the numerous statutory means of regulation and control that exist to deal with these practices in other jurisdictions. Such an account would, perforce, in the present context, be largely descriptive and would therefore serve little purpose but, more importantly, it would be only partly relevant to the analysis of 'personal information' attempted in this book. Nor is any attempt made to consider in detail the numerous forms of surveillance in its broadest sense that arise as a result of the manifold activities that are often conceived to be intrusions, investigations by the police, the security services and private detectives, or activities such as social enquiries and the Census. While reference is made to some of these issues in this chapter, the principal legal questions to which they give rise concern the use to which the information obtained is actually put; this was discussed in Chapter 6. The object, therefore, of the present chapter is to investigate the problems generated by the kinds of activities mentioned above and *in so far as they relate to 'personal information'*, to explore the manner and extent of existing and proposed methods of protecting such information.

The word 'intrusion' is used here to include, in particular, prying, spying, telephone-tapping, 'bugging', interception of correspondence, searches, and other physical intrusions. It is plain that without some controls over these activities, the extent to which 'personal information' is protected would be considerably diminished. As one writer puts it:

Free conversation is often characterised by exaggeration, obscenity, agreeable falsehoods, and the expression of antisocial desires or views not intended to be taken seriously. The unedited quality of conversation is essential if it is to preserve its intimate, personal and informal character.[1]

My objection to being watched or to having my telephone tapped is not necessarily that 'personal information' about me has been obtained, for the activities that are observed or the conversations that are monitored do not necessarily involve 'personal information'. Certainly, it is the main purpose of the intruder to obtain *information* about an individual, and some of the information may well be 'personal'. But since it would not be wholly correct to say that what I object to when I am the subject of unauthorized or unknown observation is principally that *'personal'* information' about me has been wrongfully seen, heard, or recorded, the issues under discussion in this work do not come into play to the same extent as they do in respect of the other matters considered in previous chapters.

The problems of 'personal information' thus tend to arise when it is sought to *use* such information; how it was obtained may then of course be a relevant consideration. But it should be stressed that there is no necessary connection

[1] L. B. Schwartz, 'On Current Proposals to Legalise Wiretapping' (1954) 103 Univ. of Pa. Law Rev. 157, 162.

between the acquisition of 'personal information' and the individual's interest is not being observed. Thus, to use the example given by the philosopher, Judith Jarvis Thomson,[2] I might spy on you to discover what it is you do alone in your kitchen at midnight. Or it might be to find out how to make puff pastry, which I already know you do all alone in your kitchen at midnight. In either case your right (not to be looked at) is violated. Your objection, therefore, arises independently of the quality of the information that has been obtained. Indeed, as was mentioned in Chapter 1, the very right of 'privacy' of which this is manifestly an element, is sometimes made to turn on the 'control over when and by whom the various parts of us can [the writer means, I think, 'may'] be sensed by others'.[3] The extravagance of definitions of this kind (whatever their validity: see Chapter 1) demonstrates perhaps a further attraction of the less ambitious (and, it is hoped, more constructive) approach adopted here. The interests protected and the issues that are raised by the various forms of intrusion mentioned above extend well beyond the present preoccupation with 'personal information'. When my telephone is tapped my principal objection is that there has been an intentional interference with my interest in seclusion or solitude. This is expressed as follows by the American *Restatement, Torts, Second*.[4]

One who intentionally intrudes, physically or otherwise, upon the solitude or seclusion of another or his private affairs or concerns, is subject to liability to the other for invasion of his privacy, if the instrusion would be highly offensive to a reasonable person.

In other words, to reiterate the point, there is no necessary relationship between intrusion and 'personal information'. What is essentially in issue in cases of intrusion is the frustration of the legitimate expectations of the individual that he should not be seen or heard in circumstances where he has not consented to or is unaware of such surveillance. The quality of the information thereby obtained, though it will often be of an intimate nature, is not the major objection. The

---

[2] 'The Right to Privacy' (1975) 4 Phil. & Pub. Aff. 395, 307.
[3] R. Parker, 'A Definition of Privacy' (1974) 27 Rutgers Law Rev. 275, 281.   [4] Para. 652B.

question of intrusion is therefore one that occupies a large and varied field. So, to mention only one example, in pursuit of trade secrets, the fairly well-established practice of what has come to be called industrial espionage relies on the full spectrum of electronic devices that are encompassed within the present concept of intrusion. Nevertheless, as will be seen below, the legislation in several jurisdictions regulating the use of electronic surveillance is normally restricted to the monitoring or recording of 'private conversations'. To that extent, therefore, there is an important connection between the question of intrusion and the problems of 'personal information' identified in this study.

Another factor that inevitably arises in relation to the subject of intrusion is the use of electronic (especially listening) devices by the police or security services. This matter raises, of course, wider questions of policy which extend beyond the protection of 'personal information'. It is clear, especially in a modern industrialized society, that the subjects of electronic surveillance, the interception of corres-pondence, and telephone-tapping call for systematic (and fairly elaborate) legislative machinery to control, in particular, the circumstances in which the law will permit the use of such devices and their legitimate application in the detection of crime and the system of administration of criminal justice. Analysis of the statutory regulation of these activities that has developed, notably in the United States[5] and Canada[6] lies well beyond the scope of the present study of the protection of 'personal information'.[7]

Nevertheless, since the object of this chapter is to evaluate the extent to which such information is accorded certain (normally adventitious and haphazard) protection by the law, it will be necessary briefly to consider the common law

[5] The Omnibus Crime Control and Safe Streets Act, 1968, 18 USC, paras. 2510–20 (1970).

[6] The Protection of Privacy Act 1973–74 (Can.) c. 50; the Privacy Acts of Saskatchewan (c. 80), British Columbia (c. 39), and Manitoba (c. 74).

[7] Even if the protected communications are restricted to 'personal communications', as in the Canadian statute (see below) this would inevitably relate not to the quality of the information, but whether the manner of communication would give rise to a reasonable 'expectation of privacy'.

and certain statutory provisions, even if their relationship to the question of 'personal information' is often a fairly tenuous one. Though they are interrelated, it is convenient to consider each of the following issues seriatim:

1. Spying and electronic surveillance
2. Telephone-tapping
3. Interception of correspondence
4. Searches and other physical intrusions
5. Gathering of information by the news media
6. Exclusion by courts of information unlawfully obtained

1. Spying and Electronic Surveillance

The eavesdropper[8] no longer has to rely on his eyes or ears to obtain the information he seeks. The range of electronic devices available render his task a relatively simple one. And in the face of these technological advances, the traditional physical or legal means of protection are not likely to prove particularly effective; the former, because radar and laser beams are no respecters of walls or windows; the latter, because, in the absence of an encroachment upon the individual's property, the common law of trespass will not assist the beleaguered victim of electronic surveillance. The interest protected is the plaintiff's property or interest therein rather than his 'privacy'.

Thus, even though an owner's land has been held to extend to the subsoil of the adjoining highway,[9] a contemporary snoop, armed with long-range lenses or sensitive listening devices may dispense with the need for propinquity and thus escape liability. Similarly, the ancient maxim *cujus est solum ejus est usque ad coelum et ad inferos*, is, in modern times, subject to certain limitations. Thus, in *Bernstein of Leigh*

---

[8] According to Blackstone, 'eavesdroppers or such as listen under walls or windows, or the eaves of a house, to hearken after discourse and thereupon to frame slanderous and mischievous tales, are a common nuisance, and . . . are punishable by fine and finding sureties for their good behaviour *Commentaries* (1761) iv. 168. The offence was abolished by the Criminal Law Act 1967, s. 13.

[9] *Harrison* v. *Duke of Rutland* [1983] 1 QB 142.

(Baron) v. *Skyviews & General Ltd.*,[10] the defendants were engaged in the business of taking aerial photographs of properties without the consent of their owners and offering the results to the owners for sale. The plaintiff objected when his country estate was so photographed and claimed damages for trespass and injunctions to restrain the defendants from entering his airspace and from invading his 'right to privacy'. Griffiths J. dismissing the maxim as a 'fanciful notion', held that neither a trespass nor an invasion of the plaintiff's 'privacy' had been committed. It was clear that section 40 (1) of the Civil Aviation Act 1949,[11] which excludes liability for trespass (and nuisance) in cases of 'reasonable' flights would be a formidable obstacle to the plaintiff's action. But he based his claim, not on the fact that the defendants' aeroplane interfered with his use of land, but that a photograph had been taken which infringed his 'privacy'. The court held that the mere taking of a photograph was not unlawful and it could not therefore transform an act which was not a trespass into one that was; and, even if a trespass had been committed, the plaintiff's remedy would not be particularly effective, for the defendants could simply fly over the adjoining land and take their photographs from there.

Nor will the tort of trespass avail a lodger or hotel guest, for he has no interest in the land.[12] If, however, actual physical entry occurs without permission or by impersonating an official or if lawful entry is abused[13] a trespass may be committed. Thus in one reported case[14] damages for trespass

---

[10] [1977] 3 WLR 136. In a similar case the US Court of Appeals, Fifth Circuit, applying Para. 757 of the *Restatement of Torts* held that the victim of aerial industrial espionage could obtain an injunction to prevent the defendant from using the information so obtained—even though no trespass or breach of confidence had taken place: *E. I. du Pont de Nemours & Co. Inc.* v. *Rolfe Christopher*, 431 F.2d 1012 (1970). But here, unlike in *Bernstein*, the plaintiff had suffered a demonstrable wrong; it is difficult to see how this is true of Lord Bernstein: see R. Wacks, 'No Castles in the Air' (1977) 93 LQR 492.

[11] Now s. 76 (1) of the Civil Aviation Act 1982.

[12] *Allan* v. *Liverpool Overseers* (1874) LR 9 QB, 180. Cf. *Lane* v. *Dixon* (1847) 3 CB 776; *Hill* v. *Tupper* (1863) 2 H. & C. 121.

[13] *Grove* v. *Eastern Gas Board* [1952] 1 KB 77.

[14] *Sheen* v. *Clegg* [1967] *Daily Telegraph* 22 June.

were awarded where the defendant installed a microphone above the plaintiff's bed.

Nuisance generally provides protection against activities which disturb the plaintiff's enjoyment of his land. It is difficult to imagine circumstances in which spying or eavesdropping could constitute a public nuisance[15] and even though private nuisance has been fairly broadly defined to include 'interference with one's enjoyment, one's quiet, one's personal freedom, anything that discomposes or injuriously affects the senses or the nerves'[16] it will not assist a plaintiff who has no interest in the land.[17]

Moreover, in *Victoria Park Racing Co. v. Taylor*[18] the majority of the High Court of Australia held that being spied upon does not amount to a private nuisance. (The facts of the case are, however, fairly special—the defendant, with the aid of binoculars, watched and broadcast commentaries of races held on his neighbours' adjoining land—and perhaps suggest a narrower interpretation of the *ratio*. Indeed, in his dissenting judgment, Evatt J.[19] remarked that it did not follow that because observing a neighbour's land was not unlawful, to do so constantly or systematically would not be unlawful.)

An owner of land cannot be prevented from opening new windows which overlook his neighbour's land.[20] In *Bernstein*[21] Griffiths J. expressed the view that,

---

[15] But see Younger, app. I, 236; R. F. V. Heuston, *Essays on Constitutional Law*, 2nd edn. (1964), 50.

[16] *St. Helen's Smelting Co. v. Tipping* (1865) 11 HLC 642, 650.

[17] *Malone v. Laskey* [1907] 2 KB 141.

[18] (1937) 58 CLR 479.

[19] At 517.

[20] *Turner v. Spooner* (1861) 30 LJ Ch. 801; *Tapling v. Jones* (1865); 11 H. L. Cases 290; *Johnson v. Wyatt* (1863) 2 De G. J. & S. 18. In *Jones v. Tapling* (1862) 21 LJ (NS) CP 110, 115, Keating J. said, 'I am not aware of any other system of law, by which the remedy of the owner of land for an invasion of its privacy by his neighbour opening new windows upon it is confined to their obstruction . . .' There is also no means of preventing a building being constructed on the ground only that it obstructs the plaintiff's view: *Aldred's Case* (1611) 9 Co. Rep. 57b. for 'in a densely populated country like England, the privacy of a man's landed property must give way to the building activities of his neighbours'.

[21] See above, 489, emphasis supplied.

if the circumstances were such that a plaintiff was subjected to the harrassment of constant surveillance of his house from the air, accompanied by the photographing of his every activity, I am far from saying that the court would not regard such a *monstrous invasion of his privacy* as an actionable nuisance for which they would give relief.

Whether or not this kind of activity is properly conceived to be a private nuisance, as a possible remedy for an 'invasion of privacy', it suffers from at least two limitations. First, it will avail only an 'occupier' of the land under surveillance (thus even if his 'every activity' were photographed a guest staying in the property would have no remedy.)[22] Secondly, the hypothetical scenario suggested by Griffiths J. contemplates '*constant* surveillance' of the plaintiff's 'every activity'; this is a fairly far-fetched situation: aerial surveillance (of individuals rather than—possibly uninhabited—land) is hardly likely to escape the attention of the victim, thereby defeating its object.

An action for breach of confidence, it was suggested in Chapter 3, may not lie in circumstances in which confidential information is acquired by the use of 'reprehensible means' which includes, of course, electronic surveillance, spying, and other forms of intrusive conduct. Apart from the acquisition by the news media of intimate facts concerning an individual, there is, of course, in the case of trade secrets often a considerable financial advantage to be derived from obtaining through various forms of industrial espionage commercial information from a competitor. The reason for this 'glaring inadequacy'[23] (which means that if confidential information is obtained by improper means (e.g. the use of bugging devices) the information receives less protection by the law than if it were confided to a party who was under an obligation not to use or disclose it) would appear to be the absence of any *relationship of confidence* in the usual sense between the party who wishes to keep the information confidential, on the one hand, and another party, on the other.

[22] *Malone* v. *Laskey* [1907] 2 KB 141.
[23] Law Commission Report paras. 5.5 and 6.28.

It has, however, been argued[24] that in these circumstances the defendant, since he knew that the information was confidential (why else would he be surreptitiously obtaining it?), is under an imputed duty no different from that which applies to the ordinary recipient of confidential information. Professor Jones[25] says,

It would be rash ... to conclude that the stranger who sells information obtained, for example, from the use of electronic bugs cannot be enjoined and is not liable to make any recompense or account for his profits to the plaintiff. Equity, to borrow a metaphor, should not be past the age of child-bearing. A defendant who has taken good care not to enter any relationship of any sort with the plaintiff and who has obtained confidential information by reprehensible means should be in no better position than a defendant who is given and deliberately breaches the plaintiff's confidence.

Certain support for this view is to be found in dicta in two eighteenth-century cases which have been interpreted to suggest that there may be a remedy where the defendant employs improper methods to obtain information. In the first, *Webb* v. *Rose*[26] the court awarded an injunction to prevent the printing of conveyancing precedents which had been removed from a conveyancer's offices. The second case, *Millar* v. *Taylor*,[27] involved the reprinting of a book of poems. In one of several detailed and lengthy judgements in the case, Aston J. declared that an injunction would lie to prevent 'surreptitiously or treacherously publishing what the

[24] G. Jones, 'Restitution of Benefits Obtained in Breach of Another's Confidence' (1970) 86 LQR 463; J. and R. Jacob, 'Confidential Communications' (1969) 119 NLJ 133; R. Goff and G. Jones, *The Law of Restitution*, 2nd edn., (1978), ch. 35; Younger, App. I, 297; Meagher, Gummow, and Lehane, *Equity: Doctrines & Remedies*, 826–7; Gurry, *Breach of Confidence*, 163–5.

[25] 'Restitution of Benefits', 482. Warren and Brandeis (212) themselves suggest (pointing to the judgment of Lord Eldon in *Yovatt* v. *Winyard* (1890) 1 J. & W. 394, in which he granted an injunction against making any use of or communicating any recipes, a book of which the defendant had acquired surreptitiously while in the plaintiff's employ) that 'it would seem to be difficult to draw any sound legal distinction between such a case and one where a mere stranger wrongfully obtained access to the book'.

[26] (1732) in (1769) 4 Burr. 2303, 2330.   [27] (1769) 4 Burr. 2303.

owner has never made public at all, nor consented to the publication of'.[28]

But in both cases the court was really concerned with copyright rather than confidence: it was the form in which the ideas were expressed rather than the ideas themselves (the major breach of confidence issue) which formed the basis for the granting of the injunction. Indeed, in *Millar* v. *Taylor* Yates J. went on to say: 'Ideas are free. But while the author confines them to his study, they are like birds in a cage which none but he can have a right to let fly; for, till he thinks proper to emancipate them, they are under his own dominion.'

Three more recent breach of confidence cases lend slightly stronger support to the view that protection is not confined to consensual disclosures of confidential information. In *Lord Ashburton* v. *Pape*[29] the Court of Appeal in a decision which involved the breach of confidence by a solicitor's clerk referred to its power to enjoin the publication of information 'improperly or surreptitiously obtained'. And more recently the Supreme Court of Queensland, in *Franklin* v. *Giddens*[30] allowed an action for breach of confidence where the defendant had, in the absence of any confidential relationship, stolen 'genetic information' in the form of cuttings from the plaintiff's unique strain of cross-bred nectarines. Dunn J. said,[31]

> I find myself quite unable to accept that a thief who steals a trade secret, with the intention of using it in commercial competition with its owner, to the detriment of the latter, and so uses it, is less unconscionable than a traitorous servant.

It should, however, be noted that, though there was not, strictly speaking, a consensual disclosure of information or a 'relationship of confidence' between the plaintiff and defendant, the defendant had been employed gratuitously by the plaintiff in the past, and had learned of the secret information in the course of this employment. This is a point which (though Dunn J. made no explicit finding on the facts that the

---

[28] At 2378–9.
[29] [1913] 2 Ch. 469, 475; approved in *Commonwealth* v. *John Fairfax & Sons Ltd.* (1980) 147 CLR 39, 50.   [31] At 80.
[30] [1978] 1 Qd. R. 72.

defendant had acquired the information in the course of a relationship imposing an obligation of confidence) may limit the extent to which the decision has been hailed[32] as tantamount to a recognition by the law of the 'right to privacy'. It is, in any event, better analysed as being based on the infringement of the plaintiff's proprietary rights in the twigs of budwood stolen by the defendant, than on the equitable obligation owed by him. Indeed, the court made an order for delivery up to the plaintiff for destruction of all the wood which produced the fruit which the defendant had acquired as a result of his theft.[33]

The third decision which is cited in support of the contention that the eavesdropper may be caught by the action for breach of confidence is, of course, *Francome* v. *Mirror Group Newspapers Ltd.*[34] where the Court of Appeal granted an injunction to restrain the defendants from using information that had been obtained (by parties unknown) through the use of radio-telephony. The case (which was discussed in Chapter 3) appears to conflict with the judgment in *Malone* v. *Commissioner of Police of the Metropolis (No. 2)*[35] in which Sir Robert Megarry VC declined to make a declaration that telephone-tapping by the police was a breach of the victim's right of confidentiality in the conversations. In his view an individual who divulges confidential information cannot complain when someone within earshot overhears his conversation. In the case of telephone conversations.

the speaker is taking such risks of being overheard as are inherent in the system . . . In addition so much publicity in recent years has been given to instances (real or fictional) of the deliberate tapping of telephones that it is difficult to envisage telephone users who are genuinely unaware of this possibility. No doubt a person who uses a telephone to give confidential information to another may do so in such a way as to impose an obligation of confidence on that

[32] W. J. Brathwaite, (1979) 95 LQR 323. See, too, Meagher *et al.*, *Equity*, 826–7; S. Ricketson, *The Law of Intellectual Property* (1984) 828–30. See now *Attorney-General* v. *Guardian Newspapers Ltd. (No. 2)* [1988] 2 WLR 805, 837–9.

[33] J. Stuckey, 'The Equitable Action for Breach of Confidence: Is Information Ever Property?' (1981) 9 Sydney Law Rev. 402, 430.

[34] [1984] 1 WLR 892.   [35] [1979] 2 All ER 620.

other: but I do not see how it could be said that any such obligation is imposed on those who overhear the conversation, whether by means of tapping or otherwise.[36]

Sir Robert was in no doubt that 'a person who utters confidential information must accept the risk of any unknown over-hearing that is inherent in the circumstances of the communication.'[37] Relying on this dictum the defendants in *Francome* argued that the plaintiffs had no cause of action against them or the eavesdroppers for breach of an obligation of confidence. The Court of Appeal rejected this contention on the ground that in *Malone* the court was expressly concerned only with telephone-tapping effected by the police for the prevention, detection and discovery of crime and criminals. Fox LJ distinguished the two forms of intrusion in the following terms:

Illegal tapping by private persons is quite another matter since it must be questionable whether the user of a telephone can be regarded as accepting the risk of that in the same way as, for example, he accepts the risk that his conversations may be overheard in consequence of the accidents and imperfections of the telephone system itself.[38]

This suggests that a telephone user's 'reasonable expectation of privacy' may be vindicated when the eavesdropper turns out to be a private individual, but not when it is the police acting under lawful authority. It is difficult to see how this distinction can be based on an 'acceptance of risk' argument: if I am entitled to assume that my private conversation will not be overheard by a private individual (since this is not a 'consequence of the accidents and imperfections of the telephone system itself') why should that assumption be any less strong when the eavesdropper turns out to be the police?

The Vice-Chancellor's more considered judgment seems, with respect, to be a more accurate statement of the law in respect of the obligation of confidence. His explicit restriction of his judgment to lawful tapping by the police does not affect his general observations concerning the inherently risky nature of communicating by telephone and, in consequence, the obligation of confidence to be imposed on the eavesdropper.

[36] At 376–8.   [37] At 376.   [38] At 900.

It has, however, been suggested that his judgment suffers from a 'fundamental misconception' 'that because equity acts *in personam* it responds to some personal dealing between the parties so that the eavesdropper is in a quite different case to the confidant. But what the maxim indicates is that equity responds to unconscionable conduct by the defendant; this may but need not flow from any consensual dealing with the plaintiff. Accordingly, it requires no great effort, no straining of principle to restrain the activities of the eavesdropper'.[39]

But if 'unconscionable conduct' by the defendant is to be regarded as the defining characteristic of a cause of action in Equity for breach of a confidential obligation, where is the line to be drawn? Such a broad test could operate to render even a casual listener to an ostensibly confidential conversation liable for the subsequent disclosure of what he happened to hear—if his behaviour was considered 'unconscionable'. A more satisfactory criterion might be the *means* used by the eavesdropper. By tapping the plaintiff's confidential telephone conversations, it could be argued, the spy is effectively receiving information which he knows to be confidential. He is therefore in the same position as one who is in a consensual relationship with the plaintiff and who obviously knows that the plaintiff wishes the information to be kept confidential.

However, a number of difficulties remain. For instance, even if the eavesdropper is caught, must the information be *used* before he is liable? What if the defendant receives the information without knowing how it was obtained? Is he expected to realize that it was acquired surreptitiously (by virtue of the information itself? or the informant?) and hence liable if he negligently, say, publishes it?

It is unpalatable that 'in a civilised society a law abiding citizen using the telephone should have to expect that it may be tapped',[40] and an attempt has now been made by the Interception of Communications Act 1985 to remedy this deficiency which, in Sir Robert's words, 'cries out for legislation'.[41] (see below.)

It is difficult to see how this unequivocal judgment by the Vice-Chancellor is to be reconciled with *Francome*—even if it

[39] Meagher *et al.*, *Equity*, 827.   [41] Ibid. at 649.
[40] Law Commission Report, para. 6.35.

is, as Sir Robert was careful to do, confined to the specific facts of the case (namely, the tapping of telephones by the Post Office on its premises in pursuance of a warrant of the Home Secretary where the police have just cause or excuse for requesting such tapping).[42] The decision appears therefore not to be applicable to circumstances in which no communication has occurred, such as where information is removed, read, or photographed. Nor is this conclusion entirely without its logic. It has been suggested[43] that if one is denied an action in these circumstances because there is a known risk of one's telephone being tapped, then 'why is it that employers, who are certainly aware that some employees are prone to infidelity, can claim breach of confidence against an employee who surreptitiously acquires confidential information which has been made available within the employment context?[44] The infidelity of some employee is a known risk in the circumstances of communication in the employment context.' But this analogy, it is submitted, overlooks the fact that the employee's obligation of fidelity arises from and is implied by *the pre-existing relationship of confidence between the parties*. In the case of telephone-tapping, on the other hand, there is no necessary relationship of this kind between the parties to the conversation. Moreover, it is considerably easier to avoid disclosing confidential information on the telephone (which may be tapped)—simply by employing an alternative means of communication—than it is for an employer to avoid or prevent an unfaithful employee from obtaining such confidential industrial information and using it for his own financial benefit.

The relationship between the improper obtaining of information, on the one hand, and the use or disclosure of such information so obtained, on the other, is susceptible of different forms of analysis. If the interpretation of the action for breach of confidence suggested above is correct (namely that it does not extend to the mere acquisition of information in the absence of a relationship of confidence) then, in order to control intrusion by simple or electronic surveillance, the

---

[42] See further, below.
[43] By Gurry, *Breach of Confidence*, 167.
[44] e.g. *Robb* v. *Green* [1895] 2 QB 1, (affirmed) [1895] 2 QB 315.

introduction of statutory provisions would be necessary. And the creation of criminal offences would clearly be the most appropriate and effective means of dealing with such activities. The disclosure or use of information acquired by these unlawful means could then be the subject of a civil action. This was the solution proposed by the Younger Committee which stated[45]

We think that the damaging disclosure or other damaging use of information acquired by any unlawful act, with knowledge of how it was acquired, is an objectionable practice against which the law should afford protection. We recommend therefore that it should be a civil wrong, actionable at the suit of anyone who has suffered damage thereby, to disclose or otherwise use information which the discloser knows, or in all the circumstances ought to have known, was obtained by illegal means. It would be necessary to provide defences to cover situations where the disclosure of the information was in the public interest or was made in privileged circumstances. We envisage that the kinds of remedy available for this civil wrong would be similar to those appropriate to an action for breach of confidence.

One difficulty with this approach is that since (as was seen in Chapter 5) the Younger Committee rejected the introduction of an action for unwanted publicity; the only remedies considered necessary in cases of 'public disclosure' were the action for breach of confidence and this one. But the former almost certainly requires the existence of a relationship of confidence, and the latter will only arise where the information was acquired unlawfully. This means that where, say, a journalist obtains 'personal information' lawfully, the plaintiff will have no remedy. But should he employ unlawful means, an action may lie—subject to the proposed defence of 'public interest'. In other words, in the view of the Younger Committee, the only circumstances under which a civil action would lie where there has been disclosure of 'personal information' are where the means used to obtain the information were unlawful. It is argued below that this is to permit a confusion between the interests in issue in 'intrusion' with those that arise in 'disclosure'.

[45] Para. 632.

Since the availability of remedy is, prima facie, made dependent upon the use of illegal means, the question of whether there has been an intrusion becomes a crucial criterion in determining whether the plaintiff has a remedy at all. And, it was submitted in Chapter 5, this factor ought not to be of primary importance in cases of disclosure. Equally, (and this point is acknowledged by the Committee's suggestion that disclosure be permitted if it is in the public interest) unlawful means ought not to be permitted merely because the eventual disclosure is justified. The two questions ought to be kept separate. (See the discussion of 'gathering of information by the news media', below.)

A further difficulty arises in respect of 'personal information'. If liability for the use or disclosure of information is made to turn on the method of its acquisition it follows that the *nature or quality* of the information ceases to be a qualifying factor. Thus, in recommending the creation of a criminal offence in respect of the improper obtaining of information, the law reformer is explicitly concerned with the *means* employed to obtain the information, rather than the information itself or its use or disclosure. In their proposal, however, that an obligation of confidence should arise in respect of information acquired in certain improper circumstances, the Law Commission[46] necessarily address themselves to defining those circumstances. But the information in issue would, presumably, need to have the necessary quality of confidence in order to be protected in the first place. They point out[47] that 'information' is used here (as elsewhere in the report) 'to mean information which is not in the public domain'.[48]

Nor is this proposal concerned with the improper means *per se*, but with the obligation imposed on the acquirer once

[46] Paras. 6.28–46.   [47] Para. 6.46, n. 635.

[48] In their report (*Breach of Confidence*, Cmnd. 9385, 1984) the Scottish Law Commission, however, whose proposals in this respect are materially different only in that they preferred a more general objective test of 'improper means' than the list of activities proposed by the Law Commission (see below), suggest that in this context the obligation of confidence should not 'depend on a test such as the nature of the information: it should extend to any information, however trivial it might seem to an outsider' (para. 4.38).

he has acquired the information. There is therefore a closer connection between this recommendation (which is confined to the use of confidential information improperly obtained) and the problems of protecting 'personal information' than there is between the latter and the proposed criminal control of intrusion itself. Nevertheless, the Law Commission's envisaged statutory tort, though it would confront some of the few issues which are related to 'personal information' remains afflicted with several of the structural and functional problems that were identified in Chapter 3. In particular, the requirement that only information which is not in the 'public domain' is capable of protection produces artificial results when applied to 'personal information'; also any damages that might be awarded would be likely to be for 'mental distress', and though the Law Commission[49] does propose that such damages should be exigible, a claim would be limited to 'the person in whose favour the relevant obligation of confidence originally arose'.[50] This could mean that the individual to whom the 'personal information' applied may not be the person to whom the duty of confidence is owed (and might raise complex questions in, say, the case of telephone-tapping or bugging: to whom does the spy owe an obligation of confidence: the owner of the property which he has bugged, the owner of the document which he has stolen, or the person to whom the information relates?) The Law Commission recognize that there is an important distinction between the imposition of an obligation of confidence in the normal case, and in the case of improper acquisition, when they state:[51]

There is undoubtedly a considerable difference in nature between on the one hand the obligation ['liability' would seem to be a preferable word] imposed on a person for breaking an undertaking to another to keep information confidential and, on the other, an obligation imposed on a person as a result of his having used improper means to gain information which may, indeed, be so secret that the plaintiff has never entrusted it to anyone, not even in confidence. Nevertheless, we believe that it is possible to encompass both forms of behaviour within the framework of our new statutory tort.

[49] Recc. 29, 176.　　[50] Ibid.　　[51] Para. 6.30.

They conclude that the common feature in both cases is that the receiver of information is in a position where it is *reasonable* to impose a duty of confidence upon him. They therefore propose a number of situations[52] in which the acquirer of information should, by virtue of the manner in which he has acquired it, be treated as being subject to an obligation of confidence in respect of such information acquired in the following circumstances:

(a) by unauthorized taking, handling, or interfering with anything containing the information;

(b) by unauthorized taking, handling, or interfering with anything in which the matter containing the information is for the time being kept;

(c) by unauthorized use of or interference with a computer or similar device in which data are stored;

(d) by violence, menace, or deception;

(e) while he is in a place where has no authority to be;

(f) by a device made or adapted solely or primarily for the purpose of surreptitious surveillance where the user would not without its use have obtained the information;

(g) by any other device (excluding spectacles and hearing aids) where he would not, without using it, have obtained the information, provided that the person from whom the information is obtained was not or ought not reasonably to have been aware of the use of the device and ought not reasonably to have taken precautions to prevent the information being so acquired.

One difficulty with this approach is that it is potentially restrictive: by prescribing a catalogue of specific forms of conduct there is a danger, especially in an area which is constantly undergoing technological change, of new methods of intrusion developing which call for legislative adaptation. A preferable analysis (suggested by the Scottish Law Commission)[53] is to refer in a general manner to the acquisition by illegal means or by means which would be regarded as improper by a reasonable person. This has the advantage of anticipating 'advances' in electronic surveillance technology.

[52] Para. 6.46.   [53] Paras. 4.36–41.

The Law Commission would impose automatic liability 'without qualification'[54] for the use of confidential information upon a person who obtains such information with the assistance of a device which is 'clearly designed or adapted solely or primarily for the surreptitious surveillance of persons, their activities, communications or property'.[55]

A distinction is drawn between such devices and those, such as binoculars or tape recorders, which are not in themselves designed primarily for that purpose, although they are capable of being so used. In the case of the latter, liability for the subsequent use or disclosure of the information should arise only if the subject was not or ought not reasonably to have been aware of the use of the device and failed to take precautions to prevent its acquisition.[56] This would seem to be a sensible distinction, though it is not entirely clear what is to be understood by the Law Commission's following observation:

It might be argued that the use of any form of surveillance device, whether or not designed primarily for that purpose, should be wrongful. However, to give a remedy merely because information is acquired by one of these means would amount to the creation of a right of privacy—a right, for example, not to be photographed even if the photographs were later never published . . .[57]

But, since the Law Commission are here concerned only with the *use or disclosure* of confidential information acquired by improper means, this would not be the case. And even the point that to allow a remedy where, say, an ostensibly innocuous device were used for spying, e.g. binoculars, would be tantamount to recognition of a 'right of privacy', seems to be misconceived for that would be true (in this context) whatever device, or even none at all, were used.

The Scottish Law Commission would impose an automatic obligation on a person not to use or disclose *any* information so acquired—'however trivial it may seem to an outsider'.[58] The obligation is therefore not dependent on the nature of the information acquired; it is not restricted (though, in practice,

---

[54] Para. 6.35.   [55] Ibid.   [56] Para. 6.38.
[57] Para. 6.36.   [58] Para. 4.38.

will normally relate) to confidential information. While consistent with the general concern to prevent intrusive activities (and not merely their consequences), this proposal again demonstrates the different objectives of the control of intrusion, on the one hand, and the protection against the misuse of 'personal information', on the other. The former extends beyond (but may accommodate) the more limited concern with confidential information and, *a fortiori*, 'personal information' undertaken here, and is, of course, in any event, more satisfactorily dealt with by the criminal law or by administrative control. The present statutory controls[59] are extremely limited in scope and there have been several attempts to introduce more explicit legislation.[60]

The Younger Committee expressed the view that 'there is a need of more protection than the law now gives' and it recommended the statutory creation of a new criminal offence of unlawful surveillance by surreptitious means[61] comprising the following elements:

[59] In particular, the Wireless Telegraphy Act 1949. Section 1 (1) prohibits the unlicensed installation or use of any apparatus for wireless telegraphy, defined in s. 19 (1) as 'the emitting or receiving, over paths which are not provided by any material substance constructed or arranged for that purpose, of electro-magnetic energy'. It was argued in *Francome* v. *Mirror Group Newspapers Ltd.* [1984] 1 WLR 892 that, the Act does not give rise to a right enforceable by a private individual, an argument which Sir John Donaldson MR was not called upon at the interlocutory stage to decide, though he did comment: 'Suffice it to say that I am far from sure that the plaintiffs do not have rights under the Act of 1949, if they have suffered damage by breach of the Act which is special to them: see *Gouriet* v. *Union of Post Office Workers* [1978] AC 435.' Cf. *McCall* v. *Abelesz* [1976] 1 QB 585. Under s. 7 of the 1967 Act the Minister of Posts and Telecommunications is vested with power to make regulations forbidding the manufacture and importation of wireless telegraphy apparatus in order to prevent or reduce the risk of interference with wireless telegraphy. An Order made under this section is, however, designed to stop the manufacture of radio-telephonic equipment which uses those frequencies employed by many VHF receivers.

[60] In particular, the Unauthorised Telephone Monitoring Bill, 741 *Hansard*, cols. 1051–5 (20 Feb. 1967) HC; the Industrial Information Bill, 775 *Hansard*, cols. 802–28 (13 Dec. 1968) HC; the Private Investigators Bill, 782 *Hansard*, cols. 1443–6 (30 Apr. 1969) HC; the Control of Interception Bill, 1161 *Hansard*, cols. 474–9 (20 Feb. 1980) HC.

[61] Para. 560.

(a) a technical device (defined to mean 'electronic and optical extensions of the human senses');[62]
(b) surreptitious use of the device;
(c) a person who is, or his possessions which are, the object of surveillance;
(d) a set of circumstances in which, were it not for the use of the device, that person would be justified in believing that he had protected himself or his possessions from surveillance whether by overhearing or observation;
(e) an intention by the user to render those circumstances ineffective as protection against over-hearing or observation, and
(f) absence of consent by the victim.

The Committee also proposed the creation of a tort consisting of the same elements as the criminal offence, except that the act need not be surreptitious;[63] it would thus extend to acts of overt surveillance. An action would lie without proof of special damage, and an injunction would be available where there is a reasonable expectation of the commission or repitition of the tort. The Committee was not favourably disposed to the prohibition of the manufacture, importation, sale, or possession of technical devices—measures which exist in several countries—largely because of the 'unjustifiable burden'[64] that it would place on industries dealing with innocuous devices which may be used for surveillance purposes, such as cameras.[65] Nor was the Committee persuaded of the need to license the use of surveillance devices: it was too difficult to define the devices to be controlled; many have a variety of legitimate uses, and their large numbers would render a system of licensing 'unduly cumbersome and probably ineffective'.[66]

In one important sense the problems generated by the legal control of electronic surveillance are directly related to the question of protecting 'personal information'—and, indeed, the method of arriving at their possible solution suggests that the analysis adopted in this study may not be entirely

[62] Para. 563.   [63] Para. 535.   [64] Para. 568.
[65] Para. 569.   [66] Para. 570.

unhelpful. The legislation of several countries[67] has, as its central focus, the protection of 'private conversations' or 'private communications'. And this is ultimately defined by reference to the 'reasonable expectation of privacy on the part of the originator'.[68] Thus the Canadian Act[69] defines a 'private communication' as:

any oral communication or any telecommunication made under circumstances in which it is reasonable for the originator thereof to expect that it will not be intercepted by any person other than the person intended by the originator thereof to receive it.

This suggests a two-stage enquiry to determine whether a communication is 'private' and hence covered by the Act. First, the originator of the communication must show that he expected that it would not be subject to interception by anyone other than the person he intends to receive it. If he is unable to satisfy this subjective test, the communication falls outside the Act's regulation. If he can demonstrate that he had such an expectation, a second test is applied: do the circumstances of the communication—*on reasonable grounds*—justify his having this expectation.[70] Obviously if the recipient is known by the originator to be an eavesdropper, the communication or conversation could not be described as 'private'.[71] In other words, the statutory controls turn on an objective assessment of the individual's expectations: the essence of the test of what constitutes 'personal information' proposed in this study.

A further difficulty concerns the standards to be applied in the case of 'non-consensual surveillance' as opposed to 'participant monitoring'. The former occurs where a private conversation is intercepted by a person who is not a party to the conversation and who has not obtained the consent of

[67] For example, Canada: the Protection of Privacy Act 1973–74, c. 50 (as amended), s. 178.1; Australia: the Listening Devices Act 1969 s. 3 Vic., NSW, and WA.

[68] D. Watt, *Law of Electronic Surveillance in Canada* (1979), 27.

[69] S. 178.1.

[70] Watt, *Law of Electronic Surveillance in Canada*, 27–8.

[71] I. D. Elliott, 'Listening Devices and the Participant Monitor: Controlling the Use of Electronic Surveillance in Law Enforcement' (1982) 6 Crim. LJ 327, 362.

any part to it. 'Participant monitoring', on the other hand, includes cases in which a party uses a listening device to transmit the conversation to one who is not a party, or where a party to the conversation, records it without the consent of the other party.[72] It is frequently argued[73] that, while non-consensual surveillance ought to be legally controlled (on the principal ground that the common law is inadequate to protect individuals against sophisticated devices, whose use they may be unaware of), participant monitoring—especially when used in law enforcement—is justifiable. So, in its recent Report *Privacy*[74] the Australian Law Reform Commission departed from its earlier suggestion[75] and (by a majority)[76] adoped the view that,

To prohibit participant monitoring would lead to the result that a participant could take accurate and complete shorthand notes of a

[72] Elliott, 'Listening Devices and the Participant Monitor', 328–9.

[73] See e.g. K. Greenawalt, 'The Consent Problem in Wire Tapping and Eavesdropping: Surreptitious Monitoring with the Consent of a Participant in a Conversation' (1968) 69 Colum. Law Rev. 189.

[74] Report No. 22 (1983), para. 1133.

[75] Expressed in its Discussion Paper No. 13, *Privacy and Intrusions*, para. 118. It opposed its regulation while acknowledging the force of 'countervailing reasons' expressed by Professor Dash as follows: 'To hold that a person can't record or allow a third person to listen to his own calls may interfere with what today has been declared to be both a necessary and a widely used business practice. In addition it may be important to note that the non-consenting party to the call is bound at his peril to evaluate ['challenge' might be a more apposite verb] the reliability of the other party, since the recipient could testify personally as to what was said' (S. Dash, R. F. Schwartz and R. E. Knowlton, *The Eavesdroppers* (1959), 391).

[76] The Chairman and one member (Professor Tay) dissented; they would have extended legal controls to participant monitoring: 'Human affairs are not yet normally conducted on an assumption of verbatim recording. The introduction, without legal redress, of unnotified recordings could have an undesirable chilling effect on personal communication which it is the place of privacy law to prevent or at least discourage . . . The Commission should ask whether it is a desirable development in Australian society that one individual should be free, without alerting another engaged in a conversation with him, to take a verbatim recording of the conversation. What is at stake is more than good manners' (para. 1134). The majority of the Commission could discern no evidence that participant monitoring had led to 'undesirable results' (para. 1135).

conversation and reproduce those notes with impunity, but would not be able to use a pocket recorder to perform exactly the same function.[77]

This neglects the distinctive interests that underpin the concern to protect the content and, perhaps even more importantly, the manner in which conversations are conducted.[78] Moreover, though participant monitoring is a useful aid in the detection of crime, and arguably constitutes less of a risk to 'personal information' than its non-consensual counterpart,[79] '[t]he party to the conversation who secretly makes a recording can present matters in a way that is entirely favourable to his position because he controls the situation. He knows he is recording it.'[80]

2. Telephone-tapping

The extent of telephone-tapping in Britain, long considered to be a fairly small-scale, spasmodic, relatively unsophisticated

[77] Para. 1133.

[78] Thus there is a distinction between what has been called 'aesthetic privacy' on the one hand, and 'strategic privacy' on the other. The former arises where the material recorded or disclosed is inherently embarrassing or distressing. This would seem to include the information categorized as 'personal' in this study. 'Strategic privacy' refers to the interest which the individual may have in restricting information as a means to some other end: (J. B. Rule, D. McAdam, L. Stearns and D. Uglow, *The Politics of Privacy* (1980), 22 ff. This is a complex typology, not only because the two interests frequently converge, but because it raises difficult questions—which have been alluded to throughout this study—concerning the acquiring of information itself and the manner of its use (or disclosure). Nevertheless, it is true that merely by listening to my intimate conversations the eavesdropper, even though he never uses or discloses them, has infringed a certain interest that is different from the interest affected by use or disclosure.

[79] The argument is usually made that participant monitoring is more selective and discriminating than non-consensual surveillance. It is also contended that since the purpose of a criminal trial is to establish 'the truth', the use of participant monitoring 'should be encouraged, not discouraged, and they should not be encumbered with administrative procedure' (American Bar Association *Project on Standards for Criminal Justice: Standards Relating to Electronic Surveillance* (1971), 126).

[80] *Privacy*, Australian Law Reform Commission, Report No. 22, Para. 1128.

and well regulated activity was, in 1980, alleged to be a highly centralized, efficient operation practised on an alarmingly large scale. The *New Statesman*[81] claimed that a national telephone-tapping centre conducted its activities under cover in Westminster, employing a 1,000-line tapping system linked to computers capable of converting telephonic speech into textual print-outs, and sending the texts directly to MI5 and MI6 headquarters. It alleged that between 2,000 and 3,000 taps are actually authorized per year.[82]

The journal alleged also that although the police follow the procedure of obtaining the requisite warrants prior to tapping a telephone, (see below) the security services had a virtual *carte blanche*. These allegations have never been officially denied, though in its White Paper, *The Interception of Communications in Great Britain*[83] issued in the heat of (and presumably in order to cool) the controversy sparked by the *New Statesman* revelations, the Government for the first time in almost a quarter of a century[84] disclosed the total number of warrants (as opposed to the number of telephones

---

[81] D. Campbell, 1 Feb. 1980.

[82] *New Statesman*, 15 Feb. 1980.   [83] Cmnd. 7873, 1980.

[84] The previous disclosure was in 1957 when the so-called Birkett Committee of Privy Councillors (discussed below) disclosed that the number of warrants issued by the Home Secretary had risen from 17 in 1937 to 159 in 1956 (reaching a peak of 231 in 1955), and gave the total number of warrants (as opposed to the number of telephones tapped—an important distinction) that had been issued in each of the preceding 22 years since the figures were revealed by the Birkett Committee. In 1958 the Home Secretary issued 129 warrants; in 1979 this had increased to 411, with the year 1975 producing a total of 468. It would not, however, be unreasonable to assume that the extent of telephone-tapping in Britain is much greater: these statistics relate only to Home Office tapping. The extent to which the Security Service in Northern Ireland, and, of course, private individuals engage in telephone-tapping is not included in these figures, nor could a reliable figure ever be obtained. The Government's chief argument against regular disclosure of the statistics is the rather curious one that such statistics would be 'bound to be of some value to those whose activities are under surveillance' (849 *Hansard*, col. 1781 (1 Feb. 1973) HC). And this assertion is reiterated in the White Paper which concurs in the similar view expressed by the Birkett Committee that '[i]t would greatly aid the operation of agencies hostile to the state if they were able to estimate even approximately the extent of the interceptions of communications for security purposes,' where it is hardly supported by the detailed

tapped—an important distinction) in each of the preceding twenty-two years. Under section 8 of the Interception of Communications Act 1985 a Commissioner is appointed who is required to report annually to the Prime Minister. His first two reports are considered below, though it is relevant

disclosures which appear therein! In its 1985 White Paper (Cmnd. 9438) the Government repeated that the arguments against discosure 'remain as strong now as they were before . . . but believes . . . that the passage of the [Interception of Communications] Bill is an occasion when exceptional circumstances arise similar to those in 1957 and 1980' (para. 11). It accordingly divulge the following figures (which exclude warrants issued by the Secretary of State for Northern Ireland: 'it would not be in the public interest to reveal these because of the nature of the terrorist threat in the Province' (ibid.). In his first report as Commissioner under s. 8 of the Interception of Communications Act 1985, para. 8. (Cm. 108, Mar. 1987) Lord Justice Lloyd said, 'I am not myself persuaded that there is any real risk in publishing the total number of warrants issued by the Home Secretary . . . So the figures are set out in Annex 1.' But they are not! The number of warrants *in force* is given, (see below) but, unlike the White Paper, the number of warrants *issued* by the Home Secretary is not stated. I presume that the Commissioner is here referring to the provision of particulars in respect of the actual *purposes* (national security, serious crime, etc.). This has never been made public (though the justification for not doing so remains weak) and they are included in a confidential appendix to his report.

Warrants issued: telecommunications.

	Home Secretary	Foreign Secretary	Secretary Scotland
1980	414	136	50
1981	402	101	49
1982	379	92	79
1983	372	109	53
1984	352	115	71

Warrants in force on 31 Dec. 1984

	217	98	18

Warrants in force on 31 Dec. 1985

	212	—	22

Warrants in force on 31 Dec. 1986

	206	—	33

Warrants in force on 31 Dec. 1987

	223		29

The number of warrants in force in 1985 and 1986 are from Lord Justice Lloyd's 1987 report. The 1987 figures are from his Report of 1988, Cm. 351.

here to point out that he reveals only the number of warrants in force, and not the number of warrants actually issued. It is not easy to see how the latter is of any real value to so-called 'hostile agencies' (even in Ulster) any more than it would be of any conceivable value to 'the leader of a gang planning a large bank raid to know that authorised telephone taps had increased from 834 to 968 in the previous twelve months . . .'.[85]

It is clear that in recent years the extent of telephone-tapping by the security services and the police has grown alarmingly.[86] The subject raises pressing questions of a political and administrative nature that lie outside the present analysis of the use of 'personal information', but, in order to determine the extent to which such information is protected, it is necessary briefly to examine the existing legal controls. This is no simple matter for, not only is the source of the state's power to tap telephones obscure, but its exercise remains shrouded in secrecy. According to the Birkett Committee[87] which reported in 1957, tapping was conducted

[85] T. Harper, 'Telephone Tapping' (1974) 124 NLJ 782, 783.

[86] For a detailed and disturbing account see P. Fitzgerald and M. Leopold, *Stranger on the Line: The Secret History of Phone Tapping* (1987).

[87] The Committee of Privy Councillors Appointed to Enquire into the Interception of Communications, Cmnd. 283, 1957. Three Privy Councillors, under the chairmanship of Lord Birkett, were appointed to enquire into the question of interception of communications following the recording by the police of conversations between a notorious underworld figure and a barrister, which implicated the barrister in certain criminal activities. The Home Secretary gave permission to the Chairman of the Bar Council to show the transcripts of the intercepted conversations to members of the Council who were investigating the barrister's conduct. When these events became known, MPs sought an explanation for what one described as a 'monstrous state of affairs' (571 *Hansard*, col. 1467 (6 June 1957) HC). The newly appointed Home Secretary, Mr R. A. Butler, assured the Commons 'that this action will never be used except in the interests of public order' (ibid.). Mr Butler added that the 'prerogative power' of intercepting calls was used 'solely in cases invading the security of the State, or for the purpose of detecting serious crime'. Information obtained was, he said, 'jealously guarded', and it was 'settled principle' that it was not disclosed to persons outside the public services: 571 *Hansard*, cols. 1565–71 (7 June 1957) HC.

under the warrant of a Secretary of State, but they could discern no legal authority for the exercise of this power, though government witnesses asserted that it lay in the royal prerogative.[88]

The Committee, with one reservation,[89] upheld the legality of telephone-tapping provided the following qualifications were satisfied before the Home Secretary issued a warrant: (a) the offence must be a really serious one; (b) normal methods of investigation must have been tried and failed, or must from the nature of things, be unlikely to succeed if tried; (c) there must be good reason to think that an interception would result in a conviction.

The Committee recommended that information acquired by telephone-tapping should 'in no circumstances' be made available to anyone outside the public service, but it did not consider that this was a cause for concern for, even where an innocent person's telephone were tapped, the information would go 'only to the police'.[90]

That this last observation should have been regarded (perhaps justifiably) by the Committee as consolation to those who expressed dissatisfaction with the use of information acquired through tapping, is, more than anything else, a comment on the—touching—faith and even innocence that once attended the discussion of police powers in Britain. When, some twenty-three years later, controversy concerning telephone-tapping *by the police and security services* arose,[91] it was precisely the fact that such officials were employing these methods of alleged crime detection and control that was

---

[88] It has since been held, in *Malone* v. *Commissioner of Police of the Metropolis (No. 2)* [1979] 2 All ER 620, by Megarry VC that the Post Office Act 1969 constituted legal recognition of the power of the Home Secretary to issue warrants to tap telephones.

[89] One of the Privy Councillors, Mr Patrick Gordon Walker, preferred to restrict the authorization of tapping to extreme and urgent cases such as where a 'dangerous criminal or lunatic' was at large and was likely to commit acts of violence.

[90] Cmnd. 283, 1957, para. 161.

[91] There was considerable publicity, e.g. *The Times*, 4 (including leader), 5, 11, 12, Feb. 1980; *Sunday Times*, 3 (including leader), 10 Feb. 1980.

the source of alarm. As a result the Control of Interception Bill was introduced in February 1980.[92]

Instead of legislation, however, the Government[93] proposed that a senior judge be appointed to 'review on a continuing basis the purposes, procedures, conditions and safeguards governing the interception of communications on behalf of the police, HM Customs and Excise and the Security Service'[94] as set out in its White Paper. The Home Secretary, Mr William Whitelaw MP, informed the Commons that in all material respects the principles and procedures established by the Birkett Committee were still observed. In respect of the general question raised by the practice of interception, he said,[95]

The interception of communications, whether by the opening and reading of letters, or by recording and listening to telephone communications, is an interference with the freedom of the individual in a democratic society. None the less, when carried out by the properly constituted authorities it is justified if its aims and consequences help to protect the law-abiding citizen from the threats of crime and violence and the fabric of democracy from the menaces of espionage, terrorism and subversion.

The White Paper stated *inter alia* that:

(a) the criteria applied in the issuing of warrants have not

[92] 1161 *Hansard*, cols. 474–8 (20 Feb. 1980) HC. It required that an application for a warrant from the Home Secretary to authorize the interception of communications be made on a sworn affidavit; any unauthorized telephone-tapping or electronic eavesdropping would be unlawful. The bill gives power to the Home Secretary to make regulations, by affirmative resolutions of Parliament, for the control of surveillance by private organizations or individuals, and the introduction of a licensing system for the private security industry. Under the bill, the Home Secretary is required to report annually to Parliament on the number of warrants that have been issued in the preceding year.

[93] In its White Paper, *The Interception of Communications in Great Britain* (Cmnd. 7873 (1980)). See 1161 *Hansard*, cols. 205–20 (1 Apr. 1980) HC. According to the White Paper, millions of pounds' worth of goods had been recovered as a result of telephone-tapping. The practice had assisted the police in large investigations, and the Department of Customs and Excise in recovering smuggled narcotics: in 1978 interceptions were responsible for assisting in the recovering of 62% of the heroin and 56% of the cocaine seized.

[94] Ibid. col. 208.   [95] Ibid. col. 206.

changed from those adopted by the Birkett Committee
(see above);

(b) the same requirements apply to customs officers;

(c) the Security Service must satisfy the Home Secretary
that there is a subversive, terrorist, or espionage
activity likely to injure the national interest;[96]

(d) the use of these criteria results in the rejection of few
applications;

(e) the first warrant in each case runs for a maximum of
two months, and any application for renewal must be
made to the minister;

(f) police warrants may be renewed for no more than a
month at a time; warrants for the Customs and Excise
for two months, and six months in the case of the
security services;

(g) postal warrants for the Special Branch in London may
also run for up to six months;[97]

(h) each warrant names only one person and one address
or telephone number, i.e. approval is not given to
intercept the conversations of a general category of
persons;[98]

(i) copies, tapes, or transcripts of intercepted conversations are made available only to the organization in
respect of which the warrant has been issued.[99]

While it is not the purpose of this chapter to examine the
general question of legislation in respect of telephone-tapping
(or other forms of electronic surveillance), it is difficult to see
how an argument against statutory regulation (of a kind that
exists in most industrialized countries) can be logically
sustained. Certainly, in his statements in Parliament, the
Home Secretary presented a singularly unconvincing case
against legislation. Thus, there is no necessary connection
between his (incontrovertible) observation that because
tapping is 'by definition, a practice that depends for its
effectiveness and value upon being carried out in secret' and
his assertion that it 'cannot therefore be subject to the normal
process of parliamentary control'.[100]

---

[96] Para. 6.   [97] Para. 11.   [98] Para. 10.
[99] Para. 15–17.   [100] 1161 *Hansard* col. 206.

It does not follow from the fact that the practice is secret that it cannot (or ought not to) be regulated in a manner that renders the minister accountable to Parliament for its use. And the proposition that statutory control and the power of the courts to 'enquire into the matter . . . in the presence of the complainant . . . limit the use of interception as a tool of investigation'[101] fails to take adequate account of the legitimate expectations of the individual who conducts conversations on the telephone. Such controls, which exist in several jurisdictions (see the discussion of the West German system below), certainly 'limit' the use of interception, but they do so no less than the rules of criminal procedure 'limit' the use, say, of interrogation. Unless it is to be argued that the apprehension of alleged offenders is to be entirely untrammelled by principles of 'fairness', the case against statutory control is unpersuasive.

Nor is the current alternative adequate. The practice of a senior judge superintending the practice of telephone-tapping has been incorporated into section 8 of the Interception of Communications Act 1985. He has access to police information in respect of the justification for its use in particular cases. This does not constitute a satisfactory method either of control or of providing information to the public of the manner and extent of tapping. The first report prior to the Act[102] did not inspire confidence in the system and subsequent reports, confined to 'findings of a general nature' and changes in the existing arrangements,[103] have not been made public. Since the enactment of the 1985 legislation two reports of the Commissioner, Lord Justice Lloyd, have been published (see below).

As a result of the appeal to the European Court of Human Rights against Sir Robert Megarry's decision in *Malone* v. *Commissioner of Police of the Metropolis (No. 2)*[104] the existing legislative provisions[105] have been supplemented by

[101] Col. 207.
[102] *The Interception of Communications in Great Britain*, Report by Lord Diplock, Cmnd. 8191, 1981.
[103] Col. 208.   [104] [1979] 2 All ER 620.
[105] They are decidedly restricted in regulating telephone-tapping. Three statutes (two of which, the Telegraph Acts of 1863 and 1868, were enacted prior to the establishment in 1879 of the telephone service) offer incidental

the Interception of Communications Act 1985 (see below). In *Malone* Sir Robert Megarry VC considered in detail the question of telephone-tapping and its legal control. The plaintiff who, at his trial on a number of charges related to the handling of stolen property, learned that his telephone had been tapped, issued a writ against the police. He raised three main arguments.

1. That telephone-tapping was an unlawful infringement of his rights of property, privacy, and confidentiality.

2. That Article 8 of the European Convention on Human Rights, as interpreted by the European Court of Human Rights, conferred on him a direct right to have his 'private and family life, his home and his correspondence' respected; or that the Convention was at least a guide to the construction and application of English law.

3. That the Crown had no legal power to tap telephones since, such a power had not been granted by legislation or the common law.

The court considered each of these arguments.

1. *Telephone-tapping and the plaintiff's rights*, (a) *the right of property*. The plaintiff contended that he had a right of property in his words as transmitted by telephone, and that tapping violated this right. The Vice-Chancellor was unimpressed with this view, stating that words transmitted by electrical impulses (as distinct from any copyright in them) could not in themselves be the subject matter of property.[106] (The argument has occasionally been made that telephone-tapping might be caught by section 13 of the Theft Act 1968 which makes it an offence dishonestly to divert electricity. The marginally stronger contention is that the Act's definition

protection. S. 45 of the former provides that it is an offence for any employee of a telegraph company improperly to divulge to any person the purport of any telegraphic message. S. 20 of the 1868 Act makes it an offence for any official of the Post Office to disclose, contrary to his duty, or in any way to make known or to intercept the contents of any telegraphic message entrusted to the Postmaster General for the purpose of transmission. Under s. 11 of the Post Office (Protection) Act 1884 (now repealed) it was unlawful for any employee of the Post Office improperly to disclose the purport of any telegram.

[106] At 630–1.

of 'property' includes information and ideas since section 4 (1) speaks of 'things in action and other intangible property'. But such an interpretation could hardly have been intended by the draftsman, nor would it appear to be correct.)[107]

(b) *The right of privacy.* Conceding that the English law did not recognize a *general* right to privacy (as accepted in the United States)[108] the plaintiff argued that there was a *particular* right to privacy: the right to hold a telephone conversation in the privacy of one's home without molestation. Sir Robert (rightly) observed that the Warren and Brandeis thesis did not support the particular right claimed. Referring to *Rhodes* v. *Graham*[109] in which the Kentucky Court of Appeals held that telephone-tapping was tortious, he said that if a similar case of private (as opposed to police) tapping occurred in England, 'it would be deplorable if English law gave the plaintiff no remedy'.[110] Nor would the Vice-Chancellor, in an appropriate case, shrink from recognizing such a right:

I am not unduly troubled by the absence of English authority: there has to be a first time for everything, and, if the principles of English law, and not least analogies from the existing rules, together with the requirements of justice and common sense, pointed firmly to such a right existing, then I think the court should not be deterred from recognising the right.[111]

He added, however, that 'it is no function of the courts to legislate in a new field',[112] and that the creation of 'wide and indefinite rights'[113] impaired the position of those who are

[107] *Oxford* v. *Moss* [1979] Crim. LR 119. See the discussion of information as 'property' in ch. 2.

[108] The plaintiff referred to the Warren and Brandeis essay, the Fourth Amendment to the Constitution (which has been employed to support the existence of a constitutional right to privacy in several cases: see Chapter 2), and two leading American decisions on telephone-tapping: *Katz* v. *United States* 389 US 347 (1967) in which the Supreme Court departed from its previous insistence on actual physical intrusion and held, by a majority that the Constitution protected an individual's 'reasonable expectations of privacy' against electronic surveillance; and *Rhodes* v. *Graham* 37 SW 2d 46 (1931).

[109] See above.   [110] At 632.   [111] At 642.
[112] Ibid.   [113] At 643.

subject to them. In any event, the specific right of 'privacy' to which the plaintiff laid claim (namely the right to hold a telephone conversation in the privacy of one's home without molestation) was inappropriate since he had not been 'molested'. The acceptance of such a right would, moreover, give rise to several difficulties not least of which was the question of the liability of a party who overheard a conversation on a crossed line. Sir Robert concluded that there was no legal basis on which to found even the limited right to privacy on the telephone.

(c) *The right to confidentiality.* This aspect of the decision was considered in Chapter 3. Sir Robert, it will be recalled, was reluctant to impose an obligation of confidence on the tapper, for when a telephone conversation is conducted the participants accept the risk of being overheard, a view which the Law Commission found untenable.[114]

There is surely a distinction between the situation where, in Sir Robert's words, a person 'utters confidential information' in public and one in which a person does so on the telephone. The 'reasonable expectation of privacy' which the American courts have held arises in the case of telephone conversations[115] hardly applies in the former situation. Indeed in certain statutory provisions relating to electronic surveillance (e.g. the Canadian Protection of Privacy Act 1973–74), the scope of legislative control is explicitly limited to a 'private communication' defined[116] as:

any oral communication or any telecommunication made under circumstances in which it is reasonable for the originator thereof to expect that it will not be intercepted by any person other than the person intended by the originator thereof to receive it.

The application of this objective test would normally exclude conversations the nature of which is such that it would be

---

[114] 'We do not think that in a civilised society a law abiding citizen using the telephone should have to accept that it may be tapped' (para. 6.35). They therefore proposed the imposition of an automatic duty when information is acquired by improper means. See above.

[115] e.g., *United States* v. *Hoffa* 436 F. 2d 1243, 1247 (1970), *certiorari* denied 400 US 1000 (1971); *United States* v. *Hall* 488 F. 2d 193, 198 (1973).   [116] In section 178.1.

unreasonable for the originator to expect that his communication is 'private'. Thus it would not extend to the telephone planning or discussion of unlawful activities or to circumstances in which the originator knew or suspected that the telephone was being tapped, but nevertheless continued to speak.[117]

In his judgment, the Vice-Chancellor, by conflating the situations in which the plaintiff has a legitimate objective expectation of 'privacy', on the one hand, and those in which he does not or should not have, on the other, considerably circumscribes the scope of protection that might otherwise be afforded by the action for breach of confidence. In addition, as far as police tapping is concerned, no breach of confidence would, in Sir Robert's view, arise if three conditions were satisfied:

(a) There are grounds for suspecting that the tapping of the particular telephone will be of material assistance in detecting or preventing crime, or discovering the criminals or otherwise assisting in the discharge of the functions of the police in relation to crime;

(b) No use is made of the material obtained except for those purposes;

(c) Any knowledge of information which is not relevant to those purposes is confined to the minimum number of persons reasonably required to carry out the process of telephone-tapping.[118]

In their proposals[119] the Law Commission recommended that where the police and security services acquire information improperly they should be under the same duty in relation to the use or disclosure of such information as any member of the general public, *except in so far as the information has been obtained in the course of the lawful exercise of their official functions* (a matter which the court will have to determine). Where the means used are *unlawful* the Law Commission would nevertheless permit its use or disclosure if two criteria are satisfied. First, if the officer in question was

---

[117] R. *v. Carothers; Richardson* v. *Brunhoffer* [1978] 6 WWR 571 (BC Co. Ct.). See R. v. *Watson* (1976) 31 CCC (2d) 245 (Ont. Co. Ct.).

[118] At 647.   [119] Law Commission Report, paras. 6.40–6.

acting in the course of the lawful exercise of an official function to acquire information *for the purposes of protecting state security or preventing, detecting, or investigating crime.* Secondly, he would be entitled to use or disclose the information, but *only for those purposes or related legal proceedings.* The following illustration is given:

if he acquired personal information not connected with his enquiry he would not be entitled to use or disclose it; nor would he be entitled to disclose information which was relevant to his enquiry to anyone other than those concerned with the purposes for which he acquired it.[120]

It also recognizes that where legislation confers powers on officials to acquire information[121]

acquisition of information by means which would otherwise be improper within our recommendations shall not impose an obligation of confidence if the information was acquired in pursuance of any statutory provision, provided that its disclosure or use was also for a purpose expressly or impliedly authorised by that, or any other, statutory provision.[122]

This sounds very much like an invitation to clothe such powers with legislative authority.

2. *The European Convention on Human Rights.* Neither

[120] Law Commission Report, para. 6.42. It adds (in para. 6.43), 'We should however emphasize that in adopting this . . . [view] we are not in any way ruling out the possibility that the methods which the police or security services may use to obtain information should be defined by statute, [as the Royal Commission on Criminal Procedure Cmnd. 8092, 1981, para. 3.57 recommended in respect of information obtained by the police by surreptitious surveillance] in which event it would be for consideration whether information obtained by methods which were not permitted should be made subject to an obligation of confidence. Nor do we imply any view on our part as to the desirability, if the police and security services' powers of surreptitious surveillance are not, or not wholly, controlled by statute, of subjecting the use of such powers to specific administrative and political control. However all these are matters which lie beyond the scope of this report.'

[121] e.g. immigration officials acting under the Immigration Act 1971, Schedule 2, para. 18 (2), or Post Office officials acting in terms of the Post Office Act 1953, s. 58 (1) (as amended) (see below).

[122] Ibid. para. 3.57.

the plaintiff's contention that Article 8 of the Convention[123] conferred direct rights (including the right of 'privacy') on citizens of the United Kingdom nor his argument that the Convention as interpreted in *Klass* v. *Federal Republic of Germany*[124] should be applied as a guide to the construction of ambiguous or unclear principles of English law, cut much ice with the Vice-Chancellor. The first, because any such right was a direct right only *vis-à-vis* the European Commission and Court of Human Rights and not in relation to English courts since the Convention has not been incorporated into our law.[125]

The second argument referred to a dictum by Scarman LJ[126] which suggested this approach in circumstances in which a statute was being interpreted and the court could either adopt a construction which was inconsistent with an international convention or treat it 'as part of the full content or background of the law';[127] the latter approach was to be preferred. But in *Malone* no statute called for construction and there was therefore no justification for this course of action. It is, of course, arguable that the case for adopting an interpretation consonant with the Convention is stronger where there is *no* applicable statute or rule of common law, since the Convention might provide useful guidance.[128]

3. *The power of the Crown to tap telephones.* The plaintiff contended that as the law had not conferred on

---

[123] It provides in (1) that 'everyone has the right to respect for his private and family life, his home and his correspondence'. Article 8 (2) limits this right with the inevitable qualification: 'There shall be no interference by a public authority with the exercise of this right except such as is in accordance with the law and is necessary in a democratic society in the interests of national security, public safety, or the economic well being of the country, for the prevention of disorder or crime, for the protection of health or morale, or for the protection of the rights and freedoms of others.'   [124] (1978) Halsbury's Abbr. para. 1501. See below.

[125] At 647. See R. *v. Chief Immigration Officer, ex parte Bibi* [1976] 3 All ER 843, 850 per Geoffrey Lane LJ.

[126] In *Pan-American World Airways, Inc.* v. *Department of Trade* [1976] 1 Lloyd's Rep. 257, 261.   [127] Ibid.

[128] *Ahmad* v. *Inner London Education Authority* [1978] 1 QB 36, 48 per Lord Scarman; *Morris* v. *Beardmore* [1980] 3 WLR 283, 296 per Lord Scarman.

anyone the power to intercept telephone conversations, such activities must therefore be unlawful. The court rejected this proposition: 'England is not a country where everything is forbidden except what is expressly permitted.'[129] Since tapping may be effected without committing a breach of the law, no statutory or common-law authorization is required.

The plaintiff therefore failed to persuade the court to recognize even a limited 'right to privacy'. Megarry VC was, however, careful to confine his decision that telephone-tapping was lawful to the specific facts of the case: it applied only to the tapping of telephones by the Post Office on its premises in pursuance of a warrant issued by the Home Secretary where the police have a just cause or excuse to request the tapping for the prevention or detection of crime or to discover the criminals, and where the material obtained is used only by the police, and solely for those purposes.[130]

Yet even if the case had concerned private tapping[131] it is unlikely that the plaintiff would have succeeded in view of the court's reluctance to impose an obligation of confidence on the party who intercepts the conversation. As Megarry VC observed:

In the present case, the alleged misuse is not by the person to whom the information was intended to be communicated, but by someone to whom the plaintiff had no intention of communicating anything and that, of course, introduces a somewhat different element, that of the unknown overhearer. It seems to me that a person who utters confidential information must accept the risk of any unknown overhearing that is inherent in the circumstances of communication . . . I do not see why someone who has overheard some secret in such a way should be exposed to legal proceedings if he uses or divulges what he has heard.[132]

---

[130] At 651.   [129] At 638.

[131] Professor Zellick has pointed to the failure of the court to distinguish between the state and the private citizen in these (and other) circumstances: 'The decision in *Malone* v. *Metropolitan Police Commissioner* is regrettable, for it reveals a lamentable weakness in our jurisprudence. To treat the State and its emanations as if they were a private individual is unrealistic and inappropriate' (Graham Zellick 'Government Beyond Law' (1985) Public Law 283, 295).

[132] At 645–6.

This would seem to sound the death-knell for many potential actions for breach of confidence where the plaintiff is subjected to telephone-tapping even by persons other than the police, and even where the 'circumstances of communication' create an 'inherent' risk (objectively, one presumes) of being overheard.

The control of telephone-tapping is manifestly a subject that, in the words of the Vice-Chancellor, 'cries out for legislation'.[133] But it required the plaintiff in *Malone* successfully to appeal to the European Court of Human Rights[134] before the government responded mildly to the cry.

The applicant submitted a complaint to the European

[133] At 649.

[134] European Court of Human Rights Series A, vol. 82, judgment of 2 Aug. 1984. The prospects for the plaintiff were always good, for the Court (in its decision in *Klass*, above) laid down the requirements of a system of surveillance which would satisfy Article 13 of the Convention which speaks of the need for an 'effective remedy' for violations of Article 8. The German legislation under consideration provides an elaborate system of control and safeguards. The minister must report at six-monthly intervals to a board of 5 members of the Bundestag on the operation of the surveillance legislation. A commission of 3 members has considerable powers over the exercise of the minister's authority to allow surveillance. These boards are independent of the officials who are responsible for conducting the actual surveillance. There is no legal remedy before the courts for unlawful surveillance, but any person who suspects that he is under surveillance may apply to the commission and from there to the Constitutional Court which has the power to require the authorities to provide information (which may include secret documents) and rule on whether it may be used. An individual, once notified of the fact that he is under surveillance, may test its legality in an action for a declaration or he may sue to obtain the destruction or restitution of documents. As a last resort, he may appeal to the Constitutional Court for a ruling that the basic law of the Republic has been breached. These controls, however, far exceed, by the admission even of Megarry VC the then prevailing methods employed in Britain. And the German system is by no means unique. The statutory controls of electronic surveillance in, for instance, the US (Title III of the Omnibus Crime Control and Safe Streets Acts of 1968) and Canada (the Canadian Protection of Privacy Act 1973–74) establish a framework for the interception of communications which seeks to strike a balance between the individual's legitimate 'expectation of privacy' and the needs of criminal prevention and detection. Moreover, the willingness of English courts to admit evidence obtained by improper methods (discussed below) provides little disincentive to the police to refrain from electronic surveillance.

Commission on Human Rights in accordance with Article 25 (1) of the Convention, alleging that his telephone had been tapped at the request of the police and that his telephone calls had been 'metered' (i.e. that all the numbers he had called had been recorded). He argued that this constituted an infringement of Articles 8[135] and 13[136] of the Convention.

Not surprisingly, the Commission[137] and the European Court[138] held unanimously that these Articles had been breached. In consequence the Government accepted that legislation was required[139] and the Interception of Communications Act was passed in 1985.

The Act is confined to the interception of communications sent by post or by means of public telecommunications systems. It covers all forms of communications, whatever their nature, passing through these systems, and thus includes not only letters, telephone calls, telegrams, and telex messages, but also other forms of electronic transmission such as computer data or facsimile. But it is confined to 'official' interceptions; the activities of private individuals remains unaffected.

The Act creates (in section 1) a general criminal offence of unlawful interception for which the maximum penalty is a fine not exceeding the statutory maximum on summary conviction or, on conviction on indictment, of two years' imprisonment or a fine or both. It is not an offence under the Act to intercept a communication in obedience to a warrant issued by the Secretary of State under section 2, or where the interceptor has reasonable grounds to believe that the person to whom, or the person by whom, the communication is sent has consented to the interception. It therefore facilitates 'participant monitoring' (see above). Nor is it an offence to

[135] See above.

[136] It provides: 'Everyone whose rights and freedoms as set forth in this Convention are violated shall have an effective remedy before a national authority notwithstanding that the violation has been committed by persons acting in an official capacity.'

[137] *Malone Report*, No. 8691/79. The opinion was expressed by 11 to 0, with one abstention.

[138] European Court of Human Rights Series A, vol. 82 (2 Aug. 1984).

[139] *The Interception of Communications in the United Kingdom*, Cmnd. 9438, 1985.

intercept a communication for the 'purposes connected with the provision of postal or public telecommunication services . . . or with the enforcement of any enactment relating to the use of those services' (section 1 (3) (a)).

The centre-piece of the legislation is section 2 which empowers the Secretary of State to issue warrants for interception where he considers it necessary, (a) in the interests of national security; (b) for the purpose of preventing or detecting serious crime; or (c) for the purpose of safe-guarding the economic well-being of the United Kingdom. A warrant, unless renewed, shall cease to have effect at the end of two months from the date of its issue. In an 'urgent case' (where the Secretary of State has expressly authorized its issue and a statement of that fact is endorsed thereon) an official of his department above the rank of Assistant Under Secretary of State may issue a warrant which is valid only for two working days after its issue. A warrant may be renewed by the Secretary of State for a maximum period of six months and may be modified or cancelled. In the case of the Special Branch, warrants are renewed on a monthly basis—even where the Act lays down a period of six months. In his first report Lord Justice Lloyd commented: 'No doubt this has been done from the best of motives . . .'.[140] Nevertheless he recommended that the periods should not in general be less than the periods stated in the Act; monthly renewal 'could be counter-productive . . . [it] may place an unnecessary burden on the Secretary of State, and might lead him to regard the renewal of warrants as a matter of routine, which it must never be'.[141]

The Act in section 7 establishes a Tribunal comprising five legally qualified persons to which individuals may apply if they believe that their communications have been improperly intercepted. It determines whether an authorization has named the applicant or has specified premises from which he sent or at which he received communications at the relevant time. If no such authorization is found by the Tribunal to exist, or, if an existing authorization is found to have been issued contrary to the provisions of the Act, the applicant is

[140] *Report of the Commissioner for 1986*, Cm. 108, para. 15.
[141] Ibid., para. 16.

to be told (without it being revealed whether or not interception had actually occurred). The Tribunal has the power to quash the authorization so that no interception could be effected in accordance with it after that date, and to order that the intercepted material be destroyed. It may also require the Secretary of State to pay the applicant such compensation as it thinks fit. The decision of the Tribunal (which is to be reported to the Prime Minister) is final.

This system suffers from a number of defects. First the Tribunal's jurisdiction is confined to determining whether a warrant exists and whether the criteria for its issue were observed. If no warrant has been issued, the tap is unlawful; if a tap has been issued without the criteria having been satisfied, the tap is wrongly authorized. It is only in the latter case that the Tribunal can act: it has power to quash the warrant, destroy the intercepted material, and order that compensation be paid to the complainant. But, in any other case, the Tribunal will simply declare that the victim was the subject of an unauthorized tap. 'There the case will end, with the plaintiff left in a Kafkaesque limbo to ponder one of three possibilities: a tap with a properly authorised warrant, an illegal tap, or a non-existent tap. The tribunal can offer no further illumination and there is no right of appeal against the decision.'[142]

Secondly the Tribunal's procedure enable a unauthorized tap to be removed and hence for the tappers to evade responsibility. As one Member of Parliament put it during the debate on the Bill:

If the Tribunal first tries to discover whether or not there is a warrant and then whether there is a tap without a warrant two things will happen. First, the tap will be taken off and secondly, the

---

[142] Fitzgerald and Leopold, *Stranger on the Line*, 151. In *R. v. Secretary of State for the Home Department, ex parte Ruddock* [1987] 1 WLR 1482 the applicant failed to show that in authorizing the tapping of his telephone, the Secretary of State had acted so irrationally that his decision should be set aside by the court. It was recognized that the court's jurisdiction in these matters was superseded by the 1985 Act, but the facts arose before the Act came into force. As the application was based largely on the deposition of a former MI5 intelligence officer, Catherine Massiter, the judgment provides an interesting insight into the manner in which warrants are sought and on what grounds.

Minister will be told that there is not a warrant. That is the wrong way round. The first duty of the Tribunal should be to determine whether the line is intercepted. Its second duty is to determine whether there is a warrant.[143]

Thirdly, it is unclear who will be the defendant before the Tribunal: those who *sanction* unauthorized interception or those who actually *administer* it.

The Tribunal inspires little confidence. Since the individual has no right to be *informed* that his calls have been intercepted (but merely that they have been intercepted *improperly*) it is reasonably safe to conclude that most of the Tribunal's proceedings will be conducted in camera. This means that the complainant has no effective means by which to challenge an *authorized* tap. He must accept the findings of a government-appointed body sitting in judgement on the decisions of its appointers.

A senior member of the judiciary will, under section 8, *inter alia* continue to review the exercise of the functions conferred on the Secretary of State and the procedures in respect of the authorized interceptions under the Act, and to report annually to the Prime Minister or, at any time, if he considers that the powers conferred by the Act have been improperly exercised. His annual reports will be published, subject to the exclusion of material likely to be prejudicial to any of the grounds on which warrants can be issued.

The Act accords some limited, indirect protection to 'personal information' or, at any rate, information which is not relevant to the grounds upon which warrants may be issued. Section 6 provides that in issuing a warrant, the Secretary of State shall ensure that 'so much of the intercepted material as is not certified by the certificate is not read, looked at or listened to by any person'.[144] And this requirement is satisfied if each of the following 'is limited to the minimum that is necessary' for the grounds on which the warrant is issued, namely:

(a) the extent to which the material is disclosed;

---

[143] Mr John McWilliam MP, 75 *Hansard*, cols. 211–12 (12 Mar. 1985) HC, quoted in Fitzgerald and Leopold, *Stranger on the Line*.
[144] S. 6 (1) (b).

(b) the number of persons to whom any of the material is disclosed;

(c) the extent to which the material is copied; and

(d) the number of copies made of any of the material . . . [145]

The practice of telephone-tapping obviously assists in the apprehension of criminal offenders and the prevention of crime. It is usually claimed that whatever misgivings civil libertarians may have about telephone-tapping, there is an overwhelming case for its use in detecting 'serious' offences and those that endanger 'national security'. Though the phrase 'serious crime' has now been defined in the Act,[146] 'national security' remains a slippery and notoriously subjective concept: '[e]vanescent anti-government remarks taken out of context can easily be made to sound more frightful than their true import.'[147]

The onus must be on those who wish to use the indiscriminate[148] method of investigation to demonstrate that there is an overwhelming need to do so, that their use is likely to be effective, and that there are no acceptable alternatives. If this cannot be established, it becomes almost impossible to justify the practice 'not because we wish to hamper law enforcement, but because there are values we place above efficient police work'.[149] As Sir Robert Megarry VC put it in *Malone*:

However much the protection of the public against crime demands that in proper cases the police should have the assistance of telephone tapping, I would have thought that in any civilised

[145] S. 6 (2).

[146] In s. 10 (3) it is defined to include crimes involving the use of violence, resulting in substantial financial gain or is conduct by a large number of persons in pursuit of a common purpose, or carries, for an adult first-offender a reasonable expectation of a minimum of three years' imprisonment.

[147] L. B. Schwartz, 'On Current Proposals to Legalize Wiretapping' (1954) 103 Univ. of Pa. Law Rev. 240, 262.

[148] A. Westin, 'The Wire Tapping Problem' (1952) 52 Colum. Law Rev. 165, 188, n. 112; B. C. Donnelly, 'Comments and Caveats on the Wire Tapping Controversy' (1954) 63 Yale LJ 799, 804; Y. Kamisar, 'The Wiretapping–Eavesdropping Problem' (1960) 44 Minn. Law Rev. 891.

[149] S. M. Beck, 'Electronic Surveillance and the Administration of Criminal Justice' (1968) 46 Can. Bar Rev. 643, 687.

system of law the claims of liberty and justice require that telephone users should have effective and independent safeguards against possible abuses.[150]

The statutory Commissioner, Lord Justice Lloyd, in his first report, searched in vain for evidence of abuse:

It would not have been possible in the time available to investigate every warrant. So I have adopted the practice, first described by Lord Diplock, and followed by Lord Bridge of Harwich, of selecting warrants at random, except in the case of warrants concerning counter-subversion, all of which I have examined. I have discussed these warrants in detail with the officers concerned, have inspected the files, and asked for any explanation that I have thought necessary. I can say at once that I have not come across a single case in which the information supplied by the Secretary of State has been incomplete or inaccurate, whether on the issue of the warrant or renewal. Nor have I come across a single case where the Secretary of State has not been justified in regarding the issue of a warrant as necessary in the interests of national security, or for the purposes mentioned in Section 2 (2) of the Act.[151]

This is no doubt reassuring. But the problem lies not so much in the manner in which the Act is *administered* as with the Act itself. It would be surprising if the terms of the Act were not being complied with, especially so soon after its introduction. It is not easy to resist the cynic's interpretation that the Act, passed merely to comply with the adverse *Malone* decision in Strasburg, simply codifies existing practice. No attempt was made by the Government to re-evaluate the justification of tapping or the conditions under which it should be permitted. Our law is out of step with that of European countries and the United States which require judicial authorization of taps, granted only as a last resort. Indeed, Belgian law goes so far as to make all tapping of

---

[150] [1979] 2 All ER 620, 649.
[151] *Report of the Commisioner for 1986*, para. 23. In his 1987 Report, Lord Justice Lloyd refers to the three incidents which gave him cause for concern: see *Report of the Commissioner for 1987*, paras. 16–21. All involved British Telecom intercepting the wrong lines. 'The three incidents show that things can go wrong. But I was satisfied by the answers I received from British Telecom, that everything which is humanly possible will be done to prevent such mistakes occurring in the future' (para. 21).

telephones, including tapping by the authorities, a criminal offence. Few would seriously advance so radical a solution in Britain, but as mentioned above, the West German model strikes a considerably fairer compromise between individual liberty and law enforcement than the British statute.

3. Interception of Correspondence

Among the allegations made in 1980 by the *New Statesman*[152] was the claim that the Post Office operates a systematic letter-opening section at its Investigation Division in Euston and at a 'special section' near St Paul's. The article described a variety of devices that it alleged were employed for this purpose.[153] As far as interceptions conducted with warrants are concerned, the number has declined fairly sharply since 1958.[154]

Two types of postal warrant are issued. The first relates to the interception of letters *to* an address certified in the warrant. The second (known as 'emanating warrants') seek the interception of correspondence *from* a particular address. Of the 76 postal warrants issued by the Home Secretary current at 31 December 1986, only 17 were 'emanating warrants'. Of the 72 outstanding on 31 December 1987, only 15 were 'emanating warrants'.[155] Intercepted letters are opened, photographed, resealed, and returned to the ordinary

[152] Feb. 1980, 158.

[153] For instance, long, thin pliers which enable letters to be rolled up and removed from their envelopes through its corners. 'Still more advanced equipment is already in service . . . allowing some mail to be read unopened. This is done by electronic scanning which can detect the carbon used in most kinds of ink' (160).

[154] The Government's 1980 White Paper revealed that the number of warrants issued by the Home Secretary had decreased: in 1958 the number issued was 109; in 1979 it had fallen to 52. According to the 1985 White Paper, the decline has tended to continue, until 1985, as follows: in 1980, 39; in 1981, 46; in 1982, 54; in 1983, 43; in 1984, 39. As at 31 Dec. 1984, 78 warrants authorizing the interception of letters (issued by the Home Secretary) were in force. The figures for 31 Dec. 1985 and 31 Dec. 1986 were 74 and 76 respectively, *Report of the Commissioner for 1986*, Annex. At 31 Dec. 1987 there were 71: *Report of the Commissioner for 1987*, Annex.   [155] *Report of the Commissioner for 1987*, para. 22.

postal system. The photograph is developed centrally. Only one print is made of each negative. The print is sent by special courier to the security service or other agency requesting the interception. The negative is normally destroyed within six months, and always destroyed within a year.[156]

Apart from the Interception of Communications Act 1985 which applies to postal communications, the law provides certain additional adventitious protection to correspondence. Unlike telephonic communications, a letter exists in a material form which, if it is appropriated may constitute theft or, if touched, trespass to goods; merely to read it will not suffice, for 'the eye cannot by the law of England be guilty of a trespass'.[157] But the plaintiff's complaint is not so much the interference with his property in the letter or telegram as the fact that their contents have been read. Hence the second form of protection, by statutes regulating the activities of employees of the Post Office, is not particularly helpful. Indeed, the power to intercept correspondence is recognized,[158] though (until the 1985 Act) not expressly provided, by statute. Thus section 58 (1) of the Post Office Act 1953 provides that no offence is committed by an officer of the

---

[156] *Report of the Commissioner for 1986*, para. 40–1. Lord Justice Lloyd acknowledges that 'emanating warrants' may not fit into the language of section 3 (A) (a). This refers to an 'address or addresses likely to be used for the transmissions of communications to or from one particular person . . .'. He remarks: 'One would not normally think of a letter being transmitted from a person's home address. It is more natural to think of it as being transmitted from the place where it is posted.' Nevertheless he did not 'wish to be thought to be casting any doubt on the legality of emanating warrants. Great care is taken to ensure that only letters emanating from the target are opened. If there is any doubt, the letter is left alone' (para. 40).

[157] *Entick* v. *Carrington* (1765) 19 How. St. Tr. 1030, 1066 per Camden LCJ.

[158] The Birkett Committee, above, accepted that this statute and its predecessors constituted a recognition of the power to intercept correspondence. It considered that officers who acted in accordance with an express warrant in writing under the hand of the Secretary of State had legal authority to intercept correspondence. Professor Street dismissed this notion as 'absurd': *Freedom, the Individual and the Law*, 5th edn. (1982) 44. Cf. L. H. Leigh, *Police Powers in England and Wales*, 2nd edn. (1985) 212.

Post Office who opens, delays, or detains a postal packet[159] in obedience to a warrant of the Secretary of State. Section 56 (1) provides that any person who is not employed by the Post Office is guilty of an offence if he 'wilfully and maliciously, with intent to injure any other person' opens a postal packet or does anything to prevent or impede its due delivery. The *mens rea* required would seem (the section has not been interpreted by the courts) to rule out its application to acts which consist merely of reading the contents of postal packets.

Thirdly, where the recipient of correspondence or a third party deliberately (or even accidentally) reads its contents and divulges them, an action may lie for breach of confidence. Of course, the proposals of the Law Commission (discussed above) in respect of the acquisition of confidential information by 'reprehensible means' would extend to the obtaining of such information by interference with correspondence, for there would, in most cases, be, on the part of the defendant, acquisition without authority, and this would be caught by the clause which covers 'taking, handling or interfering with any document, record, model or other thing containing the information'.[160]

4. Searches and Other Physical Intrusions

To those who conceive of 'privacy' as consisting in the 'right to be let alone' (see Chapter 1), virtually any physical encroachment upon an individual's 'private space' constitutes a violation of this right. Thus the whole range of activities associated with law enforcement[161] are taken to be prima-facie intrusions: searches and seizure of property, arrest,

---

[159] 'Postal packet' is defined in s. 87 (1) to include a letter, printed packet, sample packet or parcel, and every packet or article transmissible by post, and includes a telegram.

[160] Clause 5 (2) (a) (i) of the Law Commission's draft bill, Law Commission Report 194, and para. 6.31.

[161] Police powers are now 'rationalized' and, in many respects, extended, by the Police and Criminal Evidence Act 1984.

fingerprinting, polygraphs, blood, breath, and urine tests. And there are dicta in some recent English decisions involving searches authorized by statute in which the rhetoric of 'privacy' has been employed.[162]

But, while 'personal information' may be acquired as a result of these measures, it is clearly not their chief object and, in any event, they raise specific problems in their own right (and are therefore best treated independently from considerations of 'privacy' and, especially, 'personal information' as understood here). There are still glimmers of life in Lord Camden's celebrated declaration in *Entick* v. *Carrington*[163] that the 'great end for which men entered into society was to secure their property. That right is preserved sacred . . . in all instances where it has been abridged by some public law for the good of the whole.' And it is not difficult to see why the language of 'privacy' is called in aid to support it. Thus in the United States the Fourth Amendment (which establishes 'the right of the people to be secure . . . against unreasonable searches and seizures' and lays down the conditions under which search warrants may be issued) has been invoked to protect the individual's 'reasonable expectation of privacy' in cases involving various aspects of police

---

[162] For example *R. v. Inland Revenue Commissioners, ex parte Rossminster Ltd.* [1980] 2 WLR 15. Lord Wilberforce in the House of Lords (though upholding the validity of a comprehensive search of private and business premises and the seizure of a wide range of documents by Inland Revenue officials under s. 20C of the Taxes Management Act 1970 (as amended by the Finance Act 1976)) declared: 'The integrity and a privacy of a man's home, and of his place of business, an important human right has, since the second world war, been eroded by a number of statutes . . . [The courts] are the guardians of the citizen's right to privacy' (at 36). Lord Scarman stated that an uncontrolled power to enter premises and seize property would be 'a breath-taking inroad upon the individual's right of privacy and right of property' (at 59). Similarly, Lord Salmon said that the section 'makes a wide inroad into the citizen's basic human rights, the right to privacy in his own home and business premises, and the right to keep what belongs to him' (at 56–7).

[163] (1765) 19 How. St. Tr. 1030, 1066. 'Lord Camden . . . articulated what has come to be the classical position and so mesmerised has everyone become by this superficially attractive approach that English law has lamentably failed to develop an appropriate doctrine of the State or of State power' (Zellick, 'Government Beyond Law', 294).

investigation.[164] But this is to confuse the issues involved and may, in the end, prove counter-productive for, in the words of one commentator,

The Fourth Amendment, then, is a grand charter for privacy which rarely lives up to its promise because of the powerful exigencies of the criminal law. Most government searches occur when the government is looking for evidence of wrongdoing. Under these circumstances it is unfortunate but not surprising that claims of privacy often run into heavy weather, and that as a practical and political matter competing claims of law enforcement are difficult to overcome.[165]

5. Gathering of Information by the News Media

Attempts to reconcile the apparently conflicting interests of 'privacy' and press freedom, frequently neglect the subject of the rights of journalists to *gather* the information. But 'the right to gather information is logically antecedent and practically necessary to any exercise of [the right to publish] and . . . cannot be given full meaning unless that antecedent right is recognised.'[166]

Yet the existence of a privilege attaching to the press to gather information has generally been resisted both in Britain[167] and the United States.[168] As an English judge has

---

[164] Especially electronic surveillance: *Katz* v. *United States* 389 US 347 (1967); *Olmstead* v. *United States* 277 US 438, 476–7 (1982) per Brandeis J. (dissenting). See discussion of telephone-tapping above.

[165] J. H. F. Shattuck, *Rights of Privacy* (1977) 43–4.

[166] Note, 'The Right of the Press to Gather Information' (1971) 71 Colum. Law Rev. 838.

[167] 'We do not think that the process of inquiry involved in investigative journalism should be treated by the law in any different way from other journalistic activities. We accept it as being in principle a legitimate function of the press provided that it is carried on within the same rules which bind the ordinary citizen and the ordinary working journalist alike' (Younger, para. 184).

[168] The existence of such a right was denied by the United States Supreme Court in *Houchins* v. *KQED* 438 US 1 (1978): the majority held that to accept such a right would license the press to do anything that

said[169]

> I do not think that it can be too strongly emphasised that in this country the press has no right to go upon private property or into private places and intrude upon private people and into private rights, and that the standard of conduct and manners demanded of them is as high a standard as should be demanded of every citizen in a civilised community.

Of course, it is not necessarily only 'personal information' that the press is pursuing when it employs intrusive methods of newsgathering or photography, though the sensationalism (and trivialization) that appears to be one of the hallmarks of many newspapers requires a steady supply of gossip relating to the most intimate features of individuals' lives. And much of this is obtained by methods that, in the rhetoric of Warren and Brandeis, oversteps 'the obvious bounds of propriety and of decency. Gossip is no longer the resource of the idle and of the vicious, but has become a trade which is pursued with industry as well as effrontery.'[170]

Apart from the common law remedies mentioned above, an individual in Britain who is the victim of (improper if not unlawful) intrusion by the press may complain to the Press Council[171] which, in its 1976 'Declaration of Principle on Privacy', adopted the view that

> Invasion of privacy by deception, eavesdropping or technological methods which are not in themselves unlawful can . . . only be

facilitated the publication of information. Cf. (on a more limited claim to receive ideas and information) *Board of Education, Island Trees Union Free School District No. 26 v. Pico* 102 S. Ct. 2799 (1982). An associated matter is the extent to which journalists have a right to refuse to disclose their sources. The Supreme Court (by 5 to 4) rejected such a right in *Branzburg v. Hayes* 408 US 655 (1972).

[169] Hilberry J. in *Lea v. Justice of the Peace Ltd.* [1974] *The Times*, 15 Mar. The question of journalists' right to refuse to disclose sources arose indirectly in *British Steel Corporation v. Granada Television* [1981] AC 1096, and is now covered by s. 10 of the Contempt of Court Act 1981 which provides that sources need not be disclosed unless necessary in the interests of justice, national security, or the prevention of crime, applied in *Secretary of State for Defence v. Guardian Newspapers Ltd.* [1984] 3 WLR 986.

[170] Warren and Brandeis 'The Right to Privacy' 196.

[171] See H. P. Levy, *The Press Council: History, Procedure and Cases* (1967); G. Robertson, *People Against the Press: An Enquiry into the Press Council* (1983).

justified when it is in pursuit of information which ought to be published in the public interest and there is no other reasonably practicable method of obtaining or confirming it.[172]

But this is to conflate the criteria by which acquisition is to be judged with those that ought to apply in respect of publication. As was suggested in Chapter 5, the application of the test of what is in the 'public interest' is properly applied where material has been published. The *means* by which the information was acquired should, however, be judged by reference to the reasonableness of the intruder's conduct. The failure to draw this distinction is not limited to the Press Council, and is adopted in several decisions of the courts as well as in the literature. In one American decision,[173] however, the point of preserving a dichotomy was well expressed:

We agree that newsgathering is an integral part of news dissemination. We strongly disagree, however, that the hidden mechanical contrivances are 'indispensable tools' of newsgathering. Investigative reporting is an ancient art; its successful practice long antecedes the invention of miniature cameras and electronic devices. The First Amendment is not a licence to steal, or to intrude by electronic means into the precincts of another's home or office. *It does not become such a licence simply because the person subjected to the intrusion is reasonably suspected of committing a crime.*

[172] Press Council Annual Report 1976, No. 23, 150. It enjoins journalists to use 'sympathy and discretion' and to avoid causing 'pain or humiliation to bereaved or distressed people unless it is clear that publication ... will serve a legitimate public interest and there is no other reasonably practicable method of obtaining the material'. Its approach is exemplified in *Press Conduct in the Lambton Affair*, A Report by the Press Council (1974), in which it concluded: 'There is a danger about being too censorious about how information that can lead to the exposure of a serious public ill is obtained ... methods may be justified which would be wholly unacceptable in some less serious case ... But that is no excuse for using such methods if more acceptable methods are available. Nor will it serve to justify activities if the affair, though ostensibly serious, turns out to be a mare's nest. In other words, the user of such methods, be he citizen or Press, employs them at the risk of the reputation and nothing but success is an acceptable excuse' (para. 75). The Council has adjudicated on several complaints relating to intrusions by reporters and photographers.

[173] *Dietemann* v. *Time, Inc.* 449 F. 2d 245 (1971). See now *X v. Y* [1983] 3 All ER 648.

By the same token, the public disclosure of personal information ought not to be proscribed on the ground merely that the means employed to acquire it are improper.

6. Exclusion of Evidence Improperly Obtained

Where evidence has been obtained by methods which are unlawful or reprehensible, a court in a criminal trial may, in its discretion, refuse to admit it. But while the American courts,[174] in interpreting the protection of the Fourth Amendment against 'unreasonable searches and seizures', adopt a fairly rigid opposition to admitting the 'fruits of a poisoned tree',[175] the English courts[176] rarely exercise their discretion to reject evidence—no matter how it was acquired.[177] It is clear that the American approach constitutes a considerable disincentive against the use of telephone-tapping and other forms of electronic eavesdropping in order to obtain evidence. And this is its principal justification; as one Supreme Court Justice declared, 'Its purpose is to deter—to compel respect for the constitutional guaranty in the only effectively available way—by removing the incentive to disregard it.'[178]

Placing probative value above concerns of morality,[179] the

[174] There is a host of decisions on the exclusionary rule, e.g. *Weeks v. US* 232 US 383 (1914), *Elkins v. US* 364 US 206 (1960), *Mapp v. US* 367 US 643 (1961). The US legislation on the subject provides that 'no part of the contents [of a communication] and . . . no evidence derived therefrom' is admissible in breach of the statutory procedures.

[175] *Nardone v. US* 316 US 379 (1937).

[176] *Kuruma v. R.* [1955] AC 197 is still the leading case, after which 'it would be hard to imagine a case where the illegally obtained evidence would ever be excluded' (J. D. Heydon, 'Illegally Obtained Evidence' (1973) Crim. LJ 603, 607); *Callis v. Gunn* [1964] 1 QB 495, 501–2, per Lord Parker CJ; *R. v. Sang* [1980] AC 402. Cf. *Jeffrey v. Black* [1978] 490, 498 (per Lord Widgery CJ).

[177] 'It matters not how you get it; if you steal it even, it would be admissible evidence' (*R. v. Leatham* (1861) 8 Cox C. C. 489, 501, per Crompton J).   [178] Stewart J in *Elkins v. US*, see above, *supra* 217.

[179] 'The method of the informer and of the eavesdropper is commonly used in the detection of crime . . . If . . . the appellants by incautious talk provided evidence against themselves, then in the view of the court it would not be unfair to use it against them' (*R. v. Maqsud Ali; R. v. Ashiq Hussain* [1966] 1 QB 688, 702, per Marshall J.).

English courts, while acknowledging the impropriety of many methods by which it is acquired,[180] nevertheless admit evidence obtained through eavesdropping,[181] the interception of telephone conversations,[182] impersonation,[183] the use of *agents provocateurs*,[184] and the obtaining of body fluid without consent.[185]

The Younger Committee[186] declined to recommend any change in the law in respect of the exclusion of evidence obtained by surveillance devices in view of the then pending report of the Criminal Law Revision Committee.[187] But that report was silent on the matter. The Royal Commission on Criminal Procedure was unpersuaded by arguments in favour of the adoption of an exclusionary rule along American lines[188] and (despite a broader amendment proposed in the House of Lords by Lord Scarman) the Government adopted its own amendment which is now section 78 of the Police and Criminal Evidence Act 1984. The section provides:

(1) In any proceedings the court may refuse to allow evidence on which the prosecution proposes to rely to be given if it appears to the court that, having regard to all the circumstances, including the

---

[180] '. . . in the Divorce Court, evidence is admitted daily which results from what many people would say is really outrageous conduct, in the sense of being an invasion of privacy or ungentlemanly conduct, prying through keyholes, climbing up and looking through windows, fixing speaking apparatus, recordings and so on . . .' (*R.* v. *Senat* (1968) 52 Cr. App. R 282, 286–7, per Lord Parker CJ). See, too, *Gabbitas* v. *Gabbitas* [1967] *The Times*, 5 Dec.

[181] *R.* v. *Maqsud Ali; R.* v. *Ashiq Hussain* [1966] 1 QB 688, 702.

[182] *R.* v. *Keeton* (1970) 54 Cr. App. R 267.

[183] *R.* v. *Stewart* (1970) 54 Cr. App. R 210.

[184] *R.* v. *Sang* [1980] AC 402.

[185] *R.* v. *Apicella* [1985] *The Times*, 5 Dec.

[186] Younger, paras. 571–2.

[187] Eleventh Report of the Criminal Law Revision Committee, Evidence (General) Cmnd. 2991, 1972.

[188] Cmnd. 8092–1, 1981, paras. 2.123–4.128. It took the view that evidence in the US did not show that the exclusionary rule significantly deterred improper police conduct. In any event, it argued, the rule could affect only the few cases in which the defendant ultimately pleaded not guilty. Moreover, it operated many months after the event. In its view the proper way to control police misconduct was by disciplining the police or by actions for damages. Cf. A. J. Ashworth, 'Excluding Evidence as Protecting Rights' (1977) Crim. LR 723.

circumstances in which the evidence was obtained, the admission of the evidence would have such an adverse effect on the fairness of the proceedings that the court ought not to admit it. (2) Nothing in this section shall prejudice any rule of law requiring a court to exclude evidence.

This provision appears to be susceptible of a fairly robust interpretation, but it is doubtful, in view of the history of the judges' attitude toward admitting evidence a probative value, whether such an approach will be adopted. Professor Zander[189] suggests,

It is conceivable that they will interpret the section narrowly and admit evidence obtained by thoroughly deplorable methods on the pretext that it does not affect the fairness of the *proceedings*. This would emasculate the discretion. The whole thrust of the policy behind the new section is to give courts the power to express their disapproval of objectionable police methods by excluding the fruits of such action. No doubt it would only be used rarely but the discretion is 'at large' and should be interpreted in a broad way.

The resolution of the problem of admissibility turns on the question whether it is 'morally correct and appropriate to a free society'[190] for the police to be seen to be acting

---

[189] *The Police and Criminal Evidence Act 1984* (1985), 116–17. The Court of Appeal has recently considered section 78: *R.* v. *Mason* (1987) *Independent*, 25 May; it held that the court has a discretion to refuse to admit a confession obtained by trickery even though there is no breach of the section. In *Matto* v. *Woverhampton Crown Court* (1987) *The Times*, 27 May, the Court of Appeal held that the section did not reduce a court's discretion to exclude evidence which it could have excluded at common law.

[190] M. G. Paulsen, 'The Exclusionary Rule and Misconduct by the Police' in C. R. Sowle (ed.), *Police Power and Individual Freedom* (1962), 87, 90. A workmanlike formulation in respect of the admissibility of intercepted conversations is to be found in the Canadian Criminal Code s. 178.16 (1) which provides: 'A private communication that has been intercepted is inadmissible as evidence against the originator of the communication or the person intended by the originator to receive it unless (a) the interception was lawfully made; or (b) the originator thereof or the person intended by the originator to receive it has expressly consented to the admission thereof; but evidence obtained directly or indirectly as a result of information acquired by interception of a private communication is not admissible by reason only that the private communication is itself inadmissible as evidence.' The court has a discretion to reject evidence

improperly or, *a fortiori*, unlawfully. It is often urged that this 'misguided sentimentality'[191] impairs the process of criminal justice[192] or (as was suggested by the Royal Commission) that there is no empirical basis for the claim that the exclusionary rule deters the police from employing these methods;[193] indeed, that the rule may actually induce them to use even less desirable methods.[194]

derived from information acquired through interception where it is of the opinion that its admission 'would bring the administration of justice into disrepute': s. 178.16.2.

[191] J. H. Wigmore, *A Treatise on the Anglo-American System of Evidence*, 3rd edn., vol. iii, para. 2184.

[192] Ibid.

[193] 'The federal exclusionary rule in effect now for nearly fifty years has not noticeably deterred illegal searches and seizures' (McGarr, 'The Exclusionary Rule: An Ill Conceived and Ineffective Remedy' in Sowle, *Police Power and Individual Freedom*, 99, 101. The difficulties of measurement are obviously considerable.

[194] J. B. Waite, 'Judges and the Crime Burden' (1955) 54 Mich. Law Rev. 169, 196; Heydon, 'Illegally Obtained Evidence', 696.

Bibliography

1. *Books and Periodical Literature*

ALSCHULER, A. W., 'A Different View of Privacy' (1971) 49 Tex. Law Rev. 872.

AMSTERDAM, A. G., 'The Supreme Court and the Rights of Suspects in Criminal Cases' (1970) NYU Law Rev. 785.

ARENDT, HANNAH, *The Human Condition*, Chicago: University of Chicago Press, 1958.

ASHWORTH, A. J., 'Excluding Evidence as Protecting Rights' (1977) Crim. LR 723.

ASKIN, FRANK, 'Surveillance: The Social Science Perspective' (1972) 4 Colum. HR Rev. 59.

BAKER C. E., 'Posner's Privacy Mystery and the Failure of the Economic Analysis of Law' (1978) 12 Ga. Law Rev. 475.

BAKER, MICHAEL A., 'Record Privacy as a Marginal Problem: The Limits of Consciousness and Concern' (1972) 4 Colum. HR Rev. 89.

BARENDT, ERIC, *Freedom of Speech*, Oxford: Clarendon Press, 1985.

BARNES, J. A., *Who Should Know What? Social Science, Privacy and Ethics*, Harmondsworth: Penguin, 1979.

BARTH, ALAN, *The Price of Liberty*, New York: The Viking Press, 1961.

BARTON, W. B., 'A Study in the Law of Trade Secrets' (1939) 13 Univ. Cincinnati Law Rev. 507.

BEANEY, W. M., 'The Right to Privacy and American Law' (1966) 31 Law & Contemp. Probs. 252.

BEARDSLEY E. L., 'Privacy, Autonomy and Selective Disclosure' *Nomos XIII* 56 (1971).

BECK, S. M., 'Electronic Surveillance and the Administration of Criminal Justice' (1968) 46 Can. Bar Rev. 643.

BENN, STANLEY I., 'Privacy, Freedom and Respect for Persons' (1971) *Nomos XIII* 56.

—— 'Protection and Limitation of Privacy' (1978) Austral. LJ 601; 686.

——, and GAUS, GERALD, *Public and Private in Social Life*, London: Croom Helm and St Martin's Press, 1983.

BERTELSMAN, W. O., 'The First Amendment and Protection of Reputation and Privacy: *New York Times* v. *Sullivan* and How it Grew' (1967–8) 56 Ky. LJ 718.

BEVAN, VAUGHAN, 'Is Anybody There?' (1980) Public Law 431.

BING, JON, 'Classification of Personal Information, with Respect to the Sensitivity Aspect' in *Proceedings of the First International Oslo Symposium on Data Banks and Society*, Oslo: Scandinavian University Books, 1972.

—— 'A Background Analysis for Information Law' (1987) 1 Int. Computer Law Adviser 12.

BLOUSTEIN, E. J., 'Privacy as an Aspect of Human Dignity: An Answer to Dean Prosser' (1964) 39 NYU Law Rev. 962.

—— 'Privacy, Tort Law, and the Constitution: Is Warren and Brandeis' Tort Petty and Unconstitutional as Well?' (1968) 46 Tex. Law Rev. 611.

—— 'Privacy is Dear At Any Price: A Response to Professor Posner's Economic Theory? (1978) 12 Ga. Law Rev. 429.

BOK, SISSELA, *Secrets: On the Ethics of Concealment and Revelation*, New York: Pantheon, 1982.

BOYLE, CHRISTINE, 'Confidence v. Privilege' (1974) 25 Northern Ireland LQ 31.

BRATHWAITE. W. J. 'The Secret of Life: A Fruity Trade Secret' (1979) 95 LQR 323.

BRAZIER, M., *Medicine, Patients and the Law*. Harmondsworth: Penguin, 1987.

BRENNAN, W. J., 'The Supreme Court and the Meiklejohn Interpretation of the First Amendment' (1965) 79 Harv. Law Rev. 1.

BRETT, P., 'Free Speech, Supreme-Court Style: A View from Overseas' (1968) 46 Tex. Law Rev. 668.

BRITTAN, LEON, 'The Right of Privacy in England and the United States' (1963) 37 Tulane Law Rev. 235.

BRODIE, D. W., 'Privacy: The Family and the State' Univ. of Illinois Law Forum, vol. 1972, no. 4.

BRYAN, M. W., 'The Crossman Diaries: Developments in the Law of Breach of Confidence' (1976) 92 LQR 180.

BURNS, P., 'Privacy and the Law: 1984 is Now' (1974) NZLJ 1.

CAM ZACHRY, H., 'The Abortion Decisions: *Roe v. Wade, Doe v. Bolton*' (1973) 12 J. Family Law 459.

CAMPBELL, DUNCAN, and CONNOR, STEVE, *On the Record: Surveillance, Computers and Privacy: The Inside Story*, London: Michael Joseph, 1986.

CANAVAN, F., 'Freedom of Speech and Press: For What Purpose?' (1971) 16 Am. J. Jurisp. 95.

CHAFEE, ZECHARIAH, JR., *Free Speech in the United States*, Cambridge, Mass.: Harvard University Press, 1941.

—— *Government and Mass Communication: A Report from the Commission on Freedom of the Press* Chicago: Shoe String Press, Inc., 1965.

—— Book Review, (1949) 62 Harv. Law Rev. 891.

CHRISTENSEN, T. R., 'Do We Have to Live with Eavesdropping: A Legislative Proposal' (1965) 38 S. Calif. Law Rev. 622.

CHRISTIE, G. C., 'The Right to Privacy and the Freedom to Know: A Comment on Professor Miller's *The Assault on Privacy*' (1971) 119 Univ. of Pa. Law Rev. 970.

COHEN, M., NAGEL, T., and SCANLON, T. (eds.), *Medicine and Moral Philosophy*, Princeton, NJ: Princeton University Press, 1981.

COLLINS, HUGH, 'The Decline of Privacy in Private Law' (1987) 14 J. of Law & Soc. 91.

COOLEY, THOMAS, M., *A Treatise on the Law of Torts*, 2nd edn. 1988.

—— A Treatise on the Constitutional Limitations, ii, 8th edn., Boston: Little, Brown, & Co., 1927.

CORNISH, W. R., Intellectual Property: Patents, Copyrights, Trade Marks and Allied Rights, London: Sweet & Maxwell, 1981.

COSMAN, R. W., 'A Man's House in his Castle—"Beep": A Civil Law Remedy for the Invasion of Privacy' (1971) 29 Faculty of Law Rev., Univ. of Toronto 3.

COUNTRYMAN, V., 'The Diminishing Right of Privacy: The Personal Dossier and the Computer, (1971) 49 Tex. Law Rev. 837.

CRIPPS, YVONNE, The Legal Implications of Disclosure in the Public Interest: An Analysis of Prohibitions and Protections with Particular Reference to Employers and Employees, Oxford: ESC Publishing Ltd., 1986.

—— 'The Public Interest Defence to the Action for Breach of Confidence and the Law Commission's Proposals on Disclosure in the Public Interest' (1984) 4 Ox. J. Leg. Stud. 361.

DASH, S., SCHWARTZ, R. F., and KNOWLTON, R. E., The Eavesdroppers, New Brunswick: Rutgers University Press, 1959.

DAVIS, F, 'What Do We Mean By "Right to Privacy"?' (1959) 5 S. Dak. Law Rev. 1.

DICKERSON, R, 'Some Jurisprudential Implications of Electronic Data Processing' (1963) 28 Law & Contemp. Probs. 53.

DICKLER, G., 'The Right of Privacy: A Proposed Redefinition' (1936) 70 US (formerly Am.) Law Rev. 435.

DIXON, ROBERT, G. JR., 'The Griswold Penumbra: Constitutional Charter for an Expanded Law of Privacy?' (1965) 64Mich. Law Rev. 197.

DONNELLY, B. C., 'Comments and Caveats on the Wire Tapping Controversy' (1954) 63 Yale LJ 799.

DOWD, W., et al., 'The Press, Privacy, and "Public" Figures: A Symposium' (1967) 12 Vill. Law Rev. 725.

DWORKIN, GERALD, Confidence in the Law, An Inaugural Lecture, Univ. of Southampton, 1971.

—— 'The Common Law Protection of Privacy' (1967) 2 Univ. Tas. Law Rev. 418.

—— 'The Younger Committee Report on Privacy' (1973) 36 MLR 399.

—— 'Access to Medical Records: Discovery, Confidentiality and Privacy' (1979) 42 MLR 88.

DWORKIN, RONALD, Taking Rights Seriously, London: Duckworth, 1977.

—— Law's Empire, Cambridge, Mass.; London: Belnap Press, 1986.

ELLIOTT, I. D., 'Listening Devices and the Participant Monitor: Controlling the Use of Electronic Surveillance in Law Enforcement' (1982) 6 Crim. LJ 327.

ELY, JOHN 'The Wages of Crying Wolf: A Comment on Roe v. Wade' (1973) 82 Yale LJ 920.

EMERSON, THOMAS I., The System of Freedom of Expression, New York: Random, 1970.

—— 'Toward a General Theory of the First Amendment' (1963) 72 Yale LJ 877.

—— 'The Right of Privacy and Freedom of the Press' (1979) 14 Harv. Civ. Rights—Civ. Libs. Law Rev. 329.

——, HABER, D., and DORSEN, N., *Political and Civil Rights in the United States*, vol. i (and suppl.) Boston: Little, Brown & Co., 1967; suppl. 1973.

EPSTEIN, RICHARD, 'Privacy, Property Rights and Misrepresentation' (1978) 12 Ga. Law Rev. 455.

—— 'A Taste for Privacy? Evolution and the Emergence of a Naturalistic Ethic' (1980) 9 J. of Legal Stud. 665.

ERNST, M. L., and SCHWARTZ, A. U., *Privacy*, London: MacGibbon & Kee, 1968.

ERVIN, SAM J., 'Privacy and the Constitution' (1972) 59 NC Law Rev. 1016.

—— 'The First Amendment: A Living Thought in the Computer Age' (1972) 4 Colum. HR Law Rev. 13.

EVANS, HAROLD, 'The Half Free Press' in *The Freedom of the Press*, Granada Guildhall Lectures 1974, London: Hart-Davis, MacGibbon, 1974.

FEINBERG, W., 'Recent Developments in the Law of Privacy' (1948) 48 Colum. Law Rev. 713.

FINN, P. D., *Fiduciary Obligations*, 5th edn., Sydney, The Law Book Co. Ltd., 1977.

FITZGERALD, PATRICK, and LEOPOLD, MARK, *Stranger on the Line: The Secret History of Phone Tapping*, London: Bodley Head, 1987.

FLAHERTY, DAVID, *Privacy in Colonial New England*, Charlottesville: University of Virginia Press, 1972.

—— *Protecting Privacy in Two-Way Electronic Services*, White Plains, NY: Knowledge and Industry Publications, 1984.

—— *Privacy and Data Protection: An International Bibliography*, London: Mansell, 1984.

FRAZER, TIM, 'Appropriation of Personality: A New Tort?' (1983) 99 LQR 281.

FRIED, CHARLES, *An Anatomy of Values: Problems of Personal and Social Choice*, Cambridge, Mass.: Harvard University Press, 1970.

—— 'Privacy' (1968) 77 Yale LJ 475.

—— 'Privacy: Economics and Ethics: A Comment on Posner' (1978) 12 Ga. Law Rev. 423.

GAVISON, RUTH, 'Privacy and the Limits of Law' (1980) 89 Yale LJ 421.

—— 'Information Control: Availability and Exclusion' in Benn and Gaus (eds.), *The Private and the Public in Social Life*.

GERETY, TOM, 'Redefining Privacy' (1977) 12 Harv. Civ. Rights—Civ. Libs. Law Rev. 233.

GERSTEIN, ROBERT, 'Privacy and Self-incrimination' (1970) 80 Ethics 87.

—— 'Intimacy and Privacy', in F. Schoeman (ed.), *Philosophical Dimensions of Privacy: An Anthology*.

GIBSON, DALE (ed.), *Aspects of Privacy Law*, Toronto: Butterworth, 1980.

GOERNER, A. A., 'Confidential Relationship: When Does Such Relation Exist?, (1927) 12 Cornell LQ 502.

GOFF, R., and JONES, G., *The Law of Restitution*, 3rd edn., London: Sweet & Maxwell, 1986.

GOLDSTEIN, R C., *The Cost of Privacy*, Brighton, Ma.: Honeywell Information Systems, 1975.

GORDON, H. R., 'Right of Property in Name, Likeness, Personality and History' (1961) 55 NW Law Rev. 553.

GOROVITZ, S., *et al.* (eds.), *Moral Problems in Medicine*, Englewood Cliffs, NJ: Prentice Hall, 1976.

GOTLIEB, A. E., 'Computers and Privacy' (1971) 2 J. Can. Bar Ass. 27.

GOULD, J. P., 'Privacy and the Economics of Information' (1980) 9 J. of Legal Stud. 827.

GRANT, HAMMOND, R., 'Quantum Physics, Econometric Models and Property Rights to Information' (1981) 27 McGill LJ 47.

—— 'Theft of Information' (1984) 100 LQR 252.

GREEN, L., 'The Right of Privacy' (1932) 27 NW Law Rev. 237.

GREENAWALT, KENT, 'The Consent Problem in Wiretapping and Eavesropping . . .' (1968) 68 Colum. Law Rev. 189.

GROSS, HYMAN, 'The Concept of Privacy' (1967) 42 NYU Law Rev. 34.

—— 'Privacy and Autonomy' (1971) *Nomos XIII* 169.

GULLEFORD, KENNETH, *Data Protection in Practice*, London: Butterworth, 1986.

GURRY, FRANCIS, *Breach of Confidence*, Oxford: Clarendon Press, 1984.

GUTTERIDGE, H. C., and WALTON, F. P., 'The Comparative Law of the Right to Privacy' (1931) 47 LQR 203.

HAIMAN, FRANKLYN, S., *Speech and Law in a Free Society*, Chicago: University of Chicago Press, 1981.

HALLBORG, ROBERT B. Jr., 'Principles of Liberty and the Right to Privacy' (1986) 5 Law & Philosophy 175.

HALMOS, PAUL, *Solitude and Privacy*, London: Greenwood, 1953.

HAMILTON, PETER, *Espionage and Subversion in an Industrial Society*, London: Hutchinson, 1967.

HARPER, TOM, 'Telephone Tapping' (1974) 124 NLJ 782.

HAYDEN, TRUDY, and NOVIK, JACK, *Your Rights to Privacy*, New York: Avon Books, 1980.

HENKIN, LOUIS, 'Privacy and Autonomy' (1974) 74 Colum. Law Rev. 1410.

HEWITT, PATRICIA, *Privacy: The Information Gatherers*, London: NCCL, 1977.

HEYDON, J. D., 'Illegally Obtained Evidence' (1973) Crim. LJ 603.

HICKSON, PHILIP, *Industrial Counter-Espionage*, London: Spectator Publications Ltd., 1968.

HILL, ALBERT, 'Defamation and Privacy under the First Amendment' (1976) Colum. Law Rev. 1205.

HIRSHLEIFER, J., 'Privacy: Its Origin, Function and Future' (1980) 9 J. Leg. Stud. 649.

HIXSON, RICHARD F., *Privacy in a Public Society: Human Rights in Conflict*, New York: Oxford University Press, 1987.

HOCKING, W. E., *Freedom of the Press: A Framework of Principle*, Report from the Commission on Freedom of the Press, Illinois: University of Chicago Press, 1947.

HOESE, W. J., 'Electronic Eavesdropping: A New Approach' (1942) 52 Calif. Law Rev. 142.

HOFFMAN, L. J., (ed.), *Security and Privacy in Computer Systems*, Los Angeles: Melville Publishing Co., 1973.

—— (ed.), *Computers and Privacy in the Next Decade*, New York: Academic Press, 1980.

HOFSTADTER, S. H., and HOROWITZ, G., *The Right of Privacy*, New York: Central Book Co., 1964.

HORWITZ, M., 'The History of the Public/Private Distinction' (1982) 130 Univ. of Pa. Law Rev. 1423.

HOWARD A., 'The Press, Privacy and the Law', *New Statesman* 8 June (1973).

HUFF, T., 'Thinking Clearly about Privacy' (1980) 58 Wash. Law Rev. 777.

HYDE, H. MONTGOMERY, *Privacy and the Press*, London: Butterworth, 1947.

JACOB, J., and JACOB, R., 'Confidential Communications' (1969) 19 NLJ 133.

—— 'Protection of Privacy' (1969) 119 NLJ 158.

JONES, GARETH, 'Restitution of Benefits Obtained in Breach of Another's Confidence' (1970) 86 LQR 463.

—— 'The Law Commission's Report on Breach of Confidence' (1982) Camb. LJ 40.

JONES, MERVYN, (ed.), *Privacy*, London: David & Charles. 1974.

JONES, R. V., 'Some Threats of Technology to Privacy' in Robertson (ed.), *Privacy and Human Rights*.

JOURARD, S. M., 'Some Psychological Aspects of Privacy' (1966) 31 Law & Contemp. Probs. 307.

KACEDAN, B. W., 'The Right of Privacy' (1937) 12 Univ. of Boston Law Rev. 353.

KALVEN, HARRY, 'Privacy in Tort Law: Were Warren and Brandeis Wrong?' (1966) 31 Law & Contemp. Probs. 326.

KAMENKA, E., 'Public/Private in Marxist Theory and Marxist Practice' in Benn & Gaus (eds.), *The Private and the Public in Social Life*.

KAMISAR, YALE, 'The Wiretapping-Eavesdropping Problem: Reflections on *The Eavesdroppers*. A Professor's View' (1960) 44 Minn. Law Rev. 891.

KARAFIOL, E., 'The Right to Privacy and the Sidis Case' (1978) 12 Ga. Law Rev. 513.

KARST, K. L., 'The Files: Legal Controls Over the Accuracy of Stored Personal Data' (1966) 31 Law & Contemp. Probs. 341.

KATZENBACH, NICHOLAS DE B., and TOME, R. W., 'Crime Data Centres: The Use of Computers in Crime Prevention and Detection' (1972) 4 Colum. HR Rev. 49.

KENNEDY, DUNCAN, 'The Stages of the Decline of the Public/Private Distinction' (1982) 130 Univ. of Pa. Law Rev. 1349.

KENNEDY, I., *The Unmasking of Medicine*, London: Granada, 1983.

KIDD, C. J. F., 'Freedom from Unwanted Publicity' in J. W. Bridge, D. Lasok, A. Plender, and D. L. Perrott (eds.), *Fundamental Rights*, Univ. of Exeter Law School, London: Sweet & Maxwell, 1973.

KING, D. B., 'Electronic Surveillance and Constitutional Rights: Some Recent Developments and Observations' (1964) 33 G. Wash. Law Rev. 240.

KITCH, E., 'The Law and Economics of Rights in Valuable Information' (1980) 9 J. Legal Stud. 683.

KONVITZ, M. R., 'Privacy and the Law: A Philosophical Prelude' (1966) 31 Law & Contemp. Probs. 272.

KOTTOW, MICHAEL H., 'Medical Confidentiality: An Intransigent and Absolute Obligation' (1986) 12 J. Med. Ethics 117.

KRAUSE, H. D., 'The Right to Privacy in Germany: Pointers for American Legislation?' (1965) Duke LJ 481.

KRONMAN, ANTHONY, 'The Privacy Exemption to the Freedom of Information Act' (1980) 9 JL 727.

LARREMORE, S., 'The Law of Privacy' (1912) 12 Colum. Law Rev. 693.

LEIGH, L. H., *Police Powers in England and Wales*, 2nd edn., London: Butterworth, 1985.

LEVY, H. PHILLIP, *The Press Council: History, Procedure and Cases*, London: Macmillan & Co., 1967.

LIBLING, D. F., 'The Concept of Property: Property in Intangibles' (1978) 94 LQR 103.

LIPSET, H, K., 'The Wiretapping-Eavesdropping Problem: Reflections on *The Eavesdroppers*. A Private Investigator's View' (1960) 44 Minn. Law Rev. 837.

LISTER, CHARLES, Book review, (1973) 82 Yale LJ 619.

LOCKWOOD, M. (ed.), *Moral Dilemmas in Modern Medicine*, Oxford: Oxford University Press, 1985.

LONG, EDWARD, V., *The Intruders: The Invasion of Privacy by Government and Industry*, New York: Praeger, 1967.

LUDWIG, F. J., ' "Peace of Mind" in 48 Pieces vs. Uniform Right of Privacy' (1948) 32 Minn. Law Rev. 734.

LUNSGAARDE, H. P., 'Privacy: An Anthropological Perspective of the Right to be Let Alone' (1971) 8 Houston Law Rev. 858.

LUSKY, L., 'Invasion of Privacy: A Clarification of Concepts' (1972) 72 Colum. Law Rev. 693.

LUKES, S., *Individualism*, Oxford: Basil Blackwell, 1973.

McCLOSKEY, H. J., 'The Political Ideal of Privacy' (1971) 21 Philosoph. Q. 303.

MacCORMICK, D. N., 'Right of Privacy' (1972) 89 LQR 23.

—— 'Privacy: A Problem of Definition' (1974) 1 Br. J. of Law & Soc. 75.

McQUOID-MASON, D. J., *The Law of Privacy in South Africa*, Cape Town: Juta & Co., 1978.

MADGWICK, DONALD, *Privacy Under Attack*, NCCL. London: 1968.

—— and SMYTHE, TONY, *The Invasion of Privacy*, London: Pitman Publishing, 1974.

MARSH, N. S., 'Hohfeld and Privacy' (1973) 89 LQR 183.

MARSHALL, G., *Constitutional Theory*, Oxford: Oxford University Press, 1971.

MARTIN, ANDRES, 'Privacy in English Law' in Robertson (ed.) *Privacy and Human Rights*.

MARTIN, J., and NORMAN, A. R. D., *The Computerised Society*, Harmondsworth: Penguin Books, 1973.

MATHIESON, D. L., '*Sim* v. *Heinz* and other Aspects of Breach of Confidence in Relation to Privacy' (1961) 39 Can. Bar Rev. 409.

MEAGHER, R. P., GUMMOW, W. M. C., and LEHANE, J. R. F., *Equity: Doctrines, and Remedies*, Sydney: Butterworths, 1984.

MEIKLEJOHN, ALEXANDER, *Political Freedom: The Constitutional Powers of the People*, New York: Oxford University Press, 1965.

—— 'The First Amendment is an Absolute' (1961) Supreme Court Review 245.

MICHAEL, D. N., 'Speculations on the Relation of the Computer to Individual Freedom and the Right of Privacy' (1964) 33 G. Wash. Law Rev. 270.

MILL, J. S., *On Liberty*, ed. Gertrude Himelfarb, Harmondsworth: Penguin Books, 1974.

MILLARD, CHRISTOPHER J., *Legal Protection of Computer Programs and Data*, London: Sweet & Maxwell, 1985.

MILLER, ARTHUR R., *The Assault on Privacy*, Ann Arbor: The University of Michigan Press, 1971.

—— 'Personal Privacy in the Computer Age: The Challenge of a New Technology in an Information-Oriented Society' (1969) 67 Mich. Law Rev. 1089.

—— 'Computers, Data Banks and Individual Privacy: An Overview' (1972) 4 Colum. HR Rev. 1.

MILLER, A. S., 'Privacy in the Corporate State: A Constitutional Value of Dwindling Significance' (1973) 22 J. Pub. Law 3.

MNOOKIN, R. H., 'The Public/Private Dichotomy: Political Disagreement and Academic Reputation' (1982) 130 Univ. of Pa. Law Rev. 1429.

MORGAN, R. G., '*Roe* v. *Wade* and the Lesson of the Pre-*Roe* Case Law' (1979) 77 Mich. Law Rev. 1724.

MURUMBA, S. K., *Commercial Exploitation of Property*, Sydney: Law Book Co. Ltd., 1986.

NATHAN (LORD), 'Eavesdropping' (1958) 225 *The Law Times* 99, 135, 149.

NEILL, BRIAN, 'Protection of Privacy' (1954) 19 Law & Contemp. Probs. 203.

NANULA, PETER J., 'Protecting Confidentiality in the Effort to Control AIDS' (1986) 24 Harv. J. on Legis. 315.

NIBLETT, B., *Legal Protection of Computer Programs*, London: Oyez, 1980.

NIMMER, M. B., 'The Right of Publicity' (1954) 19 Law & Contemp. Probs. 203.

—— 'The Right to Speak from *Time* to *Time*: First Amendment Theory

Applied to Libel and Misapplied to Privacy' (1968) 56 Calif. Law Rev. 935.

NIZER, L., 'The Right of Privacy: A Half-Century's Developments' (1941) 39 Mich. Law Rev. 526.

NORTH, P. M., 'Disclosure of Confidential Information' (1965) JBL 307; (1966) JBL 31.

—— 'Further Disclosures of Confidential Information' (1968) JBL 31.

—— 'Breach of Confidence: Is There a New Tort?' (1972) JSPTL 149.

NOTE (ANONYMOUS) 'Legal Protection of the Physician–Patient Relationship, (1952) 52 Colum. Law Rev. 383.

—— 'Right of Privacy v. Free Press: Suggested Resolution of Conflicting Values' (1953) 28 Ind. LJ. 179.

—— 'Medical Practice and the Right to Privacy' (1959) 43 Minn. Law Rev. 943.

—— 'The Right of Privacy: Normative–Descriptive Confusion in the Defence of Newsworthiness' (1963) 30 Univ. of Chicago Law Rev. 722.

—— 'Credit Investigations and the Rights to Privacy: Quest for a Remedy' (1965) 57 Georgetown LJ 765.

—— 'Privacy, Defamation, and the First Amendment: The Implications of *Time, Inc.* v. *Hill,* (1967) 67 Colum. Law Rev. 926.

—— 'Right to Privacy: Social Interest and Legal Right' (1967) 51 Minn. Law Rev. 531.

—— 'Privacy, Property, Public Use, and Just Compensation' (1968) 41 S. Calif. Law Rev. 902.

—— 'Protecting the Subjects of Credit Reports' (1971) 80 Yale LJ 1035.

—— 'The Right of the Press to Gather Information' (1971) 71 Colum. Law Rev. 383.

—— 'The Court and Electronic Surveillance: To Bug or Not to Bug: What is the Exception?' (1972) 47 St John's Law Rev. 76.

—— 'Right of Privacy: Freedom of the Press does not Justify the Invasion of Privacy through Subterfuge' (1972) 50 Tex. Law Rev. 514.

—— 'Electronic Eavesdropping: A Victim's Primer' (1973) 49 Notre Dame Lawyer 162.

—— 'On Privacy: Constitutional Protection for Personal Liberty' (1973) 48 NYU Law Rev. 670.

—— 'Privacy in the First Amendment' (1973) 82 Yale LJ 1462.

—— 'Right of Privacy in U.K.' (1973) 117 Sol. J. 421.

O'BRIEN, DAVID, *Privacy, Law and Public Policy*, New York: Praeger, 1979.

O'BRIEN, W. W., 'The Right of Privacy (1902) 2 Colum. Law Rev. 437.

OGELSBY, D. L., 'Freedom of the Press v. the Rights of the Individual: A Continuing Controversy' 47 Oreg. Law Rev. 132.

PARENT, W. A., 'A New Definition of Privacy for the Law' (1983) 2 Law & Philosophy 305.

PARKER, RICHARD, 'A Definition of Privacy' (1974) 27 Rutgers Law Rev. 275.

PEDRICK, W. H., 'Publicity and Privacy: Is it any of our Business?' (1970) 20 Univ. of Toronto LJ 391.

PENNOCK, J. R., and CHAPMAN, J. W., (eds.), *Privacy, Nomos XIII*, Univ. New York: Atherton Press, 1971.

PETERSON, J., and TURN, R., 'Systems Implications of Information Policy' (1967) 30 *AFIPS Conference Proceedings*.

POLYVIOU, P., *Search and Seizure: Constitutional and Common Law*, London: Duckworth, 1982.

POOL, I., and SOLOMON, R. B., 'Intellectual Property and Transborder Data Flows' (1980) 16 Stanford J. Int. Law 113.

POSNER, RICHARD, *Economic Analysis of Law*, 2nd edn., Boston, Mass.: Little, Brown & Co., 1977.

—— 'Interests of Personality' (1914–15) 28 Harv. Law Rev. 343; 445.

—— 'The Fourteenth Amendment and the Right of Privacy' (1961) 13 Wes. Res. Law Rev. 34.

—— 'The Right of Privacy' (1978) 12 Ga. Law Rev. 393.

—— 'Privacy, Secrecy, and Reputation' (1979) 28 Buff. Law Rev.1.

—— 'An Economic Theory of Privacy' in Schoeman (ed.) *Philosophical Dimensions of Privacy: An Anthology*.

POUND, ROSCOE, *Jurisprudence*, iii, St. Paul: West Publishing Co., 1959.

PRATT, W. F., 'The Warren and Brandeis Argument for a Right to Privacy' (1975) Public Law 161.

PRICE, RONALD R., 'Of Privacy and Prisons' in Gibson (ed.), *Aspects of Privacy Law*.

PROSSER, WILLIAM L., *The Law of Torts*, 4th edn., St Paul: West Publishing Co., 1971.

—— 'Privacy' (1966) 48 Calif. Law Rev. 383.

—— and KEETON, W. P., *The Law of Torts*, 5th edn., St Paul: West Publishing Co., 1984.

RACHELS, JAMES, 'Why Privacy is Important' (1975) 4 Phil. & Pub. Aff. 323.

REIMAN, JEFFREY, 'Privacy, Intimacy and Personhood' (1976) 6 Phil. & Pub. Aff.26.

RHENQUIST, WILLIAM, 'Is an Expanded Right of Privacy Consistent with Fair and Consistent Law Enforcement? or Privacy, You've Come a Long Way, Baby' (1974) 23 Kan. Law Rev. 1.

RICHARDS, D. A. J., 'Constitutional Legitimacy and Constitutional Privacy' (1986) 61 NYU Law Rev. 800.

RICKETSON, S., *The Law of Intellectual Property*, Sydney: Law Book Co., 1984.

—— 'Confidential Information: A New Proprietary Interest?' (1977–8) 11 Melb. Univ. Law Rev. 223.

ROBERTSON, A. H. (eds.), *Privacy and Human Rights*, Manchester: Manchester University Press, 1973.

ROBERTSON, G., *People Against the Press: An Enquiry into the Press Council*, London: Quartet Books, 1983.

ROGERS, WILLIAM, P., 'The Case for Wire Tapping' (1954) 63 Yale LJ 792.

RUEBHAUSEN, O. M., and BRIM, O. G. JR., 'Privacy and Behavioral Research' (1965) 65 Colum. Law Rev. 1184.

RULE, JAMES B., *Private Lives and Public Surveillance*, London: Allen Lane, 1973.
——, McADAM, D., STEARNS L., and UGLOW, D., *The Politics of Privacy*, New York: Elsevier, 1980.
RYAN, E. F., 'Privacy, Orthodoxy and Democracy' (1973) 51 Can. Bar Rev. 84.
SAVAGE, NIGEL, and EDWARDS, CHRISTOPHER, *The Data Protection Act 1984*, London: Blackstone Press, 1984.
SAXONHOUSE, A. H., 'Classical Greek Conceptions of Public and Private' in Benn and Gaus (eds.), *The Private and the Public in Social Life*.
SCANLON, THOMAS 'Thomson on Privacy' (1975) 4 Phil. & Pub. Aff. 315.
—— 'A Theory of Freedom of Expression' in R. M. Dworkin (ed.), *The Philosophy of Law*, Oxford: Oxford University Press, 1977.
SCHAUER, F., 'The Role of the People in First Amendment Theory' (1986) 74 Calif. L. Rev. 761.
—— *Free Speech: A Philosophical Enquiry*, Cambridge: Cambridge University Press, 1982.
SCHOEMAN, F., (ed.), *Philosophical Dimensions of Privacy: An Anthology*, Cambridge: Cambridge University Press, 1984.
—— 'Privacy and Intimate Information' in Schoeman (ed.), *Philosophical Dimensions of Privacy: An Anthology*.
SCHROEDER, R. H., 'The Fourth Amendment, Electronic Eavesdropping and the Invasion of Privacy' (1972) 17 S. Dak. Law Rev. 238.
SCHWARTZ, B., *A Commentary on the Constitution of the United States*, vol. i, pt. 3, New York: Macmillan Co., 1968.
SCHWARTZ, L. B., 'On Current Proposals to Legalise Wiretapping' (1954) 103 Univ. of Pa. Law Rev. 240.
SEDLER, R. A., 'The First Amendment in Theory and Practice' (1971) 80 Yale LJ 1070.
SEGAL, W. D., ' "False Light" in California' (1971) Calif. Law Rev. 357.
SEIPP, DAVID J., 'English Judicial Recognition of a Right to Privacy' (1983) 3 Ox. J. of Leg. Stud. 325.
SHAPO, M. S., 'Media Injuries to Personality: An Essay on Legal Regulation of Public Communication' (1968) 46 Tex. Law Rev. 650.
SHARP, J. M., *Credit Reporting and Privacy: The Law in Canada and the U.S.A.*, Toronto: Butterworth, 1970.
SHATTUCK, JOHN H. F., *Rights of Privacy*, Skokie, Ill.: National Textbook, 1977.
SHILS, EDWARD, *The Torment of Secrecy*, New York: Free Press, 1956.
—— 'Privacy: Its Constitution and Vicissitudes' (1966) 31 Law & Contemp. Probs. 281.
SIEGHART, PAUL, *Privacy and Computers*, London: Latimer, 1976.
SIMITIS, SPIROS, 'Reviewing Privacy in an Information Society' (1987) 135 Univ. of Pa. Law Rev. 707.
SKEGG, P. D. G., *Law, Ethics, and Medicine: Studies in Medical Law*, Oxford: Clarendon Press, 1984.
SKELLY, WRIGHT, J. 'Defamation, Privacy, and the Public's Right to Know:

A National Problem and a New Approach' (1968) 46 Tex. Law Rev. 630.

SMITH, ROBERT ELLIS, *Privacy: How to Protect What's Left of It*, New York: Anchor Books, 1980.

SOUTHAM, CHRISTOPHER, and HOWARD, GILLIAN, *AIDS and Employment Law*, London: Blackstone Press, 1987.

SOWLE, C. R., (eds.), *Police Power and Individual Freedom*, Chicago: Aldine Publishing Co., 1962.

STERLING, J. A. L., *Data Protection Act 1984: A Guide to the New Legislation*, London: CCH, 1984.

STIGLER, G. J., 'An Introduction to Privacy in Economics and Politics' (1980) 9 J. Legal Stud. 623.

STOLJAR, S., 'A Re-examination of Privacy' (1984) 4 Leg. Stud. 67.

STONE, JULIUS, *Social Dimensions of Law and Justice*, London: Sweet & Maxwell, 1966.

STOREY, H., 'Infringment of Privacy and its Remedies' (1973) 47 Austral. LJ 498.

STREET, HARRY, *Freedom, the Individual and the Law*, 5th edn., Harmondsworth: Penguin Books 1982.

—— 'What the Law Can Do' *New Society*, 25 , May 1967.

STRÖMHOLM, STIG, *Right of Privacy and Rights of the Personality*, Working Paper prepared for the Nordic Conference on Privacy organized by the International Commission of Jurists, Stockholm, May 1967, Stockholm: PA. Norstedt Söners Förlag.

STUCKEY, J. E., 'The Equitable Action for Breach of Confidence: Is Information Ever Property?' (1981) 9 Sydney Law Rev. 402.

TAPPER, COLIN, *Computers and the Law*, London: Weidenfeld & Nicolson, 1973.

—— *Computer Law*, 3rd edn., London: Longman, 1983.

TAYLOR, G. D. S., 'Privacy and the Public' (1971) 34 MLR 288.

TEFF, H., 'Consent to Medical Procedures: Paternalism, Self-determination or Therapeutic Alliance' (1985) 101 LQR 432.

THOMSON, JUDITH JARVIS, 'The Right of Privacy' (1975) 4 Phil. & Pub. Aff. 295.

TREECE, J. M., 'Commercial Exploitation of Names, Likenesses, and Personal Histories' (1973) 51 Tex. Law Rev. 637.

TURN, REIN, *Classification of Personal Information for Privacy Protection Purposes*, Santa Monica: Rand Corp. 1976.

—— *Privacy and Security in Personal Information Databank Systems*, Santa Monica: Rand Corporation, 1974.

TURNER, A., *The Law of Trade Secrets*, London: Sweet & Maxwell, 1962; supplement, 1968.

VAN DEN HAAG, E., 'On Privacy' (1971) *Nomos XIII* 161.

VAN NIEKERK, BAREND, 'Unplugging the Bug, or the Right to be Left Alone in Criminal Law: Some Reflections' (1971) 88 SALJ 177.

WACKS, RAYMOND, *The Protection of Privacy*, London: Sweet & Maxwell, 1980.

—— 'The Right to Privacy' in R. Wacks (ed.), *Civil Liberties in Hong Kong*, Hong Kong: Oxford University Press, 1988.

—— 'Pop Goes Privacy', *Woodward* v. *Hutchins* (1977) 1 WLR 760, (casenote) (1978) 31 MLR 67.

—— 'Privacy and the Press', (1977) 93 *New Statesman* 554.

—— 'Breach of Confidence and the Protection of Privacy' (1977) 127 NLJ 328.

—— 'No Castles in the Air', *Lord Bernstein of Leigh* v. *Skyviews and General Ltd.* (1978) QB 479, (casenote) (1977) 93 LQR 491.

—— 'The Poverty of "Privacy" ' (1980) 96 LQR 73.

—— ' "Privacy" and the Practitioner' (1983) Public Law 260.

—— 'Controlling AIDS: Some Legal Issues' (1988) 138 NLJ 254, 283.

—— *Rights of Privacy*, J. H. F. Shattuck; *The Law of Privacy in South Africa*, D. J. McQuoid-Mason (book review) (1979) 42 MLR 602.

—— *Privacy, Law and Public Policy*, D. O'Brien (book review) (1980) 43 MLR 95.

—— *Privacy in Britain*, W. F. Pratt (book review) (1980) 43 MLR 359.

—— *Law of Electronic Surveillance in Canada*, D. Watt (book review) (1981) 97 LQR 178.

—— *Aspects of Privacy Law*, (ed.) Dale Gibson (book review) (1981) 97 LQR 663.

—— *Privacy and Government Data Banks*, D. Flaherty (book review) (1981) 97 LQR 664.

—— *People Against the Press*, G. Robertson (book review) (1984) 46 MLR 93.

—— *Secrets: On the Ethics of Concealment and Revelation*, Sissela Bok (book review) (1987) 50 MLR 125.

WADE, J. W., 'Defamation and the Right of Privacy' (1962) 15 Vand. Law Rev. 1093.

WAGNER DeCEW, JUDITH, 'The Scope of Privacy in Law and Ethics' (1986) 5 Law & Philosophy 145.

WAITE, J. B., 'Judges and the Crime Burden' (1955) 54 Mich. Law Rev. 169.

WAKEFIELD, P. W., *The Duty of Confidence and the Profession*, (unpublished thesis, 1972). Univ. of Manitoba.

WALKER, C. P., 'Police Surveillance by Technical Devices' (1980) Public Law 184.

WARNER, M., and STONE, M., *The Data Bank Society: Organizations, Computers and Social Freedom*, London: George Allen & Unwin Ltd., 1970.

WARREN, S. D., and BRANDEIS, L. D., 'The Right to Privacy' (1890) 4 Harv. Law Rev. 193.

WASSERSTROM, RICHARD, A., 'Some Arguments and Assumptions' in R. Bronaugh (ed.), *Philosophical Law: Authority, Equality, Adjudication, Privacy*, Westport, Conn.: Greenwood Press, 1978.

WATT, DAVID, *Law of Electronic Surveillance in Canada*, Toronto: Carswell, 1979.

WEINSTEIN, MICHAEL, A., 'The Uses of Privacy in the Good Life' (1971) *Nomos XIII* 88.

WEINSTEIN, W. L., 'The Private and the Free: A Conceptual Inquiry' (1971) *Nomos XIII* 27.
WESTIN, ALAN, F., *Privacy and Freedom*, London: Bodley Head, 1967.
—— 'The Wire Tapping Problem' (1952) 52 Colum. Law Rev. 165.
—— and BAKER, M., *Databanks in a Free Society*, New York: Quadrangle Books, Inc., 1972.
WIGMORE, J. H., 'The Right Against False Attribution of Belief or Utterance' (1916) 4 Ky. LJ 3.
WILLIAMS, E. B., 'The Wiretapping-Eavesdropping Problem: Reflections on *The Eavesdroppers*. A Defence Counsel's View' (1960) 44 Minn. Law Rev. 855.
WILLIAMS, J. S., 'Invasion of Privacy' (1973) 11 Alberta Law Rev. 1.
WILLIAMS, K., 'Privacy and the Private Bank Account' (1974) 124 NLJ 613.
WINFIELD, PERCY, 'Privacy' (1931) 47 LQR 23.
WINTOUR, CHARLES, *Pressures on the Press*, London: André Deutsch, 1972.
YANG, T. L., 'Privacy: A Comparative Study of English and American Law' (1966) 15 ICLQ 175.
YOUNG, JOHN B. (ed.), *Privacy*, Chichester: John Wiley & Sons, 1978.
ZANDER, M., *The Police and Criminal Evidence Act 1984*, London: Sweet & Maxwell, 1985.
ZELLICK, GRAHAM, 'Government Beyond Law' (1985) Public Law 283.
ZIMMERMAN, D. L., 'Requiem for a Heavyweight: A Farewell to Warren and Brandeis's Privacy Tort' (1983) 68 Cornell Law Rev. 297.

2. Reports and other documents

(a) United Kingdom

Report of the Committee on the Law of Defamation, (chairman: Lord Porter), Cmd. 7536, 1948.
Report of the Committee of Privy Councillors Appointed to Inquire into the Interception of Communications (chairman: Lord Birkett) Cmnd. 283, 1957.
Report of the Committee on Consumer Credit (chairman: Lord Crowther), Cmnd. 4596, 1971.
Interim Report of the Committee on the Law of Defamation (chairman: Mr Justice Faulks) Cmnd. 5571, 1974.
Report of the Committee on the Law of Defamation (chairman: Mr Justice Faulks), Cmnd. 5909, 1975.
Report of the Committee on Privacy (chairman: Kenneth Younger), Cmnd. 5012, 1972.
Royal Commission on the Press 1947–1949, Cmnd. 7700, 1949.
Royal Commission on the Press 1961–1962, Cmnd. 1811, 1962.
Royal Commission on the Press 1977, Cmnd. 6810, 1977.
Report on the Future of Broadcasting (chairman: Lord Annan) Cmnd. 6733, 1977.

Report of the Committee on the Law of Rape (chairman: Mrs Justice Heilbron), Cmnd. 6352, 1976.

Report on the Committee to Consider the Law on Copyright and Designs (chairman: Mr Justice Whitford), Cmnd. 6732, 1977.

Report of the Committee on Data Protection (chairman: Sir Norman Lindop), Cmnd. 7341, 1978.

Report of the Committee on Obscenity and Film Censorship (chairman: Prof. B. Williams), Cmnd. 7772, 1979.

Report of the Committee on Privy Councillors on Ministerial Memoirs, Cmnd. 6386, 1976.

Home Office, *Computers: Safeguards for Privacy*, Cmnd. 6354, 1975.

Home Office, *Data Protection: The Government's Proposals for Legislation*, Cmnd. 8539, 1982.

Home Office, *The Interception of Communications in Great Britain*, Cmnd. 7873, 1980.

Home Office, *The Interception of Communications in Great Britain*, Cmnd. 9438, 1985.

First Report of the Data Protection Registrar, June 1985, London: HMSO, 1985.

Law Commission, *Breach of Confidence*, Working Paper No. 58, Cmnd. 5012, 1972.

Law Commission, *Breach of Confidence*, Cmnd. 8388, 1981.

Scottish Law Commission, *Breach of Confidence*, Cmnd. 9385, 1984.

JUSTICE, *The Law and the Press*, London: Stevens & Sons, 1965

JUSTICE, *Living It Down: The Problem of Old Convictions*, London: Stevens & Sons, 1972.

JUSTICE, *Privacy and the Law*, London: Stevens & Sons, 1970.

Press Council, *The Press and the People* (Annual Report of the Press Council) 1954–81.

Press Council, *Privacy, Press and Public* (Booklet No. 2), 1971.

Press Council, *Press Conduct in the Lambton Affair* (Booklet No. 5), 1973.

Press Council, *Declaration on Privacy*, 1976.

Press Council, *Press Conduct in the Thorpe Affair* (Booklet No. 6), 1980).

Press Council, *Press Conduct in the Sutcliffe Case*, 1983.

Report of the Commissioner under Section 8 of the Interception of Communications Act, 1985, for 1986 (Commissioner: the Rt. Hon. Lord Justice Lloyd) Cm. 108, March 1987.

Report of the Commissioner under Section 8 of the Interception of Communications Act, 1985, for 1987 (Commissioner: the Rt. Hon. Lord Justice Lloyd) Cm. 351, March 1988.

(b) *Europe*

Council of Europe, *Explanatory Report on the Convention for the Protection of Individuals with Regard to Automatic Processing of Personal Data*, Strasburg: 1981.

Organization for Economic Co-operation and Development, *Guidelines on the Protection of Privacy and Transborder Flows of Personal Data*, Paris: OECD, 1981.

(c) *International*

Australia Law Reform Commission, *Privacy* (Report No. 22), Canberra: 1983.

Australia Law Reform Commission, *Unfair Publication: Defamation and Privacy* (Report No. 11), Canberra: 1979.

Australia Law Reform Commission, *Privacy and the Census* (Report No. 12), Canberra: 1979.

Australia Law Reform Commission, *Privacy and Intrusions* (Discussion Paper No. 13), Sydney: 1980.

Australia Law Reform Commission, *Privacy and Personal Information* (Discussion Paper No. 14), Sydney: 1980.

Canada Department of Communications, *Post Industrial Canada and the New Information Technology*, Ottawa: 1972.

Canada Office of the Privacy Commissioner, *Annual Report, Privacy Commissioner, 1983–1984*, Ottawa: 1985.

Canada Privacy Commissioner, *Report of the Privacy Commissioner on the Use of the Social Insurance Number*, Ottawa: 1981.

Canada Departments of Communications and Justice, *Privacy and Computers: A Report of a Task Force*, Ottawa: 1972.

US Privacy Protection Study Commission: *Personal Privacy in an Information Society*, Washington DC: 1977.

US Commission on Federal Paperwork, *Confidentiality and Privacy: A Report of the Commission on Federal Paperwork*, Washington DC: 1977.

US Congress, House Committee on Government Operations, Government Information and Individual Rights Subcommittee, *Implementation of the Privacy Act: Data Banks*. Hearings, 94th Congress, 1st Session, 3 June 1975, Washington DC: 1975.

US Congress, Senate Committee on Government Operations, and Committee of the Judiciary *Ad Hoc* Subcommittee on Privacy and Information Systems. Subcommittee on Constitutional Rights, *Privacy: The Collection Use, and Computerization of Personal Data*, 93rd Congress, 18–20 June 1974, Washington DC: 1974.

US Department of Health, Education and Welfare, Records, *Computers, and the Rights of Citizens*, Report of the Secretary's Advisory Committee on Automated Personal Data Systems, Washington DC: 1973.

US General Accounting Office, *Automated Systems Security: Federal Agencies Should Strengthen Safeguards over Personal and Other Sensitive Data*, Report to the Congress by the Comptroller General of the US, Washington DC: 1979.

US Library of Congress, Congressional Research Service, *Information and Telecommunications: An Overview of Issues, Technologies and Applications*, Report for the Subcommittee on Science, Research and Technology, US House of Representatives, 97th Congress, Washington DC: 1981.

US National Commission for the Review of Federal and State Laws Relating to Wiretapping and Federal Surveillance, *Electronic Surveillance*, Washington DC: 1976.

US Privacy Protection Study Commission, *Privacy Law in the States*, Washington DC: 1977.

US Privacy Protection Study Commission, The Privacy Act of 1974: *An Assessment*, Washington DC: 1977.

US Privacy Protection Study Commission, *Technology and Privacy*, Washington DC: 1977.

US Library of Congress, Congressional Research Service, *Legislation Related to the Right of Privacy*, 96th Congress, Washington DC: 1980.

Index